D1403118

Stealing
The National Parks

Stealing The National Parks

The Destruction of Concessions and Park Access

by DON HUMMEL

A FREE ENTERPRISE BATTLE BOOK

The Free Enterprise Press
BELLEVUE, WASHINGTON

Distributed By 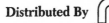 MERRIL PRESS

FIRST EDITION
Published by The Free Enterprise Press

Typeset in Caledonia typeface on Mergenthaler computers by
Nova Typesetting, Bellevue, Washington.

The Free Enterprise Press is a division of the Center for the
Defense of Free Enterprise, 12500 N.E. Tenth Place, Bellevue,
Washington 98005.

This book distributed by Merril Press, P.O. Box 1682, Bellevue,
Washington 98009. Additional copies of this book may be ordered
from Merril Press at $19.95 each.

LIBRARY OF CONGRESS CATALOGING-IN-PUBLICATION DATA

Hummel, Don, 1907–
    Stealing the national parks.

    "A Free Enterprise battle book."
    Bibliography: p. 383–403.
    Includes index.
    1. National parks and reserves—United States—History. 2.
Concessions (Amusements, etc.)—United States—History.
3. United States. National Park Service—History. 4. National
parks and reserves—Government policy—United States—History. 5. Concessions (Amusements, etc.)—Government policy—
United States—History. I. Title.
SB482.A4H85   1987   363.6'8'0973   86-29539

ISBN 0-939571-01-3

PRINTED IN THE UNITED STATES OF AMERICA

To my wife
Eugenia
A staunch supporter
and a stern critic.

Contents

Contents

DENOUEMENT

Foreword

A merica's system of national parks is one of this nation's greatest contributions to the world's cultural and natural resource heritage. From the huge, 12 million-acre Wrangell-St. Elias National Park in Alaska, to small but significant historic landmarks, battlefields, seashores or monuments in every state of the union, the park system protects our national treasures and allows people to experience and learn from them.

But as our nation grows, the National Park Service's dual mission—to both protect these resources and to let people have access to them—has led to increasing friction and conflict. The parks are not, unless they are otherwise so designated, wilderness areas. They are meant to be seen, enjoyed and experienced by people. To do that, we have to provide them with certain services—places to stay, places to eat, tours, interpretive facilities and the like. But who should provide services? Should government do it or private enterprise? Under what terms and conditions? At what point does the people's right to experience the parks begin to harm the parks?

These questions have been debated for many decades. In 1965, the Congress formalized the role private enterprise has to play in accommodating the visitors to the parks. It established standards for the legal and economic rights of these concessioners. Unfortunately, the debate was not abated.

In this volume Don Hummel describes what he sees as the systematic erosion of park concessioners' rights and with it, the erosion of services to visitors in the parks. He argues that conservationists have allied with the Park Service to destroy the economic security necessary to private concessioners in an effort to remove all such operations from the parks. Such an effort would have major impact on how the public relates to park lands. Already, he argues, their activites have harmed the public's ability to fully experience their parks.

I have known Don Hummel for many, many years. There are few people in America who know as much about park concession operations as he does. He is a tough and out-spoken man and I know of no one better able to tell the park concessioners' side of the story than Don Hummel. I do not agree with everything he says, but he raises interesting and difficult questions that should concern everyone who cares about our parks.

MORRIS K. UDALL
Member of Congress

Preface

I have long been concerned over National Park Service efforts to remove visitor facilities from our national parks. This book is my protest against elitist environmental organizations that have pressured the Park Service into its present anti-people posture. It is a documentation of National Park Service policy, past and present. It is an explanation of the historic system that provided for private enterprise in the parks. It is a shocking tale of how the American people are losing their right to fully enjoy their parks.

This book is also the story of national park concessions and concessioners. I believe the reading public will find in these pages a new and refreshing viewpoint on the national parks. It is long overdue. It is of vital importance to the survival of our national park system as Congress originally intended it to be.

The reader will find this book filled with personal anecdotes from my many years in national park concessioning. My fellow concessioners will probably feel that there's too much Don Hummel in these pages, and I can only beg their forbearance. I have stressed my personal experience not because I think it's the best experience, but rather because, like a nature interpreter, I wanted to accompany the reader into an area I have worked hard to understand myself and hope to make understandable to others.

Any national park concessioner could have written this book, and probably better. I am certain that every concessioner will think of many important points I have left out. This book is the best I could do. I have tried to say the things here that all concessioners want the public to know. So take this as the voice of one among many.

This book could not have been written without the able assistance of many people. I first want to thank the crew at the Free Enterprise Press who helped with their time, knowledge and research assistance. Managing editor John Versnel kept the book on schedule and aided with many research tasks. Press editor-in-chief Ron Arnold—although a stern taskmaster of rewrites—generously offered many valuable suggestions and performed extensive fact-checking duties. Research editor Janet Arnold spent many thankless hours digging out endless details at university and federal libraries. My thanks to Alan M. Gottlieb, president of the Center for the Defense of Free Enterprise for accepting this project for publication.

My greatest debt of gratitude is to legendary former National Park Service Director Horace M. Albright. Along with first Director Stephen T. Mather, Mr. Albright shaped the great concessioning ideas that are today known simply as the Mather-Albright principles. Mr. Albright's records, both in university archives and his own personal collection, proved invaluable in every phase of writing this book. Mr. Albright's daughter Marian Schenck provided assistance in her own right and as a relay point for messages to her father while he recuperated from his 1986 heart attack.

Harold K. Steen, Ph.D., executive director of the Forest History Society at Durham, North Carolina, kindly gave permission to use extensive materials from the Society's *Journal of Forest History*. Charles S. Cushman of the National Inholders Association offered insights into possible political solutions to the theft of our national parks for chapter nineteen.

The U.S. Department of the Interior and the National Park Service provided access to many documents otherwise unavailable. To Chief Historian Ed Bearss and historian Barry Mackintosh, my thanks for providing the "Chapman memo" and "Drury Memo" and Solicitor's Opinion of 1946 among other key documents.

University of California at Los Angeles special collections librarian Lilace Hatayama located the Conference of National Park Concessioners' first annual report (1930) in their Albright Collection. Mildred Mather, librarian at the Herbert Hoover Presidential Library, West Branch, Iowa, located the Ray Lyman Wilbur speech to the first Conference meeting in 1929.

My wife Genee spent many hours helping to edit and clarify language and made life bearable in general while this book was being written. My thanks to Emily Moke and Lynda Karjola for their patience and expertise in typing and computer services.

Whatever virtue this book may have comes from these fine people. Any errors of fact or judgement in these pages are my responsibility alone.

1

Thieves

A powerful political lobby is stealing America's national parks. This powerful lobby is methodically taking over our natural heritage, cheating us out of the nation's "crown jewels" one by one—Lassen, Yosemite, McKinley (Denali), Yellowstone, Mammoth Cave, and on and on. Despite voluminous laws and regulations that forbid such an outrage, this deliberate plunder of America's wonderlands has been going on for more than a decade and continues unabated this very minute. What's worse, some bureaucrats in the National Park Service itself and a few key Congressmen have allied themselves with the thieves and work in collusion with them, all under the banner of preserving our natural resources.

After that inflammatory introduction, the average reader might expect a tirade against "profit-mad developers encroaching on the national parks," or "corporate capitalists wrecking precious wilderness." Naturally, the guilty bureaucrats and politicians would be "on the take from big-spending industrial interests." We're accustomed to that sort of rhetoric.

But my message is different, almost diametrically different. My introductory paragraph refers to a special interest that we seldom think of as a special interest: it is not some private-sector corporate lobby that is stealing the national parks, but the environmental lobby. Yes, the environmental lobby. You may wonder how I can make such harsh accusations against a popular movement the public has embraced so wholeheartedly. The answer is complex; it will take us nineteen chapters to unfold. I assure you that I am utterly sincere and that my charges are well documented.

The Environmentalists

The basic problem is this: The nation's environmental groups seem devoted to what you could call the "lock-it-up-and-keep-'em-out" philosophy. As we shall see, leading environmentalists use the catchword of "ecological sensitivity" to "protect" America's scenic treasures from the people who own them. Environmentalists contend that a massive crush of national park visitors is destroying the very wonders the parks were meant to preserve. It makes no difference that the facts show quite another story. The contention is a matter of dogma, a feature of environmental ideology. A certain breed of environmentalist wants the great outdoors returned to a state of "pristine nature" and "ecological integrity." In practical application, those glowing terms mean *limiting people access*—and that means denying the American public its rightful use of our national parks.

Listen to their own voices. Martin Litton, long-time board member of the Sierra Club, told *Time-Life Books* writer Robert Wallace in 1971, "The only way we can save any wilderness in this country is to make it harder to get into, and harder to stay in once you get there."

Connie Parrish, California representative of Friends of the Earth, told a KABC-TV (Los Angeles) reporter on June 14, 1975, "What Friends of the Earth, the Sierra Club and other conservation groups have proposed is to phase out national park visitor accommodations."

The Wilderness Society, also in 1975, recommended in its *Wilderness Report* "that the National Park Service adopt and implement a firm policy of phasing out unnecessary concession facilities in the parks."

The National Parks and Conservation Association recommended that visitor services in Yosemite National Park be removed from "the heart of scenic Yosemite Valley," the very place where people want to be.

Edward Abbey, author of *The Monkey Wrench Gang* and "ecotage" advocate (he glorifies sabotage against man's works to save nature), condemned the National Park Service in the early 1980s for freely allowing visitors into the parks. He derisively claimed the national parks had become "national parking lots."

We could go on with this recitation for many pages. But the point should be obvious: the seemingly populist environmental movement has something against people in the national parks. Environmentalists' actual attitudes are far less savory than their public image would indicate.

We may legitimately ask: How is it that the "citizen saviors" of our environment could get the plain raw power to dictate how we use the national parks? We're accustomed to thinking of environmentalists as being outnumbered and outfinanced by "big business." But the fact is that environmentalism *is* big business. The top ten American environmental groups rake in more than $110 million each year. The National Wildlife Federation alone took in some $43 million in 1986. The hired lobbyists of these affluent environmental organizations have been recognized by the media as wielding some of the most effective clout on Capitol Hill. And there are no anti-trust laws to keep powerful environmental groups from forming more powerful coalitions. Yes, the environmentalists are powerful. Powerful enough to steal the national parks.

But is anyone *smart* enough to pull off such a monumental hijack? Demographic studies tell us that environmentalists, particularly the elite who prefer wilderness to developed campgrounds, constitute one of the best educated segments of the American public. A typical study, *Wilderness Users in the Pacific Northwest—Their Characteristics, Values, and Management Preferences*, states that "Wilderness users have been found to be a special group in that most of them are highly educated, more so than other recreationists." Respondents in this study came from less than the top ten percent of the U.S. population in terms of educational attainment. Forty-nine percent of California's High Sierra Wilderness users, for example, had gone to college and 33 percent had done graduate work. Yes, environmental purists are smarter than the average national park visitor. They are very clever folks. Clever enough to steal the national parks.

Then what about the motivation to limit human use of the national parks? Are environmentalists really so snobbish and greedy? Are they really such elitists? Some are honest enough to say so. Writer Peter Steinhart admitted in the July 1981 issue of *Audubon Magazine* that environmentalists "are elitists in that they fear a life in which men substitute speed for curiosity, sensation for knowledge, and mass culture for individuality."

Author Theodore Roszak expressed his disgust for park visitors in his book *Where the Wasteland Ends*: ". . . the worst came on the day we decided to visit Old Faithful. At the site we discovered what might have been a miniature football stadium: a large circle of bleachers packed thick with spectators devouring hot dogs and swilling soft drinks while vendors passed among them hawking souvenirs." Mr. Roszak was particularly upset with a family sitting beside him taking pictures of the famous geyser: ". . . no sooner did the geyser begin to blow than their eyes vanished behind their cameras, as if for sure the best way to have this experience was through a lens and on film." Mr. Roszak evidently feels he's better than people who eat and drink and take pictures. He concluded that we should "stay away" and spare the parks "such desecration." His feelings are common among environmentalists.

The March 10, 1983 issue of *New York News World* featured the comments of an environmentalist at Yosemite to then-Interior Secretary James Watt, who had just mentioned the need to improve access to national parks:

"The environmentalist was enraged. He roared, 'You are

not speaking to the real problem. The real problem is people and the degradation they bring to the National Park resource. We have to prevent people from coming here, not make it easier for them.' "

Notice the attitude: *We* have to prevent *them*. *We* represent the sensitive and the appreciative. *They* represent only "desecration" and "degradation." Yes, environmentalists are snobbish and greedy. Greedy enough to steal the national parks.

The National Park Service

The national parks are entrusted, logically enough, to the care of the National Park Service. How could the very agency that is supposed to manage the national parks for the benefit of all Americans allow special interest groups such as environmental organizations to deny these public treasures to the public? Citizens who are accustomed to thinking of the National Park Service as a spotless custodian of our natural heritage—and public opinion surveys show the Park Service as the most highly regarded agency in the entire federal government—find the idea that the national parks are being stolen impossible to believe. But the sad truth is that the National Park Service not only *allows* this to happen, but some of its officers also work to *make it happen*.

Why doesn't the public know? The reasons are not too difficult to grasp. The vast majority of people who visit America's national parks each year see the beauties of nature, marvel at their experience and then go on to the next destination. They don't see the immense bureaucracy that runs the parks. They don't see the legions of regional officials, the armies of Washington bureaucrats. They don't see certain key Park Service officials bending to environmentalist pressure. They don't see hard core environmentalist sympathizers in the Park Service making decisions to block off access roads and tear down fine old lodges and demolish public camping grounds and say who can get into the national parks and who will be turned away. The plain truth is that our highly esteemed colleagues in the National Park Service are ordinary bureaucrats, some of whom are susceptible to political pressure and special interest lobbying just like other bureaucrats. But the touring public sees only the national parks, never the national park bureaucrats.

The American public can hardly be blamed for not understanding the Park Service bureaucracy. Bureaucracy is by nature complicated and obscure. Many don't even realize that the National Park Service is an agency of the Department of the Interior of the United States of America. A political appointee runs the Interior Department: the Secretary of the Interior, a cabinet officer nominated by the President and confirmed by the Senate. But the Interior Secretary isn't the direct boss of the National Park Service—that would be unbureaucratic. There's another layer of political appointees called "Assistant Secretaries" between the Secretary and the Park Service. These Assistant Secretaries are also nominated by the President and approved by the Senate.

The Assistant Secretary for Fish & Wildlife and Parks is the boss of the Director of the National Park Service. The Director is appointed by the Interior Secretary, and at this writing is former California state official and Reagan friend, William Penn Mott, Jr. All these people work in the big gray Interior Department building on the corner of 18th and C Streets N.W. in Washington, D.C.

The First Park

Both the national parks and the National Park Service were created by Congress. Interestingly, the parks came long before the Park Service. The first national park was Yellowstone. The mysterious region had been shrouded in legendry since the end of 1807 when mountain man John Colter passed through its snowbound fastness, possibly the first white man to do so. He had been with Lewis and Clark in 1805 and requested leave on the expedition's return journey to trap in the headwaters of *La Roche Jaune*, (the River of the Yellow Rock). Colter's wide-eyed reports of gigantic fountains, mud volcanoes and huge boiling springs fell on deaf ears, as did rumors brought by other trappers and prospectors—including Jim Bridger, who claimed to have seen a fish there swimming across the Continental Divide. Such men were regarded as notorious liars, but stories of "Colter's Hell," a fantastic place walled off by high mountains and surrounded by fierce Indians, kept trickling in year after year. The yarns were too incredible to swallow, yet too persistent to dismiss.

Finally in 1870 a nineteen-man party of Montana dignitaries financed by Jay Cooke, an agent for the Northern Pacific Railroad, pierced the veil of mythology and put Yellowstone on the cartographers' map, giving many features the names they bear today, including Old Faithful geyser. A military escort of one corporal and four privates commanded by Lieutenant Gustavus C. Doane accompanied expedition leader Henry D. Washburn (the Surveyor-General of Montana), Judge Cornelius Hedges, prominent citizen Nathaniel Pitt Langford and other noted Montanans into the hidden high world. The Folsom-Cook expedition of 1869 beat the Washburn expedition to Yellowstone, but did not publish its findings in a timely manner and lost the distinction of "discoverers."

In 1870 the stunned Washburn expedition discovered the legends were all true, even Bridger's story of fish swimming a stream that flowed to two oceans. This party credited itself with originating the idea of national parks. Langford's journal tells us that one night at the confluence of the Firehole and Gibbon Rivers the explorers fell to discussing schemes for exploiting their discovery. Langford wrote:

> The proposition was made by some member that we utilize the result of our exploration by taking up quarter sections of land at the most prominent points of interest, and a general discussion followed. One member of our party suggested that if there could be secured by pre-emption a good title to two or three quarter sections of land opposite the lower fall of the Yellowstone and extending down the river along the canyon,

they would eventually become a source of great profit to the owners. Another member of the party thought that it would be more desirable to take up a quarter section of land at the Upper Geyser Basin, for the reason that that locality could be more easily reached by tourists and pleasure seekers. A third suggestion was that each member of the party pre-empt a claim, and in order that no one should have an advantage over the others, the whole should be thrown into a common pool for the benefit of the entire party.

Mr. Hedges then said that he did not approve of any of these plans—that there ought to be no private ownership of any portion of that region, but that the whole of it ought to be set apart as a great National Park, and that each one of us ought to make an effort to have this accomplished. His suggestion met with an instantaneous and favorable response from all—except one—of the members of our party, and each hour since the matter was first broached, our enthusiasm has increased.

Even though Langford gave the credit for the national park idea to Hedges, history buffs know that the first published reference to the desirability of establishing national parks appeared nearly forty years earlier in 1833 when the *New York Daily Commercial Advertiser* published a series of letters by famed artist-explorer George Catlin, who had visited the Indian country of the Upper Missouri in 1832. Catlin urged the establishment of a *"nation's Park*, containing man and beast, in all the wild and freshness of their nature's beauty."

Regardless who gets credit for the idea, under Langford's leadership the Washburn expeditioners mounted a great lobbying campaign in the winter of 1871-72. A U.S. Geological Survey party led by geologist Ferdinand V. Hayden had trekked that summer through Yellowstone with eighteen members including the outstanding pioneer photographer William Henry Jackson and the noted landscape painter Thomas Moran. Jackson's 400 superb photographs coupled with Moran's fine paintings did much to further the cause of the first national park. The Northern Pacific helped, too, for obvious reasons: Every new attraction they could bring rails to would mean more passengers and each passenger would mean a net profit—odd how history's dread capitalists seem to have been a driving force behind the ideas environmentalists now take credit for.

N.P. Langford lobbied the public by writing articles in *Scribner's Magazine* and lecturing in New York and Washington, D.C. As the brother-in-law of a Northern Pacific promoter, he also had friends in Congress. On December 18, 1871, Kansas Senator Pomeroy and Delegate Clagett of Montana introduced a bill to set aside Yellowstone as a public park. Geologist Hayden's scientific report and his testimony before Congress stressed the worthlessness of Yellowstone for mining, logging or grazing—nothing would be lost to the nation by making it a park. The legislators felt reassured. The lobbyists were about to convince Congress to accept Hedges' visionary idea.

Congress created the world's first national park by the Act of March 1, 1872, dedicating and setting apart Yellowstone "as a public park or pleasuring-ground for the benefit and enjoyment of the people." There was no Park Service until 1916, and Congress in 1872 placed Yellowstone "under the exclusive control of the Secretary of the Interior." The Secretary was instructed to make and publish regulations which "shall provide for the preservation, from injury or spoliation, of all timber, mineral deposits, natural curiosities, or wonders in said park, and their retention in their natural condition."

The Double Mandate

Notice that the Yellowstone National Park Act of 1872 set forth two mandates: the park was to be *used* ("pleasuring-ground," "benefit and enjoyment") and its wonders were to be *preserved* ("from injury or spoliation," "retention in their natural condition"). This double mandate of use *and* preservation is the crux of historical conflict over the national parks. There has always been an ultra-primitivist faction that wanted to reinterpret the law to put preservation foremost and use hindmost.

But this was never the intent. The Yellowstone Act itself clearly states that "The Secretary may in his discretion, grant leases for building purposes for terms not exceeding ten years, of small parcels of ground, at such places in said park as shall require the erection of buildings for the accommodation of visitors." While it's true that N.P. ("National Park") Langford, who after his exertions appropriately became Yellowstone's first superintendent (without salary), was not overwhelmed by tourists at Yellowstone—the nearest railroad was still five-hundred miles away—Congress wrote similar "leases for accommodation of visitors" language into nearly all subsequent national park Acts. It was present in the Acts creating Sequoia and General Grant National Parks (California, 1890); Yosemite (California, 1890); Mount Rainier (Washington, 1899); Crater Lake (Oregon, 1902); Wind Cave (South Dakota, 1903, including a clause allowing accommodations *inside* the cave); Sullys Hill National Park (North Dakota, 1904, transferred to the Department of Agriculture in 1931 as Sullys Hill National Game Preserve); Platt National Park (Oklahoma, 1906, Act provided for a townsite, park redesignated Chickasaw National Recreation Area, 1976), Glacier (Montana, 1910); and Rocky Mountain (Colorado, 1915, Act specifies regulations "primarily aimed at the freest use of the said park for recreational purposes by the public"). Our modern environmentalists who want to exclude people from the parks have a lot of contrary history to rewrite.

When Congress created the National Park Service on August 25, 1916, the dual mandate reappeared: "to conserve the scenery and the natural and historic objects and the wild life therein and to provide for the enjoyment of the same in such manner and by such means as will leave them unimpaired for the enjoyment of future generations." Here again we have the troublesome dichotomy between use ("enjoyment" of present and future generations) and preservation (the actual word in the law is "conserve" and not "preserve," conservation implying "wise use" rather than "non-use").

Unfortunately for the American public, overzealous environmentalists have prompted some Park Service officials to tamper with this original intent, rewriting the law without consulting Congress. The Service's primitivists who wrote the Master Plan for Yellowstone in the 1970s dismissed the original Yellowstone Act's dual mandate by telling us "it was stated in 1872, at a point in this Nation's history when only a handful were convinced that America's natural resources were limited and that the public could not have its cake and eat it too. Today, with the Nation and the park facing an environmental crisis, it should be apparent that to have both is to have neither. In light of this, the original purpose must be translated in terms of contemporary connotations; as such it should read: To perpetuate the natural ecosystems within the park *in as near pristine conditions as possible for their inspirational, educational, cultural, and scientific values for this and future generations.*" (Emphasis in the original.) The Park Service bureaucrat who wrote this affront ignores the people's right to use and enjoy their parks.

What's worse, he and his environmentalist colleagues misdirect our attention by trotting out the "environmental crisis" image. Such special pleading might be appropriate for parts of the Eastern Megalopolis, but it is absurd in Yellowstone's two million acres—yes, *two million* acres—of pristine backcountry that seldom sees a visitor and suffers *zero* human impact. Today only three percent of Yellowstone is available for general public use, including roads, parking lots, campgrounds, Park Service and concessions buildings. This is not national park management, it's rank discrimination against the general public.

The Threat That Isn't

The Park Service uses many approaches to reduce the people's access to the parks, one of the shrewdest being misapplication of visitor-use statistics. The public sees visitor figures such as 350 million or 450 million people annually in the national parks (see *U.S. News & World Report* for May, 1986 for these horrifying numbers) and gets the impression that our great nature parks are being ruined by throngs of humanity. But it's lying with statistics: The national park system contains so many different kinds of units (337 individual areas in 1985, divided into 20 separate classifications) that such alarming total figures convey a false impression.

For example, in 1985 NPS gave its usage figures as 346 million total visits. Admittedly, that's a lot of people. But where was this horde? It wasn't in the nature parks because Park Service statistical abstracts show only 50 million people visiting the 48 areas officially called National Parks (places such as the Grand Canyon, Yosemite and Yellowstone). And that 50 million figure applied only to day visits. **Only 9.2 million people stayed overnight in a National Park in 1985.**

Well, you might ask, if all those mega-visitors didn't go to the nature parks, then where *did* they go? The remaining 296 million visitors were spread out over the other 289 units managed by the National Park Service. They went to places you don't even think of as national parks: 27.1 million people visited city parks in San Francisco and New York City (Golden Gate National Recreation Area and Gateway NRA). 49.3 million drove on roads (Natchez Trace Parkway, George Washington Memorial Parkway, and the Blue Ridge Parkway). 17.3 million went to the beach (Colonial National Historical Park on Jamestown Island, Lake Mead behind Hoover Dam, and Cape Cod National Seashore). 8.3 million visited Washington, D.C. city parks. And so forth. Although the National Park Service manages these places and hundreds of others like them, they're not exactly what you think of when you say "national parks."

To understand the hodgepodge of different units managed by the National Park Service, you have to grasp that NPS divides up their 337 areas into three broad categories: Natural Areas, Recreation Areas, and Historical Areas. (These divisions are falling out of use within the Service, but help the outsider look in.)

Natural Areas include National Parks, National Monuments, National Preserves, National Environmental Education Landmarks, and Registered Natural Landmarks. A National Park is usually large in area and contains a variety of resources; National Monuments are usually smaller than National Parks and lack their diversity, but preserve at least one nationally significant resource, such as Devils Tower, Wyoming. National Preserves generally protect some specific resource such as Big Thicket in Texas and Big Cypress in Florida. The other two classifications are relatively minor areas.

Historical Areas include National Historic sites, National Historical Parks, National Memorials, National Military Parks, National Battlefields, National Battlefield Parks, National Battlefield Sites, National Cemeteries, and National Historic Landmarks. This bewildering array of labels covers the home of Abraham Lincoln in Springfield, Illinois (a National Historic Site) and the Lincoln Memorial in Washington (a National Memorial), and many other history-related areas.

Recreation Areas include National Parkways (roads), National Recreation Areas, National Seashores, National Lakeshores, National Scenic Trails, National Scenic Riverways, and National Wild and Scenic Rivers. National Recreation Areas originally designated the reservoirs impounded behind federal dams, but nowadays encompass a variety of different sites. Wild and Scenic rivers preserve ribbons of land bordering free-flowing streams and are used primarily for hiking and canoeing.

Now that you understand the mish-mash of the national park system a little better, we can talk more sensibly about all that visitor load on the national parks. What about those 50 million who went to the 48 magnificent wonderlands officially called "National Parks?" The most-visited nature parks had fewer visitors than the Lincoln Memorial. The memorial had more than 3.8 million visitors while Acadia National Park had

3.7 million, Yosemite 2.8 million, the Grand Canyon 2.7 million, Olympic 2.5 million, Rocky Mountain 2.2 million, Yellowstone 2.2 million, and Glacier 1.6 million. Only Great Smoky Mountains National Park had more visits than the Lincoln Memorial at 9.3 million people. However, most of them drove through without stopping. The fact that only 478,600 people stayed overnight in the Great Smokies gives you a clue about how many people actually got out and walked around, but *everybody* who visited the Lincoln Memorial walked into it.

The thirty-odd other national parks had much lower visitation than those listed above. But you'd never know any of this listening to the National Park Service. They use big numbers to scare the public, to convince us that people should be discouraged from visiting and using their own parks.

Other spoilers in the Park Service take more direct action to eliminate park visitors: they methodically demolish visitor facilities. Park Service zealots tore down the wonderful old lodge and cabins at Utah's Cedar Breaks National Monument in 1975—they would have ravaged Zion and Bryce Canyon lodges as well if Utah's congressional delegation had not angrily stepped in to stop them. In Virginia, NPS superintendent Albert A. Hawkins ordered Mammoth Cave National Park's beautiful lodge at Historic Entrance to be demolished. Park Service nihilists had the boundaries of Rocky Mountain National Park changed to exclude majestic Grand Lake Lodge from the park, leaving no overnight facilities to any except camping visitors. The charming rustic lodge, cabins, and store at Lassen Volcanic National Park in California fell to Park Service barbarians one at a time from 1974 to 1985. The overnight facilities at Yellowstone's Old Faithful have been scheduled for closure and the campground, service station and store at West Thumb have been removed. This sad list seems to have no end. What priceless history is being obliterated! What a defeat for the American people, and at the hands of those sworn to defend our heritage! Most bitter to contemplate, all these destroyed in the name of preservation!

The Congress

Congress is the source and head of national park policy. The Senate and the House of Representatives each contain a special committee that oversees the Department of the Interior and its National Park Service. In the Senate, the Energy and Natural Resources Committee handles legislative matters related to the parks. Its Subcommittee on Public Lands and Reserved Water deals with most national park issues. In the House, the Interior and Insular Affairs Committee, chaired by Morris K. Udall (D-Arizona), covers park legislation. It was Udall who authored the Concession Policy Act of 1965 intended to secure facilities for park visitors. The Subcommittee on National Parks and Recreation passes on all park matters.

Other congressional committees also get involved with the national parks in some capacity: Senate and House Appropriations Committees approve all park budgets and monies for park expenditures. On occasion, the Senate Committee on Governmental Affairs and its subcommittees and the House Committee on Government Operations and its subcommittee on Environment, Energy and Natural Resources, will deal with specific issues touching upon the national parks. Likewise, the Small Business Committee gets involved occasionally. At times Congress also orders the General Accounting Office to undertake hostile investigations of concessions.

In Congress, as in the Interior Department, a few key players agree with the anti-people plans of the environmental lobby and work in collusion with them to steal the national parks. For many years the late Rep. Phillip Burton (D-California), Chairman of the Subcommittee on Parks of the House Interior and Insular Affairs Committee, was known as "the congressman from the Sierra Club" and did more mischief for the environmental elite than any other legislator. Upon his death in 1984 the mantle passed to Rep. John Seiberling (D-Ohio), another high-ranking member of the "Interior Committee" with an environmentalist bias.

The obligation of Congress to oversee the National Park Service is more honored in the breach than the observance. The public popularity of NPS makes it a difficult target for meaningful congressional reforms. Then, too, bureaucrats and environmental groups protect NPS interests for their own mercenary reasons: A revolving door exists between congressional staffs, Park Service staffs, and environmental group staffs—the list of individuals who have worked for all three would fill a book.

In due course we will meet many federal legislators and staff members who act to sabotage public access to the public parks. Fortunately, we will also encounter many who champion the right of the people to freely use and enjoy their national parks.

The Concessioners

If you've ever visited Grand Canyon and gazed upon the long rambling native stone and log grandeur of the El Tovar Hotel, or entered the massive "forest" lobby of Glacier Park Lodge with its sixty immense Douglas fir columns, their bark still intact, or savored the old-mountain-cabin feel of Le Conte Lodge in the Great Smoky Mountains, or luxuriated in the stately magnificence of The Ahwahnee in Yosemite, you were looking at private enterprise. Surprised? Most people are. The National Park Service neither owns these park concessions nor operates them.

The same is true throughout the park system: Crater Lake Lodge, Death Valley's Furnace Creek Inn, the Lake Crescent Lodge in Olympic National Park, and the Chateau at Oregon Caves National Monument, all are privately owned and operated, as are most other visitor accommodations and services in the national parks—grocery stores, saddle packers, filling stations, photo studios, souvenir sales, float trips, scenic flights, everything. With some important exceptions we'll see in later chapters, it's been that way for the entire history of the national parks and even before. And it's a good thing for America, because the private national park concessioners are the true champions of public access and reliable front-line fighters for the right of the people to use and enjoy their parks. Concessioners have the most trustworthy of reasons for being so public-spirited: their economic survival and their way of life depends on it.

But it would be wrong to assume that concessioners are only in the game for a fast buck. It would be all too easy for critics to fall back on the outworn anti-business slogan that profit is a dirty word in and of itself. One can make a profit and still respect nature and the spirit of the parks. Concessioners are living proof of that proposition. Because concessioning is one of the riskiest businesses on earth, with short seasons, supply problems, a demanding (and changing) public, rigid government regulations, uncertainties about vacillating federal policy, and chronic low profits, most concessioners got into the business because they love the outdoors and are devoted to the parks. They understand nature with a deep personal insight. They were selected for concession contracts because they understand park values.

In fact, it was a concessioner who pioneered the concept of nature interpretation: Enos A. Mills, who in 1901 established Longs Peak Inn near Estes Park, Colorado, was among the first to outline nature-guiding principles and qualifications of nature guides. For years he conducted a "trail school" in the Estes Park area. He was instrumental in the establishment of Rocky Mountain National Park in 1915 and also opened opportunities for women in nature guiding. Esther Burnell, the first nature guide licensed by the government, later married Mills. Concessioners were doing nature interpretation long before the Park Service even existed. They have contributed a great deal to America's national parks. They are part and parcel of the national park idea. As Congressman Wayne Aspinall, Chairman of the House Interior and Insular Affairs Committee that developed the Concession Policy Act of 1965 said, "We must think of the concessioner as an integral part of our national park system. He is there to serve the public and he must be selected with this in mind."

Invitation to Discovery

I can lay claim to a modicum of experience in the national parks, and have some right to speak on these issues. I have spent most of my life in the national parks as a ranger and park concessioner. I was one of the partners that started the first concession in Lassen Volcanic National Park in 1933. I operated the Mount McKinley concession in Alaska, was President and Chief Executive Officer of the Yosemite Park & Curry Company, and finally headed up Glacier Park, Inc., where I retired in 1981. As chairman of the Conference of National Park Concessioners for fourteen years I had the opportunity to meet most of the nation's concession people. They're good honest people who care about the parks and their visitors. They're my friends. They're your friends. They're a precious national resource just as the parks are a precious national resource. They may be the only thing standing between parks for the people and the total elimination of people from the parks.

The national park concessioners are a good part of the reason I'm bestirring myself out of retirement to write this book. Not much has been written about them. Virtually nothing has been written about the environmentalist campaign to destroy the concessioners as a major step in keeping people out of the parks. I want to remedy that. I don't know that I'm the right person to do it, but people keep telling me that nobody knows as much about national parks, their concessions and concessioners as I do. Maybe I'm beginning to believe them. I'll have to let you judge that for yourself after you've finished with me.

But for now I want to extend an invitation to you. Come with me. Come discover the world of the national park concessioners, the men and women who provide people-services in America's parklands. You'll find yourself in a lively fellowship of dedicated private enterprisers working to protect and keep open America's pathway to the parks. When you have read their story I hope you will be moved and concerned enough to make your voices heard in their defense. When you awaken to the multitude of threats facing your right to use and enjoy your own national parks I hope you will join me in spreading the story nationwide.

I propose that we now set to work to explore that story together.

2

The Discovery Trail

You CAN FULLY understand how the parks are being stolen only by knowing the story of the parks, including the story of the concessioners. Of course, I can't literally guide you down the whole parks trail—no one person can—but I'll point out those vistas I believe to be most important. From there you can make your own decisions.

I can't think of a better place to start than my own discovery of the national parks. Don't we all cherish our first experience in a national park? I certainly do. It was back in June of 1928. It all came about by chance while I was a junior studying history and political science at the University of Arizona in my hometown of Tucson. One spring night after classes my married sister Villette invited me over to meet some friends. These friends turned out to be Minor R. "Tilly" Tillotson, Superintendent of Grand Canyon National Park, and his wife Winifred. I was surprised and pleased that my sister had such distinguished acquaintances. We were all visiting when much to my astonishment Superintendent Tillotson offered me a summer job as a temporary ranger in Grand Canyon.

I gratefully accepted and sent in my application. However, when I got the instructions back I saw that the pay was only $150 a month, minus fifty cents per meal, and the price of the ranger's uniform would consume most of my remaining summer's salary. I told my dad, who ran a modestly successful law practice in Tucson, that I would probably turn the job down. He looked at me a moment and said I should take it. He'd even help with my finances. He told me, "The people you'll

meet may mean a lot more to you than the money you earn."
How right he was. As things turned out, I worked at Grand
Canyon four seasons while finishing up at the University of
Arizona and later as a law student at the University of Mich-
igan. That park experience changed my whole life: it led to
my career as a concessioner.

Grand Canyon

I reported to the Park Service at Grand Canyon at the
beginning of summer. What a different place from anything
I'd seen before! It was nothing like home in Tucson, and I'd
always thought of home as spectacular in its own right. I had
grown up with colorful sunsets over the nearby Tucson
Mountains and almost every day had looked up to the saw-
toothed Santa Ritas and the rugged Santa Catalina Mountains. But it hadn't prepared me for the Grand Canyon. Even
the approach was an experience. The smell of the pine trees
and the freshness of the air invigorated me. But when I
looked over the rim into the canyon depths my vigor seemed
to evaporate: gazing into that abyss I felt weak with awe. It's
just too big to comprehend.

Thirteen miles of empty space from rim to rim! The myriad
peaks and ridges within the canyon, massive though they
were, did little to alleviate the overpowering sense of empti-
ness. You could feel instinctively that great earth forces were
at work here. Down at the bottom, I knew, as much as half a
million cubic feet of water explode through the Inner Gorge
every second during spring floods of the Colorado River,
scouring millions of tons of silt over bedrock each day. But the
dominant fact of the Grand Canyon is simple empty space.
And every visitor asks, "How did that empty space get there?"

As a ranger I was to learn that the question is very old and
has many answers. The Southern Paiutes had an ancient
answer that still fascinates those who appreciate Indian lore.
It is said that long ago the wife of a wise chief died and was
taken to a happier land. The chief mourned so deeply that the
god Tavwoats appeared and took him to visit his wife, leaving

behind a barrier so great no mortal could follow: the Grand Canyon.

Scientists, of course, give us a more familiar answer. The Grand Canyon is the result of river erosion over eons of time—eons impossible for the mind to grasp. That was the Grand Canyon as I first experienced it: time and space too vast to encompass. Like most first-timers, I gazed long at all those purple chasms and rainbow-colored rocks and the sun changing all the canyon's forms with every change of light. I sat down overwhelmed. The poet Carl Sandburg was right when he said of this spectacle, "There goes God with an army of banners."

I found my way into the Park Service office and began filling out the employment forms. One of the blanks stunned me: I realized I was not of age—only 20 years old—and the minimum was 21. I lied about my age, writing my birthdate as 1906 instead of 1907. Nobody seemed to notice, for Assistant Superintendent Pat Patrow duly swore me in as a temporary ranger. Since the federal government at Grand Canyon had concurrent jurisdiction with the county and state, I was also sworn in as a deputy sheriff.

After a few days of orientation the powers that be assigned me to the Hopi fire tower to watch for forest fires in the vast pinyon and ponderosa pine stands spreading from the Coconino Plateau south of the canyon rim to the Kaibab Plateau beyond the north rim. I was also supposed to patrol the roads while driving to and from Hopi tower. Since we had only one tower, and thus couldn't pinpoint smokes scientifically by triangulation, I had to estimate fire distances as they used to say "by guess and by God." If you were too far off on your estimate, you could send the fire crew on a wild goose chase, which did not win you any friends. When the smoke lay beyond the horizon, guessing exact locations became particularly difficult. Despite it all, I gained a reputation as a dead-eye smoke spotter.

Then there was rim patrol duty. Every evening until 9:00 p.m. I'd meander back and forth on the canyon rim walkways and trails answering questions and enforcing park regulations. Other rangers and Park Service people frequently joined me, as sitting on the rim watching the girls go by—and sunset over the canyon—was a favorite pastime.

Canyon Concessions

One day I wandered into the marvelous stone and pine-log lodge on the south rim and discovered concessions. El Tovar, the lodge is called, operated by the legendary Fred Harvey Company. You walk into its impressively spacious Rendezvous Room whose massive rafters and dark log walls give way to bright white hallways decorated with handdrawn Indian designs. Its history is the history of concessions in miniature.

Railroads and national parks seem to have been inseparable in the early days of the national parks, and Grand Canyon is no exception. Even so, commercial interests came to the Canyon in the 1880s when the nearest rails lay sixty miles south and tourists had to take an eleven-hour stagecoach ride over dirt roads that alternated between choking dust and mud-bogged washes. Legendary early Canyon settler John Hance built the old Bright Angel Hotel at the head of Bright Angel Trail in the 1890s. Hance is reputed to have tried his hand as a miner in the 1880s until he found dragging asbestos out of the Canyon to be hard work and appointed himself the area's first official guide and hotelier. While leading visitors along his mining trails to the river, he'd tell some wild tales. For example, he claimed he once stopped to take a drink of the mighty silt-laden Colorado and almost choked to death before he could get out his knife to cut the drink off. Hance had a gift for colorful expression. He was only caught speechless once, when a little girl holding her mother's hand looked over the rim and asked, "How come it's there, Mister?" Without hesitation, Hance replied, Because I put it there."

"Where'd you put the dirt?"

Hance opened his mouth, but nothing came out.

I was surprised to discover that not all visitors are thrilled with the Canyon. The determined investigator can still find this amusing entry in one of Hance's yellowed and fraying guest books: "July 12, 1892. This is a warm place. I fainted when I saw that awful-looking canyon. I never wanted a drink so bad in my life. Goodbye. Gertrude B. Stevens." Then as today, concessioner service was available to the whole public, including visitors with little appreciation for nature.

But on September 18, 1901, the Santa Fe Railway officially opened a branch line running from Williams, Arizona, to the South Rim near the Bright Angel Hotel, which soon overflowed with guests. Ralph Cameron, another early Grand Canyon settler, opened a second hotel on an old mining claim between the railroad terminal and the Bright Angel Hotel, which the Santa Fe had bought from Hance. Disembarking Santa Fe passengers thus had to pass by the Cameron Hotel before reaching the Bright Angel. This did not please the railroad, which had contracted Bright Angel's operations to Fred Harvey Company, the Atchison, Topeka, and the Santa Fe's restaurant and hotel partner since 1876—the Fred Harvey that gained renown for civilizing the West with his starched fleet of gracious waitresses known as the Harvey Girls, "young women of good character, attractive, and intelligent." The railroad solved the Cameron problem by simply extending its tracks several hundred feet eastward to its own hotel's portals.

The Santa Fe had already begun plans for a luxury hotel at the south rim when the rails arrived in 1901. They asked architect Charles Whittlesey to design them something with the best features of the world-famous Swiss and German mountain inns, yet appropriate to the Canyon's rugged environment—you have to understand that after the turn of the century something of a scandal had erupted over America's lack of efficient highways, comfortable accommodations, and a palatable cuisine to go with the magnificent scenery. As Stephen T. Mather was to say in 1915 just before he became first Director of the National Park Service, "Scenery is a hollow enjoyment to a tourist who sets out in the morning after an indigestible breakfast and a fitful sleep on an impossible bed." Concessioners had done their best to provide digestible breakfasts and possible beds long before Mather arrived on the scene, but German-style highways to the scenery and Swiss-quality accommodations were virtually non-existent.

In 1905, the opening of the El Tovar brought quality accommodations to the Grand Canyon: the dining room boasted a spectacular view of the canyon as well as the ambience of sterling silverware, fine china and crystal set on white linen. The best meats and produce came in daily on Santa Fe trains; milk, cheese and butter all came from the Harvey Company's own dairy herd at the hotel; eggs came from chickens kept at the dairy—and in later years fresh flowers from a local greenhouse graced the tables.

And all this was done by private enterprise with private capital on privately owned land within what was then the Grand Canyon Forest Reserve, managed not by the Interior Department, but by the U.S. Department of Agriculture. Thus, the firm that became Grand Canyon's first major concessioner arrived nearly twenty years before Congress declared the area a national park February 26, 1919. You can tell I was impressed by Fred Harvey's Grand Canyon concession.

One of my favorite concession buildings at Grand Canyon is known as Hopi House, which opened in 1905 a few months before the El Tovar. There's something special about Hopi House: It was designed by Mary Jane Colter, who had a genius for blending man-made structures into the canyon's natural environment. Hopi House was a replica of an actual unit of homes from the Hopi village of Oraibi. When Hopi House opened, Colter decided to bring in the craftspeople along with the crafts: For quite a few years Hopi and Navajo families lived in and around Hopi House, making and selling their wares to the tourists. The Hopi also performed a dance each evening for the tourists.

The National Park Service eventually followed Colter's lead in designing their own buildings, only one of many examples of concessioners leading the way to sound park policy. One of

Colter's designs fit in with the rimrock surroundings so well that hikers on the Bright Angel Trail below couldn't see it even though it stood in plain view, molded perfectly into the canyon edge. This was the Lookout Studio, Santa Fe's tactical answer to the Kolb brothers, Emery and Ellsworth, pioneer photographers of the Grand Canyon. Santa Fe negotiators had failed to buy out the Kolb Studio at the head of Bright Angel Trail. The Kolbs are as legendary as John Hance: they racked up many photographic firsts in the Canyon, among them a daring 1911 venture down the tumultuous Colorado in a wooden boat with a heavy hand-cranked movie camera—in the days when many had never even heard of motion pictures. If the Santa Fe couldn't remove the Kolbs, they could give them some competition, and thus Colter was commissioned to design the Lookout Studio practically next door to the Kolb Studio.

Colter ultimately built six public buildings for the Santa Fe at Grand Canyon: Hopi House (1905), The Lookout Studio (1914), Hermit's Rest (1914), Phantom Ranch (1919), the Watchtower (1932), and Bright Angel Lodge (1935). See Bill McMillon's fascinating 1983 book *The Old Lodges & Hotels of our National Parks* for the whole story. Of couse, the Watchtower and Colter's Bright Angel Lodge hadn't been built when I worked for the Park Service at Grand Canyon, but Phantom Ranch was there along with the old Bright Angel Lodge.

On The Trail

Because I had stock and packing experience—I grew up on a ranch outside Tucson—the Park Service gave me special assignments packing supplies to the canyon bottom and across the Colorado River to the north rim, which took me to Phantom Ranch many times.

One day park superintendent Tillotson called me in and said he and his wife Winifred and I would be crossing to the north rim the next day to pick up some important Park Service guests. He gave me the details and I told him I'd have the requisite 14 head of saddle horses and pack mules ready from the corral bright and early. I had never seen the particular mules assigned to me next morning, six with full packs, the balance with saddles. I knew that once we reached Phantom Ranch after descending the Yaqui Trail I would have to turn them into the canyon-bottom corral with 75 other mules assigned to the packing contingent. The following morning I would be expected to identify my mules and pack them for our trip up to the north rim where our VIP visitors waited. Thus I spent the entire trip down trying to memorize the mules and their respective packs so I could get the right packs on the right mules in the morning and avoid a lot of adjusting of harnesses and packs.

We crossed the Kaibab Suspension Bridge over the Colorado in late afternoon. This bridge, actually a narrow line of 2x12 planks hung from cables across the Inner Gorge about 75 feet above the water, had been completed in 1922. It allowed Fred Harvey Company to open its canyon-bottom camp just north of the Colorado on Bright Angel Creek, the camp that became Phantom Ranch. The bridge had been preceded by a crossing contraption in 1907, when one David Rust, who operated a hunting camp on the north rim, built a cable tramway to transport the adventurous across the Colorado so they could hike out to the north.

The raging river beneath our spindly bridge has been inextricably tied up with the name of John Wesley Powell, a one-armed Civil War veteran who floated the Colorado from Green River, Wyoming, with nine others in 1869, the first humans to do so since the days of Tavwoats. Major Powell named most of the tributaries that flow into Grand Canyon, dubbing one of them the Dirty Devil because it gave no relief from the muddy water his party had been drinking for weeks—in John Hance's inimitable argot, it was "too thick to drink and too thin to plow." To make up for the Dirty Devil's uncomplimentary name, when Powell found the clear creek we now headed for, he dug into his literary knowledge and named it after "the Angel bright" of Milton's *Paradise Lost*.

Three of Powell's men died during the expedition, but not from the terrors of the river: they could stand the battering of rapids and rocks no more, and climbed out of the Canyon only to be killed by hostile Indians on the rim. Powell and the six who stayed with him returned safely to Washington and gave the world its first map of the river. But not until 1923 did the U.S. Geological Survey send an expedition to definitively chart its course. The Canyon itself was mapped completely only in the 1970s, and it still contains many remote places where, as John Hance would say, the hand of man has never set foot.

After Grand Canyon was declared a national park in 1919, the NPS decided to replace Dave Rust's cable car with a suspension bridge. After only six seasons NPS once again had crews working on a replacement, this time with a steel bridge (but it would still be so narrow as to restrict the number of animals that could cross it at any one time). Building this new bridge occupied all the regular packers and gave me this singular opportunity to do the special packing chores.

After we reached Phantom Ranch that evening and I went to bed, I kept saying to myself, "I have to get up at four o'clock, I have to get up at four o'clock." I'd need that time to pick out the mules, get them saddled and packed and be ready to start up-trail at 7:00 a.m. with the superintendent and his wife. After dozing fitfully, I awoke with a start, lit a match to look at my dollar watch, and saw it was 11:30 p.m. I slipped off again. It was the same every 45 minutes or so until I finally got up at 3:30 a.m. and went down to the corral. I found the superintendent there ahead of me. Between the two of us we located our mules and got them packed. I suspect my boss was apprehensive about my ability to get us rigged in time, but he said nothing. The trouble was that we were loaded so early the mules had to stand several hours with a full pack; they were as tired as I was by the time we reached the North Rim.

At the top we picked up our notables, nationally-known naturalist and president of the Carnegie Institution of Washington, John C. Merriam; noted geographer and president of Clark University in Worcester, Massachusetts, Wallace W. Atwood; Mr. Charles L. Gable, Senior Auditor in Interior's Branch of Operations, Washington, D.C. (he would soon become Chief, Public-Utility Service Operators Division—they called concessions Public-Utilities in those days); and one of Gable's assistants, Wilson A. Blossom. We made Phantom Ranch again before nightfall. I took care of the stock while the others retreated to their quarters.

By 1928 Mary Jane Colter's original Phantom Ranch had been expanded to include new stone cottages, a recreation hall, a blacksmith shop, showers and toilets—it even approached self-sufficiency with its own orchard, an alfalfa field for livestock, rabbits and chickens near the mule barn, and water from a reservoir built above the ranch on Bright Angel Creek. The added amenities brought so many of the rich and famous that Phantom Ranch's guest register looked like *Who's Who*.

After I got cleaned up and had some supper, senior auditor Gable and two others invited me to make a fourth for a game of bridge. We sat down and suddenly somebody turned off the electric lights. Gable got up and turned them back on. Then the culprit, Fred Harvey Company's manager-chef of Phantom Ranch, jumped up and turned them off again. Gable told the man that we wanted to play bridge. The manager made no effort to explain that the camp was having generator problems—a fact we discovered later—and proceeded to berate the concessions chief in less than complimentary tones. Gable, even though a man of small stature, was definitely not one to tangle with: He offered to fight this irascible (and six-foot-two) manager-chef. I stepped between the two and told Gable he could handle the problem at the Fred Harvey office the next morning.

At daybreak we rode our mules up to the South Rim. Gable stopped in at the concession office to report their cantankerous employee. Much to Gable's surprise, the manager-chef had realized the seriousness of his misdeed, hiked out ahead of us, gave his employer an accurate report of the incident, and submitted himself for dismissal. The Fred Harvey people had already paid his last wages and let him go when Gable arrived.

What a job, being a National Park summer ranger! I had a variety of duties: fire detection, rim patrol, packing for VIPs, even accompanying Chief Ranger James C. Brooks to catch bootleggers and robbers. The job I liked best, though, was taking a horse and a couple of pack mules down in the canyon for several weeks seeking out springs and building catch-basins around them to provide water for the wildlife. To be alone in the vastness of Grand Canyon is an experience beyond compare.

Origins

The fact that I had enough outdoor background to make it as a park ranger is just another illustration of the old saw that life is what happens while you're making other plans. Here I was at the University of Arizona, hoping to enter law school later, when the ranger opportunity unexpectedly appeared. Rangering takes a good deal of physical stamina, and I had plenty of that because I grew up on a ranch outside Tucson. And my ranch life came about by a strange twist of fate.

I was born September 9, 1907, in an elegant room with hand-decorated walls and hand-carved furniture at "Sweet-wine," my family's country home in Cincinnati, Ohio. My father Louis G. Hummel ran a thriving law practice and held extensive business interests. At the time of my birth, he was about to join the ranks of the wealthy with a chemical formula which promised a low-cost substitute for gas street lights. Three months later he lost everything in the "financial crisis" of 1907. All he had left was a mining interest in Greaterville, Arizona.

And so we went West. My father Louis went first, followed by my mother Emma, who brought my brothers Louis and Gene, my sisters Villette and Floss and Della and three-month-old me. We arrived in Tucson Christmas eve. It was not a happy time. Nothing seemed to work out, including the mining interest. Finding his prospects dim, my father took up a homestead near Cortaro, a dozen miles northwest of Tucson, amid the dust and the brush. The homestead laws required settlers to build a house. Dad was flat broke and trained as a lawyer, not a rancher or a carpenter. But he was resourceful. He built our Cortaro home from abandoned box-car doors enclosing a dirt floor, quite a contrast for my mother who left the comforts of a fine home back in Ohio.

We soon moved to the Santa Rita Placers, a not entirely reputable mining community in the Santa Rita Mountains southeast of Tucson, and a staging point for substantial smuggling operations out of Mexico. I do not know the exact occupational arrangement my father had, but we lived in an old frame house in Santa Rita Placers. Magnate George MacInney established the placer mining operations there, one of a "big five" successful early mine developers including newspaper baron William Randolph Hearst and Leland Stanford, founder of Stanford University.

We evidently didn't stay there long. My mother and maternal grandmother Yockey (who had joined us after we moved to Arizona) filed a homestead claim about eight miles north of Sonoita in the watershed of Cienega Creek, above what old-timers called the "Sacaton bottoms" where Sacaton bunch-grass still grows six feet tall in the valley between the Santa Ritas and Apache Peak. Some people think of Southern Arizona as an ancient scrub desert, but the mesquites and other brush are recent invaders. When I was a kid there was much less brush and vast stands of tallgrass stretched for miles around. Before the immense cattle herds of the 1894 season grazed it down, this was a sea of grass tall as a horse's belly. We lived in this favored valley for a number of years in an old frame house which had been moved down from somewhere else.

It was here that my brother Gail was born on January 11, 1911. I will never forget the day, because my sister Villette's daughter Aline and I were told to leave the house, to go up into the pasture. We didn't want to because it was raining, but the family insisted. While we were gone my father delivered Gail. Grandmother Yockey was bathing him on the oven door when we returned. Children were often bathed there because it was the warmest place in the house.

The freedom of the ranch is one of the most powerful memories of my young life. We played, roped calves, milked cows and rode horseback. Before I was old enough to go to school, I hunted rabbits every morning. I remember getting a B-B gun at the age of four and a single shot .22 caliber rifle at the age of six. Our whole family was taught to handle guns, that guns were always loaded (ours were) and that even pointing a make-believe gun at someone was absolutely taboo. My hunting provided most of the meat my family ate until we moved to Tucson years later. We seldom butchered our stock for food; it brought in our scanty cash revenues.

While I never became a good bronc rider, I broke my share of horses. By the time I was ten years old, we got all except our dray horses from the wild herds that roamed the southern Arizona country. Rounding up wild horses and driving them into our corral provided plenty of excitement. When we spotted a band of wild horses, my older brothers would get two or three riders and we'd circle the hills trying to drive the beasts into our corral. It would be a frenzied chase with one horse after another trying to break away and avoid capture.

My brother Gene would turn furious if I failed to move the running herd the way he wanted. Yet he also fretted that my horse would fall with me as I galloped across the arroyos and ditches. Maybe I was a little reckless. Ten-year-olds are naturally fearless; I sometimes marvel at the fact I ever survived childhood.

My packing experience came from the Boy Scouts, and my experience with them came from another unexpected event. When I was twelve years old my father gave up ranching and established a law practice in Tucson, finally returning to his chosen profession. We moved into town, leaving my older sister Floss in charge of the ranch. I attended Safford School not far from our new home and found the transition from rural to city school difficult. I hadn't started in the one room country school house near our ranch until I was nine, and then I covered three years of classwork in two and passed to the fourth grade with large gaps in my education. After great struggle in my new school in Tucson I caught up, and that year had the distinction of being singled out first as the dumbest and then as the brightest kid in the class. My manual training teacher, a man named Byron Morton, seemed to sense that I could benefit from some guidance and invited me into Boy Scout Troop 4, of which he was scoutmaster. He was an excellent leader and inspired those who joined. The scouts provided one of the few outlets for youngsters of that time.

One year I particularly wanted to attend the Boy Scout Summer Camp held at Camp Lawton on Mount Lemmon in the Santa Catalina high country, but couldn't afford it. Imagine my joy when the scoutmaster offered me and two others, Frank Beetson and Burton Hall, a chance to work out the camping fee by packing bedrolls and supplies to the campsite. We'd never done anything like it before, but heartily accepted the job.

On the appointed day the three of us met at the starting point in Tucson. We were given 12 burros and pack frames. We couldn't figure out what was wrong with the packs for a while. Then we realized they were for *mules* and much too large for burros. Despite the troublesome packs, we started out walking from Tucson driving these burros, many of which had never been packed before. After a fifteen mile hike to lower Sabino Canyon a truck met us with the scouts' bedrolls and clothing which we packed on the burros as well as we could and started the long trail up Mount Lemmon to Soldiers Camp, thirty miles and two days away.

The only road to Mt. Lemmon in those days looped north clear around the Santa Catalinas by way of Oracle, a 75-mile trip, so nobody was too eager to haul a bunch of Boy Scouts to camp by automobile. Then too, once this route climbed into the mountains the road was restricted to one-way traffic only, alternating up and down, which further discouraged scout-masters from auto-ferrying their troops to camp. They trucked most of the supplies to a place called Soldiers Camp and it was our job to pack them the last three miles to Camp Lawton. When our job was done, the rest of the scouts would then hike up the trail from Sabino Canyon.

But now we had to drive the pack burros to Soldiers Camp ahead of the main body of scouts. After two upward days, Beetson, Hall, and I arrived at Camp Lawton with the burros and unpacked the bedrolls and other gear. Then we trekked the three miles to Soldiers Camp, packed the tents and food supplies, and hauled them back to Camp Lawton. Aside from the fact that the packs didn't fit well, some of the burros bucked and ran into trees trying to dump their loads and we had supplies strewn all along the trail. One burro had knocked off a pack loaded with toilet paper which left streamers for some little distance. In fact, when some families drove their youngsters up to Soldiers Camp and asked the rangers for directions to Camp Lawton, they were told to just follow the toilet paper. A slight exaggeration!

When the first contingent of thirty Scouts was ready to begin their journey up to camp, we drove our burros down to lower Sabino Canyon to meet them, pick up their luggage and escort them back—thirty miles each way. This first batch was scheduled to overnight at The Basin, a good campsite some fifteen miles above Sabino. Many of these boys were tender-feet with poorly assembled bedrolls, so we found ourselves along the trail picking up bars of soap, toothbrushes and an assortment of articles falling out of the packs.

The Scoutmaster had gone on ahead of the pack animals with his enthusiastic charges and, upon reaching The Basin in early afternoon, decided to press on to the top—without reckoning that their equipage tarried far behind. Beetson, Hall, and I arrived at The Basin midafternoon and realized what had happened. Since we had all their blankets and sleeping gear, we decided to push on after them. About halfway to the Camp, the burros laid down and refused to move. They'd worked hard enough. Period. We had no choice but to make camp on the trail where we were, so we opened some bedrolls and went to sleep.

About midnight we were awakened by a periodic whistle on the trail above us. One Sutton Menard appeared, sent by the Scoutmaster to urge us on to Camp Lawton. We explained the situation to him and suggested he take a bedroll and go to sleep. Being a sensible fellow, he did. We made Camp Lawton about ten o'clock the next morning. The disgruntled scouts had spent a cold night in front of a flickering campfire. Thereafter, Tucson scouting officialdom decided to truck their boys up to Soldiers Camp by way of the roundabout Oracle road.

I never explained to the Park Service just exactly what packing experience I had. I only mentioned that I could pack. Fortunately, that was enough to get me the assignments.

It should be plain by now that some things in my life were "just happening." I was trying my best to arrive at a definite goal, to be a lawyer like my father. But those unexpected events kept cropping up in my path. Yet when you stop to think about it, what better way to strike out on the discovery trail than by accident?

3

Concessions and Conflict

PERHAPS ALL THIS personal history seems rambling and a little disjointed. It is, but now I want to make a point with it: The whims of fate that led me into the National Park Service are no different from the caprices that shaped the national parks themselves. National park history is as rambling, random and ragtag a story as you're ever likely to hear. The concessions grew up with the national parks, which should forewarn you not to expect any pattern in their history, either. In this chapter I'll guide you through the maze to reveal why *private enterprise* is the preferred approach to serving the public in the parks.

When Congress created the first national park at Yellowstone in 1872, it never contemplated a *system* of national parks. It certainly never contemplated a National Park Service. Moreover, Congress gave its new park (remember, it was *the only one*) no appropriations whatsoever for five years. In fact, Congress thought of Yellowstone, when it did at all, less as an aesthetic playground than as a utilitarian forest reserve or potential settlement site. Senator George Graham Vest of Missouri called it "a great breathing place for the national lungs," but his California colleague Senator Cole expressed the more general view, "I do not know why settlers should be excluded from a tract of land forty miles square." As we saw in Chapter One, only the sedulous advocacy of the Langford partisans had convinced a skeptical Congress to make Yellowstone a national park at all.

It was seven years before Congress established another

national park, this one on Mackinac Island in 1879, but it didn't survive long before it was granted to Michigan as a state park in 1885. Congress seemed more interested in getting rid of scenic wonders than in keeping them. For instance, in the Yo-Semite Valley Act of 1864 Congress gave Yosemite and the Mariposa Big Tree Grove to the state of California for "public use, resort, and recreation." However, Congress gave away only the valley itself, the "Cleft" or "Gorge," not the high Sierra country surrounding it.

People for Parks

Most of the early national parks resulted not from national clamor, but from intensive lobbying by local interests. Not until 1890 was the next permanent national park established, and then three of them came at once to California. But they came only after local nabobs pressured Congress, and the Act withdrawing them didn't even mention the word "park," but instead created "reserved forest lands."

It was Secretary of the Interior John W. Noble who later named these reserves Sequoia National Park, General Grant National Park (only four square miles in area—it was eventually enlarged to become Kings Canyon National Park), and doughnut-shaped Yosemite National Park in the high country surrounding the famous valley Congress had given to California as a state park. So Yosemite National Park at first didn't even include the place we all think of when we say "Yosemite."

The first two reserves had been promoted by prominent Visalia, California, citizen George W. Stewart and the town newspaper, the *Weekly Delta*. The campaign for Yosemite had been vigorously prosecuted by naturalist John Muir— and the Southern Pacific Railroad. Muir could hardly believe it, but grudgingly wrote, "Even the soulless Southern Pacific R.R. Co., never counted on for anything good, helped nobly in pushing the bill for [Yosemite] park through Congress."

Both Muir and the Southern Pacific followed in the footsteps of noted landscape architect and Yosemite-friend, Frederick Law Olmsted, who had designed New York City's

Central Park as a retreat from the "nervous exhaustion" of high-pressure urban life. Olmsted's early arguments for the preservation of Yosemite (as a state park in those days) are worth considering: today's preservation-versus-use controversy could gain much from it. Although Olmsted had argued in an 1865 advisory report to the California legislature that such "natural scenes of an impressive character" as Yosemite should never become "private property," his reasons were completely use-oriented. He asserted that scenic beauty had a favorable influence on "the health and vigor of men," especially their "intellect." He agreed that "the power of scenery to affect men is, in a large way, proportionate to the degree of their civilization and the degree in which their tastes have been cultivated." This view opened the door to today's high-minded elitism among some park supporters, yet Olmsted insisted that "the enjoyment of scenery employs the mind without fatigue and yet exercises it; tranquilizes it and yet enlivens it." That includes everybody. Thus scenic preservation as originally advocated was to function strictly in the service of human visitors.

By the time Yosemite's high country became a national park in 1890, concessions had been down in the valley for more than thirty years. Two crude hotels stood in the great glacial canyon by the late 1850s. The place had been popularized by James M. Hutchings, editor of the *California Magazine*, who took the first sightseeing party there to spend "five glorious days in luxurious scenic banqueting" in 1855 and soon after wrote the first promotional article about Yosemite.

White men had first seen the fabulous valley in 1833 when the Joseph Walker emigrant party went by. In October 1849 two gold miners, one of whom kept a journal, viewed Yosemite Valley. But it was little known until 1851 when a posse calling itself the Mariposa Battalion under the leadership of James Savage chased a band of raiding Yosemite Indians to the camp where they lived under Chief Tenaya. The posse ironically named the natural wonder after the Yosemite tribe (Indian for "great full-grown grizzly bear")—

who themselves called the place Ahwahnee ("deep grassy valley in the heart of the sky mountain").

Yosemite is one early major park where the railroads had little to do with any of the concessions (yet as Alfred Runte noted in his *Trains of Discovery*, the Yosemite Valley Railroad began bringing visitors in 1907 but its tracks did not enter the park proper). The valley's first amateur hotels have faded into history with a certain charming notoriety as fleabags. The Lower Hotel, built of hand-riven boards near the base of Sentinel Rock (at the foot of the present Glacier Point trail) in the fall of 1856 by four miners, has been described as "a shed partitioned by eight-foot-high split planks into four stalls, used as bedrooms; it had gaps in the roof and no floor except the earth itself." Shirley Sargent says of it in her *Yosemite & its Innkeepers*, "its function was more that of a saloon until snow crushed it." Hutchings House, or its predecessor known as the Upper Hotel, actually, has been unkindly called "a two-story crate on the banks of the Merced facing Yosemite Fall" by historian Robert Shankland, whose telling of the story I paraphrase:

The Lower Hotel was replaced by Black's Hotel in 1869. But five years earlier, James Hutchings gave up magazine editing and writing about Yosemite to become an innkeeper there: he bought the crate on the Merced in April of 1864. Hutchings House catered to its early female guests by making them retire together in the single room of the second story while herding their male escorts to repose in the open lower floor. Hutchings soon gave in to the requests of married couples and divided the lower floor into bedrooms. The doors and walls were cheesecloth and provided the most interesting magic-lantern shows to shadow-watchers.

Finally Hutchings hard-walled the place in 1869, built a sawmill to shape the necessary lumber, and hired a man to run it who called himself an "unknown nobody in the woods." In fact, it was none other than the High Priest of the Sierra himself, John Muir, "John o' Mountains," the naturalist who made a career of these "mountains of light." So devoted was

Muir to this place he once lashed himself to a valley tree during a severe thunderstorm so he could experience Yosemite to the hilt.

While Yosemite operated as a state park, new hotels proliferated along with concessions of all kinds. More came when the surrounding national park was declared in 1890 (California didn't cede the valley itself back to the federal government until 1906). The most notable arrivals of the post-park era were David A. Curry and his wife Jennie, who later became known simply as "Mother Curry." In 1894 the two ex-Hoosiers began operating covered wagon summer tours to Yellowstone from Ogden, Utah, where they had settled as schoolteachers. That was the same year, incidentally, that Congress relaxed concessioner rules, increasing a single concessioner's permissible lease-holding from ten to twenty acres maximum, and allowing construction as close as one-eighth of a mile from the natural curiosities, not that it did the Curry tours any good.

In 1895, Stanford University President David Starr Jordan invited the two schoolteachers to come live in Redwood City south of San Francisco. Jordan had taught Jennie Foster and David Curry geology at Indiana University in 1883 (three years before the youngsters were married). Here began a long "Stanford Connection" with park service concessioners. Soon after the Currys' move they shifted their summer operations to Yosemite. There they established a permanent camp similar to W.W. Wylie's famous 1896 tent camps in Yellowstone. By 1899 Camp Curry stood on the very spot in Yosemite where it stands today.

The Unsystematic System Grows

Eighteen-ninety-nine also brought America its fifth national park, Mount Rainier in Washington State. The majestic stratovolcano stands dominant on the crest of the Cascade Mountains, its 14,410-foot summit visible for over a hundred miles on a clear day in western Washington. Its visibility, glaciers and inaccessibility drew many early settlers who tried to climb the behemoth. One of them, James Longmire, in 1883 discovered a fair meadow with mineral springs on the mountain's western flank, a site he considered perfect for a lodge to house the explorers and climbers beginning to trickle toward the mountain. His Longmire Springs Hotel and Baths still stood when Congress declared Mount Rainier a national park.

The campaign to make Mount Rainier a national park was different from most. It began in 1893, pushed by a consortium of John Muir's Sierra Club, the National Geographic Society, the Geological Society of America, the American Association for the Advancement of Science (founded, incidentally, by the Grand Canyon's own Major John Wesley Powell), and the Appalachian Mountain Club. This was the first genuine national campaign for a national park. These five nature groups prepared a memorial to Congress in 1894 which Washington Senator Watson C. Squire introduced and led in 1899 to the establishment of the national park.

Some eight years later, Rainier became another railroad park like Yellowstone: The Tacoma and Eastern built the National Park Inn across the road from Longmire's place, which burned not long after the new inn came. Up in the alpine meadows of Mount Rainier, a small entrepreneur named John Reese built a seasonal tent camp in what Longmire had named Paradise Meadows. George Hall ran another tent camp at Indian Henry's Hunting Ground.

Next came Crater Lake in Oregon. It owes its 1902 designation to the assiduous advocacy of local interests, particularly William Gladstone Steel, who came out from Kansas in 1885 and got his first glimpse of the dazzling azure lake lying in the caldera of its collapsed volcano. He was impressed by its rockribbed walls reaching a thousand feet above waterline. Steel instantly decided it was worthy of the same recognition given to Yellowstone, and in only five months convinced President Cleveland to withdraw the area from settlement. But making it a national park took seventeen long hard-fought years of lobbying and concession-building by Will Steel—and all of his money.

Wind Cave National Park was established in South Dakota in 1903, enshrining limestone caverns with intricate boxwork and fairylike calcite crystal formations in the scenic Black Hills. The truth is it was a small and not very distinguished place that later national park administrators did not regard as being of national park quality. In 1906 Mesa Verde in southwestern Colorado gained the cachet of Congress, an archaeologist's park established to stop raiders from plundering the hundreds of ancient Indian dwellings in the cliffs of a vast tree-crowned plateau.

Now let me beg your patience. All this discourse on the whens and wheres of these early park days has a reason: It helps to understand modern events in the national parks. Without this context, we remain ignorant, and today's theft of the national parks by environmentalists can remain cloaked in high-sounding generalities, which is exactly what the environmentalists want. I won't let that happen.

We can already see that indeed no system accompanied the founding of the national parks. Not only was there no National Park Service to provide consistent administration, but there was also no single individual within the Department of the Interior assigned exclusively to the parks. The few clerks in the Department who had been saddled with the parks generally ignored them—they had more important things to do.

The national parks grew not only without plan or supervision, but also without immunity to politics. The political machinations of the two decades from 1890 to 1910 threw the future of the national parks into near-chaos. The trouble, as you might expect, centered around the preservation-versus-use controversy.

Titans of Conservation

The early controversy revolved primarily around the ideas of two men, John Muir and Gifford Pinchot. The two could hardly have been more different. Muir was an "aesthetic" preservationist, as differentiated from Pinchot's "practical" conservationism. Muir, born into modest circumstances in

Scotland and reared in Wisconsin, despite his hortatory agitation for the national parks idea was personally shy and inward-looking. His approach to nature has been called "essentially religious," by historian Robert Shankland. Robert Underwood Johnson, editor of the popular 1890s magazine *Century* tagged Muir as "great Nature's high priest." Muir's preoccupation with nature earned him an international reputation as writer, naturalist and scholar. Muir's writings on Yosemite exerted great influence in Congress, enough to thwart strenuous objections to a new national park by California settlers.

Gifford Pinchot, on the other hand, was the scion of a wealthy Eastern family, a European-trained professional forester and political confidant of Theodore Roosevelt. Roosevelt appointed Pinchot the first Chief of the Forest Service when it was established in 1905 in the U.S. Department of Agriculture. Pinchot is credited with coining the term "conservation" as applied to nature, meaning "the wise use of resources." Although wise use might encompass preservation in selected places, Pinchot used the term primarily to indicate economic timber harvesting, protection of watersheds for agricultural and urban water supplies, and other utilitarian goals of the Progressive Era. Historian Samuel P. Hays has characterized Pinchot's vision of conservation as "the gospel of efficiency."

All this is important to know because of an intricate string of events that was to shape the future of the parks: Congress had passed an Act in 1891 that empowered the President to establish forest reserves by proclamation, and that led fourteen years later to the creation of the Forest Service. This in turn led to political maneuvering by Pinchot to get the national parks transferred from the Interior Department to his Forest Service so he could manage them for utilitarian as well as scenic purposes. Reaction to Pinchot's maneuvering led to the campaign that created the National Park Service. Complicated? Yes, indeed.

It happened like this: The power to designate forest reserves previous to the 1891 Forest Reserves Act rested in the hands of Congress. In fact, the three 1890 forest reserves that Interior Secretary Noble unilaterally turned into national parks in California had been established by Congress. But the Forest Reserve Act of 1891 gave the President proclamation power over forest reserves, and it's much easier for one man to create preserves by proclamation than for Congress to thrash it out among several hundred individuals of diverse origin and opinion.

President Harrison immediately withdrew 13 million acres of America as forest reserves and President Cleveland shortly added 5 million more, but said he would add no more until some real protection measures were taken. Congress had given the president the mere power to create such reserves, not to manage them.

But the Forest Management Act of 1897 did provide for managed use of the forest reserves, to be administered by the General Land Office of the Department of the Interior. Preservationists hoped that the Interior Department would convert more of these forest reserves into national parks. But it was not to be. Under heavy pressure from the Pinchot faction Congress transferred this forest administrative duty to a new bureau in the Department of Agriculture in 1905: the Forest Service, Pinchot presiding. The reserves began to be called "national forests" in 1907, and no more national parks could be carved from them—agency rivalry saw to that.

Pinchot's boss, Teddy Roosevelt, established forest reserves left and right, bringing the total up to 150 million acres. Settlers became alarmed by all this public land vanishing into the government's grab-bag and screamed their opposition. Congress prudently took the proclamation power away from the president, but not before Roosevelt and Pinchot selected last-minute reserves from everything that looked good on a map—including an embarrassing fifty-thousand-acre stretch of what turned out to be treeless sagebrush in Inyo County, California. Visitors still laugh at the Forest Service sign welcoming them to the desert lowlands of Inyo

National Forest, but they stop laughing when they drive up to the sparse ancient bristlecone pines atop White Mountain, the oldest living creatures on earth at 8,200 years.

The National Monuments

In 1906, the year I told the Park Service I was born, things really got complicated. Pinchot's suddenly burgeoning Forest Service empire alarmed not only the settlers, but also the preservationists. They quickly enlisted Iowa Congressman John F. Lacey to introduce a bill giving the president the power to set aside by proclamation any lands owned by the United States that contained "historic landmarks, historic or prehistoric structures, and other objects of historic or scientific interest." These lands would be known as national monuments. Lacey had just successfully promoted Mesa Verde for a national park and threw his considerable legislative talents into convincing his colleagues to pass the Preservation of American Antiquities Act of 1906, called by some "the Lacey Act." And this is where the fun began.

Teddy Roosevelt proclaimed the first national monument on September 24, 1906 at Devils Tower, Wyoming, an 865-foot tower of columnar rock, the remains of a volcanic intrusion; in the same year the Rough Rider proclaimed El Morro, New Mexico and Montezuma Castle in Arizona as national monuments. The Antiquities Act got a lot of use. It eventually encompassed everything from Arizona's ten acre Tumacacori National Monument (1908, a Spanish Catholic mission building) to the two and a half million acres of Katmai in Alaska (1919, a vast nature reserve including the highly volcanic "Valley of Ten Thousand Smokes").

Here's the rub: jurisdiction over the national monuments and their various concessions was divided between three agencies. The Interior Department managed those taken from the public domain, the Agriculture Department had jurisdiction over those from the national forests, and the War Department had control over military reservations.

Even worse, there was no uniformity within the national

parks themselves. The appropriations that went to any particular park got there because of the influence of that park's particular friends. Park superintendents ran their parks more or less as each saw fit. Concessioners operated under widely divergent regulations from park to park.

And to make things completely absurd, even within a given park authority was split according to historical accident. In Yellowstone, for example, all improvements and the appropriations for those improvements were controlled by an officer of the Army Corps of Engineers who was not answerable to the Interior Department or the park superintendent (the result of that 1883 Sundry Civil Expenses Act). Even though the original 1872 Yellowstone law said "exclusive control" of the park rested with the Secretary of the Interior, the park superintendent himself was an Army officer appointed by the Secretary of War. At Mount Rainier and Crater Lake Army engineers built the roads and improvements but the park superintendents were civilians appointed by the Interior Secretary. Yosemite, General Grant and Sequoia, on the other hand, had no engineers but the park superintendents were Army officers appointed by the Secretary of War. It was quite a zoo. And Gifford Pinchot was trying to herd it into the Forest Service.

The Prophet of Parks

Obviously, something had to be done, but no one was quite sure what. J. Horace McFarland changed all that. He was a civic leader, editor of a Harrisburg, Pennsylvania, newspaper, president of the American Civic Association, and ardent national parks advocate. He felt that Pinchot's utilitarian urges were out of place in the national parks, and the two crossed swords over the celebrated "Hetch-Hetchy steal" in the Yosemite country. Hetch-Hetchy Valley had become part of Yosemite National Park in 1890, but in 1908 Pinchot publicly supported its development as a water supply reservoir for the city of San Francisco, giving the project the impetus it needed for success. San Francisco, built on a sandy

peninsula, had been devastated by the earthquake and fire of
1906 and obviously needed a good fresh water supply. National Park or no, Pinchot thought Hetch-Hetchy's water
should, as he put it, "serve the public utility."

When Pinchot appealed to McFarland for his association's
support in the Hetch-Hetchy matter, he asserted that the
aesthetic side of conservation in this dispute could not be
allowed to "go ahead of the economic and moral aspects of the
case." McFarland angrily retorted, "I feel that the conservation movement is now weak, because it has failed to join
hands with the preservation of scenery." The proper view,
said McFarland, is "that the preservation of forests, water
powers, minerals and the other items of national prosperity in
a sane way must be associated with the pleasure of the eye
and the mind and the regeneration of the spirit of man."

McFarland realized that if he was to make all this high talk
mean anything, he must take a leaf from the "efficiency boys"
and get Congress to create a special bureau to take care of the
national parks and nothing else, something on the lines of the
Forest Service, but in the Interior Department, not in the
Agriculture Department. McFarland turned out to be a great
lobbyist. He started on Secretary of the Interior Richard A.
Ballinger. In 1910 the Secretary's annual report to the President recommended the creation of "a bureau of national parks
and resorts, under the supervision of a competent commissioner, with a suitable force of superintendents, supervising
engineers, and landscape architects, inspectors, park guards,
and other employees."

Pinchot fumed against this proposal, arguing that a National Parks Bureau was "no more needed than two tails to a
cat." But now the parks forces took the offensive, and history
was on their side: The automobile had come into its own, and
the American public was ready to travel. Railroad promotion
agents had sensed the flow of tourist dollars to well-developed
and accessible European scenic spots and had coined the
slogan "See America First." This slogan rapidly gained
enough partisans to take on the character of a social move-

ment. William Howard Taft was President and had named Walter L. Fisher, a friend of the national parks, as Secretary of the Interior in 1911. Now, as one of his first official acts in office, Fisher called a national parks conference in Yellowstone, the first historic activist mobilization of park officials, See-America-Firsters, and park boosters such as McFarland.

By 1911 there were eleven national parks and twenty-one national monuments, most administered by the Interior Department, and their problems were well known: how to get enough money, enough visitors, enough governmental recognition, enough public supporters. The conference dealt with these issues straightforwardly.

Louis W. Hill, president of the Great Northern Railway, promoter and concessioner of the year-old Glacier National Park, told the conference: "We do not wish to go into the hotel business; we wish to get out of it and confine ourselves strictly to the business of getting people there just as soon as we can. But it is difficult to get capital interested in this kind of pioneer work. With the cooperation and assistance of the government, we hope within two or three years to get financial people interested in the park and then we can get out and attend to railroading."

It sounded like a replay of the Northern Pacific's 1883 plaintive cry in Yellowstone, and it was. For many years railroads were to be the most reliable source of venture capital necessary to provide visitor accommodations in the national parks. It was not surprising considering the short business seasons, demanding work conditions, and meager profits to be had in concessioning. You had to have a lot of capital to weather such storms, and few had as much capital in those days as the railroads.

The under-capitalized park concessioner was doomed to slow destitution. Congress might provide Army engineers to build a few roads in the parks, but was not about to spend a dime on visitor accommodations. Will G. Steel told the 1911 conference about his experience promoting the creation of the sixth national park: "Aside from the United States govern-

ment itself, every penny that was ever spent in the creation of
Crater Lake National Park came out of my pocket, and besides that, it required many years of hard labor that was freely
given. When that was accomplished, I felt that my long labor
was finished, and was so green, so simple-minded, that I
thought that the United States government would go ahead
and develop the proposition. In this, I found that I was mis-
taken, so I had to go to work again. All the money I have is in
the park, and if I had more, it would go there too. This is my
life's work, and I propose to see it through."

The conference closed after hearing many speakers besides
concessioners come to the same conclusion: a national parks
bureau was badly needed. Concessioners supported the bureau idea because they thought it would mean government
help with their concessions. The bureau idea caught on.

The Bureau Campaign

McFarland ran around Washington telling everybody who
would listen, "Nowhere in official Washington can an inquirer
find an office of national parks or a single desk devoted solely
to their management." One of the listeners was President
Taft, who agreed to address the 1911 annual convention of
McFarland's American Civic Association. Taft told them:

> Now we have in the United States a great many natural
> wonders, and in that lazy way we have in our government of
> first taking up one thing and then another, we have set aside a
> number of national parks, of forest reservations covering what
> ought to be national parks, and what are called "national monu-
> ments." We have said to ourselves, "Those cannot get away.
> We have surrounded them by a law which makes them neces-
> sarily government property forever, and we will wait in our
> own good time to make them useful as parks to the people.
> Since the Interior Department is the 'lumber room' of the
> government, into which we put everything that we don't know
> how to classify, and don't know what to do with, we will just
> put them under the Secretary of the Interior." That is the
> condition of the national parks today.

President Taft was hooked: On February 2, 1912, he sent this special message to Congress:

> I earnestly recommend the establishment of a Bureau of National Parks. Such legislation is essential to the proper management of those wonderful manifestations of nature, so startling and so beautiful that everyone recognizes the obligation of the government to preserve them for the edification and recreation of the people . . . Every consideration of patriotism and the love of nature and of beauty and of art requires us to expend money enough to bring all these natural wonders within easy reach of our people. The first step in that direction is the establishment of a responsible bureau. . . .

When Woodrow Wilson became President, he appointed another parks supporter as Secretary of the Interior, Franklin K. Lane. Fate seemed to be on the side of the national parks now: Lane liked the idea of a parks bureau. He hired an old friend of independent means to be Assistant to the Secretary at the ridiculous salary of $2,750 a year and make sense of the parks mess: Professor of Economics Adolph C. Miller of the University of California, Lane's alma mater. However, President Wilson soon discovered Miller's talents and whisked him away from Lane on loan to the Treasury Department to draft legislation creating the Federal Reserve Board. Wilson told the Secretary, "Go find another millionaire with an itch for public service."

Easier said than done. Yet against all odds, one morning in the fall of 1914 the problem solved itself: a classmate of Adolph Miller's at California sent the Secretary a scorching letter protesting the lack of protection in the national parks, a self-made millionaire who got his start with the famed 20 Mule Team Borax firm. His name was Steve Mather.

Lane sent him back the now-famous reply, "Dear Steve: If you don't like the way the national parks are being run, come on down to Washington and run them yourself."

4

Steve Mather

NOW WE COME TO the most decisive episode in the entire
history of our national parks. It gave the people real
access to the parks. It made the private concessioner advocate
of that access. It is the story of a genuine American hero,
Stephen Tyng Mather, a name to conjure with in the National
Park Service. To know his story is to know why the national
parks must never be stolen by our environmentalist neigh-
bors. Let's see what happened after he got that terse reply
from Franklin K. Lane.

Running the national parks was not what Steve Mather had
in mind when he dashed off his furious complaint to Secretary
Lane. Even so, the note was something of a put-up job:
Secretary Lane had earlier arranged to visit Mather in
Chicago through a mutual friend named John H. Wigmore.
After sizing Mather up and liking what he saw, Lane actually
asked for the letter. He was pleased with Mather's forthright
criticism of conditions in the parks, because it gave him the
excuse he needed to fire back the famous message.

Mather, however, was not prepared to accept the job. He
was a dynamic and powerful businessman, unwilling to be
wrapped in red tape. As historian John Ise described him in
Our National Park Policy, Mather was "a man of prodigious
and explosive energy, a tireless worker, a born promoter, 'a
practical idealist of the live-wire type,' with a generous devotion to his job which is reminiscent of some of America's
greatest—Washington, Thomas Paine, and Gifford Pinchot."
NPS historians Harlan D. Unrau and G. Frank Williss noted

that Mather's "success in the private sector rested as much on his publicity skills as it did on organizational ability." Horace Albright said, "He was like a wound spring." Mather was used to getting things done by whatever means possible, not going through channels. Work for the government? He'd strangle on red tape.

But Mather actually stopped and considered the idea. Run them yourself. He liked Lane's attitude. Run them yourself. Mather had a mind to do just that: he was a member of the Sierra Club, had met John Muir, had climbed Mount Rainier with Sierra Club bigwigs, considered himself a conservationist. He'd been born in Connecticut, educated at the University of California, Berkeley, and settled in Chicago. He held an active membership in McFarland's American Civic Association, too. Run them yourself. After much cajoling by friends and family, and assurances from his business partner that their Chicago borax firm could survive without him for a while, Mather reluctantly agreed to visit Lane in Washington. He got there on a stormy December morning and listened to Lane's blandishments.

The proposition went something like this: You come to work here for a year, visit the parks, see their problems for yourself, figure out what to do with them, and we'll back your recommendations before Congress. If that includes creating a national parks bureau, you can hand-pick its first commissioner. You'll be back to your borax business next year and America will be eternally grateful for your service. We'll even provide a man to steer you through the red tape so you don't strangle.

Enter Albright

Lane introduced Mather to the second man this story is about: a young fellow named Horace Marden Albright. A law student from the University of California, Albright had been brought to Washington on May 31, 1913, by Adolph Miller—and was anxious to get back home. But when he met Steve Mather it was instant rapport. Mather wanted to know if Albright knew his way around the government. Albright said he pretty much did. The way historian Robert Shankland tells the tale, Mather said, "Okay, I'll think about giving a year to the national parks if you'll think about staying and keeping me out of jail." Horace Albright's 1985 telling of the incident in *The Birth of the National Park Service* leaves out the part about keeping Mather out of jail. Horace has a phenomenal memory, so he's probably right, but since I believe every bureaucrat needs that kind of assistance, I can't help but think the Shankland version is how it ought to have gone.

On January 21, 1915, Stephen Tyng Mather was sworn in as Assistant to the Secretary of the Interior. Thus began the partnership with Horace Albright that lasted all the years of Mather's life. Together these men were to shape the destiny of the national parks.

Mather quickly determined that getting a parks bureau from Congress was imperative. But he realized that the necessary political backing could only come from a populace that knew and appreciated the parks. Getting people to the parks and accommodating them once they got there was therefore the first order of business.

That meant two things: Improving automobile and rail access, and straightening out the tangle of concession leases. Mather went to Yellowstone and saw that the Northern Pacific had long departed from the concession scene except as mortgage holder. In 1901 the railroad had become nervous about the wavering attitude of Congress toward concessioners and turned their Yellowstone Park Association hotel properties over to Harry W. Child, a stagecoach operator in the park. Now Child ran a chain of five hotels and two lunch stations. He and two others ran their own stagecoach lines, and three other firms operated low-cost permanent camp systems. A passel of small operators ran travelling camps that took visitors on a wide variety of pack trips through the park.

At first Mather was impressed by the enterprise of these concessioners, but stood appalled at the high-pressure sales tactics they used to sway disembarking Northern Pacific passengers at the park boundary. In one instance two competing stage drivers grabbed a customer one by each arm and ripped his coat in half. Mather also didn't like concessioners' efforts to sabotage each other to dominate the market, and decided free market competition was not what government parks needed.

Shaping Concession Policy

In one of the great ironies of American history, Steve Mather, free enterpriser *par excellence*, decided to establish a regulated monopoly system for the national parks. As things turned out, it was probably the wisest alternative. Mather was faced with a number of unyielding historical facts that influenced his decision. To begin with, Congress had never given approval to a general policy of government ownership of public accommodation facilities in the parks although many individual members had favored it during the course of time. That being the case, it was essential to enlist private capital to provide park accommodations.

Owners of private capital had erected the buildings, furnished transportation equipment and provided the organization necessary to care for the public staying in the parks. Congress had originally stipulated that no concession lease could be granted for more than ten years. Ten years proved too short a period to enable private companies to install the proper types of accommodations—particularly buildings, which take a long time to amortize—and furnish regular service with any assurance of a fair return on their investment.

Mather discovered that the economic problems of park concessions were staggering: Money came in only during the two or three snow-free months—mostly on weekends—but went out ll twelve in the form of interest, depreciation and obsolescence. Food and supplies had to be hauled in over long distances. Crews with the proper skills, sensitivity to the visitor's needs, and willingness to take seasonal work were hard to find. Repairing storm damage was a perennial problem—the roof of Crater Lake Lodge caved in one winter under heavy snow. Vandalism by people and bears became an annual headache. And those are only a few concessioner worries.

To recoup even a small investment in ten years you had to get *most* of the business. The result was a chaotic situation in the parks, as hotel competed against hotel and agents of various transportation companies hounded, harassed and misinformed prospective passengers. Park visitors were the sufferers. While on vacation the average American neither likes to be besieged by representatives of various caterers to his comfort nor to take time to shop around on the ground to secure the best accommodations at the lowest rates.

Congress recognized the problem posed by short-term leases and allowed the Interior Secretary to grant 20-year terms to approved concessioners in all existing national parks in 1914, just before Mather arrived. But even 20-year terms were not enough to entice well-capitalized businessmen into the risky world of park concessions, and attracting sound concessioners became one of Mather's major problems.

Realizing that some order had to be brought out of this confusion, Mather settled on the ideal plan to license one prime concessioner for each park, one firm to do everything, run the hotels, transportation, camps, everything—a regulated monopoly (just what Congress forbade after the 1882 Yellowstone concession flap). Mather realized that any time the word "monopoly" rustled through Congress in connection with park concessioners, he could expect roars of outrage. Americans had learned to detest monopolies. Mather, as the prime mover of park policy, knew he had to get his arguments lined up in defensible form.

The Public Utility Theory

This is how he thought it out: Government parks were perfect settings for regulated monopolies, primarily because there was not enough business in any single park to yield much profit. He had seen with his own eyes that too many businesses in Yellowstone had created less than desirable results. Mather had personal experience with Chicago municipal reform societies that advocated regulated telephone monopolies. Public utilities were "natural monopolies" according to some economists of the day, and national park concessioners were public utilities in Mather's view. Concessioners willing to operate under a regulated monopoly would of necessity be looking not only for profits, but would also have to possess a strong sense of park values and public service. He would sell his idea to critics with the public utility argument.

In fact, Mather never once used the word "concessioner" as a heading for the concession section of his annual reports to the Secretary of the Interior, instead titling the subject "Public-Utility Services." As an amusing sidelight to Mather's struggle with concessions, it's interesting to see how many different names the government later applied to them. After Mather's tenure ended in 1928, the Secretary of the Interior's Annual Reports called them "Public-Utility Services" until 1934. In 1935 and '36 the concession section of the report was titled, "Accommodations for the Public Furnished by Private Capital." Then in 1937 it changed to "Services by Park Concessioners" and in 1938 "Accommodations Furnished by Concessionaires" (note the two spellings). In 1939 it was "Services Furnished by Park Operators" and stayed that way until the Second World War. In the 1940s the word "concessioners" became dominant and remains so to this day.

When Mather first came to the parks in 1915, the main factor that prompted his regulated monopoly idea was the problem of too many concessioners in each park competing for too little business. But there were other problems. Mather felt that the multiple operations in Yellowstone, which had the strongest "public-utility services" array in any of the parks, were pre-empting too much park space.

Then too, there was the matter of poor service. Each concessioner wanted to provide only the profitable services and no one wanted to provide the unprofitable. The lessees wanted to open for July and August and close as soon as the visitor count dropped off. This meant that early park visitors in June and late visitors in September usually found few, if any accommodations. Mather knew that the visitor had to come first, and racked his brain for practical ways to install regulated monopolies.

Birth of the Park Service

While Mather struggled with his plans to improve services for the park visitor, the focus of national park action shifted to Congress. It was time to create that bureau. When the first park bureau bill had been introduced in 1912, it quietly died in committee. In 1913 another effort fizzled. But now in 1915 the McFarlands of the country had done their homework, dragging Congressmen around the parks all summer and drowning the newspapers and magazines in national park stories. With Mather's help they had convinced independent Congressman William Kent of Chicago to introduce a fresh, well-drafted parks bureau bill. A highly respected confederate of the parks clan, Frederick Law Olmsted, Jr.—who had taken his father's position as a leading landscape architect—wrote a short but crucial section of the new bill.

Olmsted's policy statement set forth the purpose of the proposed new national park service: "To conserve the scenery and the natural and historic objects and the wild life [in the parks] and to provide for the enjoyment of same in such manner and by such means as will leave them unimpaired for the enjoyment of future generations." Even though Olmsted's father had made it clear that preservation was justified only by its benefits to people, this dual preservation-use mandate was to create endless conflict in the years ahead. Nonetheless, Congress liked the draft and passed the National Park Service Act on August 25, 1916. Seventeen parks awaited the new service, along with 22 national monuments, some of which belonged to other agencies. And Congress had wisely included the new 20-year concession lease period in this new Act.

Unfortunately, the bill came after the Interior Department's 1916 appropriation had been passed—without funds for any National Park Service. Thus, an "interim service" had to be set up with Mather's hand-picked leader, Director Robert B. Marshall, who had been chief geographer in another Interior agency, the U.S. Geological Survey (no, this is not the same Bob Marshall who explored the Alaska Arctic and later founded the Wilderness Society). Even so, now Mather could return to his Chicago borax business and Albright could go into a long-awaited law practice in California. They had got their bureau from Congress and their public service was done—they thought.

The Mather-Albright Principles

Mather and Albright expected great things of Marshall. As those things turned out, Bob Marshall was a better geographer than administrator: he quickly botched the new Park Service budget for a powerhouse at Yosemite and annoyed the public by shutting down Yellowstone two weeks early for fear of a railroad strike that never materialized. Mather gave him back to the Geological Survey, which welcomed him, but Marshall resented the demotion and accused Mather of wanting the directorship for himself. Whether he wanted it or not, Secretary of the Interior Lane appointed Mather Director April 17, 1917, with Albright as assistant director. Neither was thrilled by the honor, but both sighed and resigned themselves to a little more public service.

Albright became a co-founder of concession policy because Mather suffered a nervous breakdown after his first high-voltage year of whipping the parks into shape. Albright actually managed the new Park Service during much of 1917. Once Mather returned to work, concessions occupied much of his time. He was determined to install his regulated monopoly idea as a national concessions policy and gradually managed the feat by whatever means proved workable, persuasion when possible, tyranny when necessary.

The truth is, he had already gone a long way toward creating his regulated monopoly system. Back in mid-1916 Mather had ordered Harry W. Child to merge his hotels, which had always lost money, with Frank J. Haynes' transportation line, which had always turned a neat profit (Haynes had originally been Yellowstone's first official photographer since 1882). Mather wanted to motorize park transportation anyway— horse-drawn transportation concessioners had stiffly resisted the incursion of automobiles in the national parks and had even convinced the Interior Department to impose a discriminatory entry fee on motorists. When Child submitted the better bid on the new Yellowstone contract in 1917, Mather let him buy Haynes out and convinced him to purchase a hundred ten-passenger buses and sixteen seven-passenger cars. Haynes went cheerfully back into the photography business.

In the fall of 1916 Mather had also revoked the franchise of one of the three permanent camp operators, the Old Faithful Camp Company, and forced the other two to merge. Now Yellowstone had only a single hotel company, a single transportation company, and a single camping company combined from two predecessors that had also dropped their own transportation business. Except for the general stores and a few minor concessions, Mather had the park well on the way to a regulated monopoly. The visitor must come first. The concessioners at Rocky Mountain, Mount Rainier, Crater Lake and Glacier national parks quickly acquiesced in Mather's consolidation program.

Mather justified his acts in Yellowstone in his first Annual Report of the Director of the National Park Service, ". . . it would be uneconomical to permit the establishment of more than one transportation line on the Yellowstone roads with each touching the same point . . . more than one line would be difficult to control by the Park authorities, as questions of right-of-way on the roads would constantly arise . . . with more than one competing transportation system the tourist would be subjected to importunities and harassment at railroad terminals by rival solicitors . . . supply stations and garages would be very large and it would be doubtful if more than one line could be operated at a profit."

The new contractual arrangement in Yellowstone was not to be the old lease format dating from 1872. Mather decided that leases would be inadequate to handle his regulated monopolies, so he brought forward the concept of *contracts* for park "public-utility service" operators (concessioners). Even though he could not immediately place all concessions under one prime contractor in each park, the contract idea would at least lead in that direction, whereas leases tended to proliferate uncontrollably. And control was what Mather wanted, for the visitor's sake.

Contracts were to replace leases. "Public-utility service" operators were to be allowed to make a profit, but, as Mather wrote, it must be "consistent with satisfactory service to the public and a fair return on capital invested, irregularity of seasons, and the otherwise generally hazardous nature of the investment being considered." Concessioners generally felt this language from Mather's 1917 contract with Child in Yellowstone to be acceptable. Similar contracts eventually became the order of the day in Yosemite and other parks.

Franchise fees to the government in Mather's contracts were based on a percentage of the net profit and were minimal. The concessioner was entitled to make six percent on his investment, which was cumulative. In other words, if he did not make six percent during any given year, he could make six percent the next year, plus any deficiency from earlier years before paying a fee to the government. If cumulative profits went over six percent, 37 percent of the excess went to the government with the balance retained by the concessioner. Under these provisions the concessioner seldom had to pay the government a fee, since he rarely made a six percent return on his investment. Revenue to the government was not a major purpose of concessions as far as Mather was concerned: service to the park visitor was.

In these early days of the Park Service, concessioners and bureaucrats for the most part got along famously. Interior Secretary Franklin K. Lane had written a long twenty-three-point policy letter to Mather on May 13, 1918—it is still regarded as the creed or manifesto of the parks—which stated in part:

> As concessions in the national parks represent in most instances a large investment, and as the obligation to render service satisfactory to the department at carefully regulated rates is imposed, these enterprises must be given a large measure of protection, and generally speaking, competitive business should not be authorized where a concession is meeting our requirements, which, of course, will as nearly as possible coincide with the needs of the travelling public.

Mather took the person-to-person lead putting this cooperative policy into effect. For example, when things got tough for the Yosemite National Park Company about 1918—their competitor Camp Curry was doing fine—Mather recklessly loaned them two hundred thousand dollars out of his own pocket at five percent interest. This gave his political enemies something to think about, but no one ever pressed the issue. Even this largesse could not keep the Company afloat, so in 1920 Mather helped them raise a million dollars by public subscription, enlisting the aid of his friend Henry Chandler, publisher of the *Los Angeles Times*. The subscription kept the Company crippling along for another five years.

The regulated monopoly policy raised some new questions. Concessioners particularly wanted to know the extent to which their contracts might be considered exclusive. Who would have preference to provide new services or accommodations, the existing concessioner or a hopeful newcomer? Could entrepreneurs from the surrounding private land enter a park to offer competitive services? The question proved to be sufficiently vexing that it was put to the Solicitor of the Interior Department (the chief legal officer) for a formal legal opinion. On February 21, 1924, a Solicitor's opinion definitely established as Department policy the preferential right of operators to provide facilities, accommodations and service authorized under their contracts. Assistant Secretary for Public Lands John H. Edwards had originally supported this position, and the concessioners thus called this policy "the Edwards decision." They regarded it, along with Secretary Lane's "parks manifesto," as the cornerstone of concession policy.

Mather had most concessions on an even keel until 1924 when petty bickering between the Yosemite concessioners flared up. Seeing the problems of competition in the parks so loudly paraded, Mather grew impatient to impose his regulated monopoly plan. The new Secretary of the Interior Hubert E. Work, an impatient man himself, told Mather in late 1924 exactly what he wanted to hear: the rival Yosemite companies would have to merge or be replaced. Albright was sent to negotiate, and his first instruction was to ask for repayment of Mather's $200,000 loan to the Yosemite National Park Company. Once that impossible request had been made, both concessioners saw the handwriting on the wall and were in a mood for serious discussions. The merger was announced February 21, 1925.

Installing the Policy

The result was the Yosemite Park & Curry Company, controlled by the Curry family, and secured in its concession by a contract dated February 4, 1926. Its president was an able young fellow named Donald B. Tresidder, who had married Mary Curry, daughter of David and Jennie Curry, cofounders of Camp Curry. Tresidder is another link in the "Stanford Connection:" he met Mary while a Stanford student working in one of many summer jobs provided to college students by the Currys. He had earned his degree as a medical doctor (but never entered medical practice) and went on to become president of Stanford University during the 1940s. The firm he headed remains Yosemite's prime concessioner to this day.

In 1926, several important concession contracts were granted specifying certain property relations that were to bedevil future concessioners. Article IX of those 1926 contracts—it was to become known as "that *damned* Article IX"—stated, "all buildings, fixtures and appurtenances, whether now on the land or hereafter placed thereon, shall at all times be part of the realty and the property of the United States." Concessioners asked the Park Service, "Does that mean we get to pay for it and you get to keep it?" The Park Service said, "Don't worry, we understand your need for security of investment. That's just to keep some creditor from legally attaching your hotel and removing it for debt. It won't be interpreted narrowly. As long as you provide satisfactory public service, your contracts will be renewed and your beneficial ownership of the buildings will remain intact. You have the good faith of the government of the United States."

Concessioners looked over the rest of Article IX and saw: ". . . if, on the expiration of this contract . . . the premises shall be leased to some one other than the [existing concessioner], the latter shall be given an opportunity to be reimbursed for the reasonable value of such of its buildings, fixtures, stock, equipment and other property thereon. . . . The value of such buildings and property . . . shall be paid . . . to the [existing concessioner] by the person to whom the premises are to be leased. . . ."

The Park Service said, "See, even if you lose your contract, you can get reimbursement from your successor, so your investment is secure." No one saw until 1946 that a quite different and absolutely devastating interpretation could be gained from reading those words. But that's getting ahead of our story.

Mather, at Albright's insistence, had discovered the beauties of Zion and Bryce Canyon on a 1919 auto trip, and went after the Union Pacific Railroad to develop concessions there and at the North Rim of the Grand Canyon. He admitted that they would probably make no money but would "accumulate enough goodwill to set back bolshevism twenty years." Mather turned on the charm and talked them into it. They incorporated a subsidiary, Utah Parks Company, which built fine lodges designed by noted architect Gilbert Stanley

Underwood at Zion, Bryce, and Cedar Breaks in Utah. When the U.P. opened the North Rim Grand Canyon Lodge in 1928, the railroad threw a huge celebration in honor of its long labors and in honor of Steve Mather.

By 1928 Mather had achieved most of his regulated monopoly plan. On April 24 he gave official approval to the policy of preferential rights embodied in "the Edwards decision," and even convinced Congress that year to include in its annual Interior Department appropriations bill a provision authorizing the Interior Secretary to grant concession contracts "without advertising and without securing competitive bids." No contracts were to be assigned "without the approval of the Secretary of the Interior," but the Secretary was authorized to permit concessioners to "execute mortgages . . . upon their rights, properties, and franchises, for the purpose of installing, enlarging, or improving plant and equipment and extending facilities for the accommodation of the public."

Now Mather's regulated monopoly policy had gained the status of law. He had insured the concessioners' private property rights in their buildings and equipment even though the land on which they were built remained vested in the United States. He had found the formula that enabled private enterprise to serve the park visitor properly, and set the stage to protect public access to the parks forever. His fourteen-year struggle to insure adequate facilities and services for the public had paid off.

It is impossible for us today to honor Steve Mather's achievements enough. His policies brought millions of Americans to their national parks for the first time, gave us an appreciation for what we had protected, and struck an intelligent balance between those old antagonists, preservation and use. It is only because we have forgotten Mather's lessons, lost our historical memory, that the environmentalists can steal the national parks.

Steve Mather's visitor accommodation policy gained Congressional approval none to soon. On Monday, November 5, 1928, while talking to his attorney in Chicago, Mather suffered a paralytic stroke. He was rushed to St. Luke's hospital. Assistant Director Horace Albright, now Mather's aide in the field, hurried from San Francisco to his side, but there was little he could do. Within days it became obvious that Mather's active life with the parks was over. He named Albright to succeed him as Director in mid-December. Interior Secretary Roy O. West and President Coolidge made it official January 12, 1929.

Now we've come back up to the time when I first discovered the parks, a summer ranger unaware of the policy and personal dramas playing themselves out far away.

5

Lassen

WHILE ALL THIS was going on in the East, I was doing my best to prepare for a career in the West. I had graduated from the University of Arizona in June of 1930 and returned to my summer job at Grand Canyon National Park—my third summer there. I was getting to be a pretty good ranger by now, but the idea of a career in the parks was the farthest thing from my mind. The day before my summer stint at Grand Canyon was over, though, fate nudged me gently and changed my future.

A fellow ranger named George Collins waited with me on the South Rim for Chief Ranger Brooks to give us an assignment. Just to pass the time, I told Collins I had been accepted into the University of Michigan Law School at Ann Arbor and intended to enter within just a few days. George congratulated me, and, just to pass the time, told me about his rangering experience at Lassen Volcanic National Park in California.

George said his brother Walker was Superintendent of Lassen, and recommended that I apply for a temporary ranger job there instead of coming back to Grand Canyon next summer. I knew nothing about Lassen except what George told me: there were no concession facilities; it was a small park, but a beautiful place to work. In fact, it was where he got his start as a ranger and was one of his favorites.

Well, I thought, why not? It sounded like a good change and a new experience in the parks. So I sent in my application and George followed up with a letter of recommendation to his brother. At summer's end I went on to my first year at law school. I quickly became absorbed in my legal studies and my job waiting table at the Michigan Law Quadrangle. I gave little thought to the Lassen job. Months passed. Nearly the entire school year passed. Nothing had come back from Lassen. One day in May of 1931 I received a telegram from Chief Ranger Brooks of Grand Canyon asking whether I was returning for summer employment. With no word from Lassen and the Depression hanging over everything, I immediately sent a wire stating that, yes, I was returning to Grand Canyon for my fourth season.

Three days later the job offer came in from Lassen. I told the ironic story to schoolmate Don Ford. He raised an eyebrow and said how lucky I was. Here he was, a year ahead of me at law school, going back home to Hollywood, California, with only a low-paying job delivering ice to homes for ice boxes. There I stood, he said, with two very respectable national park job offers. Unheard of! Would I recommend him to Superintendent Collins for the job at Lassen? Of course, I would— what are friends for, anyway? But I warned Don that I knew neither Mr. Collins nor anyone else at Lassen. What's more, Collins knew nothing about me except what his brother had told him. I doubted whether my recommendation would carry much weight. Don agreed with my skepticism, but even a slight hope for a better job was worth the try. At any rate, I sent off a letter. Much to our surprise, Don got the offer!

Both of us westerners had jobs, so we decided to buy a secondhand 1929 Ford Roadster for transportation from school. Don's roommate Lawrence Curfman asked if he could pay his way west with us. Don not only agreed, but also made arrangements for Curf to take his old ice-delivery job and stay with Don's folks in Hollywood for the summer. Another law student in need of a ride made a fourth. We set out on our trek. I said goodbye to my school friends at Grand Canyon in June, performed my summer of rangering, and joined up with Don and Curf again in September for the return trip to Michigan—by way of Coos Bay, Oregon, so Don could see his girl friend.

On to Lassen

The following season Don and I applied for and received jobs as Lassen temporary rangers, to be stationed at Summit Lake Ranger Station, located roughly in the middle of the park. I was eager for this new assignment in unfamiliar territory. When we arrived I found the place exceeded my expectations.

Here in the midst of majestic conifer forests lie fifty or more alpine lakes amid vast jumbles of mountains. Towering above it all looms the 10,457 foot plug-dome volcano named for early California emigrant guide Peter Lassen. Once thought extinct, Mount Lassen had been proclaimed a national monument in 1907, steamed into life May, 1914, exploded violently on May 22, 1915, and gained Congressional designation as a national park August 9, 1916, the year the National Park Service was created.

The sweet-smelling and sparkling land surrounding Lassen belies the violent upheavals that formed it. As Stewart L. Udall wrote of Lassen in *The National Parks of America*, "In the order of nature, often where there is chaos, great beauty is nearby." High up in the alpine forests grow California red firs in perfect Christmas-tree shape, given the technical name *Abies magnifica*—*magnifica* suits them, as writer Richard L. Williams once remarked—and surrounded by vivid wildflower meadows rich with bird and mammal life. Around Lassen Peak itself lie seething mudpots, steaming fumaroles, active hot springs, and brightly painted sulphur pits appropriately called "hells." Ominous names such as Bumpass Hell, Sulphur Works and Devils Kitchen dot the map of Lassen, which tells the knowledgeable that it is only the last, southernmost rampart of the long volcanic Cascade Range that marches 600 miles northward, even into Canada. The Cascades are crowned by slumbering thunder-mountains with names such as Shasta, Thielsen, Diamond Peak, the Sisters, Jefferson, Hood, Adams, Rainier, Glacier Peak, and Baker.

Today's Lassen contains the remnant of an enormous

predecessor peak known as Mount Tehama, which is thought
by some to have reached as high as 20,000 feet, although most
believe that 12,000 feet is nearer the truth. Master interpreter Freeman Tilden tells its story in *The National Parks*:

> Three miles southwest of Lassen Peak once stood a mighty
> mountain known as Tehama, whose top towered more than
> four thousand feet over the present Sulphur Works, in the
> southwestern corner of the park. A succession of quiet lava
> flows had built this Tehama mountain. Later it collapsed in-
> ward, perhaps as Mazama did to form Crater Lake. Brokeoff
> Mountain, with its precipitous sheared side, is the largest
> remnant of this old crater rim.

Lassen's present highway was built in the caldera of ancient
Mount Tehama. Mount Saint Helens far to the north in
Washington State reminds us that one day all these Cascade
sleepers may awaken into holocaust as Lassen did in 1914 and
1915.

Lassen's awakening blast in 1914 merely opened a new
crater, but soon a series of eruptions proved that Lassen had
something big up its magma-filled sleeve. A brave young man
(or foolhardy, take your pick) climbed to Lassen's summit
between outbursts prior to the final climactic explosion,
taking two companions. "Just as I turned to leave the crater's
rim," wrote Lance Graham, "there was a puff of blue smoke,
followed by a tongue of red flame. . . . In a trice I was en-
veloped in a cloud of smoke, while a perfect hail of small
volcanic bombs and cinders beat down upon me. Then I was
struck by a stone about twice the size of my fist that felled me
to the ground." Lucky for him, his companions pulled him out
and down the mountain.

On the night of May 19, 1915, with tremendous explosions,
lava spilled through a notch on the west side of the crater rim
and down the slope for a thousand feet. Snowmelt sent a
torrent of mud carrying 20-ton boulders tumbling down Lost
Creek and over the divide into Hat Creek, sweeping every-

thing before it. A tremendous low angle blast much like the 1980 cataclysm of St. Helens mowed down trees on Raker Peak three miles distant. A 1915 photograph copyrighted by B.F. Loomis shows the towering mushroom cloud over Lassen Peak, visible the next day for hundreds of miles, to be at least the equal of the latest St. Helens outpouring. Lassen grumbled intermittently for more than seven years before sinking back into dormancy.

Here I was in 1932 in the middle of all this wonder and being paid for it. Don Ford and I reported for duty and took up our station at Summit Lake, under Hat Mountain and not far from Dersch Meadows. It was down to practical matters right away. Even though the landscape was about as different from Grand Canyon as you could imagine, the job had the same elements, and going into the back country on patrol was one of them.

Rangering

Don and I had been assigned a pickup truck, but no horses. Without horses, no back country patrol. We asked for them through regular channels. A week went by, then two. The Park Service, in its plodding way, delivered no horses. But, like most NPS employees, Don and I had learned a few things about cutting red tape. Don came up with the solution: confront the superintendent, but do it nicely. We would invite Superintendent Collins and his wife to a dinner, a very special dinner. We wrote up a regular menu and sent it with an invitation subtly labelled, "Horse Bait Dinner."

As usual, I did the cooking, but I couldn't cope with dessert—we wanted a pie to impress our guests. A cook by the name of Eddie in the park construction camp had a reputation as an excellent baker, so we had him bake us a raisin pie. We put on our spread, heated the pie in the oven and lavishly entertained the superintendent and his wife. We got our horses three days later.

In time we settled into the ranger routine: back country

patrol, road patrol, occasional fire suppression, visitor contact in the campground. The Park Service made a point of showing the flag at the campgrounds, answering questions and helping with problems. Don and I made many friends on campground duty. Often when campers left for home they had some supplies left over and dropped them off for us at the Ranger Station. They understood perfectly well that rangers weren't rich. This lightened our grocery bill considerably; in fact, with the campers' donations, Don and I lived frugally on $7.00 a month each. As the cook, I found that Spanish rice was a very inexpensive dish, easy to fix and good to eat. My frugality became known locally as "Hummelizing." Maybe I got carried away with it, because Ford tells to this day how he lived on Spanish rice that summer.

Occasionally we went to a dance in Chester, California, nicknamed "Little Reno" for its wide-open gambling. It was a typical small town dance lasting into the wee hours of the morning and about the only diversion to be had.

Toward the end of the season, the Superintendent assigned Don to work at headquarters helping prepare the budget. He had worked ably on it the previous year, and his aid was appreciated. After that, he returned to Los Angeles. So there I was alone at Summit Lake. I got to thinking about our back country patrols. There weren't many trails in Lassen at the time, and we badly needed a trail from Summit Lake to Echo Lake two miles east.

I decided to do something about it. I laid out a trail upcountry following pretty much the contours of the land so as not to require too much cutting and filling. Building a trail turned out to be harder than I expected, fraught with endless marking and backtracking to check alignment. I laid out the route by trial and error and finally wound up at Echo Lake. I was greatly pleased when the park adopted it officially. The following year a trail crew came in and took out the rough spots and cut some of the banks level, but they followed my route. If you ever hike that trail, you know how it got there.

The Idea

Toward the end of the 1932 season, I had patrol over the Lassen Peak Road and began to arrange my schedule to end up at Manzanita Lake, where Charles Keathley lived—Lassen's ranger-naturalist. We prepared our evening meal together because it was more efficient that way. At one of these dinners I told Keathley that someone was going to make money if they put in some concessions at Lassen. I'd given away quite a bit of gasoline that day to tourists who came into the park expecting services, only to discover that they did not have enough fuel to get out to a service station.

I jokingly suggested that maybe we ought to put in for the concession. Keathley didn't take it as a joke. He thought it was an excellent idea. After talking it over we got genuinely enthused about the possibilities. Finally I agreed to see the superintendent the next day and ask if there was any possibility of us applying for the concession.

When I saw Superintendent Collins the next morning he told me the Park Service was actively looking for a concessioner. In fact, Yosemite Park & Curry Company had already turned it down—Lassen was too small for them to bother with. I asked Mr. Collins if he would recommend Keathley and me for the concession, and he agreed. He told me the people who ran a lodge at Childs Meadows on Highway 36 between park headquarters in Mineral and the town of Chester were also interested.

I went back to Manzanita Lake and told Keathley. He was elated. Together we went to work on our application. We proposed a store, cabins, a service station, and a lodge at Manzanita Lake. When we came to the part about financing the facilities, we were stumped. "What do we put here, Charlie?" I asked. "I don't know," replied Keathley, "what do you think?" We muttered and mumbled and finally ended up writing that we had "sufficient financial backing to insure this venture." This was a slight overstatement—I had signed notes for all my tuition at law school and waited table for my board. Keathley was in worse condition: he had to borrow money from his fiancée to buy his ranger-naturalist uniform!

As the season closed I received notification of my promotion to head waiter back at school, meaning I would receive my room as well as board as compensation. I bought a coach ticket on the Southern Pacific and went east by way of Tucson to see my parents before going back to Ann Arbor.

About Easter time 1933, while putting on my waiter's coat to go to work, a friend brought me a telegram from Charles L. Gable, NPS Chief of Public Utility Service Operators, the man I had played bridge with at Phantom Ranch. The NPS would like a "more definite statement of our financial position." I made some hurried telephone calls to Keathley at the University of Missouri. This was it, either fish or cut bait. After serious discussion, we decided to try raising funds for the venture.

Luck was with us. One of my friends at law school was a fellow named Dallas W. Dort, a graduate of Princeton University reputed to have some money—his father had been one of the organizers of General Motors. I approached Dal, who had heard of national parks but not Lassen Volcanic National Park. I produced the wire from Gable and described the opportunity. I told him about Keathley, about the need for visitor services, our plans to develop those needed services. Dal and I worked out an agreement—he would put up the immediate cash and own a one-third share in the firm, Keathley and I would sign notes to him for our one-third shares, and I would direct the firm as president. That afternoon we sent NPS a wire giving Dal Dort's financial position.

Concession Building

The reply came back "Yes." But we could only have a temporary four-year permit. Only four years. I was quite disturbed—how could we possibly recoup our investment with such a short-term permit? The Park Service assured us, however, that if we performed satisfactorily, the permit would be extended. We decided to proceed on their assurances. I called my dad and asked him to set up a California corporation, which he did under the name Lassen National Park Camps, Ltd.—rather an ostentatious name for such a small outfit. Keathley immediately quit work on his doctoral degree in paleontology and married his fiancée Mary Ann Hutchinson. He bought a second-hand Ford and headed for Lassen with his bride.

I could hardly wait the two weeks until graduation. When Dal and I finished law school, he went with me to Flint, Michigan, and bought a second-hand Ford van for $200. We drove a hard bargain for the car, pleading poverty. When Dal gave the car salesman his check signed "Dort"—a name well-known in Flint, of course—he thought we had taken advantage of him.

Now we were ready to start on our epic journey. Dal would go his way to seek employment as an attorney, but I would travel west to Lassen, taking Lawson Baxter, a longtime schoolmate who decided he'd like to work for us in this new venture. We soon found that Dal and I had not made as good a deal as we thought on the automobile. The tires were so old and rotten we spent about half our traveling time fixing flats—all the way to Lassen.

Keathley had arrived at the park two weeks ahead of us. He had contacted Superintendent Collins, who by then knew that NPS had granted us the concession permit. Superintendent Collins had immediately helped Keathley make contact with various suppliers for materials to build our facilities. Our principal supplier was Diamond Match Company, who agreed to deliver lumber for our construction start, no questions asked. They shipped us about $5,000 worth of lumber without even a credit rating. The fact that it was for construction in the park led the company to believe their sale was secure without credit references or down payment—another sign of the Depression: every business was willing to take a chance in order to sell its product.

But what about construction workers? Walker Collins again came to the rescue. He gave Keathley a list of employees who had worked in the park either as laborers or carpenters but were now unemployed awaiting congressional approval of emergency funding—workers we'd known from the past summer. Keathley hired the necessary crew and put them to work on the store building. Our dream that started as a joke was materializing!

We paid carpenters $5.00 per day and laborers $1.00. The Saturday I finally arrived I was greeted with our first two-week payroll—$750, due NOW. Dal Dort had given me a checkbook on a Flint, Michigan, bank, but I didn't know if the account had any money in it yet. Here it was Saturday afternoon. All our employees were anxious to get to town to cash their checks—most had been out of work for some time. I telephoned every number I could think of, but couldn't find Dort to see if he'd made a deposit.

Keathley and I put our heads together. This was serious. We couldn't tell our new employees they'd have to wait for their money. They all knew us as ranger and ranger-naturalist. This year I was still officially a ranger and only held a stockholder interest in the company—I wasn't even a working concessioner like Keathley was. Our employees knew that we personally had no money. A delay in payroll would have been disastrous. We swallowed hard and sent our workers into town with their paychecks, which would take a week to clear the Michigan bank—and held our breath. Later that night, Dal Dort called and told me he had deposited $2,000 in our account. I still shudder when I think what would have happened if those checks had reached the bank before Dal made the deposit.

The architect for Yosemite Park & Curry Company, Eldridge (Ted) Spencer, designed our lodge at Manzanita Lake, which was to be a rock building—specifications called for rock no larger than one man could handle. The Park Service sent up an architect to supervise construction. He, of course, wanted huge boulders, which we were not prepared to handle. I stopped by on my regular ranger patrol one day to watch the work and saw our crew taking an hour or more to lay one stone. We couldn't go on that way. I told Superintendent Collins of the problem and he cleared me to drive the fifty miles west to Redding to see if I could get a truck with a boom strong enough to lift large rocks. (You can see by this just how closely early concessioners worked with Park Service officials. In those days we could work out our problems face to face.)

Keathley had been offered a truck at $25 per day—we furnish the driver, maintenance and fuel. Absolutely unreasonable. In Redding I heard about a farmer whose truck had just been returned from another job, and that it might be available for hire. I went to see the farmer and talked with him as he lay in bed inside a shadowy screened sleeping porch. To this day I have never seen the man's face. We agreed that he would rent us the truck for $15 per day and he would provide a driver, maintenance and fuel. His truck came up the following day and we had the capability to handle those big rocks the architect wanted.

As the lodge slowly took shape, honeymooners Charles and Mary Ann Keathley lived nearby in a tent that doubled as our store. It was quite romantic, set beside a clear mountain stream in a stand of huge yellow pines. Their bed was separated from the public by a counter at which we sold candy, beer and groceries, along with sandwiches Mary Ann made. Not a classy operation, but practical.

Although we stocked perishables, we had no refrigeration to protect them from spoiling. So we built a screened box and placed it by Manzanita Creek under the bridge behind our tent in such a way that cool water flowed over its burlap cover. Evaporation kept the perishables in reasonable condition. We kept this primitive refrigerator the next year even after completing the lodge. It amused our customers mightily to order groceries in the lodge lobby, only to have the clerk run out the door, go down under the bridge, and scurry back up with a bottle of milk, then have to go back again when they decided to buy a pound of butter. This arrangement worked reasonably well until the Park Service brought in a Veterans'

CCC Camp in the summer of 1934. These hearties were stationed about twelve miles down the road from our gradually rising lodge, but worked nearby in the park. The astute vets learned where we kept the beer and we never had a moment's peace thereafter.

At Work

While carrying on my duties as park ranger I set aside time to study for the California Bar, poring over law review books and getting acquainted with sales, mining and water law, partnership and other courses I never had in law school. The California Bar examination had a reputation for being one of the most exacting in the United States, a three-day test, eight hours each day. I signed up to take the August exam in San Francisco.

One late July day in 1933 we got a pleasant shock: Herbert Hoover walked into our tent-store. The former President of the United States, who had recently lost the election to Roosevelt, was an avid fisherman and often came to Lassen to enjoy his sport. We thought we had struck a real bonanza— not only did we have a world-famous celebrity for a customer, but his party also bought out our tent-store and left half the goods for our own use.

Our workaday world didn't provide many such diversions. Most of our attention stayed on construction. The lodge abuilding was a small structure, something like thirty by sixty-five feet interior measurement, I don't recall exactly, but we had five upstairs rooms to house employees, and on the main floor a lobby, a six-seat food counter, a few shelves for groceries, a kitchen, a counter for cabin registration and another for gift sales. We also had a slot for a Post Office; Mary Ann Keathley was appointed Postmistress. We finished two bungalows which stood ready for visitors.

Outside we built a two-pump service station. We pumped the gasoline by hand into high glass cylinders, as common in those days. To our chagrin, the architect had laid the station out in a less-than-ideal location: our gas customers blocked the side entry into the lodge.

Our financial backer Dal Dort (who had been married for a year or so) went touring the country with his wife Betty, sightseeing and trying to land a job with some law firm. Dal decided to come to Lassen and see what we were doing with his money—with no advance warning. When they showed up we greeted them with happy surprise and put them to work. Dal took over painting the lodge interior, laying on brown stain, covering it with green paint, which he immediately wiped off to leave a pleasing gray mottled overglaze. Dal became a familiar sight with paint on his clothes, his arms, head and hair. Betty went to work as a maid and subsequently became our first waitress. Dal received no wages and Betty's were minimal.

We also had 10 duplex cottages under construction, each with two bedrooms, an individual bath with showers and a connecting kitchen. The kitchen was arranged to be shared for a family party, or could be locked off with one side rented as a bedroom only and the other as a bedroom with kitchen. Wood stoves provided heat for the cottages. We had to put them out in the middle of the room—the architect had placed them in an alcove where they would have burned the cabins down. Our hot water was heated by propane gas, using a Swedish invention called a Watrola, a very efficient unit that required no storage tank, but heated the water as it went through a series of copper coils.

It was a cheerful, exuberant time. The future grew before our very eyes. Our dream was nearly a reality. But not quite. The lodge and cottages remained unfinished that first season, and brought us no revenue. When the tourist season closed in September, our total receipts for the summer of 1933 came to $15,000, all from over the counter sales in the tent occupied by the Keathleys. Even so, it wasn't bad for a bunch of inexperienced upstarts.

But now it was time to think about what we'd do until the next season opened, the 1934 season when I could go to work as a concessioner. And that was not so cheery. My note to Dal Dort was coming due and I had no idea how I could pay it. Looking ahead to the winter in depression time, my economic prospects seemed less than encouraging.

6

Getting Organized

WHEN THE 1933 Lassen season ended I went home to
Tucson and started work in my father's law office. I had
qualified for the California bar in August, one of a scant
twenty-three percent who passed the rigorous exam that
year. Now I prepared for the Arizona bar examination to be
held early the next year. By March, 1934, I was a member of
the bar in California and Arizona. Dad was delighted. I entered practice with him and found that despite the client
traffic no one had any money and we seldom collected any
fees. I was a working attorney, but with little or no compensation.

In May I decided to go back to Lassen. The winter snow
was gone from Manzanita Lake by then and my two partners
Dort and Keathley agreed I would be paid $30 a month for my
first year's active duty as a national park concessioner. You
have to understand that when I say "$30 a month," I mean
only for the three or four summer months of tourist season.
All three members of our concession company stayed on the
payroll only for short periods each year and then sought other
jobs during the winter so we wouldn't create too much
overhead.

Growth

My first task of 1934 was to get the financing necessary to
finish our lodge and cabins and purchase equipment. I went
to Redding and arranged for a $15,000 loan from a banker
named Frisbie and our crew went back to work.

The loan was large enough to accommodate a new and expanded development plan. We decided to add a real dining room to the back of the lodge with space beneath for a grocery store. Our revised Manzanita Lake Lodge would be a creditable destination resort. The ground contour made our addition easy, dipping sharply from the rear of the unfinished lodge, enabling us to cut into the bank and attach the new dining room at ground level with the store beneath it partially below grade. We wanted a dining room fireplace, so we would have to find a lot of large rocks to match the lodge's existing stonework. We also planned a new full-size service station about 100 yards from the lodge, removing the previous year's annoying side-entrance obstruction.

When construction began that spring on the expanded lodge, we found things weren't as easy as we'd expected. The terrain dictated a tall chimney for our new dining room so it would draw properly and not smoke out our customers. Getting large rocks up so high presented a real challenge. We finally borrowed a power winch from the National Park Service, dug a hole in the ground, cut a pine tree, put it in the hole, and guy-wired it to several other trees. Then we ran the power winch cable through a block and tackle lashed to the top of our spar tree. Nobody else seemed to want the job, so I was nominated winch operator.

Our truckers dumped the rocks around the spar tree so our rock mason could pick and choose with ease. Of course, he always selected rocks from the inaccessible middle of the pile. I had to pull ton-sized rocks out from their hiding places and over the whole heap. When I revved up the power to pry loose a thousand-pound rock lodged in the pile, the spar tree bent like a bow and onlookers ran for cover. When my rock finally came clear, the tree snapped back quivering. With a little practice I soon found myself deftly raising and flinging boulders out of the pile up to the chimney masons who guided them neatly into place. I had perfect confidence in my skill, but one day our insurance agent came up to watch. When he saw all these huge rocks flying through the air, narrowly missing the lodge walls, he climbed into his car and left. He didn't want to know anything about this operation! He never came up again, but business in the depression was prized. He didn't cancel our insurance policy.

Once a week we had to go to Red Bluff and Redding for supplies, an all-day trip going down Lassen Peak road and into the Sacramento valley. In Red Bluff we picked up fruit, vegetables, melons and produce. (We bought them from an oriental farmer who turned out to be a Japanese intelligence agent, as we heard years later when World War II broke out.) We bought the balance of our supplies in Redding and returned on Highway 44 to Manzanita Lake, a 170 mile round trip taking a whole day, often to midnight. Our three-quarter ton panel truck was always overloaded, making for a slow climb from almost sea level to 4,800 feet.

Managing

Our concession employee roster for the 1934 season included Charles and Mary Ann Keathley, Mary Ann's sister Harriet Hutchinson, and me—not counting our construction crew. In addition to my power winch duties, I managed the lodge and played cat-skinner excavating for the new dining room and grocery store using a Caterpillar tractor borrowed from the Park Service. When I asked about borrowing the "Cat", the chief ranger told me it had been left out in the forest after a job and I would have to go get it. I slogged through the underbrush, found the tractor and clattered back with it over the manzanita thickets, when suddenly the machine lurched on its side and stopped. I had run over a pine log that lodged between the Caterpillar tracks. Only the dense manzanita brush had kept me from turning over completely. I climbed under the tilted tractor, pulled the logging chain from the rear winch, wound it around the offending log and anchored the chain onto the left track. I got back in the operator's seat, gunned full power to the right track and flipped the log out behind me. When I saw the path the chain had taken, I realized it could just as easily have swung over the top of the tractor and cut me in half. I still break into a sweat just thinking about it.

By mid-June we had enough of our cabins complete to take visitors—which was a mixed blessing for the visitors. One day while excavating for the dining room and store, I went into the lodge covered with dirt and grease, altogether a disreputable looking person. I stepped behind the registration desk to check our construction plans when a woman came up and said to the clerk on duty, "I want to see the manager." The clerk, of course, pointed to me and told the lady, "This is the manager." I still remember the look of disgust on her face.

Fortunately, most of our customers had a better opinion of us, and the 1934 season ended on a high note. Travel to Lassen had been better than we expected. We had demonstrated our capacity to finance and operate a successful national park concession. Park visitors liked our cabins and our service. We enjoyed working with the public and didn't mind when we had to reinvest all of our meager profits. That year we didn't pay a stockholder dividend, which became a permanent condition as perennial expansion demands took all our cash. We paid our bills and we did our job well.

At the close of the 1934 season, I contacted the National Park Service and asked for the extended contract we had been promised. We still had two years to go on our permit, but visitor loads were so great that the Park Service insisted we make major new investments in expanded facilities. We obviously needed a long-term contract if we were to recoup our investment. I went to Washington, D.C. to negotiate the contract with Chief of Park Operators Charles L. Gable. I was getting to know him quite well. He showed me the papers and I read them thoroughly, putting my recently acquired legal education to work.

I asked Gable about numerous contract provisions that gave the Secretary of the Interior absolute discretion, saying the document was completely one-sided. The Park Service could tell us when to open and when to close the season. They could tell us how much to charge for accommodations. They could tell us what kind of facilities to build and when and where to build them. But one point particularly upset me.

"Mr. Gable," I complained, "Look at this Article IX."

"What about it?" he asked.

"Right here at the end it says, 'all buildings, fixtures, and appurtenances, whether now on the land or hereafter placed thereon, shall at all times be part of the realty and the property of the United States.' Does that mean the concession buildings I pay for automatically belong to the government? I don't own them?" I didn't realize that I must have been the umpteenth concessioner to ask him that.

Gable looked at me and said, "Hummel, that language has been used for many years now. Nothing you can say or do and nothing I can recommend will change it. You have to rely on the good faith of the United States Government. We'd never take concessioner property without paying for it. In fact, I can't remember us taking concessioner property at all. All other contracts have the same language and concessioners have operated under those conditions for nearly thirty years. The policy of the government is that if you perform satisfactory service your contract will be renewed and you keep the beneficial ownership of your buildings."

I was a little worried about Article IX—that *damned* Article IX—but I signed the papers. In early 1935 I received a 10-year contract from the Park Service signed by Director Arno B. Cammerer, who had succeed the legendary Horace Albright after the Roosevelt administration came in. The contract was to expire in May of 1946. On the basis of this contract we built additional facilities. Every cent of earnings plus everything we could borrow went into construction of facilities for Lassen Volcanic National Park.

I didn't know it until years later, but the Secretary of the Interior's Annual Report for 1934 would give the concessioners a big pat on the back: "The wisdom of the concessionaire system has been fully demonstrated during the 5 years since 1929, for during that period of depressed conditions the usual high standards of service were furnished by operators of public accommodations, and in many instances at substantially lower rates."

One Among Many

Our lodge at Lassen was only one among dozens in the national parks by the mid-1930s. The really famous ones such as Crater Lake Lodge in Oregon and Mammoth Cave Hotel in Kentucky and Wonderland Club Hotel in Tennessee's Great Smokies and Olympic National Park's Lake Crescent Lodge in Washington State and Glacier Park Lodge in Montana and of course Yellowstone's Old Faithful Inn and Yosemite's Wawona Hotel had been going concerns for decades by this time.

But others that have since become famous were just getting started, just as we were. Oregon Caves Chateau at the national monument near Cave Junction, Oregon, was designed by local architect Gust Lium for a group of Grants Pass businessmen who started Oregon Caves Company in 1923 but didn't have the chateau ready until the 1934 season.

Death Valley National Monument's Furnace Creek Inn opened its doors less than ten years earlier, in 1927, after Pacific Coast Borax Company, the original investor, put up $30,000 for construction and talked Beulah Brown and her concession crew from Yellowstone's Old Faithful Lodge to work their off season in Death Valley for the winter clientele (Horace Albright, while Mather's Field Assistant Director of NPS and Superintendent of Yellowstone, helped talk her into it).

And there was The Ahwahnee that opened in 1927 in Yosemite—The *The* is always capitalized and *Hotel* is never added. First NPS Director Steve Mather, completely departing from his policy that the national parks and their facilities should be forever inexpensive so that all citizens could enjoy the natural wonders set aside by Congress, ordered construction of The Ahwahnee, so the story goes, because Lady Astor had refused to spend the night in Yosemite, Mather's favorite park. She had turned up her nose at all the hotels, saying they were too primitive for her elevated sensibilities. Mather was uncharacteristically embarrassed by the incident and vowed to put a world-class hotel in Yosemite that *nobody* could snub.

That, some park historians claim, is the real reason why Mather forced the merger of Yosemite's two major concessioners, although I think it's just another example of his intent to gear each park to a single "principal concessioner"—but it is a fact that Mather wrote a clause into the Yosemite Park & Curry Company's first contract calling for construction of a new, fireproof hotel in the valley. It was The Ahwahnee and it cost a million dollars in 1926, and the interior decoration cost another quarter-million by itself. In its heyday an English butler attended the foyer and icily asked the common herd who stumbled in whether they had reservations. Distinctly uncharacteristic of Mather-Albright policy!

Internal Dissent

My own story as a concessioner now began to take the first of many unforeseen turns. As had become my custom, I alternated summers at Lassen with winters in Tucson working as a struggling attorney. The concession season of 1935 brought our first glimpse of problems to come—not in providing visitor services, which the public seemed to approve—but differences of opinion on management arose between Charlie Keathley and me. Keathley was turning out to be arbitrary, and didn't get along very well with our employees, whose number had increased to include my nephew, Al Donau, and Charlie's youngest brother Marshall. These differences were to smoulder for over six years before coming to a head.

The 1935 season at Lassen closed on a high note despite our partnership problem. Even though we hadn't finished our dining room (and had planned more improvements), visitors enjoyed our Manzanita Lake cabins and lodge facilities and began to book ahead to next season. We were a going concern. We were no longer upstarts, but emerged as professionals at concessioning. And that meant it was time to join ranks with concessioners in the other parks. I'd heard of the Western Conference of National Park Operators, the official concessioners' organization, and asked around to find out about membership. I discovered that the Conference had been founded barely six years earlier, in December of 1929, but already enjoyed a wide reputation for effective cooperation with the Park Service. In February of 1936 I joined up.

The Conference Idea

This was another one of those fateful decisions like taking that summer ranger job at Grand Canyon: it introduced me to people who would become centrally important later in life. Looking back on it I can see that while I had been studying political science at the University of Arizona in 1929, preparing for an eventual legal career, destiny had other plans for me. Converging forces in that year brought together an organization I would one day serve as chairman: the Conference of National Park Concessioners, as it is called today. The group has labored under four names, National Park Operators Conference (1929 to 1933), then by majority vote of concessioners, Western National Park Operators Conference, used interchangeably with Western Conference of National Park Operators (1933 to 1939), Western Conference of National Park Concessioners (1939 to 1966), and from 1966 on, the Conference of National Park Concessioners.

The modern Conference serves as the park concessioner's representative to the National Park Service, a rather arm's-length relationship. Today's environmentalists constantly try to drive wedges between concessioners and the NPS by attacking the legitimacy of the concessioners' organization. But back in the organization's early days, teamwork was the watchword between Park Service and park concessions, the closer the better for the park visitor. The legitimacy of such a close relationship was unquestionable. In fact, I'm about to tell you the story of how the Secretary of the Interior himself created the concessioners' national organization. And to unfold that story we must backtrack to 1929.

Horace Albright's first year succeeding Mather at the helm of the National Park Service, although revealing him as a masterful administrator, brought many challenges. Park travel was up, for one thing. Albright could note with a smile that park visits had amounted to only 334,799 people in 1915 when he had teamed up with Mather. During the season ending September 30, 1928, just before Mather's debilitating stroke, 2,522,188 had visited the national parks and 502,656 the national monuments. 1929 travel promised to top that. Albright quickly sought and got legislation enlarging the boundaries of nine national parks: Yellowstone, Mount Rainier, Crater Lake, Lassen Volcanic, Yosemite, Zion, Bryce, Rocky Mountain, and Mesa Verde. It was small wonder, for Albright personally knew more than a hundred members of Congress when he took over from Mather, and was on a first name basis with nearly fifty of them.

Most momentous, Herbert Hoover entered the Presidency and drafted Stanford President Ray Lyman Wilbur as Secretary of the Interior. President Hoover, it was known, intended to reorganize the government, providing for the transfer of the Forest Service to the Department of the Interior, or possibly for the establishment of a Conservation Department which would combine all federal land-use agencies, both ideas that Albright supported. The ideas, incidentally, never had any result other than to show Hoover as a concerned conservationist.

Wilbur was an excellent choice as Interior Secretary when it came to the National Park Service, the park concessioner and the park visitor. As Albright had expected, Wilbur turned out to be a friend of the parks, working for their improvement as well as increasing their size.

In personal terms, Wilbur was an astonishingly accomplished individual. He had been a member of Stanford's second graduating class, where he met Hoover, a member of the first. Wilbur went on to become a doctor of medicine, then dean of Stanford's medical school and in 1916, president of Stanford University. When Hoover called him to serve his country in the Interior Department in 1929, Wilbur at first refused, but the President convinced him to come. Once in office, Wilbur took on the job with vigor.

Albright found Wilbur to be a natural leader, yet self-effacing. While Wilbur became famous as a leader of Hoover's "Dark Horse Cabinet," so called because most were unknown, he also refused a large office in the Interior Department building on F Street between Eighteenth and Nineteenth Northwest (today it houses the General Services Administration one block north of the present Interior building). Much as he had done at Stanford, Wilbur selected an unpretentious room which he affectionately called "The Secretary's Cubbyhole."

Wilbur, incidentally, is the person responsible for changing the Interior Department's symbol from an eagle with outspread wings to the American bison. He felt it gave the Department its own unique identity and helped morale. He certainly set an example for high morale: He worked at such a level of intensity that employees soon called him the "executive buzz saw." Albright could hardly have hoped for a better Secretary. Wilbur spent substantial time during the summer of 1929 visiting the national parks with Albright and familiarizing himself with their problems.

Both Wilbur and Albright felt that the growing national park visitor traffic had given rise to new questions about concessions which ought to be addressed. Providing some uniformity in rates, services and facilities between the major parks loomed as a particularly pressing problem: visitors didn't like being charged more for the same service in one park than in another. The automobile and the increasingly popular multi-park vacation meant that this problem would only grow worse unless something was done.

Assistant Secretary for Public Lands John H. Edwards had for some time thought the answer lay in a formal concessioner organization. A formal organization would make it easier for the Park Service to standardize services for the public. The organization itself, working with the Park Service, could make and enforce binding decisions. But the concessioners would have none of it: like the rugged individualists they were, they refused to be bound by the dictates of any general organization. The Park Service was enough boss.

Not that concessioners didn't like each others' company. Quite the contrary. I have found correspondence between concessioners from the 'Twenties describing convivial annual meetings that had evidently been held for many years, probably back to 1919 (the record is unclear on the year but concessioner mythology holds it to be true). These meetings were always informal and more for "conversation and gossip" than banding together to forward the cause of the park visitor.

Edwards suggested that if the Secretary of the Interior himself sent out the call to organize, and if the Secretary provided the proper setting, then the concessioners might go along with the idea. It was worth a try. Wilbur agreed and invited all national park concessioners to a special meeting in Washington to be held December 6 and 7, 1929. Ostensibly, it was "to consider certain problems confronting the Government in the administration of the Parks." Albright handled the organization of the meeting.

The Birth of the Conference

December 3, 1929, Albright sent Secretary Wilbur a memo asking him to "bring up several important questions" in his opening remarks to the impending national park operators' conference. The memo told the Secretary emphatically that "The conference is very important," explaining, "Nearly all operators will be here and they represent a total investment of over $20,000,000." After the stock market crash two months earlier, that was big money indeed.

The day of the big meeting arrived. There were 29 principal operators in the national parks in 1929 and some 25 of them sent representatives. At the appointed time, 10:00 a.m., Friday, December 6, 1929, the park operators gathered in the "Secretary's Cubbyhole" for Ray Lyman Wilbur's opening remarks. This is how he began:

> The success of the development of the national park system depends upon a joint medium of which the Government, as represented by the National Park Service, is one part, and individuals or corporations acting under franchise to furnish service to the public, is the other. This is the American method of trying to bring together Government and business, in such a way that private business many be maintained. We must work out a joint program to handle the whole matter on a larger basis, we protecting the parks and their visitors, providing good roads and trails, and generally supervising; you public utility operators, providing the machinery for developing the peculiar type of accommodations necessary in order to care for the public adequately.
>
> In this connection we must remember that the visiting public looks upon the whole thing as a national enterprise. If visitors find adequate accommodations in one park, and then find inadequate facilities in another, they wonder why the Government does not do something about it. Therefore we must work toward standardization of service; or perhaps I should say uniformity. We do not, of course, want to make everything alike in the parks; that would be a calamity. Rather we want to work for uniformity in types of accommodations available and in prices charged. Broadly speaking, so far our joint endeavor has been a big success, and such difficulties as have occurred have been primarily due to failure in certain areas in keeping up with improvements in others. This is what we want to strive to overcome.
>
> The national parks have a unique relationship to our national life, as I have discovered upon my visit to several of them during the past summer. We are in charge of the finest spots on the American continent, and our people have discovered this and have begun to visit them in great numbers. When they arrive, you of the public utilities become hosts to them all.

Secretary Wilbur did not raise the question of forming a concessioner organization, but he did provide a written list of the questions he wanted the concessioners to consider.

Next came Representative Louis C. Cramton of Michigan, one of Albright's long-time backers and Chairman of the House appropriations subcommittee of the committee handling Interior Department funds. He told the concessioners:

> The operators are, generally speaking, performing a great part in the task of determining and maintaining the proper use and essential preservation of these great areas. The appropriations committee realizes that the foundations are now being laid of the great national park system of the United States, and that they, and the public utility operators, are privileged to be in at the beginning, helping to lay the foundations for a wonderful system which it is hoped for centuries to come will continue to serve and aid in the proper development of our people.

Cramton also praised the railroads for financing the development of many national parks, particularly Northern Pacific at Yellowstone, Santa Fe at the South Rim of the Grand Canyon, Great Northern at Glacier, and Union Pacific at Bryce, Zion, and the North Rim of the Grand Canyon. He said, "I hope, and really feel confident that these expenditures will be good investments, but it took vision and a public spirit on the part of the executives of those railroads to convince boards of directors that such expenditures were justified. Their pioneer work did much to bring the development of the parks up to the point we have now reached."

The questions Albright and Wilbur had posed for the concessioners could not be answered without substantial investigation. Late in the two-day conference, Assistant Secretary Edwards suggested that Secretary Wilbur would be pleased if the concessioners formed a permanent organization to deal with such questions—just something informal, nothing with binding power over individual concessioners. The concessioners agreed.

The organization, which named itself The Conference of National Park Operators, elected as its first chairman Yosemite Park & Curry Company president Donald B. Tresidder. Its first report to the Secretary of the Interior included a statement of purpose.

The Conference of National Park Operators was formed:

a. To learn the facts and report findings to the Secretary of the Interior on the problems submitted to the Operators in writing on December 6, 1929.

b. To provide a mechanism by which, at the invitation of the Secretary of the Interior, the Park Operators could from time to time present or consider questions of policy affecting the common interest of all concerned.

c. To encourage better understanding and closer affiliations among the Operators themselves in the interests of better service, greater operating economies, and more effective cooperation.

d. To cooperate with the National Park Service in general publicity and all activities designed to increase the popularity of the National Parks.

e. To cooperate with the National Park Service in placing the contractual status of the Operators on a more logical, uniform, and secure basis.

Edwards left it to the concessioners to iron out their organizational details in interim meetings. Before the new Conference adjourned its Washington sessions, committees were appointed to study Secretary Wilbur's questions and the next meeting was scheduled for April 8 and 9, 1930, in San Francisco.

Horace Albright wrote of the Washington meeting in his Annual Report of the Director of the National Park Service on June 30, 1930:

An outstanding accomplishment of this meeting was the formation of an organization of operators to work together for their mutual benefit and for the best interests of the visiting public.

The concessioners were generally wary of their new organization and took pains to keep it informal lest it grow too powerful. Even though Director Albright later wrote "at conferences held in the West during the year [1930] the details of organization were perfected," those "perfected" details left a highly informal organization with no dues, and annual expenses that were simply picked up by the chairman's firm and later billed proportionately to the rest of the concessioners. As typical with informal organizations, the Conference's leadership selection system was not very democratic. Tresidder of Yosemite remained chairman until he got tired of it in 1933 when Frederick Harvey of Grand Canyon took over. Later the chairmanship went to a Yellowstone concessioner. It rotated between these "Big Three" concessions at Yellowstone, Yosemite and Grand Canyon until the 1960s. By then the Conference had become highly formalized.

Progress

The second annual meeting of the Conference, and its first as a permanent organization began December 4, 1930 in Washington. The Great Depression had brought hard times to park concessions as it had everyone else. At the meeting concessioners reported that the 5-year development plans requested by the Park Service had fallen behind in almost every park. And despite the economic situation, this second meeting centered on obtaining clarification of the department's policy for the administration of the parks and the public utilities, the relations of the operators with the Government and with each other, and definitions of the rights of operators under their franchises. Tresidder of Yosemite, as I have already noted, was re-elected chairman.

During 1931 the Depression deepened and other problems just as serious arose. An opinion delivered by the Comptroller General of the United States threw the status of concessions into complete turmoil. The opinion involved contracts. The Secretary of the Interior had routinely authorized temporary four-year contracts to new concessioners with the assurance that if they succeeded in rendering good public service, the temporary contract would be canceled in favor of a new full 20-year contract—just as they did for me at Lassen. But in late 1931 the Comptroller General ruled that the Interior Secretary had no such authority. The only possible interpretation was that all 20-year contracts made under such circumstances were illegal and void.

When the National Park Operators Conference held its third annual meeting in Washington in November 1931, the Comptroller's opinion was the main agenda item. Many concessioners at the time operated under just such canceled-temporary-and-newly-issued-20-year contracts. If these documents were illegal and without effect as the Comptroller said, millions of dollars of concessioner investments could vanish into thin air. *And* all incentive to invest in much-needed expansion projects would vanish with them.

After lengthy discussion, the conference concluded that it should request the government to resubmit the question to the Comptroller for clarification. Secretary Wilbur complied and resubmitted the question March 31, 1932. He received a positive reply April 28: In proper cases for the benefit of the public, the Secretary *could* legally cancel old contracts and issue new 20-year contracts within the authority granted him by Congress. Horace Albright wrote in his report to Secretary Wilbur on June 30, 1932:

> This decision is a further assurance to the operators of the integrity of their contracts and the stability of their investments.

The early spirit of cooperation and mutual concern between the Interior Department, the Park Service and the concessioners is unmistakable in this episode. When an outside threat to concessioners appeared, all three banded together and solved the problem. As we'll see in later chapters, the public would benefit from a good dose of such unity today.

Albright's 1932 report also told the story of economic disaster: "The full effect of the general economic conditions of the past three years was not felt in the national parks until the season just passed . . . With the amount of business in 1929 considered as an index at 100 per cent, we find that the volume has decreased to 21⅛ per cent in 1932."

A confidential report sent by concession officer Noble Wilt to Director Albright dated March 9, 1932 revealed what that meant in dollars: Yosemite Park and Curry Company had made a profit of $262,000 in 1929, $9,524 in 1930, and showed a loss of $126,005 in 1931. Yellowstone Park Hotel Company made a profit of $119,714 in 1929, showed a loss of $77,621 in 1930, and a loss of $162,161 in 1931. The Union Pacific concessions at Zion, Bryce and North Rim of the Grand Canyon, just as Mather had predicted, never made a dime. They may have set bolshevism back twenty years, but they didn't do the railroad's balance sheet much good either with losses of $167,000 in 1929, $169,000 in 1930 and so forth down the years.

The fourth annual Conference meeting in Washington in November 1932 dwelt on transportation and rate policies for the coming 1933 season. Visits to national parks had declined so drastically—1933 was projected to bring only 15 percent of the 1929 volume—that Director Albright decided to restrict bus services in the parks to those licensed by the Secretary of the Interior—which dampened unlicensed Greyhound's plans to offer cut-rate transcontinental tours through the parks. Despite layoffs among concessioner employees, the same high standard of service was demanded by the Park Service. Low cost cafeteria service supplanted regular meal service in many parks.

But most shocking to the Conference was the news that rail travel had declined so steeply that various gateway facilities serving the railway traveler would not be opened at all: Mammoth and Lake Hotels and the Lake Lodge in Yellowstone, the Cut-Bank and St. Mary's Chalets in Glacier, and the Prince of Wales Hotel just outside Glacier on Waterton Lake in Canada.

The Interior Secretary's Annual Report for 1934 states that "no general conference of park operators was held in Washington during the past year," but I have a letter from Howard H. Hays, concessioner of Sequoia and Kings Canyon National Parks to Roe Emery, concessioner at Rocky Mountain National Park describing just such a meeting on December 4, 1933. Emery had empowered Hays to represent him at the Conference sessions. The letter was Hay's report on the proceedings. Several important issues were decided, but that is not what strikes me about the letter. Reading Hays' roll-call of attendees reminds me of something I have not thought of for years: How closely and personally each concessioner belongs to his national park.

Hays wrote, "Present were Tresidder of Yosemite, Nichols of Yellowstone, Sceva of Rainier, Harvey of Grand Canyon, Mauger of Sequoia," and so on, the person *of* the park. This was no simple tag stating where the people came from, it was a proprietary honorific denoting ownership. Only it was the men who were owned by their parks, not the other way around. They were truly Tresidder *of* Yosemite, Sceva *of* Rainier, and Mauger *of* Sequoia. How evocative those words are to me! How strong those bonds!

Another sentence in that letter also hits home: "Sceva of Rainier reported that he understood Price of Crater Lake had decided to go it alone, and would not attend further conferences." Even a Conference with no power to bind its members to collective decisions didn't suit some of these independent-minded people.

This 1933 concessioners' meeting had to deal with an unthinkable change: "It was agreed that we had all lost our right arms when Albright left the National Park Bureau." The founding era had ended: Horace Marden Albright resigned on July 17 as Director of the National Park Service. He had received a number of highly attractive offers from United States Potash—which he had turned down for several years—and retired from government work. But he did not retire from the cause of the national parks: he remains a vocal supporter at the age of 96 as I write this in 1986. To this day, the original private enterprise concessions policy of the National Park Service is referred to as the Mather-Albright policy.

His loss in 1933 was felt keenly by the concessioners. Hays tells that the Conference assessed his absence and "felt that it would be a good move to have someone in Washington as a representative." The immediate need, as Hays colorfully put it, "is for some big bird to watch our interests during the next six months—a man who knows the President, Ickes and the Parks."

The Ickes Era

January of 1933, of course, had seen the inauguration of Franklin Delano Roosevelt as President, swiftly followed by the confirmation of Harold LeClaire Ickes as Secretary of the Interior. During those winter days Horace Albright had harbored some concern that he would be replaced by the incoming administration, but the new Secretary asked him to stay on. Within a short time, Albright emerged as a close and influential advisor to the irascible Ickes.

Interior Secretary Harold Ickes, a colorful, irritable, energetic, pragmatist-visionary that FDR called "the old curmudgeon," came in with vast ambition. When Albright told him of Hoover Administration efforts—in which Albright was instrumental—to bring all the military parks and national monuments under National Park Service jurisdiction, Ickes made sure Albright gained access to the one man who could guarantee the project's success: FDR. On April 9, 1933, Albright was among the invited guests on a presidential excursion to former President Hoover's camp on the Rapidan River in Virginia. Roosevelt listened, asked no questions, and agreed it should be done.

Congress soon authorized President Roosevelt to reorganize the government by executive order, and on June 10, 1933, FDR signed Executive Order 6166 reorganizing the National Park Service, to take effect sixty days later. The order was broadly inclusive: "All functions of administration of public buildings, reservations, national parks, national monuments, and national cemeteries are consolidated in an Office of National Parks, Buildings, and Reservations [a new name for the National Park Service] in the Department of the Interior." The Park Service, incidentally, did not like its new name and changed it back on March 2, 1934. One effect of this reorganization was to create a large number of national park units in the eastern United States.

This turn of events prompted the December 1933 concessioners' meeting to action. "The Conference voted to change the official name of our group to *Western* National Park Operators Conference," wrote Hays. He explained, "When I saw Albright he told me so much about the Eastern National Parks that I think there is a danger of our taking in too much territory, and also a danger of becoming involved with Park Operators who do not have our problems." Regionalism was creeping into the concessioners' outlook.

When Albright left that July, Ickes wanted an "outsider" as Director of the National Park Service, not somebody "in lock-step with the Civil Service that can't change his mind." Newton B. Drury, executive secretary of the Save-The-Redwoods League and former University of California classmate of Albright, refused the job, and Ickes gave his grudging approval to Arno B. Cammerer. Cammerer had a long Park Service background: Since 1919 he served as associate director and later as Albright's assistant director. It would be up to the quiet, hardworking Cammerer to deal with the huge reorganization of the NPS. In the final days of 1933 he helped bring all national monuments, military parks and the national capitol parks under Interior jurisdiction, along with major responsibility for the Civilian Conservation Corps program.

Not many people today realize how involved the Interior Department became with the CCC. Interior Secretary Ickes was the head of the CCC. At the peak of the CCC program in 1935, the Park Service would be allotted 600 CCC camps, 118 of them assigned to NPS areas and the rest to state parks, employing 120,000 enrollees and 6,000 professionally trained supervisors including landscape architects, engineers, foresters, biologists, historians and archaeologists. The Interior Department empire was to grow large indeed.

When the park operators met in conference in Washington on November 22, 1934, it was in conjunction with a meeting of Park Service field officers—and under Director Cammerer. The principal agenda item was still regulations governing the admittance of buses into the parks. But now rumbles appeared suggesting that Ickes was no friend of the park concessioner. As noted historian John Ise wrote, "When Ickes came in he had a theory that the government should build, own, and operate the concessions." It would mean the end of the private sector in the national parks and the end of the hard-won Mather-Albright concession policy.

Ickes had floated a proposal for the United States government to nationalize all concession companies in the parks and operate them itself. This was but one part of his grandiose master plan to create a new Department of Conservation that would include the Forest Service with all current Interior functions, the same idea that went nowhere in the Hoover administration. In 1934 he stripped Cammerer of authority to approve new roads in the parks, reserving all approvals to himself in an anti-road "aesthetic purist" move strikingly similar to modern environmentalist approaches. Ickes was gaining quite a reputation as an incipient dictator: he threatened to use his withdrawal authority to close public lands to livestock grazing if Congress refused to pass reforms, a threat which prompted the passage of the Taylor Grazing Act of 1934. He had also curtailed citizen rights under the Homestead Act.

It was Gifford Pinchot, the original wise-use conservationist, who used his influence to quash the imperial designs of Ickes. Pinchot had been ousted from the Forest Service in 1910—after a fierce battle with the Interior Secretary of that time, Richard A. Ballinger—then served two terms as Governor of Pennsylvania, and in 1936 worked as a professor at

Yale's Pinchot School of Forestry. Pinchot opposed every aspect of Secretary Ickes' Conservation Department idea, and quietly told his friend, Franklin Delano Roosevelt, a relative, remember, of Pinchot's old boss Teddy Roosevelt. The support for a Conservation Department that Ickes thought he had from President Roosevelt failed to materialize—Roosevelt decided he didn't need a power struggle between his Interior and Agriculture Secretaries—and the whole plan fizzled. But Ickes never gave up.

7

Hard Times

THE FIRST MEETING I attended as a member of the Western Conference of National Park Operators in February of 1936 proved to be quite educational. To be honest, I didn't even know that any of these horrendous concession policy problems existed. I had joined simply because I thought it would help the professionalism of our Lassen concession. My first conversations with fellow concessioners, however, didn't do much for my image as a professional.

I couldn't help overhearing concessioners commiserating with each other over how difficult it was to provide facilities at uniform rates from park to park, particularly for the depression-induced low-cost "shelter cabins." Billie Nichols, who ran the Yellowstone Park Company—Billie Nichols of Yellowstone—asked Paul Sceva of Mount Rainier National Park Company, "What do you get for your shelter cabins, Paul?"

Sceva said, "I get two dollars."

Nichols asked, "What's in them?"

Sceva replied, "Well, there's a table with a wash basin and pitcher, a chair and a cot with a mattress, and people bring their own blankets."

"Where do you get your water?" asked Nichols.

"There's a spigot outside, one for about each ten cabins."

Nichols said, "That's about right."

I foolishly stepped up to Nichols as he walked away and volunteered, "We're only charging a dollar-seventy-five at Lassen, and we have a hot and cold shower in the cabin, and we furnish the blankets—we're fully equipped."

Nichols called, "Hey, Paul, come listen to this," and had me repeat my story to the Mount Rainier concessioner.

Sceva listened intently and asked, "Did you make any money?" As I learned later, we hadn't—I didn't grasp the difference between a positive cash-flow, which we had, and a net profit, which we didn't. So I said, "Yeah, we made some money."

Nichols then called all the concessioners around the room over to our corner: "Hey, you guys, come listen to this!"

A little intimidated by now, I repeated my story again. I could tell that everybody thought I was underpricing myself out of business. Nichols, perhaps the biggest of the "Big Three" concessioners then told his peers, "I suggest we all go home before the Park Service puts a gold medal around this guy's neck and makes us out a bunch of sons-of-bitches."

Welcome to the Western Conference of National Park Operators, Don Hummel!

Down to Business

They must have been a tolerant bunch, because nobody refused to talk to me during the rest of the meeting. And Adolph A. Aszmann, general manager of the Glacier National Park operations of the Great Northern, even had the good grace to take me aside and say confidentially, "Now look, these guys are supposed to be working for everybody, but they're very sensitive to their own interests. Don't be deterred if they razz you a little. And if you ever need any assistance, just give me a call."

But I definitely learned more with my mouth shut than with it open at that meeting. Many concessioners expressed concern over the Ickes plan to nationalize all park concessions, even though it had become obvious he did not have the political clout necessary to pull it off. Ickes had a reputation for getting things done circuitously if he couldn't act straightforwardly. If he couldn't talk Congress into taking over private concessions immediately, he'd find a way to slowly ease them out, and that way seemed to be the authorization of not-for-distribution-of-profit concessioners.

Word went about at this February 1936 Conference meeting that a non-profit organization was operating accommodations for the public in the National Capital Parks, a group called the Welfare and Recreational Association of Public Buildings and Grounds, Inc. (WRAPBG). This nonprofit distributing agency paid one-half of its net profits directly to the federal government as revenue with the remaining half used for welfare and recreational purposes within the District of Columbia.

But more disturbing was the news that Mammoth Cave in Kentucky had been taken over by a nonprofit concessioner after more than a hundred years of operation by private owners. The story was complex. Visitor services at Mammoth Cave had continued uninterruptedly from 1816 when it was first opened to visitors. It was strictly a private business venture from its beginning until 1929. For ninety years, from 1839 to 1929, it was operated by Dr. John Croghan and a trusteeship under the provisions of his will.

In 1924 a small group of Southcentral Kentucky businessmen decided that Mammoth Cave deserved national park status. It was commonly accepted that Niagara Falls and Mammoth Cave were the top two American tourist attractions in those days. The Kentucky boosters formed a stock company called Mammoth Cave National Park Association and began the classic local lobbying job that produced most national parks. The response was not encouraging: the President, the Secretary of the Interior and Congress made it clear that any new national park had to have a certain minimum of government land, that no funds would be made available for such an enterprise, and that, besides, Mammoth Cave was not really of national park quality.

The Association went ahead soliciting funds for land acquisition anyway, converting from a stock company to a not-for-profit company. They also lobbied the Kentucky legislature for support, this time with better luck. The state created an agency called the Kentucky National Park Commission with the mandate to acquire lands for a Mammoth Cave National Park. Now the Association and the Commission set about buying up all the available land around the cave. The park was authorized by Congress May 25, 1926, but only with many stipulations, among them the further acquisition of private land. The National Park Service sent an agent to the area, which was identified as a National Park *Project.*

In a decisive final sweep, the Association and Commission pooled their resources to jointly purchase the historic entrance to the cave and the Mammoth Cave Hotel. Now the question arose, who would do the operating? After heated arguments, the two groups decided to form a Joint Operating Committee composed of representatives of both bodies so service to the public would not be interrupted. W. W. Thompson, who had been identified with the national park movement as secretary to the Association and the Commission, was appointed general manager. The Park Service had just found their operating managers in a husband-wife team with long experience at Yellowstone: Henry S. and Beulah Brown Sanborn. Before she married Hank, Beulah had also operated Death Valley's winter concession, as I mentioned earlier.

All the concessioners liked the Sanborns, but they were uneasy about a non-profit concession company. It looked too much like Ickes was sneaking his nationalization plan in the back door. All the profits from the Mammoth Cave Operating Committee were donated to the United States for the purpose of additional land purchases to complete the Mammoth Cave National Park. To free enterprisers, this looked suspiciously like a model for all future national park concessions.

Perhaps most disturbing, the government had recently built a visitor-use dock at Colonial National Historical Park in Virginia and a concession building at Shiloh National Military Park in Tennessee. Government ownership of concessions was definitely creeping into the American scene.

Diluting the Parks

Another important Park Service move was also afoot. Ickes had begun lobbying Congress to give him authority over recreational areas. The National Conference on Outdoor Recreation held in 1924 had warned, "it is an inescapable fact that recreation as a public use of Federal lands cannot be turned aside." The development of the automobile had prompted Henry S. Graves, Chief Forester of the Forest Service to say as early as 1920, "Thousands who formerly spent their vacation days abroad or at some nearby resort are traveling long distances by rail or motor to visit the mountains, lakes, and forests of our country." Ickes wanted a piece of that pie for the Interior Department. His efforts would soon result in the comprehensive Park, Parkway and Recreation-Area Act of 1936 which initiated four new types of National Park Service area: recreation demonstration areas, national parkways (roads), national seashores, and national recreation areas.

Most crucially for the public, the addition of historical areas (1933) and recreational areas (1936) to Park Service responsibility would eventually result in more non-scenic areas under their jurisdiction than natural areas. This increasing emphasis on non-scenic areas would in 1956 lead to a de-emphasis on concessions, which serve predominantly scenic park areas. That de-emphasis would in the 1960s play into the hands of zealous environmentalists bent on removing both concessions and visitors from our national parks. But that problem lay far in the future.

I left my first concessioners' meeting much wiser than I had arrived. February of 1936 brought another major change in addition to my new membership in the Western Conference of National Park Operators. Winters were becoming more difficult to survive. The Tucson law practice brought in only enough cash for my dad. I had to do something. Only the government had jobs for a young aspiring lawyer, so I began to inquire.

The WPA

Dal Dort, our concession partner, had taken a job with
President Roosevelt's Works Progress Administration. He led
the investigative division, a position created in the aftermath
of Idaho Senator Borah's charges of graft in the agency.
Shortly after returning to Tucson from the concessioners'
conference in February 1936, I applied to Dal for a job. A
WPA agent interviewed me and said I met their qualifications. After the normal application processing period I was
hired, shipped to Washington, D.C. for training and soon
found myself assigned to Nathaniel Rogers, Field Agent in
Charge of the Portland, Oregon, office. I was not to return for
summers at Lassen for many years, and left Charley Keathley
in charge, retaining my office as founder and president of the
recently renamed Lassen National Park Company.

My first investigative case took me to the Seattle, Washington, area and produced spectacular results. The WPA Administrator was fired for irregularities and the State of Washington agency completely reorganized. By chance, my time in
Seattle turned up another important case, one that a fellow
concessioner alerted me to. One Sunday I drove the seventy
miles or so from Seattle up to Mount Rainier to see the
concession operation of Paul Sceva, the man Billie Nichols
had introduced me to at the concessioners' conference.

Steve Mather himself had helped put the Mount Rainier
National Park Company together back in 1915 after finding no
local volunteers to finance a lodge in the high alpine
meadows. Mather gathered a group of Seattle and Tacoma
civic leaders and told them if they didn't come up with the
cash he'd get Eastern money to finance the project. They
came up with the money, founded the concession company,
and built an inn at Paradise Valley. The Alaska cedar logs for
Paradise Inn were salvaged in 1915 from the site of a tremendous forest fire that had scorched the western slope of
Mount Rainier back in 1885. The logs were hauled to Paradise
by horses and milled on the site. Almost all the woodwork in

the huge lobby was done by an old German carpenter who stayed in the building during the heavy winter of 1915-16 (snowfall covered the third-story windows of the inn). The tireless craftsman hand-hewed the cedar logs with an adze and built much of the rustic furniture—huge tables, a hand-made piano, and the ornate grandfather clock that stands beside the vast fireplace.

While I looked over Paul Sceva's Mount Rainier operation that Sunday, he told me in confidence that WPA was building a lodge to be used for commercial purposes on Mount Hood, just east of Portland. Sceva didn't think it proper for the government to use relief funds for a hotel to compete with private sector lodges. The man behind it was WPA's Oregon administrator E. J. Griffith, Sceva said, and somebody ought to look into it. I sent in the complaint, disclosing only that it came from a confidential source.

Washington approved the case for investigation, so I quietly began examining documents and making discreet inquiries. I soon found that the WPA Administrator had authorized diversion of most of the non-labor costs of practically every project in the State of Oregon to build Timberline Lodge on Mt. Hood. The federal land of the building site, incidentally, did not belong to the National Park Service, but to the Forest Service of the Department of Agriculture. The Park Service was no part of this scandal.

I went up to examine the project and discovered they had spent almost a million dollars on a beautiful lodge with sumptuous lobby and dining room, but had provided only 19 guest rooms. I found numerous other design flaws, such as three huge fireplaces with no place to store firewood. The kitchen crew had to cross through the lobby to get from their quarters to work. Most incredible, the lodge had been oriented toward the prevailing maritime winds so that snow drifts piled up at the front door and totally blocked the entrance. The government later had to construct a huge culvert-like structure so people could get in during snow season.

In the middle of my investigation, our Washington office

called and instructed me to meet with administrator Griffith, our principal defendant. He had complained to his friend Eleanor Roosevelt about this investigation being conducted without his knowledge or approval. Following instructions, my boss Nat Rogers and I went to Mr. Griffith's Portland office. He was irate and greeted us haughtily, demanding to know who made the complaint and asserting it was one of his political enemies. I felt safe, as only I knew the complainant.

After his initial tirade, Griffith turned to me and said, "Well," as though now giving me permission to speak. I was determined to keep control of the investigation, so I said as innocently as I could, "Mr. Griffith, you sent for us; what do you have in mind?" He blew up! I let him rave for a while, then proceeded to question him about the diversion of non-labor funds and the secret agreement I had discovered that Mount Hood's Forest Service Supervisor C. J. Buck had given to Jack Meier, of Meier and Franks Department Store in Portland, to operate Timberline Lodge after its completion. Mr. Griffith responded as little as possible to my questions and ended the interview.

As soon as we left, he apparently telephoned Washington, and told them I was an "investigator of extreme youth who employed badgering tactics." Thereafter, the agents in the Portland office referred to me as The Badger.

My investigation led to some changes in WPA, threw out the agreement with Jack Meier, and put the contract out for public bid. Even so, WPA had to authorize about another million dollars to build dormitories for skiers and provide other facilities so the lodge could operate at a profit.

Marion

The years 1937 and '38 were times of personal extremes for me, joy and sorrow. On the joyous side, the Lassen concession seemed to be thriving beyond our expectations, expanding and upgrading facilities practically every year.

Another joy was Marion. I had noticed the secretary in the WPA office, an attractive Scottish girl named Marion Chris-

tison, and began to date her. She lived with her widowed
mother and two brothers. The Depression had hit her family as it had most, and Marion was the only one with a job.
In time she confided that her family frequently irritated
her, everybody telling her what to do and where to go—
and she was the one supporting them! We spent a great
deal of time together, and soon it became obvious we were
in love.

Tragedy

But Marion had respiratory problems that soon worsened.
One day she could no longer work regularly and resigned her
secretarial job. I arranged for her to live at my parents' home
in Tucson, where she spent several months in the warm dry
climate that has helped so many respiratory cases. She was
then able to return to Portland, but within weeks we got word
that my mother was dying of cancer of the pancreas. If I
wanted to see my mother again, I would have to go home
immediately. I resigned my WPA job, married Marion September 27, 1937, and took her to my folks' home. Less than
two weeks later my mother died.

Once more I practiced law with my father, but Marion was
soon diagnosed with tuberculosis, and needed constant medical care in a rest home—at $350 per month, money I didn't
have. I went back to work for WPA's Division of Investigation, assigned to San Francisco. Within days I was called to
Albuquerque, New Mexico, where a huge WPA scandal had
erupted involving U.S. Senator Dennis Chaves and his son-
in-law Stanley Miller, the Assistant U.S. Attorney for New
Mexico—a serious case of diversion of funds for political
purposes that kept me there for eleven months. At least I
could drive home to visit my wife frequently. It was hard
watching her deteriorate. On our first wedding anniversary
Marion greeted me with a poem entitled "Marion Christison
to Don Hummel - A Year Ago Today." The poem
read:

To have lived long years and never to have
    your lips soft on mine;
Never to have your arms with mine entwined;
Never to know the thrill of sweet surrender;
Heard your whisper—gentle, tender "mine all
    mine";
Oh, better short sweet days of living, loving,
    dreaming,
If one brief year is all there is to be,
My joyous thanks for moments shared, for our
    loves' immortality.

Toward the end of May, 1939, Marion had to be taken to St. Mary's Hospital in Tucson. Her attending physician, Roy Hewitt, gave her the best care medical science could offer in those days. Despite his best efforts, about ten days later a lung collapsed. Then an associate physician installed a butterfly valve to prevent compression of the lung. This meant that the pleural lining could not heal. I knew from Dr. Hewitt's expression that this was a consignment to death. On her 15th day in the hospital, Marion awoke and said to her mother and me, "Last night I crossed too many hills of understanding. I've gone too far and I can't turn back. I'm going on. It's going to be hard on you both, but I want you to be brave."

At that moment Dr. Hewitt came in and Marion told him, "Doctor, I had confidence that if anyone could help me, you could, but we've lost the fight and you've lost a patient." She died two days later. I buried her next to my mother on June 6, 1939.

8

The Parks and War

D URING THE YEARS just before Pearl Harbor I stayed with
WPA, advancing to the job of field-agent-in-charge in
Denver and later in Atlanta. I managed the Lassen concession
in absentia, making policy decisions and advising by telephone.

Concession policy was gradually hardening into the Ickes
mold of government-built, government-operated services.
One at a time his new facilities took shape. In 1937 the
National Park Service undertook construction of a hotel at
McKinley Park Station, at the entrance to Mount McKinley
National Park under an allotment of funds by the Public
Works Administration to the Alaska Railroad, which itself was
a government-owned agency of the Interior Department. The
railroad was to operate this concession.

Authorization also came in 1937 for remodeling the government-owned Painted Desert Inn at the Petrified Forest
National Monument in Arizona, and work continued on the
new government-owned concession buildings at Bandelier
National Monument in New Mexico.

In 1938 Ickes made his move. He promoted a bill in Congress to authorize the acquisition and operation by the government of concessioners' facilities throughout the park
system. Other bills were introduced for the purchase of accommodation facilities in certain areas only, such as Mount
Rainier, Olympic, and Mount McKinley National Parks.
None became law.

Ickes wrote in his Interior Secretary's annual report for 1939:

While considerable thought has been given to the acquisition and operation of Government-owned facilities, the old, established policy under which concessions are granted to private interests for the establishment and operation of accommodations for the public was continued and further developed during the 1938 season.

. . . Government-built and Government-owned facilities at Bandelier National Monument were opened to the public during May 1939 . . . This is the first distinct step in the policy of the Government's construction of new facilities in national parks for operation by private concessionnaires. While there have always been many Government-owned facilities in national parks and monuments heretofore utilized for accommodations of the public, these facilities had all been acquired only incidentally in land purchases or similar transactions.

Despite this hard-line Secretarial "concessionaire" policy, the National Park Service itself did not completely agree with Içkes and continued its good relations with concessioners. At the National Park Service Conference held in Santa Fe, New Mexico, October 2 to 8, 1939, attended by both Service and concessioner representatives, nothing but the usual "nuts-and-bolts" issues occupied the agenda, such as rates charged for accommodations and the types of facilities that would best serve public needs.

Which is not to say that NPS was slacking off or getting unduly "buddy-buddy" with concessioners: the Service initiated a tough policy at that same conference requiring operators to include with plans of public facilities submitted for approval, data on costs of construction, proposed rates, and estimated revenue, expense and resulting net profit, to provide reasonable assurance of satisfactory operation of the proposed facilities on a sound economic basis.

In early 1940 our Lassen concession developed an agreement with the Western Pacific and Southern Pacific Railroads for all-expense trips to Lassen Volcanic National Park, which also involved a bus service franchise between Redding and the park. In anticipation of the increased traffic, we expanded our operation with a type of better-quality visitor facility for the Manzanita Lake area. We built a number of these units and called them "hotel bungalows."

Drury

On August 20, 1940, Ickes saw an old wish come true: Arno Cammerer resigned as NPS Director, his health broken, and "outsider" Newton B. Drury left his cherished Save-The-Redwoods League to take over the Park Service. The new Director took on his duties with dedication and energy, but he didn't escape the wrath of Ickes: the Secretary frequently insulted and ultimately excoriated even such a dyed-in-the-wool conservationist as Drury. And, true to form, Ickes decided that if he couldn't take over the concessioners, he could at least keep them out of the parks, as he wrote in his 1940 annual report:

> In the newer eastern park areas, a policy is gradually being formulated whereby only the daytime needs of visitors for gasoline, oil, food, and picnic supplies shall be met by operations within the parks. The Deparment favors development of overnight accommodations by private enterprise outside park boundaries.

By early 1941 concessioners could feel the war approaching. We received notification that employment of aliens in national park areas was prohibited. The Park Service obtained the agreement of concessioners to offer uniformed military personnel reduced rates for accommodations.

Interior Secretary Ickes chose this time of unsettled conditions to install one of his pet projects. On June 21, 1941, National Park Concessions, Inc., a non-profit-distributing membership corporation began operating the public facilities at Mammoth Cave National Park, Kentucky. The corporation's purpose, according to Ickes, was "to furnish adequate accommodations for the public at reasonable rates and to develop these facilities solely in the interest of the public welfare." Since NPCI was a strictly membership corporation, it could issue no capital stock and yield no profit to the incorporators.

The NPCI directorate of five included W. W. Thompson, president, H. S. Sanborn and Mrs. Beulah Brown Sanborn as treasurer and secretary, respectively, A. J. Knox, National Park Service attorney, and Charles L. Gable, Chief, Park Operators Division, Branch of Operations. This looked too much like the long-suspected master-plan organization upon which the government would pattern all future concessions. Even though it soon became evident that the government treated this new company no different than a private enterprise concessioner, for many years the Western Conference of National Park Operators would not permit National Park Concessions, Inc. into their membership.

War

Then, of course, December 7, 1941, changed everything. On December 16, Interior Secretary Ickes called upon all bureaus of the Department for "full mobilization of the Nation's natural resources for war . . . upon a basis best suited to serve our military and naval forces without waste, and with a view to saving all that we can of such resources for future generations." Congress immediately cut national park appropriations more than 50 percent. In all, 125 permits were issued to the War and Navy Departments to make use of National Park Service lands, buildings and facilities.

With the onset of World War II many national parks were virtually shut down, despite NPS interest in keeping as many open as possible—Lassen was one of the few that managed to stay open through the entire war. Gasoline rationing meant that park visits originated nearby, for the most part. Military personnel on leave made up a substantial fraction of wartime visitors. The Park Service itself was shoved out of Washington, D.C. in 1942 to make way for defense activities and relegated to a tiny Chicago office. Many Park Service employees were shuffled to defense-related jobs: 40 Service employees found themselves immediately assigned to a pig-iron survey in 900 foundries throughout the country.

The differences of opinion between Charley Keathley and me developed to such a point by 1941 that Dal Dort and I thought it best to buy out Keathley's interest. We offered to buy Charlie's one-third interest in the company and he agreed to sell for $20,000 in early 1942. This was a pretty good return for an individual who had gone in with nothing—$20,000 in those days was a lot of money, when a laborer got $1.00 a day and carpenters $5.00 and lumber went for $20.00 a thousand. The Keathleys left for San Francisco, where Charlie found work with the General Services Administration. He continued there until his retirement many years later. My brother Gail took over the Lassen concession for the next season.

I sought a transfer from the Works Progress Administration and found a position in the Office of Price Administration inspection unit for a while, but in 1942 entered the military, bound for China duty. Faced with the uncertainties of war, I gave three shares of Lassen Company stock to Dal Dort's wife Betty so they could hold stockholder meetings in my absence. Dal now served in the State Department and would remain in Washington for the duration. With wartime regulations forbidding expansion of "recreational facilities," we didn't have to worry about making improvements to our concession. I was off to war.

Wartime brought serious problems to the national parks. Visits declined from over 21 million in 1941 to 6 million in 1942. Reduced travel meant trouble for concessioners. By June 1943 no accommodations were offered at Crater Lake. There had been three lodges at Isle Royal in Michigan; two were closed. Hotels in many parks just shut down completely. In some parks "minimum service" was offered, meaning cabins and simple meals. The Navy took over The Ahwahnee in Yosemite and remodeled it as a convalescent center, primarily for submarine crews. In Hot Springs the Eastman Hotel and Bathhouse was bought by the War

Department for use as a hospital. The McKinley Park Hotel at Mount McKinley was turned into a recreation center for soldiers.

The CCC camp at the South Rim of the Grand Canyon became a military training camp. The Paradise section of Mount Rainier found use for training troops in mountain warfare. At Joshua Tree National Monument desert warfare training units built a road across the natural area. Military equipment and clothing were tested at Shenandoah, Mount Rainier, and Yosemite. Nearly every coastal unit of the Park Service, Pacific, Atlantic, and Gulf, became a defense installation, aircraft warning posts for the most part. The military services drafted even the trained personnel of the Park Service, which then had to get along with inexperienced men on a temporary basis. Vandalism in the parks increased. Wartime had unmistakably come even to the national parks.

War certainly occupied all my thoughts. After serving for a year in my China combat station, one day I received word that the Lassen concession faced a crisis: My brother Gail had completed his year as manager as agreed, and with the draft taking everyone, we could not find a replacement. How could we meet our operating contract obligations to the Park Service? Who would actually manage Lassen for us?

Arthur E. Demaray, NPS Associate Director, said he would get National Park Concessions, Inc. to operate the Lassen facilities if we would agree. I had less worry about NPCI than many concessioners, and didn't hesitate to accept their offer. We made a profit-splitting contract with them and NPCI assigned one of their employees named Claude Galloway to manage the operation. Another war year went by.

Then the Lassen concession faced another crisis. While I served at my combat post in China, National Park Concessioners, Inc. informed Dal Dort and me that they intended to exercise their right to get out of our contract at the end of 1943 and no longer manage Lassen for us. However, they were shutting down another park facility and had no immediate need for Galloway, so we hired him directly on a salary basis. Even a war could not keep me from having to deal with concession problems.

The only unexpected bright spot was travel. Park visits, which had hit an all-time peak in 1941 at 21,050,426 and slumped to about 6 million in 1942, surprisingly increased in 1943 to 8,193,090. But travel decreased again in 1944 to 7,455,271, of which 2,149,398 were military personnel.

In 1944, Ickes wrote in his annual report that his "policy that concession facilities wherever possible should be installed and owned by the Government was further crystallized . . . Post-war construction programs were broadened to include plans and estimates for new Government-owned concession facilities in many areas." Ickes' National Park Concessioners, Inc. operated wartime concessions at Isle Royal, Rosemary Inn at Olympic National Park, and Vanderbilt Inn in the Vanderbilt Mansion National Historic Site, and was designated concessioner at Big Bend National Park in Texas. But perhaps most ominous was Ickes' statement:

> In the older national parks the original lay-out of visitor facilities, under then-prevailing slow modes of travel, was based on the need for overnight accommodations within the park and near points of major interest. In general, this condition no longer prevails. The question, therefore, arises: Should future planning envision only such facilities as are necessary for daytime use, depending upon nearby communities to furnish sleeping accommodations as in the case of the Great Smoky Mountains National Park?

Years later the environmentalists would forcefully take up this argument as their main weapon to completely eliminate concessioners from the parks as the first step in stealing the national parks.

Business Leave

I could tell you some interesting personal war stories here, but I won't. At the end of 1944 I received word in China of another Lassen crisis, this one serious. Claude Galloway had been recalled by National Park Concessions, Inc., leaving Lassen without a manager. Dal Dort couldn't take leave from the State Department so I took 30 days R&R and returned to the United States to find another manager for Lassen. How ironic that Uncle Sam allowed me to fly home to take care of my own personal business! But I had the relief time coming, and it was my choice to take it that way.

I flew into Oakland, California, and interviewed Fred L. Taber, a school principal who had worked a summer season or two at Lassen. We spent about an hour talking and reached an agreement. I gave him the keys to the Lassen facilities, authorized him to sign on our bank account.

While I was in the States, I decided to telephone my partner Dal Dort. He told me that he had just taken an option to buy the Yosemite Park & Curry Company for $1,750,000. There was a catch, though. Government Services, Inc., a not-for-distribution-of-profits corporation that had for some years provided newstands, cafeterias and other services to government buildings in Washington, D.C., had first rights. GSI was headed by NPS Associate Director Arthur Demaray, Dal told me. That appeared to be a conflict of interest to me, but that's what we had to deal with. Dal asked if I would go to Yosemite, look over the operation, and send him a buy/no-buy recommendation.

Hilmer Oehlmann, president of Yosemite Park & Curry Company, met me in San Francisco and we drove to Yosemite. We spent about a day going over their facilities. Things had changed in Yosemite. Don Tresidder had been president of Yosemite Park & Curry Company when the war started, but now sat as President of Stanford University, leaving the concession under Oehlmann's management. The principals were worried how long the war would last and wanted to sell the operation. It was a fabulous deal. I wired Dal to do everything possible to acquire Yosemite Park & Curry Company. He wanted to know if I could come to Washington to discuss it with him. I told him yes and caught a series of military transports to the nation's capital. It was good to see Dal and Betty again, but there was only time for business. I went over the details with them and all too soon found myself on the military transport route and back in California. Then it was back to active duty where I spent the rest of the war.

Dal didn't get the Yosemite concession because of Demaray, who kept requesting extensions of his first option from Don Tresidder, even though he couldn't comply with the terms. By the time Demaray dropped his option because of inability to pay, the war with Japan was coming to an end. Not long afterward, rationing and price controls were removed, releasing pent-up demand for recreation and filling up the parks overnight. Of course, Yosemite Park & Curry Company decided against selling. I ended up president of the Yosemite concession anyway, but that's getting ahead of our story.

After what seemed an eternity, the war was over. Japan surrendered and in time we all came home. The war years had been hard on the national parks: appropriations had shrunk from $21 million to $5 million. Government facilities had fallen into disrepair. Concession facilities had also deteriorated. Many areas lay closed and unoccupied. Others had been converted for wartime use and needed refurbishing. None were ready for the crush of visitors waiting in the wings. But as bad as the war had been, coming home was more traumatic.

9

New Challenges

I RETURNED TO the United States in January of 1946, after release from active duty with the Air Force. One of my first priorities was Lassen. I telephoned our school-principal-turned-manager Fred L. Taber and found he had done a good job under difficult conditions. He told me we had about $15,000 in our bank account—but I knew it would take much more to put things in post-war order. As soon as I could, in early February, I travelled to San Francisco and negotiated a concession loan with Crocker National Bank. With our finances assured, I stopped in to see the Congressman for Lassen's district, Clair Engle, and discussed my hopes and plans for the park's postwar operation. Congressman Engle received me cordially and wished me the best, but reminded me, "Lieutenant Colonel Hummel, don't forget that you have to be out of uniform and dressed in 'civvies' within a month of mustering out." I was on duty until my leave expired in April, so this detail posed no problem. With my congressional courtesy visit taken care of, I drove up to Lassen to evaluate our situation.

Return to Lassen

No maintenance had been done during the war years and I dreaded to see what our Manzanita Lake facilities looked like. When I arrived in Northern California I received a different shock: While I was still in China the Public Service Commission had revoked our franchise certificate to operate bus service between Redding and the park. I realized I'd have to deal with our Park Service concession contract, too, which would expire in May. There was a lot to do in a little time.

As long as I was in the area, I tackled the bus franchise problem first. I knew we had records to prove our right to that certificate somewhere in the Manzanita Lake Lodge, but in early March deep snow still covered the ground. There was nothing to do but snowshoe in. After hours of slogging, I turned the last bend and saw the old lodge again. How long it had been. How dismal and forlorn the old place looked. When I got in, I found that much of our equipment was missing, taken during the years when people could not buy blankets and bedsheets and pots and pans. Memories flooded back of better days, building days.

I went up to the attic with a flashlight—the electricity had been shut off—to see if I could find anything to support our franchise. I didn't know if the records still existed and if so, in what form. After a couple of hours shuffling through old documents, I recovered enough material to prove we owned the franchise and had complied with its terms.

We petitioned to reopen the case. The man who had been given our franchise naturally enough opposed the reopening, but to no avail. After the hearing, our franchise was restored, and the man asked if I wanted to sell. I said "No," which turned out to be a bad mistake, since the operation never made money.

Then I hastened to Washington and negotiated a new concession contract. Park Service concession chief Oliver G. Taylor had taken Gable's place—I never found out what became of Gable—and together we went over the contract. Nothing much had changed. The Park Service could still tell us when to open and when to close the season. They could still tell us what to charge for accommodations. They could still tell us what kind of accommodations to provide, and when and where to build them. They dictated sanitation measures, wages and hours of my employees, and how to house them. Even the amount of beef put into a hamburger was carefully evaluated to approve the price charged to the public. I asked them again about that Article IX: "Are you guys going to own the buildings I pay for?"

Oliver smiled, "Don, you've been concessioning in the parks for ten years. Do you need to ask?"

"Just checking," I said.

They sent the contract on for approval, which was, as usual, a mere formality. I returned to the West satisfied that everything was in order and shortly received a memo from Assistant Secretary of the Interior C. Girard "Jebby" Davidson insisting that despite any obstacles every effort must be made to expand facilities for the anticipated crush of post-war travel. I had already intended to provide more visitor rooms, but this memo included specific instructions to build a new cafeteria at Lassen to be in full operation by the 1947 season—an ill-conceived idea, I thought, but orders were orders. They wanted to see plans immediately.

The Surplus Saga

Coming as it did in the months just after the war, this expansion order presented a huge problem. Congress had passed an Act requiring all new building materials to be used only in homes for veterans; no new lumber could be used for any recreational development and this included Lassen. Even if I could find the materials, how could I pay for them? So there I was, faced with making instant plans, obtaining instant financing and locating instant materials in a market that didn't exist.

First, the plans. Lassen superintendent Jimmy Lloyd and I snowshoed to the Manzanita Lake Lodge over three feet of snow in March to settle upon a site for the new cafeteria. Lloyd was a man of contradictions; he could be pleasant as possible one minute and completely obstreperous the next. While selecting the cafeteria site he was in his pleasant mood. I sketched out a plan on the spot and Lloyd signed it, agreeing for time's sake that I would go to San Francisco that night and present it to Regional Director Owen A. Tomlinson the next day.

Approval came back from Washington: "The plan you submitted directly to the Regional Office for cafeteria construction has been approved." When Jimmy Lloyd saw the approval he was in his obstreperous mood. He decided to "go by the book," and wrote me a two-page letter citing regulations requiring me to go through his office and not directly to the Regional Office.

I decided to put a stop to this pettiness once and for all. I wrote back a complete description of each step in our joint decision, including the fact that Lloyd had personally signed my plan and approved its submission directly to the Regional Office. I copied my reply to Park Service Director Drury and Lloyd never crossed me again.

Next, the additional capital. I went to the bank and told them my situation. They looked at my operating statement, asked what the terms of my new contract were, and I told them they were substantially as before. Banks that had been stymied during the war now anxiously sought borrowers and weren't as particular as usual. I got the loan.

Finally, the materials. Here began a grueling eight-month struggle in which my only friend was the War Assets Administration, fancy words for war surplus camps. As a veteran, I had preference in all surplus sales. Even so, that preference could not perform miracles for the Lassen concession. New cabins were out of the question. The only way to provide additional accommodations was to build tent units on platforms. The time pressure weighed heaviest: I had to get the cafeteria and tent platforms under construction in order to comply with my concession contract terms. Agonizing as it would be, my only realistic source of materials was an endless string of scattered army surplus sales. And the problem with army surplus sales was always the same: I had to buy more than I needed if I wanted anything at all. It was the army's insistent way getting rid of materiel it no longer wanted.

I learned in April that Standard Oil Company was dismantling an abandoned defense plant down in the Bay area and seeking bids for building removal. My bid won, I got a crew together, and we started tearing down the buildings to retrieve the lumber. But I had no way to get the secondhand lumber to Manzanita Lake.

I hurried to a war surplus sale and bid on two big 6x6 Army trucks when I only needed one, but they were packed two together, no separation allowed. I bought a pair, unpacked the crated truck parts and hired some mechanics to assemble them.

While the mechanics prepared my trucks I scrounged for cafeteria equipment at another war surplus sale (stoves, cutting tables, deep fat fryers, pots and pans, dishes and silverware, everything including kitchen sinks). Here again it was all or nothing. I needed only enough to serve a hundred-fifty guests, but ended up with equipment adequate for twenty thousand. When the trucks were ready, I hauled my kitchen equipment and used lumber to Manzanita Lake in their beds. My used lumber provided fifty platforms and sides, but I could find no tents.

I hurried to another war surplus sale. This one listed Army tent material. I bought it and had tents made. It was excellent material, but had been fireproofed, which left no breathing pores and made for a very hot tent.

Now I needed beds. I scurried to another war surplus sale and bid on a number of Army cots.

Now I needed mattresses. I dashed to another war surplus sale and bid on a batch of Army mattresses listed as fitting the cots. The only mattresses available were a little larger than our cots, and hung over the sides. But they were mattresses!

Now I needed blankets. I rushed to another war surplus sale and bid on a great number of Army blankets.

But we were still without pillows. I hurriedly searched for pillows. When I finally located them at another Army surplus sale—as usual—I had to buy considerably more than we needed: you took all or none. We had pillows, pillows and more pillows! I think I attended every Army surplus sale in the State of California. And there were a *lot* of them.

Rendezvous with Confusion

I don't mind such problems—they are the heart of management responsibility. But now, as December, 1946, approached, I had to set these happy problems aside for some distinctly ugly ones, new and potentially devastating challenges to concessions.

It started innocently enough as I flew to Washington for the second post-war meeting of the renamed Western Conference of National Park Concessioners (no longer "Operators"). I looked forward to a time of renewed acquaintances and renewed activity. The Conference had lain for the most part dormant during the war years with Daggett Harvey of the South Rim Grand Canyon concession as caretaker. The Conference had held its first post-war meeting in Chicago on December 3 and 4 in 1945—the Park Service was still relegated to the Merchandise Mart building in Chicago—and many members of Director Drury's staff attended some of the meetings to discuss return to full prewar operations, wage and hour regulations, winter operations, and the possible need to limit the length of stay at park hotels and lodges. But some concessioners still served in war-related jobs at the time—I was in China—and it was poorly attended.

Things were different by December of 1946. All of us that were coming home had come home. Most of the Park Service had been moved back to Washington. Our old nemesis Ickes had been ousted in a dispute over President Truman's nomination of Edwin W. Pauley, an oil executive, as Undersecretary of the Navy. A new, inexperienced Interior Secretary, Julius Krug, sat in the big chair and Oscar Littleton Chapman, an ardent New Dealer with Interior since 1933, was elevated to Undersecretary to keep Krug "out of jail," as Mather had once used Albright. Krug was also reputed to have a drinking problem and didn't devote full time to Department business. Everybody thought of him as "the absentee landlord." But the redoubtable Newton B. Drury still served as Director of the National Park Service, and that pleased most concessioners. The 1946 concessioners' Conference convened on December 3 amid high spirits and hope for the future.

During the first day of our Conference proceedings an invitation came from the Park Service asking all concession representatives over to discuss the renewal of our contracts. This didn't strike any of us as unusual or ominous since many 20-year concession contracts dated from 1926 and were up for renewal this year. At the appointed time we went to the big Interior building on the corner of 18th and C Streets.

They had set up the meeting room with chairs arranged theater-style, all facing forward. As I took a seat next to Yosemite's Don Tresidder, it became obvious that the Interior Department considered this get-together of more than passing importance: They trotted out the generally quiet and congenial Assistant Secretary for Public Lands C. Girard Davidson (everybody called him "Jebby") and Assistant Solicitor for Parks Harry Edelstein. Davidson was one of Krug's "bright young men," a Louisianan transplanted to Oregon and the man who, along with Under-Secretary Chapman, actually made many of the decisions issued over Secretary Krug's signature. Davidson disagreed with Chapman and Krug on many issues, but never balked at cooperating with them. Edelstein was respected as a sharp attorney and one to be wary of.

After brief niceties, Jebby Davidson announced that he wanted us to hear a legal opinion from the Department of the Interior's Solicitor's Office. The Solicitor is the Department's chief attorney. His word has the power of law in certain Interior matters, and this legal document called an "opinion," as we knew, would have binding force on us. Jebby wanted our reaction. Edelstein stood before us and made the presentation.

"I have here a Memorandum to Assistant Secretary Davidson from Solicitor Mastin G. White dated today, December third, nineteen-forty-six. Its subject is 'Proposed Renewal of Concession Contract with Sequoia and Kings Canyon National Parks Company.'"

Edelstein continued: "It states, "On June 6, Acting Secretary Chapman returned to the Director of the National Park Service the proposed draft of a renewal contract with the Sequoia-Kings Canyon National Parks Company. In this memorandum the Acting Secretary raised certain questions with respect to the term of the contract, the rate of the franchise fee, the ownership of the buildings, and the method of valuation if the government should purchase the company's properties. The Director resubmitted the proposed contract with minor changes with his reply memorandum of July 8th. Action on this contract was temporarily deferred pending the receipt from the Park Service of its reply to the memorandum concerning the Bernice Lewis contract in Glacier National Park which you transmitted to the Park Service on July 12 and which raised related issues. The latter issues were largely resolved by your memorandum of November 1 to the Director. Copies of these memoranda are attached."

We were a little puzzled about why we had all been called in to listen to the details of renewing two concession contracts. As Edelstein came to the substance of the opinion, though, we realized why we were there. One blow at a time, the Solicitor's opinion methodically knocked the underpinnings from beneath the entire private enterprise concessioner system. The room grew silent. Article IX of our old contracts, Edelstein said, "vested in the United States the complete title to the buildings erected by the concessioner Company and left in it only the right to have an opportunity to secure from its successor reimbursement measured by the value of the buildings."

This was contrary to all past practice. Interior was going to narrowly interpret that damned Article IX! Our rights to the structures we had built and paid for had just vanished with the stroke of a typewriter key! When our contract expired, our buildings belonged to the government! We retained the right to try getting money for the buildings from a successor concessioner—as if anyone would become a successor under those conditions. If we signed a new contract, all our property rights would be forfeited and no "just compensation" would be paid. It was the Ickes plan multiplied to the hundredth degree. Someone working for "the absentee landlord" was formidable indeed.

Edelstein continued: The term of contracts should be reduced from 20 years to as short as practicable. Franchise fees should be raised from 3 percent to 5 percent.

Not only would we be stripped of our buildings and equipment, our contract terms were to be slashed! Our franchise fees were to be raised enough to wipe out every cent of profit in the entire park concession system!

While we were trying to absorb these pronouncements, we kept noticing a great deal of reference to the June 6 "Chapman memo" and the reply July 8 "Drury memo," which mystified all the concessioners. Evidently these new policies had been under study within the Interior Department for some time.

While Edelstein droned on I watched Don Tresidder, President of Stanford University and board member of Yosemite Park & Curry Company. He was without question the most respected concessioner in all the national parks. Here was a man long accustomed to facing adversity with reserve and tact, the very embodiment of the ancient Greek motto of "grace under pressure." I could see Tresidder's urbanity dissolve as he squeezed the chair in front of him until his knuckles turned white.

Edelstein read the closing paragraph recommending total revision of the standard depreciation formula and method of valuation of concession buildings. The economic viability of the national park concession system had just been totally destroyed. Edelstein read the authorizing signature, "Mastin G. White, Solicitor."

Tresidder was on his feet instantly, protesting in the strongest imaginable language that White's Solicitor's opinion repudiated the whole history of national park concessioning. It was an unthinkable breach of the long understanding held between concessioners and the National Park Service. It was an act of dishonor that could never be allowed to prevail.

I looked around the room and saw that the Solicitor's opinion had appalled the Park Service people as much as it had the concessioners. They were definitely on the concessioners' side in this dispute, but dared say nothing. As we heard a few days later, even former Secretary of the Interior Ickes was aghast: He told Tresidder, "I wanted to take your concessions over, but I didn't intend to steal them from you."

But now, sitting in the room with Edelstein's words echoing in our heads, the tension was palpable. Jebby had wanted our reaction. He got it. When the meeting adjourned, there were no polite goodbyes. Paul Sceva of Rainier muttered, "If they want to steal our concessions, I'll have my congressman get the government to buy me out!"

Casting the Gauntlet

The Western Conference of National Park Concessioners sessions resumed in turmoil. No one had thought to obtain a copy of the Solicitor's opinion. We had only our memories and emotions to go on. For two days, no matter how we analyzed it, discussed it, or cussed it, we always ended with the same conclusion: "It'll have to be settled in Congress."

Someone, I recalled, had mentioned a congressman from Iowa by the name of Ben F. Jensen who sat on the House Appropriations Committee. He had evidently been following the six-month ruckus over concessions in the Interior Department and appeared sympathetic to our cause. I couldn't stand the confused inaction of the Conference. During a recess I went to Jensen's office on Capitol Hill and discussed our troubles. He seemed to understand the problem in some depth and indicated a willingness to intercede on behalf of the concessioners.

When the Conference reconvened for its final session, I reported on my visit with Jensen and his offer of help. I was astonished to see that no one in the audience responded. With no comment on my report, Conference Chairman Byron Harvey announced that he would entertain a motion for adjournment. I strongly protested, saying that I had listened for two days to their discussions and the general consensus that we would have to go to Congress for relief, and now that a congressman had expressed interest in pursuing this problem on our behalf, we were going home without consulting him. I told the Conference that if I were in the congressman's shoes and they didn't follow through now, but came around later asking for help, I would tell them all to go to hell!

As a result, the Chairman appointed Conference attorney Herman H. Hoss and me to go see Congressman Jensen. Hoss, as I learned later, had seen this Solicitor's opinion coming. He had given Howard H. Hays, President of Sequoia and Kings Canyon National Parks Company, an analysis of the building ownership problem just a few months earlier. The Park Service had even quoted his letter to Hays in their opinion—but not by name.

Jensen proved to be as solicitous as we had expected. He advised us to take the matter to the House Public Lands Committee, predecessor of today's House Interior and Insular Affairs Committee, which had legislative jurisdiction over the Department of the Interior. We followed his advice. In 1946, Congressman J. Hardin Peterson of Florida chaired the Public Lands Committee, and quickly agreed to place concessioner problems on the committee's agenda.

Peterson knew what we didn't: Six months prior to our Conference sessions a quiet but intense civil war had broken out inside the Interior Department over the concessions issue. The "Chapman memo" and the "Drury memo" that Edelstein had referred to so many times in the Solicitor's opinion represented in effect the two feuding parties. On June 6, 1946, Under-Secretary Chapman had sent to Park Service Director Drury a 5-page single spaced typed memorandum. It specifically dealt with the renewal of Howard Hays's contract as concessioner of Sequoia and Kings Canyon National Parks. But it raised universal questions about the four cornerstones of national park concession policy: building ownership, term of contract, rate of franchise fee and method of valuating concession buildings.

Just over a month after the Chapman memo, on July 8, National Park Service Director Newton B. Drury wrote a 13-page single-spaced typed memo to Secretary Krug in which he defended the private enterprise concession system and disagreed with virtually every conclusion of the Chapman memorandum. Drury sympathized in principle with eventual government ownership of concessions, but recommended "that we recognize the realities and, while pressing forward toward the goal of ultimate Government ownership of facilities . . . do not meanwhile disrupt the pattern of operations that has, by and large, proved successful and has rendered good public service, without having something to substitute for it."

"We now have 85 concession contracts," Drury reminded Chapman, "under which accommodations, meals, transportation, stores, and other services are furnished in the national parks. Most of these contracts are with concerns that have been induced to make investments in plant, running in some cases to several millions of dollars, with the expectation of a reasonable return upon the capital invested. As long as we have this system we shall have to make contracts on terms that those investing the capital will accept."

Point by point Drury took Chapman's nationalization-by-contractual-seizure plan apart.

Franchise fee rates: "Some believe that the concessions should pay more into the Government treasury. My own opinion is that even more important is the obtaining of moderate rates for the public patronizing the concessions."

Term of contract: "In order to secure the concessioners that we now have, it was necessary to grant them 20-year contracts to obtain the developments required. On numerous occasions, after a 20-year contract has run for ten years or more, in order to meet increased public requirements, the concessioners have applied to the Department for new 20-year contracts in order to obtain greater security for the substantial investments required. Their reason has been that the period remaining in their contracts was so short that it was not reasonable to expect them to make the investment without the additional security. From a business viewpoint, this was a reasonable requirement, and in most cases the Department approved a new 20-year contract. This reasoning has been accepted by the Comptroller General of the United States as providing sufficient benefits to the United States to warrant the cancellation of a partially expired contract and the execution of a new 20-year contract."

On Chapman's plan to replace existing concessioners in response to charges of "monopoly:" "I think we shall regret it if we take a course of action that will supplant some of the present tried concessioners with fly-by-nights that are an unknown quantity and will probably not give the public nearly as much and surely will not be as ready to conform to park policies and regulations."

Ownership of concession buildings: Drury explained carefully why the Park Service had never narrowly interpreted Article IX. "While, in the interest of continuous public service, it was desirable to assure the continuance of the buildings on the Park lands free from possible attachment of legal title by creditors of the concessioner Company, nevertheless it was both fair and necessary at the same time to assure the Company its beneficial ownership. This was to be accomplished by vesting legal title to the buildings in the United States, precluding the Company or a creditor from removing them, and on the other hand providing for the Company's right to reimbursement of the reasonable value of buildings in the event it no longer had the beneficial use of them under a contract."

Then, in one of the more elegant slanders in government literature, Drury wrote, "Anyone familiar with the history of concessions in the national parks knows that it was on such understanding that private capital was induced to invest in buildings on Federal lands for these operations. Without this assurance there would have been no such concessions as the public for thirty years have used and enjoyed."

Although politely worded and properly deferential in tone,

Drury's memo was a document of extraordinary defiance and bravery. He undoubtedly knew it put his job on the line. But he steadfastly refused to budge.

Seeking a Solution

Deadlock. Chapman, already the Acting Secretary although listed as Under-Secretary, had his eye on the Secretariat, a position he was fated to achieve. He could not retreat without a severe political setback. Drury had no such ambitions, but knew the National Park Service's integrity and honor were at stake. Integrity and honor might seem intangible to the cynical, but they are of weighty import to Congress and the public.

Both men were ready to fight it out.

Another discordant note quickly joined the cacophony: In their mid-1946 report on the upcoming Fiscal Year 1947 Interior Department appropriations, the House Appropriations Committee—without Ben Jensen's approval—commented unfavorably on national park concession operations and demanded that the Service make a study designed to effect improvements. Someone had encouraged members of the House Appropriations Committee's parks subcommittee to examine park concession records armed with three questions: 1) How much gross income is the concession making? 2) How much money is the concession paying the United States government for its franchise? and 3) How many competitive bidders are there for the concession? To anyone unfamiliar with the Mather-Albright concession principles the answers to these carefully one-sided questions would make concessioners appear to be unconscionable monopolists cheating the government out of revenue. It was clear what kind of study the appropriations committee would insist on.

Before Director Drury wrote his defiant memo, he too had thought of a study of concessions. He also realized what a double-edged sword such a study could be. If the Krug and Chapman faction undertook a concessions study in the name of the Interior Department, the conclusions would be foregone. The instant-nationalization-by-contractual-seizure program would become a reality. Drury hit on the solution: He suggested that an impartial citizen panel be appointed to study the concession issue and make recommendations. His argument to Krug was twofold. First, the Park Service had no personnel available for such a huge study, and second, as one of the principal parties of interest, the Service—and by implication, the Interior Department—could hardly conduct the impartial and dispassionate study necessary to garner respect from Congress and the general public. And if they could act fast enough, the Park Service could steal a march on any House Appropriations Committee-ordered investigation.

Drury had quietly obtained Krug's blessings for such a study before he wrote his July 8 memo. Once Drury released his memo, which mentioned Krug's approval of a citizen advisory group study, the Chapman faction was boxed in. On July 22, 1946, Interior Secretary Krug publicly announced the study project and by fall a five-man Concessions Advisory Group had been assembled.

Krug appointed Clem W. Collins of Denver as chairman, a past president of the American Institute of Accountants. The other four "persons of the highest character and specially qualified in their several fields" included George D. Smith of San Francisco, a past president of the American Hotel Association; Elmer Jenkins, of Washington, D.C, head of the Touring Bureau of the American Automobile Association; Charles G. Woodbury, also of Washington, a member of the board of both the National Parks Association and the Wilderness Society. Charles P. Taft, of Cincinnati, a nationally-known leader in civic and religious affairs, was chosen to represent the general public. Their task would occupy two years.

But by the time we concessioners came to Congressman Peterson on December 4, 1946, almost every concession contract in the parks hung in limbo. The Chapman-Davidson faction held tight to their confiscatory contract renewal plan and Director Drury refused to enforce it. Nearly all concessioners refused to sign new contracts since to do so would forfeit their property rights once and for all. Director Drury granted a blanket extension of our old contracts until December 31, 1948. We had come home from one kind of war only to be faced with another.

I say "nearly all" refused to sign because one concessioner, Union Pacific's Utah Parks Company, decided it could not afford the enormous refurbishing bill at North Rim Grand Canyon, Bryce and Zion. They had lost $150,000 or more each year simply operating these scenic money losers, and figured that was enough public service. Union Pacific signed the new contract and wished the government luck on its new possessions. But they stayed on to operate the concessions.

To the Grindstone

While all this was going on in Washington during mid-1946, I was still at Lassen scurrying from one war surplus sale to another trying to accommodate a horde of tourists letting off some of that "pent-up demand for recreation" they'd stored up during the war. My nephew Al Donau and his new bride Mary Frank (everybody called her "Frankie") joined me as permanent employees that summer. Things were looking up. At the 1946 season's end we had made a profit of $10,000. Not much for all that work, perhaps, but something to be proud of. In November Assistant Secretary Jebby Davidson wrote, "Although the amount of your profits are small, you must, regardless of the obstacles to be overcome, arrange for the expansion of your overnight facilities." Jebby, however, had not talked Congress into letting me buy new materials.

The 1946 Lassen season had not been without its managerial snafus. I found that a great change had taken place in American society during the war years. It was impossible to get experienced employees, just the very young who had worked only in cost-plus defense industries where "productivity" was an undefined term. New businesses were starting everywhere and "manpower shortage" was becoming a by-word. Our wartime manager Fred L. Taber proved an invaluable help in locating new employees.

I will never forget the day Fred sent us a waitress who had been a cocktail hostess. She arrived in a fancy low-cut dress and had a feather in her hat—appropriate for a lounge, but not a dining room in a national park. She was pretty independent and resented our demanding working conditions. Our visitors routinely gathered early and lined up at the dining room door before opening time. As soon as the doors opened the crowd filled all our tables, putting real pressure on the whole crew, waitresses and kitchen. One evening our cocktail princess didn't show up to serve her assigned tables. I was embarrassed to find guests going without service, so I served them water and said the waitress would be down soon. I then went upstairs to the employees' quarters and there she was, lounging and clad only in a bra and panties.

I said, "Your tables are full and the people are waiting for you downstairs." She said, "I'll be right down." I went down and tried to placate the guests. When she didn't arrive, I went back up and found her pretty much in the same position. I told her she should be down in five minutes or she didn't have to come down at all. I went back and told the customers I was having trouble with their waitress and would appreciate it if they didn't tip her. She finally graced us with her presence, finished serving, but never got a single tip. That was it. She exploded. I got a car out and drove her into Redding where she presumably found a more congenial atmosphere.

I offered the waitress job to a young girl on our housekeeping crew, an excellent employee and a good worker with a jovial personality. While I hated to disrupt the housekeeping crew, I felt it only fair to give her first choice at this opportunity to increase her earnings through tips. I was amazed when she turned it down. I asked her why. She said, "Well, when you're cleaning a toilet, it doesn't talk back to you."

That summer I also survived my first brush with unionized

workers. Most of the construction crew I had recruited early in the year was union labor. At first I never even thought about it, but agreed to pay union wages and honor union work hours. Like any other crew, there were conscientious workers and goof-offs. The union crew didn't like Earl Potter, my non-union carpenter foreman, an old standby from earlier years. They tried to give me a hard time about him, saying he was "riding on their backs." And it seems that in one of his more colorful moments he'd called them "a bunch of communists." I told them I regretted his poor choice of words, but I knew perfectly well who worked how much and not to tell me who was riding on whose back.

Several weeks later when Saturday payday came, the union group visited my office with an interesting piece of news.

"You've shorted our checks," said the crew spokesman.

"I don't understand," I ventured.

"Wages went up the beginning of the week by 25 cents an hour," said the spokesman. "It's not reflected in our checks."

"Don't you think it's a little late to be telling me this?"

"Maybe so," he agreed.

"Well, next week I'll start the new wage."

"No good. The union'll fine us."

"Well, do you think it's fair to come in at the end of the week and tell me about this?"

"Prob'ly not. But that's the way it is."

I got mad. I said, "Do you realize that room and board went up $2.00 a day this last week?"

The union workers' faces sort of fell and they left grumbling. As they went out the door I added that the tourist season was starting and they would have to move out of the cabins into construction tents. This didn't go over very well, but they said nothing further.

I was at the lodge desk Sunday night when some of the crew returned from Red Bluff and Redding. One carpenter who was obviously about half-drunk came up to me and said, "I've got two nots."

I said, "You have what?"

"I've got two nots," he repeated.

Then I tumbled and said, "Okay, what are they?"

He said, "I'm not going to sleep in a tent and I'm not going to pay that extra $2.00 per day for board and room."

I said, "That's fine, but haven't you forgotten the third not?"

"What do you mean?"

I replied, "You're NOT working for me."

That was the end of my union troubles. We understood each other.

Still, I was exasperated and finally called Hil Oehlmann to ask his experience at Yosemite. I thought maybe I had been out of the country too long and didn't understand employees any more. Hil assured me that everybody had the same problem.

High Grumbles

1947: Back in Washington, the concession policy issue still smouldered despite the progress of Secretary Krug's Concessions Advisory Group—or rather *because* of it. The House Appropriations Committee report on the upcoming 1948 appropriation act criticized the establishment of an outside group to undertake the task—they obviously resented being outflanked by Drury's quick action. The committee report was insistent that with respect to concession services, (a) prices be decreased, (b) the Treasury receive a greater return and (c) concession "monopolies" in the parks be brought to an end. This without regard to the economics involved!

Despite this harangue from the Appropriations Committee, Clem Collins and his Concessions Advisory Group carried on unperturbed. While deep in their investigation, they received a statement of substantial importance from former National Park Service Director Horace M. Albright on March 19, 1947:

"Congress, even in its days of willingness to be extravagant in the appropriation of public funds, never showed any signs of being liberal in voting funds for the acquisition of private holdings in the National Parks. . . . It is simply humanly impossible for the National Park organization to operate Parks, giving care, protection and interpretive service to the public and at the same time operate tourist facilities. . . . The great objection to authorizing government agencies to construct buildings for the accommodation of tourists is that the National Park Service policy may dictate locations . . . too far away . . . to make them attractive to visitors. . . . The Service might regard its policy of protecting scenic features of the Park more important than providing accommodations attractive to the public and profitable to the operator." What a gift of prophecy Horace Albright displayed there!

And as if to underline his prophetic utterance, as Albright spoke, the Sierra Club repudiated its roots: The Club revised its 1892 general Declaration of Purpose conceived by John Muir himself, "to explore, to enjoy, and to render accessible the mountains of the Sierra Nevada." Club leaders of 1947 struck three vital words from the original: "to render accessible." What a falling off was there! As recently as the 1930s Sierra Club president Bestor Robinson had admonished wilderness lovers: "One should fight for wilderness but know when to compromise: I want wilderness to contribute to the American way of life." The Sierra Club now betrayed its honored founders and the ideals of its native land: it turned to the dark path of misanthropic exclusionism. No longer would all people be welcome to the mountains. In the years ahead the Sierra Club's unstated but implicit purpose would be "to render inaccessible the mountains."

Genee

The year 1947 proved to be significant for me personally. During Lassen's summer rush when space was at a premium, a young woman and a nice gray-haired lady—her aunt— showed up at Manzanita Lake Lodge looking for a room. We were able to accommodate them in a tent, but not in a cabin—disappointing, but not completely.

There was something about that young woman, something

that caught my attention, but I gave her no further thought until the next day. Then she came in and asked if I had any summer jobs available. Her name was Eugenia Mitchell— she said to call her Genee—a high school teacher in Sunnyvale down in the Bay Area. She told me that she and a fellow teacher named Lou Ann Large needed summer work. The two had planned on going to Hawaii, but heard there were no jobs. At the last minute she joined her aunt and came to Lassen. Here again fate intervened.

Certainly there was work, I assured her. For her and her teacher friend. When could they start?

She said she had to visit her parents in El Paso, Texas, but would return and join her friend Lou Ann in the Bay area in a few days. I urged speed. For the concession's sake, of course. The operation needed a slightly more mature worker than we had been getting. Two school teachers would know how to take some responsibility. But they failed to report for several days. I sent my nephew Al to San Francisco to hire some additional cooks. I was upset when he didn't bring Genee and Lou Ann back with him.

"What's the matter with you?" he said. "You didn't even ask about the cooks I hired."

"There's nothing wrong with me," I retorted. Of course not.

Genee and her friend showed up within a day or two and we put them on the front desk. Al wondered why I was so happy to have a new desk clerk.

I started dating Genee. Whenever she had time off, I took time off. One afternoon we took two horses into the Bear Lake backcountry to explore new scenery away from the public. About dusk, Al and Dick Hemstead, the wrangler, came riding up looking for us. This aggravated me.

"Why are you guys here?" I demanded.

Al smiled, "Just thought maybe something had happened."

"Nothing happened. You knew we took some steaks for a cook-out."

Al smiled again, "If I take bacon and eggs, that doesn't mean I'm goin' to stay all night."

I didn't appreciate Al's gift for cryptic comment.

Toward the end of the 1947 season, Genee and I drove to Redding and called her folks. We told them we were engaged and wanted to be married on their wedding day that November.

Genee's dad Cornelius—everybody called him Mitch—was not pleased. "You haven't known each other very long," he said.

"But Don's a nice man, dad," said Genee. "He's responsible, he's a partner in the company that runs the summer lodge in Lassen National Park."

"Don't get stars in your eyes up in that park. What's he do in the winter? You've got to eat then, too, you know."

"He's a lawyer in Tucson. He's going to be the Assistant United States Attorney. Oh, daddy, say yes."

"Well. . . "

The date was set for December 27, 1947. I spent the Christmas vacation in El Paso with her family. My brother Gail came over from Tucson to be my best man. We were married in the Episcopal church in El Paso, reception at the Mitchell home. Gail, Genee and I drove back to Tucson. I started as Assistant U.S. Attorney the next Monday, the fifth of January, 1948.

Living space was tight in Tucson. I had to pay six months in advance to rent a small but comfortable apartment in Frontier Village. My new job soon proved less than ideal. My fellow Assistant U.S. Attorney K. Berry Peterson handled all the government's criminal cases. He was a brilliant attorney but, unfortunately, had a drinking problem and often failed to appear when cases were called. I had to fill in for Peterson on several occasions, but told Frank Flynn, U.S. Attorney in Phoenix, that I had been hired to handle civil litigation, and wanted no further part of criminal law. To make matters worse, a new federal judge had just been appointed, a man named Howard Speakman. A short time after his appointment he had a heart attack and seldom held court. I had a difficult time carrying out the government's business, but found myself with time to start building up a private practice—an activity entirely permissible by government regulations. By February my personal life settled into a reasonable pattern and the issue of park concessions livened up.

A Small Victory

On February 19, the Concessions Advisory Group report was released vindicating the general policy of the Service in the preceding thirty-one years.

Clem Collins and his four fellow advisors had produced a report generally favorable to the time-honored Mather-Albright policies. Among its most important conclusions:

> It is recommended that the policy of operations of concessions be continued under contracts that will not only protect the interests of the Government, but will give the concessioner the security to which he is entitled and sufficient incentive to provide a high standard of service to the public.
>
> . . . Contracts should be awarded to selected operators of known reliability and, assuming that they render satisfactory service, their contracts should be renewed.
>
> . . . As a general rule, the interests of the public will be best served by the present policy of granting preferential contracts to concessioners.

Historian John Ise described their report thus:

> Unsympathetic with criticism of monopoly in concessions, the advisory group ruled that contracts to a single concessioner for all operations in a given area represented sound policy, considering the hazards involved in many concession operations and the need for adequate and continuous service, and that the Director should be free to select operators on the basis of known qualifications, not only as to adequate financing but also as to sympathy with the objectives and policies of the National Park Service.
>
> The advisory group ruled that while "service at cost," with a reasonable return on investment included in cost, was sound in principle, it was not actually practicable; that a franchise or

contract fee should be levied against net profits; that the concessioner should get a fair minimum return of perhaps 6 per cent on investment, and should get a fair percentage of the profits above this to offset occasional lean years. The group did not believe that the concessioners generally made excessive profits.

The advisory group also approved the general policy of government ownership of concessions, but not government operation, and suggested that Congress should establish a definite policy of acquisition and maintenance. The advisory group found that the facilities provided by the federal government as well as the personnel in the parks were "taxed beyond capacity." They wrote, "All this results in situations for which the Service is often criticized but over which it has little control. Much of this criticism would not arise if the appropriations for the Service were more nearly commensurate with responsibilities on it and the public service expected from it."

Under-Secretary Chapman was not altogether pleased with the advisory report, and wrote to Horace Albright asking for his comments. Albright, in the private sector since 1933, had followed the ups and downs of the parks with keen interest, and his opinion was about the best that could be had. In his reply to Chapman, which was published in the *Congressional Record*, he said there was little in the report that he disagreed with. Albright thought that in the end it would be best for the government to own all concession facilities, with private operators, but that this would not come soon. This last point appears to reflect a change of mind on Albright's part from his March 19, 1947 position generally opposing government-built concessions.

Even though this advisory report seemed definitive, in 1948 Representative Dawson of Utah presented House Resolution 639 authorizing the House Public Lands Committee to study concessions, and Senator Butler of Nebraska offered Senate Resolution 254 for the same purpose. Not surprisingly, both measures died in committee.

The Plan

And now came one of the more baroque pieces of political maneuvering concessions have witnessed. Congressman J. Hardin Peterson had promised support for concessions, but realized that none of the parties involved were prepared to present a concession policy bill to Congress—Herman Hoss had a draft of a model concession bill written up, but the concessioners hoped things could be cleared up without resorting to legislation. Yet without a bill, there was nothing on which to hold hearings. All sides agreed that speedy hearings were desirable. Enter Representative Thor Tollefson from the State of Washington: Paul Sceva had been boiling mad about the Solicitor's Opinion from the day he heard it. As he had vowed at the end of Jebby Davidson's session, Sceva went to Congressman Tollefson and told him his plight.

Sceva's Mount Rainier National Park Company had been losing money steadily. The buildings were run down and needed extensive rehabilitation. With the government's breach of good faith on possessory interest and long term contract security, Sceva refused to invest another dime. He insisted instead that the government buy him out and pay just compensation for the tremendous investment he'd made over the years. Congressman Tollefson told Sceva that the government would be unlikely to appropriate funds for such a buyout. Other concessioners resented Sceva even thinking of selling out to the government. But Sceva was adamant. Tollefson promised to take the matter up with the Public Lands Committee and followed suit.

Peterson, upon hearing Sceva's tale of woe, realized that a bill to buy out the Rainier Concession would have no chance of passage whatsoever, but that it would provide just the forum he needed in which to examine general concession policy. Peterson encouraged Tollefson to enroll H.R. 2313, "a bill authorizing the Secretary of the Interior to acquire on behalf of the United States government all property and facilities of the Rainier National Park Company." When the bill was duly introduced, Peterson convinced Subcommittee on Public Lands Chairman Frank A. Barrett of Wyoming to schedule hearings on the bill for May 21, 27, June 1, 11, 12, 15, and 16, 1948—ridiculously extensive hearing time for what amounted to a personal relief bill. It was obvious to insiders that this was a front for some greater purpose. When the word went out from Washington, nobody paid the slightest attention to the official title, but prepared full scale evidence for hearings on overall concession policy.

I was one of three concession Conference members invited to testify. None of us even realized that the hearings were supposed to be about the Mount Rainier buy-out—the hearing title clearly stated what H.R. 2312 was all about, but it never registered on any of us. Concessioners in those days were somewhat naive lobbyists—"hicks from the sticks," as the saying goes. When June and the hearings approached, I prepared my testimony and hoped for the best.

Talking to Congress

The first two days of the hearing, March 21 and 27, were filled with testimony from Congressman Tollefson, who mentioned Paul Sceva's concession among many other issues, National Park Service Director Newton Drury and his staff. Drury's superior, Assistant Secretary for Public Lands Jebby Davidson, as usual, spoke for the Department. Associate NPS Director Arthur E. Demaray, Chief of Concessions Oliver G. Taylor, and Chief of Lands Conrad L. Wirth all bore up under heavy fire from Subcommittee Chairman Frank A. Barrett of Wyoming. Barrett was a friend of the private enterprise concession system and not particularly pleased with the Solicitor's opinion or its implications. Barrett spent little time inquiring about Paul Sceva.

During the first June days of hearing testimony, Union Pacific lobbyist Howard Blanchard told of their Utah Parks Company's problems with the Zion, Bryce and North Rim Grand Canyon concessions. Herman H. Hoss, attorney for the Western Conference of National Park Concessioners, methodically ripped apart the Solicitor's opinion, using many of Drury's arguments. Hoss hoped to find an opening to explain his model concession bill, but none came up. And nobody mentioned Paul Sceva except in passing. Finally, on Saturday, June 12, 1948, the fifth day of these hearings, at two in the afternoon, as the next-to-last witness I got my big chance before Congress. Subcommittee Chairman Barrett said, "The first witness this afternoon will be Hummel. Will you come forward, Mr. Hummel?" I came forward and began my testimony:

> I am Don Hummel, president and general manager of the Lassen National Park Co., a concessionaire in Lassen Volcanic National Park. My statement today will attempt to show the position that some of the concessionaires find themselves in as a result of the change of policy. I will make this as succinct and brief as I can.

I told my story as well as I could and seemed to be getting a warm reception. Chairman Barrett appeared particularly sympathetic, and asked a number of personal questions:

Mr. Barrett. Were you in the service?

Mr. Hummel. Yes, sir.

Mr. Barrett. For how long?

Mr. Hummel. Four years.

Mr. Barrett. What branch of the service were you in and where did you serve?

Mr. Hummel. Army Air Forces. I served in north Africa, India, China and the Philippines.

Chairman Barrett, Congressman Wesley A. D'Ewart of Montana, and Congressman Clair Engle of California, a man I had known for some time, all seemed to ask questions that deliberately revealed the hardship under which concessioners labored and emphasized the unfairness and outrage represented by the Solicitor's opinion. We did not mention Paul Sceva. When the subcommittee was finished with me, Congressman D'Ewart said:

I would like to thank Mr. Hummel for appearing before this committee and presenting his case as a veteran who is doing his best to serve the public as a concessionaire in a national park under conditions that seem almost insurmountable. It is not only discouraging to him but to others. How he can proceed from here and give the people who visit his area the services they are entitled to is hard for me to understand. I sincerely hope that this committee will proceed with this investigation and work out a solution that will encourage just such men as Mr. Hummel in the carrying on of their operation and the continuance of their facilities so they will be available to the public over the years.

I think that is something this committee has to undertake right away. In the meantime, I sincerely hope you will not be disturbed in the use of your facilities until this committee can act and write a policy that will be in the interest of the public as a whole.

Then Mr. Engle said:

May I concur, Mr. Chairman, in the statement made by my friend from Montana. I have known Mr. Hummel for several years. The first time he came to my office he was in uniform. Since then I have had rather close contact with him in connection with his operation in my district. I know that he runs a good facility there for the public, and that he is sincerely interested in doing a good job in running his concession. He has also indicated a real interest in the public welfare.

All this sweetness and light must have rankled Congressman Fred L. Crawford of Michigan, ranking majority subcommittee member behind Chairman Barrett. He was one of the few who took the ostensive purpose of the hearings seriously—to buy out Paul Sceva—and could not see what I had to do with Mount Rainier. Crawford asked pointedly, "Why is the Concessioners Conference pushing you out in front as the principal witness?"

Of course, I had nothing to do with Mount Rainier, but neither did I know this hearing was supposedly about government acquisition of Paul Sceva's concession. I answered, "I'm a very small concessionaire and a returning veteran, sir. As I see it, the loss of our facilities at Lassen would be contrary to everything Congress is doing to enable returning veterans to reestablish themselves."

Crawford must have thought I was playing games with him. In frustration he zeroed in on my veteran's status. He proceeded to belittle my testimony, debunking any privileges that I might have as a veteran: "You're just one of millions of veterans, aren't you, Mr. Hummel?"

"Yes, sir."

"You're not entitled to any more consideration than any other veteran, are you, Mr. Hummel?"

"No, sir."

"Then you can't present this committee with special pleading for your private business interests and claim to be speaking as a veteran, can you, Mr. Hummel?"

"No, sir."

I was as frustrated as Crawford. I thought of all the sharp answers a week too late. How I wish I could have retorted that I was not asking for special consideration! How I wish I could have told Crawford I had used up all my veteran's preference to reestablish the Lassen operations, and would lose it completely if another concessioner or the government were allowed to take over our operations! But I was too green in the ways of Congress to make these points—and it wasn't until later that I discovered Peterson's clever ruse using Sceva of Rainier as bait for a full scale concession policy hearing.

Evidently Crawford's conscience bothered him: when the committee print of the hearing testimony was published, I saw that he had ordered his hostile exchange with me expunged from the record.

10

Drakesbad and McKinley

THE HOUSE Public Lands Subcommittee hearings had ended on an upbeat note despite the drubbing I took from Congressman Crawford. Congress, we could see, felt generally sympathetic to concessioner problems. Even the press was treating national park concessions with less hostility. Conference attorney Herman Hoss had shown Congressman Peterson his model bill that would give statutory authority to the proven Mather-Albright concession principles. We felt it had a good chance of winning the cachet of Congress. Things could hardly have looked better. And we had a friend in Congress.

Democratic Congressman J. Hardin Peterson of Florida, who had lost his Chairmanship of the House Public Lands Committee when the Republicans took control of the Eightieth Congress in 1947, still served as ranking minority member of the Public Lands Subcommittee and second ranking minority member of the committee of the whole. (All House and Senate Committees are chaired by a member of their respective majority party.) At the conclusion of the Concessions in the National Parks hearings on Saturday, Peterson called a few Conference members aside. As the saying goes, he had good news and he had bad news.

First the bad news. Peterson told us, "I'm sorry, gentlemen, we're going to hold a couple more days of these hearings, but there's no time to enact any legislation this session. I know you're disappointed, and I think Mr. Hoss's draft legislation is good. Save it for another day. This session there's just no time to introduce it."

155

Then the good news—but it certainly didn't sound good at first: "You go negotiate new contract terms with the Department of the Interior," Peterson said. That did not sound very promising, given our current relations with Chapman and Davidson. But the Congressman explained, "I've already told those folks there's going to be no money to acquire your facilities. I've told them Mr. Tollefson's bill is never going to get out of committee. And I've told them they'd better make their peace with you concessioners. Get your Conference to send somebody on over to Interior next Monday and start dealing."

Negotiating

If there was to be no legislation, this was our best chance for future stability. The Conference leadership immediately decided to negotiate and I found myself agreeing to stay over until Monday and serve as one of its two negotiators. We made a few calls and it was all set: Interior Department Assistant Solicitor Harry Edelstein and National Park Service General Counsel Jackson Price were to act for the government. Attorney Herman Hoss and I were to act for the Western Conference of National Park Concessioners.

Monday morning. Hoss and the two Park Service negotiators met in Director Drury's office on the third floor of the big gray Interior Department building. They had just come out when I intercepted them in the hall on their way to our small meeting room.

"Well, Don," said Hoss, "Drury just gave us our instructions."

"What did he say?" I asked.

"Go into the room I reserved for you. Negotiate new contract language. And don't come out until you've reached an agreement."

That was plain enough.

We all sat down around the little table, bracing for what we knew would be a grinding ordeal. We immediately dug into a highly technical problem: the exact nature of the concession-

ers' property interest in their facilities, given the government's legal title to the land under those facilities. As we
talked, it became obvious that we already knew each other's
position. But Edelstein had always been a little gun-shy of
Hoss, a man considered unflappable and so precise in expression that Interior officials habitually called him "that technical
bastard." But Herman had come into the session with uncharacteristic jitters. A doctor had taken him off smoking because
of a growth on his tongue. Edelstein, quickly realizing Herman's disadvantage, began to needle him.

Herman proposed to designate the concessioner's property
right as a "possessory interest," to be defined as all incidence
of ownership except legal title, which remained in the United
States. Hoss had borrowed the term from California tax law,
wherein the State taxed private buildings constructed on
public land by assigning a "possessory interest" to the owner
of the buildings.

Edelstein shrewdly taunted Hoss: "Can't do that, Herman.
The concessioners don't possess those buildings."

"Of course they do," snapped Hoss. "They're occupying
them right this minute."

"Doesn't matter. The United States possesses them."

"By what right?"

"Ever hear of federal marshals? Don't forget that Steve
Mather took Huntley Child's concessions in Yellowstone."

"You wouldn't. You don't have the authority."

"The police power of the United States is fully vested in the
Department of the Interior."

"That Mather thing happened in 1918, Harry. And it was a
personal argument between Mather and Child anyhow."

"Mather took those hotels."

"I've heard the story. Mather gave them back." By now
Herman was getting upset. "Besides, Congress would never
stand for that high-handed approach nowadays!"

Edelstein said, "Why don't we just drop the possessory
interest concept?"

Whereupon Herman got up, walked to the window and

said, "Oh, hell, what's the use?"

Harry said, "Yes, what's the use," took his papers and walked out of the room.

Jackson Price and I argued and pleaded to get these two men back together. It took us two hours to get them to the negotiating table. But once we got them there, we got the job done: We agreed upon acceptable "standard language" for concession contracts. "Standard language" is the "boilerplate" section of any contract that spells out general terms and conditions into which the names of the specific parties and special circumstances are inserted.

The new standard language contained eight crucial provisions: 1) concessioners owned a possessory interest in structures erected with the approval of the secretary on government land with private capital; 2) if taken for public use, just compensation must be paid for this property interest; 3) government policy must not prevent the concessioner from earning a reasonable profit; 4) a substantial private investment merits a long-term contract.

5) If a concessioner's service is satisfactory to the secretary, it merits a preferential right to contract renewal; 6) rate approval is to be based primarily on comparisons with similar services outside park jurisdiction; 7) private investment in the parks is to be encouraged by promoting continuity of operations, including cancellation of unexpired contracts and issuance of a new longer term contract when major investments are required; 8) a satisfactory concessioner may be given the preferential right to provide additional services of a similar kind.

These provisions were to prove historic. They were the source of many future restatements of park concession policy and eventually became the law of the land. However, the thrust to nationalize all concessions remained embedded in these Mather-Albright principles. A provision was included that "an option to purchase the concessioner's facilities may be exercised by the Secretary only at the end of the contract period or other termination of the contract; funds shall be available to the Department 12 months prior to the exercise of the option by the Government, and when the option has been exercised a valid contract between the parties shall exist." In the main, needless to say, Harry Edelstein was not pleased. But the potential for the government to take concessions by unreasonable measures would one day come back to haunt us.

I returned to Tucson happy and turned my attention to work and domestic matters. As things turned out, no major concession policy crises would emerge for nearly ten years, despite the fact that our legislation had not even been introduced. Hoss's draft bill was put aside. We placed our trust in our new contracts.

I carried on as Assistant U.S. Attorney, found a new home for Genee and me on East 3rd Street, and on November 8, 1948, our first daughter Donna was born. On November 1, incidentally, Interior Secretary Krug announced new concession policies that embodied most of our negotiated contract language, but he was not enthusiastic about it and retained his belief in government construction and operation of concessioners' facilities. The elections that month brought the Democrats to control again in Congress. The next year, on November 10, our daughter Diane was born.

Treachery

During August of 1949, unbeknownst to any concessioner that I know of, Krug's Interior Department made one last attempt to steal our concessions. Behind our backs, Chapman's crew released a list of 19 contracts which had expired or would expire by December 31, 1949, and invited proposals for taking over and operating the concessions. I can find no evidence that the Park Service joined in this perfidious effort, or even knew about it. If word of such an outrageous maneuver had leaked out, you cannot imagine the outcry that would have arisen from the entire concessioners' Conference.

But, as Krug noted in the Secretary of the Interior's 1949 Annual Report on page 301, "The response was slight and mostly by persons with little capital to invest." I never had an inkling of this treachery until I began research on this book and in the normal course of fact-checking ran across the story in Krug's last Annual Report (1949). Nor as far as I know did any other national park concessioner—obviously we should have made a routine practice of reading those dry government documents.

In a way I find it surprising that Secretary Krug allowed that account into his report: he didn't record in earlier years how he intended to take over our concessions through a strict reading of contract language. And because of that fact, the casual reader of his 1949 report would have no background by which to understand the whole concession situation. I was completely disgusted to see the following self-serving account of Interior's failed attempt at calling in bids for concession takeovers: "Where no other proposals have been received, negotiations are under way with old concessioners who have given satisfactory service. The inability of concessioners to finance needed expansion is the major difficulty in current negotiations." What a whitewash!

The fact is that not a single negotiation was going on. No concessioner—except Utah Parks Company—would think of signing a new contract that abrogated his property rights. And the Interior Department itself had created that "inability to finance needed expansion" by threatening to confiscate concessioner property: what sane banker would loan money to a business facing dispossession?

But what really makes my blood boil is a complete falsehood that the 1949 Krug report states about me: "At Lassen Volcanic National Park, the Lassen National Park Co., which has accepted an extension of its contract to May 1, 1950, has advised that it cannot enter into a new contract, due to inability to finance new developments. Consequently, a new concessioner is being sought who will be able to furnish the service required."

It is true that I accepted an extension on my old contract to May 1, 1950—the Park Service allowed all concessioners such extensions of their existing contracts on a year-by-year basis as Drury's means of thwarting Chapman's nationalization plan. It is false that I advised Interior that I could not enter into a new contract due to inability to finance new developments. I never told them anything of the sort: I wasn't communicating with them at all until a Mather-Albright-principle contract was made available.

And had I known Interior was seeking another party to take over our concession, I would have taken immediate legal action as well as contacting the House Public Lands Committee. Lassen Park Company always prided itself on public service. We initiated every new expansion investment in the park with no prompting from the Park Service—with the sole exception of that post-war cafeteria idea, with which we disagreed but readily complied.

But the failure of this last gasp at taking over the concessions seems to have impressed upon Oscar Chapman the futility of his plan: When he succeeded Julius Krug as Secretary of the Interior in December of 1949, he delegated Assistant Secretary for Public Lands Dale E. Doty to put our negotiated settlement into a definitive policy statement. It was formally released on May 6, 1950 as a memorandum from Secretary Chapman to NPS Director Drury and then summarized in the Interior Secretary's Annual Report for 1950. The Chapman statement contained ten specific policy points which appeared to reestablish the Mather-Albright policies, but which also retained a troublesome *possibility* of government takeover. But now we had in print the long-recognized right of concessioners to the security of their investment in the national parks.

The Clincher

However, Congressman J. Hardin Peterson, who had returned to his Public Lands Committee chairmanship when the Democrats regained control of Congress, wrote a Committee Resolution released July 18, 1950, stating:

Whereas, the Secretary of the Interior issued a memorandum on May 6, 1950, to the Director of the National Park Service clarifying the concessions policy of such department, and

Whereas, the policy announced by the Secretary on May 6 seems to meet many of the problems which had arisen and would enable the concessioners to give good public service and provide adequate facilities; and

Whereas, such clarifying policy by the Secretary seems to adopt the principles of proposed legislation being considered by the committee . . .; and

Whereas, the matter relating to security of investment by the concessioners, although not covered in the memorandum, . . . may be covered to the satisfaction of all parties concerned in new contracts between the concessioners and the Park Service.

Whereas in view of the announcement by the Secretary it would not appear to be necessary to pass further legislation at the present time, Now, therefore be it

Resolved: That the policy . . . under date of May 6, as attached and made part of this resolution, is approved; . . . the Secretary of the Interior and the Director of the National Park Service are requested to give notice . . . of any change in policy . . .; any breakdown in negotiations . . . relative to recognition . . . of the investment security (including the possessory interest) of the concessioner.

> J. Hardin Peterson, *Chairman.*
> Claude E. Ragan, *Clerk.*

On October 13, 1950, a definitive 20-point statement entitled "Concessions Policies of the National Park Service" was issued over the signature of Dale E. Doty as Acting Secretary of the Interior. Although this policy statement, like the one of May 6, avoids the words "possessory interest," it does specify that "it is the policy of the Department to recognize that the concessioners have substantial property rights in [their buildings, structures, and other improvements] and appropriate provisions on this subject shall be included in concession contracts."

In addition, Peterson advised the Interior Department that any concessioner contract had to be deposited with the Public Lands Committee for 30 days before the Park Service could sign. I have never been able to document this fact anywhere, but Congressman Peterson told me about it personally in a face to face meeting and I have no reason to doubt it. I also know of specific contracts that were thus deposited, and a later bill Congress passed with similar provisions. Peterson's move gave the concessioner a chance to complain to Congress if the Park Service or the Department of the Interior did not live up to our newly negotiated contract provisions.

Peterson undoubtedly knew about Interior's last-ditch effort to go around the concessioners with its call for new bids. Although the record is silent, I suspect that it led to his 30-day deposit requirement, which was a highly unusual slap at a major governmental department. The concessioners welcomed the move because we had so often in the past reached an oral agreement with the Department of the Interior only to find the later written version unrecognizable. I might also mention that almost exactly six years later, on July 14, 1956, Congress passed an act requiring that all concession contracts in excess of five-year terms, or which had a gross income of more than $100,000, be submitted to the House Interior and Insular Affairs Committee 60 days before the award was made.

We had won our five-year post-war conflict.

A Call from Drakesbad

With the arrival of the 1950s I felt it was time for a change. I resigned my position as Assistant U.S. Attorney in 1951 and set up my personal law practice in Tucson's Valley National Bank building. The family was not yet complete. My son Cliff arrived August 8, 1951. I still ran the Lassen operation, rotating between summer concessioning in Lassen and wintertime law practice in Tucson.

The National Park Service felt it was time for some changes, too. On All Fools Day, April 1, 1951, Arthur

Demaray was promoted to Director. Perhaps his date of appointment was an inauspicious omen, for he lasted only eight months and left a lackluster legacy. On December 9, 1951, Conrad L. Wirth became the sixth Director and was to keep the seat for more than twelve years.

May, 1952: A call came in from Roy Sifford, owner of an operation in the southeastern part of Lassen Volcanic National Park known as Drakesbad. He had a problem. A record snowfall had blanketed Lassen that winter.

"Don, last week Pa and I hiked into Drakesbad from Lee's."

"You hiked in?" I asked. "Was the road still snowed under?"

"Snow's gone," said Roy, "but you can sure tell it was there. The county Cat was mired in one big mudhole. My pickup couldn't get past it. When we got up to the place we found the dining room caved in. The porch and the lobby had pulled loose. Every cabin had some damage—and the corral is in bad shape."

"How terrible, Roy."

"There's more. The Park Service is pressuring private landowners in the park worse than ever. My mother just died. There's no cure for my sister Pearl's undulant fever. Pa's not well. It's all just too much for me. Old Doc Jensen says I better make some other arrangements for the operation."

Roy's first thoughts had gone to the many patrons who had been with him year after year.

"I called everybody and canceled their reservations," he said.

But Roy didn't want to lose Drakesbad. He'd considered a way to save it, had thought it over carefully. Now he was certain. He asked me, "Would you take over the operation on a lease basis?"

This was a real surprise but I immediately agreed.

"I think we can do it. In fact, we'd love to have it."

Roy and I worked out the terms and soon got approval from Park Service regional headquarters.

I told Al Donau my decision: I would go to Drakesbad and

see what could be done with the place. Al thought I was crazy, because Drakesbad had a capacity of only about 50 people. It was more like a guest ranch than like our resort operation at Manzanita Lake. Earl Potter, the master carpenter who helped us build everything at Manzanita Lake, went with me to Drakesbad to evaluate the damage and see how best to get the operation going again.

Drakesbad's facilities were primitive, to say the least. The lodge building had a desk in the lobby for an office and six guest rooms overhead. A dozen or so separate cabins and six tents rounded out the accommodations. No power lines came to Drakesbad: coal oil lamps served the cabins and tents and Coleman lanterns lighted the lobby and dining room. The only refrigeration it had was a small propane-operated domestic unit.

A corral held twelve horses for the guests, which Roy Sifford had agreed to handle for us. Horseback rides were Drakesbad's main daytime activity, with occasional evening "hot dog rides" taking all the guests to some spot in the park where they roasted hot dogs over an open fire and returned by moonlight.

It was exactly what its small but devoted clientele wanted. And it was clothed in romance and history. Historically, the place itself epitomized Lassen Volcanic National Park with active volcanism encompassing a boiling lake and hot springs, and a group of fumaroles and steam vents called Devils Kitchen. Its spacious grassy meadow bordered the headwaters of the Feather River, the sort of trout stream that fishermen keep secret.

The place had originally been known as Hot Springs Valley. A German immigrant by the name of E. R. Drake homesteaded a portion of the valley, which he called Drakes Place. Drake had built a small hand-hewn-timber bathhouse which gave the place its current name, Drakesbad, from the German *Drakes* + *bad* = Drake's bath. Drake's wood tubs were supplied with natural hot water by a scooped-out log trough, which also fed a small swimming pool.

Roy's father Alex bought the homestead in 1900 and at the seller's request retained the name. On June 6th, the Sifford family moved to Drakes Place from their home at Susanville, taking three days to travel the 54 miles because they had to ford high streams. Alex Sifford drove the big wagon, Roy's mother and sister Pearl the spring wagon, and seven- year-old Roy himself herded the milk cows with their calves tied to the cows' tails to keep them in tow while crossing high water.

The Sifford family built up Drakesbad as a resort during the big 1905-1910 camping years, hosting up to three-hundred visitors in August. The crowds were brought by publicity surrounding the declaration of Lassen Peak and Cinder Cove as National Monuments in 1907, managed by the Forest Service. Philenda Spencer, a frequent Drakesbad visitor and mother-in-law of Congressman John E. Raker, proposed a petition to make this area a national park. Congressman Raker took the petition to Washington in 1911. As I mentioned in Chapter 5, Mount Lassen was cooperative enough to begin its series of dramatic, well-publicized eruptions starting May 30, 1914, following which Lassen Volcanic National Park was established in 1916.

But now, in the summer of 1952, we rebuilt the dining room. All the furniture had been crushed beyond repair. Genee was able to buy hickory tables and chairs in Arkansas which fit in very well with this rustic, simple dining room lighted by Coleman lamps. It was rugged going back and forth from my full-time management work at Manzanita Lake to the refurbishing of Drakesbad. Maybe I had made the wrong decision. Some of the pressure was relieved when late in the summer my brother Gail and his wife Helen promised to come operate the facility for the next season.

Democratic Politics

Shortly after Christmas of 1952, I received a call at my Tucson home from John Molloy, who said he represented a group that wanted to know if I would run for mayor. I said, "What's the joke?" He replied, "It's no joke—we're interested in coming out and talking with you about running for mayor of Tucson."

A group of about 10 arrived at our home and asked if I would be interested in declaring my candidacy. I said I could hardly afford it. I was just getting my law practice reestablished after serving four years as Assistant United States Attorney. One of the group said that we all talk about good government, but when it comes to doing our share, we all say that we can't afford it. I agreed to run for mayor.

They didn't tell me who they had asked before coming to me, but I know they had been turned down by a number of people. The problem was the Eisenhower landslide and Richard Nixon's talk about 20 years of treason—his opinion of the long-held Democratic national administration. With that going on, not many wanted to run on the Democratic ticket. In fact, many didn't want to admit being Democrats. Unlike many cities, the Tucson Charter calls for a partisan government, and somebody had to run on the Democratic ticket. We talked it over and decided I should run.

Then came the hunting to get three councilmen to run with me. We were able to get two, but not a third. If elected, we would have four councilmen opposed to us. The prospect didn't deter us and we started campaigning.

I enlisted the help of many Democratic officeholders who controlled Pima County government, including Lambert Kautenberger, Chairman of the Board of Supervisors. Lambert had quite a political machine. He agreed to use his organization and put up a number of signs announcing my candidacy. I went to see Bill Matthews, publisher of the *Arizona Daily Star,* and a dominant force in the Democratic party. Matthews indicated that he intended to support my opponent Fred Emery—the incumbent—and was very negative toward my candidacy.

After my campaign got some momentum and victory appeared imminent, Matthews interfered behind my back, calling Kautenberger and the other Democratic officeholders, warning them that he would oppose anyone supporting my candidacy. To my dismay, three days before the election,

Kautenberger ordered his men to take down all my political signs. We were defeated by a small number of votes. But that's politics.

Idylls at Drakesbad

Getting the Drakesbad operation going again in 1953 proved to be a task. Roy had contacted most of his regular guests and urged them to return, promising that conditions would be much as they had been in the past. Roy's people were skeptical—he'd spoiled them like pampered grand-children—but decided to try us. I don't believe they were disappointed, because they came back to us for many years. My brother Gail told me he and Helen wouldn't be able to continue after their first season at Drakesbad, and I'd have to find someone else. But there wasn't anyone else. I decided to run it myself. In June of 1954 I appointed Al Donau general manager in charge of the Manzanita Lake operation and turned my attention to Drakesbad.

Genee and I and the four children—Charlene had been born in 1953—began our new adventure. Some of our em-ployees lived in the loft above the storage room, and our family moved in over the dining room, where we shared the space with some of our female employees. Separation was effected by hanging up a blanket partition—shades of the old 1850s Hutchings House in Yosemite! We all shared one tiny upstairs bathroom.

We had about eight employees besides Genee and me and Roy Sifford. Benny, a Chinese cook who had worked for Roy many years, fortunately stayed on with us. He was a Drakes-bad favorite, a cook with the magic touch, a congenial com-panion and a good friend. All the guests knew him personally.

As the facilities were primitive, so our supply system was primitive. We had to go into Chester three or four times a week to pick up our food and soft goods. We had arranged to arrive about 6:00 in the morning and take our dirty linen to the laundry. The proprietor was cooperative and got it washed immediately, so by the time we had finished our purchasing and running other errands in Chester, we could pick up the laundry and return to Drakesbad, arriving around noon. It was a little frantic, but saved us having to keep a large laundry inventory.

After my first season there, I decided I liked Drakesbad for our children and was just as happy to have my nephew Al running the big operation at Manzanita Lake. But I had second thoughts when we came back the next spring. At the end of my first Drakesbad season we had put some canned goods, sugar, flour and other nonperishables in a little walk-in box in the kitchen to prevent it from freezing during the long winter. We gave no thought to what this might attract. When we returned the following spring to open up the facilities, we found that a bear had tromped across the snow and entered a second story window, which was about snow-height. The bear had ripped up all our beds, for one thing. For another, it apparently saw itself in our long mirror, because its broken shards lay scattered all over the upstairs.

Undoubtedly sniffing the food we had thoughtlessly left behind, our furry friend went downstairs and broke into the walk-in storage box. It proceeded to bite into all the canned goods, dripping fruit and vegetable juice over the floor. The bear then ripped open the flour and sugar bags, mixing their contents with the previously prepared vegetable and fruit cocktail. The mess thickened until it spread nearly eight inches deep. Then, instead of going out the way it came in, our ursine visitor went back upstairs and created an exit of its own. For some reason or another, the bear also pulled a mattress halfway through the hole it had torn in the wall. Needless to say, we never left any end-of-season food in the kitchen again.

The bathhouse was one of our favorite places at Drakesbad. It receives natural hot water from mountain-slope volcanic springs on one side of the valley, which we mixed with the icy water of our trout stream arising from snowmelt springs in the upper valley, giving us a naturally-heated temperature-controlled swimming pool. It was a popular place, but difficult to keep clean—algae grew very rapidly. Our last child Charlene learned to swim at the age of one in this pool. It was perfect for children—the water soothingly warm and the pool small enough for a child to learn to swim without fear.

Roy Sifford handled Drakesbad's horseback parties, but I led some of the rides. Our children came with us on many rides in the park; in fact, while she was still a toddler, Charlene usually rode on my saddle in front of me.

George Collins, my old friend from Grand Canyon, began writing to me in 1954. George had reported as a permanent ranger, subsequently received promotion to the Park Service's Washington office, then went on assignment to Alaska to develop a master plan for Mount McKinley National Park. George wrote me a number of times trying to entice me up to Alaska to run the McKinley concession. I thought Alaska was sled dogs and year-around snow, and, besides, I had no money, so I declined.

Mayor of Tucson

The year 1954 was momentous for me in another direction: I once more sought election as Tucson's mayor, with council candidates Bill Wisdom, Limey Gibbings and John Hardwicke. This time we ran a better campaign and all won except John. The problems started before we were even sworn into office in April 1955. Before our inauguration, City Manager Luther Davis resigned to take over the presidency of Tucson Gas, Electric Light and Power Company. One of our campaign promises had been to select only a professional city manager. But when we assumed office there was no such person available and we had a vacancy to fill. We appointed Phil Martin as acting city manager—he had long City of Tucson experience as head of the Water Department and had even served from time to time in acting capacity as city manager.

The *Tucson Daily Citizen* immediately lambasted us for appointing Martin, suggesting we had no real intention of keeping our promise to hire a professional. We assured everyone that we were conducting a nationwide search for the best possible city manager. It took considerable time and the *Citizen* constantly complained we were dragging our feet. But we made good on our promise and hired Kansas City, Missouri's director of research and budget as our new city manager, a man named Porter Homer.

The mayor's position was considered part-time, and the position only paid $200 per month. It turned out to be the fullest full-time job I ever had! With all my mayoral duties, the 1955 Drakesbad opening was hectic, but we made it on time—an absolute necessity with all our pre-registered guests. We were barely into the operation when a call came from Tucson: the bus operators had struck. I had to return immediately. There was nothing to do but to turn the Drakesbad operation over to Genee. It would be her first time with full management responsibility for our four children, eight employees, and fifty guests.

Park operation is not an easy job, and managing employees is one of its touchiest parts. One of our Drakesbad employees was a nephew of mine named Dale "Jake" Fenter. Jake had an obstinate streak and caused Genee no end of concern. He didn't like the way she gave orders and refused to follow them. Genee fired him.

I wondered what was wrong when I called in the next day, because Genee sounded edgy and apprehensive. Then she explained how she had fired my nephew. I laughed and assured her that I would have done the same. From then on she took her management job in stride.

That summer Al and I decided that the small store under the Manzanita Lake dining room was no longer adequate for our visitors. We proposed to the Park Service a separate new store building, which they approved. We obtained the financing and built it at a cost of $90,000. That same year, we added cabins at Manzanita Lake at a cost of $30,000.

Even during these good years, I took only a small salary from the Lassen concession and only during actual operating months. My law practice and Mayor's salary combined with this was still not enough to live on with a family of four children. Had I not bought and sold real estate as a sideline, I could not have made it.

In 1956 I was elected President of the League of Arizona Cities and Towns and to the National Board of the American Municipal Association, subsequently named the National League of Cities. These activities demanded more of my time.

The Lure of McKinley

One day in August of 1957, a letter arrived at Tucson from Duane Jacobs, superintendent of Mount McKinley National Park. He said he understood that I would be representing the Conference of National Park Concessioners at the upcoming Superintendents' Conference at Yellowstone in September. He wanted to encourage me to take over McKinley's concessions. I wrote back agreeing to meet with him after the conference in Yellowstone.

Genee and I took our two daughters Donna and Diane with us to Yellowstone. Our fellow concessioner Daggett Harvey and his wife Jean took the two girls under their care. All four had a wonderful time, our girls somehow ending up calling Daggett "Dagwood" and Jean "Blondie."

After the conference I had my meeting with Duane Jacobs. He showed me that traffic to Mt. McKinley National Park had increased to a total of 25,000 for the season since the opening of the Richardson Highway—an impressive increase. He urged me to come up to Alaska and look over the operation.

"What about the concessioner who's running it now?" I asked.

"Oh, Lawson?" said Jacobs. "He declared bankruptcy. National Park Concessions, Inc. is operating it now just to keep the place open. But we need a regular concessioner."

"What about all the costs of running it?" I wanted to know.

"The operation is losing about $50,000 a year," Jacobs admitted candidly. "More visitors are coming, but winter costs are a real burden. We're paying National Park Concessions for their services and picking up the tab for the losses. But I think with all the visitors we're getting, a good concessioner can turn it around."

Jacobs thought I could do the job. I agreed to look at it.

When I returned to Tucson, I called Al Donau in Lassen and told him to get ready to go to Alaska with me. He didn't even ask why. When his wife Frankie asked him, he said he didn't know, but I had asked him and that was good enough. We bought tickets on Alaska Airlines and headed for McKinley in early November.

Alaska Airlines in 1957 was not what it is today. Back then they must have rarely seen a passenger. When Al and I boarded their aircraft in Seattle, all the seats had been removed and we sat on strapped-down cargo. Despite these opulent accommodations, we managed to sleep most of the long haul up to Anchorage.

We transferred at Anchorage to the Alaska Railroad, which took us to Mount McKinley Station. Acting Superintendent Sam King met us and said that Superintendent Jacobs had been transferred. King arranged to take us out in the park in a four-wheel-drive vehicle where we were greeted by about six inches of snow. We were intrigued by the abundant wildlife, mostly caribou. Then we came back to the hotel.

In 1936, during Secretary of the Interior Harold L. Ickes' regime, "the old curmudgeon" insisted as part of his government concessions plan that the National Park Service provide hotel facilities in Mt. McKinley National Park. Ickes' 1937 annual report states, "In addition to the hotel structure itself, a complete utility plant must be constructed to provide heat, light, water, and sewage disposal facilities. This hotel, located along the line of the Alaska Railroad, will be operated by that organization, but will furnish much needed accommodations to McKinley Park visitors." The Alaska Railroad, as I've mentioned before, belonged entirely to the Interior Department.

NPS Director Cammerer sent Chief Landscape Architect Tom Vint to Alaska in 1937 with instructions to have a hotel erected and available for the summer season, 1938. Cammerer told Tom not to return until the hotel was finished. There was no time to design a proper structure for Alaskan conditions, so Vint rummaged around and found some old hotel blueprints that looked adequate for overnight accommodations and took them to McKinley Park. The hotel was hurriedly built according to these plans along with a more or less standard powerhouse.

Now, twenty years later, I examined Ickes' brain-child with a critical eye. Having been designed without regard for permafrost conditions, the original foundations later had to be braced with huge timbers to prevent the surrounding arctic soil from heaving the foundations inward. The hotel's plumbing was a complete disaster: it could not be drained properly for off-season shutdown. Thus the entire hotel had to be heated all winter long—with no guests—just to keep the pipes from freezing. Sam King told me that one year they didn't heat it and had to break into the walls to repair the burst pipes. It cost about $50,000 to get the operation going that year.

I thought I had seen enough to understand McKinley's problems and decided to return home. Al and I took the Alaska Railroad back to Anchorage. When we got there, we learned that our plane would be leaving shortly with no other flight to the "Lower 48" for two days. We rushed to the airfield and arrived just before departure time. The ticket girl wasn't at the check-in counter—she doubled as a freight handler—and we went scurrying to find her.

She had just loaded the plane and latched its doors. She refused to sell us tickets. We didn't relish the idea of waiting two days in Anchorage. While I argued with the ticket-seller Al ran out onto the apron and stood in front of the aircraft, waving to the pilot to let us on. The pilot shouted his okay to the ticket girl and we caught the plane back to Seattle. Things were a little informal in those days.

A week later—it was early December now—Al and I kept an appointment with NPS Regional Director Lawrence C. Merriam in San Francisco. We had decided to negotiate a contract for the McKinley concession. Our reception was cordial. We began to deal. I told Merriam that despite its miserable financial record I'd be happy to take over the operation with all facilities in place as is. But I wouldn't pay the cost of heating the hotel during winter for a three-year period, 1957 to 1960.

Merriam looked puzzled. "Why not?" he asked.

I said, "Your heating problem is the source of most of McKinley's losses. I want time to see what can be done."

"I don't know how you can make any improvements," he protested. "We've explored every avenue."

"I want time to make a study," I said. "Maybe I can come up with a solution."

"But you'll pay the cost of operations during the season?"

"Yes."

"And you'll pick up the winter heating bill after the third year?"

"If there's a winter heating bill, yes."

He said, "If Washington approves your application, you're the new concessioner at Mount McKinley National Park."

Washington approved.

And so a new and important stage of my life began. I was a principal in two national park concessions. As I expected, our first problem at McKinley was credit. Our predecessors had just gone through bankruptcy and we found credit hard to establish. Suppliers didn't differentiate between Lawson— the bankrupt—and us.

We could have struggled along with a status-quo operation, but we wanted to erect a new service station and store to serve the increased automobile traffic coming to McKinley. Financing became critical. Years earlier we had obtained financing at Lassen through Standard Oil Company of California. They had advanced money for our service station operation in exchange for agreement to sell their products. We contacted Standard Oil with the same proposal for McKinley and they agreed.

We built a new Standard Oil service station and turned what should have been the grease rack into a grocery store. It was handy for truck and car campers, one-stop for gas and groceries.

Policy Progress

A highly significant milestone in park concession policy came on June 28, 1958, when Congress established the Outdoor Recreation Review Commission by Public Law 85-470:

> *Be it enacted by the Senate and the House of Representatives of the United States of America in Congress assembled,* That in order to preserve, develop, and assure accessibility to all American people of present and future generations such quality and quantity of outdoor recreation resources as will be necessary and desirable for individual enjoyment, and to assure the spiritual, cultural, and physical benefits that such outdoor recreation provides; in order to inventory and evaluate the outdoor recreation resources and opportunities of the Nation, to determine the types and location of such resources and opportunities which will be required by present and future generations; and in order to make comprehensive information and recommendations leading to these goals available to the President, the Congress, and the individual States and Territories, there is hereby authorized and created a bipartisan Outdoor Recreation Resources Review Commission.

Along with that windy overture, the commission received a mandate to:

1. Inventory the nation's outdoor recreation facilities;
2. Determine how they should be made available for use;
3. Examine the question of government ownership of recreation facilities;
4. Examine concessioners' interest in structures built on government lands (possessory interest);
5. Examine government supervision and changes in government policies and their effect on outdoor recreation in the United States.

The commission was composed of prominent citizens such as legendary forestry professor Samuel Trask Dana; Bernard L. Orell, an executive of Weyerhaeuser Company; and Joseph W. Penfold, Conservation Director of the Izaak Walton League. Also enlisted were members of Congress including Senator Henry M. "Scoop" Jackson of Washington and Representative John P. Saylor of Pennsylvania. Commission chairman was Laurance S. Rockefeller, Chairman of New York's Rockefeller Brothers Fund. Francis W. Sargent served as commission executive director and Henry L. Diamond served as Editor of the commission's report. The commission's study was destined to take four years. Its conclusions were to prove invaluable in a future we could not yet envision.

Fixing McKinley

Back to McKinley: During the summer of 1958 I talked for a couple of hours with the power plant operator, learning everything about heating the hotel. I soon found that no one had ever thought about monitoring the structure's circulation system. One part of the hotel would be down to 50 degrees and another up to 80 degrees. The prevailing north wind predictably left the north wing coldest.

I contacted the 3M Company in Minneapolis and had them send me high/low temperature recorders. I put one on each floor in each wing and soon charted the hotel's heat loss pattern. Then it was a simple matter to reroute the hot water pipes through the coldest parts first and thermostatically control temperature levels elsewhere in the building. I reduced the heating bill to one-third what the government had been paying.

The first winter after developing this control system, I wanted to reduce the hotel's shutdown temperature as low as possible to save on winter-long fuel consumption. I tested various temperature levels, lowering the heat in five-degree increments to see how cool I could safely keep the hotel. When I got down to 55 degrees and wanted to try 50, the Park

Service objected. They said that in event of a powerhouse breakdown there would be insufficient time for repairs before the temperature dipped below freezing and burst the pipes. I told them if they were going to participate in the decisions, they'd have to participate in the cost. We finally agreed that each would pay half of the winter heating bill. Since I had already reduced it by two-thirds, the government didn't object.

Our contract included transportation facilities for tours taking visitors into the park to see the majesty of McKinley. The equipment was deplorable, so we had to finance new buses. Regular buses were out of the question: they ran about $65,000 to $75,000 each, and we needed three. We solved the problem by having the Bluebird Bus Company of Phoenix, Arizona—a well-known school bus manufacturer—build us three bus bodies on Chevrolet chassis. Each bus held twenty-two passengers and served our purposes very well.

Our standard sightseeing trip went some 65 miles into the park to the Point Eilsen visitor center. Park tours originated in Anchorage at 8:00 a.m. on the Alaska Railroad and arrived at the McKinley Park Hotel at noon. We welcomed the visitors to their overnight rooms, fed them dinner and got them up at 3:30 a.m. for a full Alaskan breakfast of sourdough pancakes, bacon, eggs and coffee. We hustled them into our buses by 4:30 a.m. You have to get an early start if you want to see any wildlife in Alaska, and there's plenty to see: moose, caribou, golden eagles, willow ptarmigans, Dall sheep, grizzlies, red foxes—the list goes on and on. Then, too, the clouds start generating around Mount Denali (McKinley) early in the day and the late starter sees only overcast. Our tour returned to the hotel in time to catch the noon train to Fairbanks.

This sounds like a terrible schedule, and to some people it was, but the 24-hour summer daylight in Alaska made it seem less objectionable. What made me uncomfortable was the narrow roads our young drivers had to negotiate in the parks, particularly Polychrome Pass, where a mishap could take a bus a thousand feet into the riverbed. We never in fifteen years had a serious accident, although one driver went to sleep and ran off the road (on level ground, fortunately), turning the bus on its side and injuring a few people, none seriously.

Al and I rotated inspection trips to Alaska, each of us making two or three visits during the summer. It really wasn't ideal for proper management. You shouldn't run an operation like McKinley from two thousand miles away. But we hired the best on-site managers we could find, occasionally sending experienced Lassen personnel we could trust on temporary assignment. One hired manager gave us some problems and we sent our Lassen maintenance man and ski-tow operator Ken Tibbet to fill in until we could replace our key man. This turned out to be a mistake: Ken never really wanted to go back to work after getting a taste of management. After McKinley he thought he should only supervise and never do any physical work himself.

Whatever its problems, a good life it was, winters politicking in Tucson, summers hosting at Drakesbad, and intermittent inspection tours at McKinley. But Drakesbad was my favorite. The hot and cold running mountain streams still linger in my memory after all these years. The taste of that pure cold stream water has no match anywhere. We needed no ice for water on the Drakesbad dining room tables. Roy Sifford put in a spring-fed running fountain on the porch of the Lodge where you could get a cold drink any time you felt like it. It ran constantly from the day we opened until the day we closed—that is, until the Park Service took it out because it was not chlorinated! Perhaps the Park Service means well, but sometimes they exhibit little common sense.

After several years we built two duplexes in the meadow at Drakesbad. The units were designed so the whole front would open up and you could roll the beds out on the porch to sleep under the stars if you wanted. Those were perfect days. Guests were our good friends. The children loved it. Unspoiled beauty. Happy times. Peaceful nights. Idyllic. I still think of Drakesbad when I need to cheer up.

But it was only the calm before the storm.

11

Glacier National Park

THE 1950s may have passed without major national park concession crises, but the material conditions were building toward real trouble. The central problem brewing was how to cope with increased visitor traffic. The Park Service of the mid-fifties was well-equipped to handle the 21 million visitors of 1940, but not the 55 million that actually showed up. Priority demands of World War II, the Korean War and the continuing cold war kept Park Service budgets thin.

Concessioners expanded and improved their visitor accommodations as fast as investment capital could be obtained—and memories of the hostile policies of Ickes and Krug did not encourage bankers to approve investment loans with any speed. Chapman too did little to inspire financer confidence. So a great many facilities in the parks, both concessioner and Park Service, grew progressively more run down and outdated.

All this was dramatically brought home to concessioners when we read an August 1954 news report that 6,000 of some 16,435 tourists who entered Yellowstone one day either had to sleep in their cars or drive back out. We sat up and paid real attention when a writer named Anthony Netboy slapped concessioners hard in an article for *American Forests* of May, 1955, asserting that some concessioners made up to 10 percent or more on their investment while providing poor and inadequate service. He lashed Yellowstone and Yosemite with special venom.

Hil Oehlmann, chairman that year of the Western Conference of National Park Concessioners, wrote his response in the July issue of the magazine: Concessioners, he said, were not to blame for the ills of the parks. Concessions, he went on, are not generally very profitable, in some parks earnings are quite dismal, and several concessions were for sale. Hil charged much of the responsibility to Ickes' threat of government ownership and the restrictive policies of Ickes and Krug, which did not create the confidence essential to long-run expansion. He also pointed out that many facilities had been considerably improved. The Park Service backed him up on the profitability question, writing that in 1953 the average rate of return was 6.87 percent, not excessive considering the hazards of the business.

Netboy's article added image problems to the actual financial difficulties some concessioners were experiencing. Inflation and rising costs of labor and supplies strained some concessions to the breaking point. In 1954 the Santa Fe Railway Company got out of its business at the South Rim of Grand Canyon, donating its power plants, boilers, water system and pumps at Indian Gardens to the government. The Santa Fe sold its El Tovar Hotel, Bright Angel Lodge, Hopi House and the Auto Lodge to the Fred Harvey Company, which remained the operator, as it always had been.

Other concessioners, however, were investing new millions in the parks. In the early 1950s new concessioners opened up Coulee Dam National Recreation Area, Big Bend National Park, Channel Islands, Katmai, and Black Canyon of the Gunnison National Monuments. Jackson Hole Preserve, Inc., a Rockefeller nonprofit group, built the Jackson Lake Lodge at an expense of $6.5 million in 1955. Private concessioners built a total of $37 million worth of improvements in 1955 and $50 million in 1956.

The Mission Called 66

Conrad L. Wirth, who had become Director of the National Park Service in late 1951, decided the root of our park problems lay in faulty Congressional appropriation patterns.

Improvement obviously could not come in the piecemeal year-by-year appropriations of the past. At home one February Saturday evening in 1955, Wirth decided a package approach was essential, "a plan that would anticipate our requirements and put areas into the kind of shape the people of the United States have a right to expect." That shape included modern roads, visitor centers, added personnel, better living quarters for rangers, more public buildings, utility systems, government campgrounds, and many, many new parks.

The next Monday Wirth put together a task-force aimed at producing a model park system by the Park Service's golden anniversary year in 1966. In January 1956 their study was done. Basing projections on 80 million estimated visitors to the parks by 1966, the Park Service figured it would cost $786 million to rehabilitate and "round out" the system. They called the project "Mission 66." They presented the plan during a Cabinet meeting to President Eisenhower.

The section dealing with concessions stated Connie Wirth's Park Service policy:

> Concession facilities shall be developed in the parks only when they are necessary for appropriate enjoyment of the areas by the visiting public. Where public accommodations are available or can be developed in adequate quantity in the immediate vicinity of a park, this will normally preclude the need of providing them within the park.

Although Wirth was talking primarily about small Eastern park units such as historical areas, unscrupulous environmentalists later quoted this statement out of context as part of their purist efforts: Take all concessions out of the parks entirely. Thus the Park Service's 1933 reorganization to include historic sites and the mid-'30s addition of recreational sites now began to work against concessions. By 1956 there were more historic and recreation sites than natural areas. The Mission 66 report de-emphasized concessions by such statements as:

Not all areas administered by the Service have concession operations; in most of the areas they are not needed. Of those that do, most have relatively small operations involving usually only the sale of refreshments and souvenirs [primarily the historic and recreational sites added in the 1930s]. It is in the large, scenic parks of the West, distant from communities which might provide lodging and dining services, that concessions are so important as to be a necessity for the park visitor.

As seen by the 1956 Park Service, concession operations had been launched originally "to offer food, lodging, and transportation," and had been "extended to include a number of other services dictated by present-day travel habits and requirements." This comment indicates how uncomfortable the Park Service was becoming over automobile travel: Obviously concessions could become much more important in a highly mobile society if not held back by policy.

The Mission 66 crew also put serious pressure on concessioners by telling President Eisenhower that although the cost value of concessioners' fixed assets had risen 23 percent since World War II to $37 million, they had produced only sixteen percent more lodging. Overnight capacity would have to be increased by about 16,600 people by 1966 in order to keep up with projections. To Director Wirth's credit, he also noted, "Concessioners find it difficult to obtain capital from private lenders because accommodations are on Government lands. To extend the authority of the Small Business Administration to guarantee loans to concessioners in the parks will go far in solving this problem."

When the Park Service presentation was finished and Interior Secretary Douglas McKay asked if there were any questions, Wirth held his breath. Eisenhower said only, "Why wasn't this request made back in 1953 when I came into office?" They had administration backing for Mission 66.

A billion dollars later, Mission 66 not only had done a magnificent job of refurbishing our rundown parks, but also quite unexpectedly wrought infinite mischief that later generations will have to undo. Mission 66 for the first time condemned private property—eradicating whole communities—to *create* new national parks. The horrors left in the wake of this well-meaning Frankenstein monster are detailed in Charles S. Cushman's forthcoming book, *Parks Against People*, which Mr. Cushman was kind enough to show me in manuscript.

One other notable concession policy changed during the 1950s: on May 29, 1958, Congress passed an Act increasing the limitation on National Park concession contracts from 20 to 30 years. Congress felt that the longer term would materially assist the concessioner in obtaining loans from sources which generally only make loans for longer periods of time than commercial banks (insurance companies, for example).

Glacier Calls

Early in 1960 I got a telephone call from James Kenady, in charge of property for the Great Northern Railway Company. He said he had heard that I might be interested in taking over their operation in Glacier National Park and the adjacent Prince of Wales Hotel in Waterton Lakes National Park, Canada. I told him yes and asked for information.

What came back was trivial. I made no response. Then Kenady called again, asking if I was really interested. They had terminated their Park Service contract, he said, and were anxious to dispose of the property. I told him I was interested, but he'd have to provide better information if he wanted a serious response. Kenady agreed to send five years of financial reports. When they arrived I saw why they hadn't sent them earlier. Glacier hadn't shown a profit during any of the previous five years.

In 1959 Glacier National Park Company (Great Northern's park concession subsidiary) lost $578,175 on a gross income of $1,467,897, in 1958 lost $588,034 on $1,189,435 gross, in 1957 lost $431,344 on $1,116,739, in 1956 lost $319,246 on $1,018,937, in 1955 lost $128,093 on $914,534. The Great Northern had been unhappy about this situation for many years. In 1958 they had retained the Knutsen Construction Company to put the facilities in physical and financial shape to sell. Knutson was authorized to manage the facilities during this period of renovation. The records showed that the more money they took in the more they lost. I learned later that Glacier had lost money consistently for twenty years.

The financial reports cooled my interest considerably, but my brother Gail happened to be on his way to Montana to look at an operation at Swan Lake, so I asked him to go on to Glacier National Park and look it over. He reported back that I should check into it thoroughly. There were tremendous numbers of facilities in the park and he thought the opportunity excellent.

Within days Jim Kenady called again warning me that they were telling their employees Great Northern would not operate its park facilities the following year. He knew I'd want to retain most of Great Northern's employees, and this was his way of spurring me into action. In early September I interrupted my duties as Mayor of Tucson long enough to meet Kenady in Great Falls and drive to Glacier National Park.

The Northern Rockies

Even pictures of Glacier don't prepare you for the reality. Everywhere you see evidence of ice without seeing the ice. About fifty small glaciers remain in the park today, but their predecessors that carved these immense gouges in the earth must have been vast beyond belief. As National Geographic's book *America's Wonderlands* so vividly states, "A million or so years ago only the highest of these peaks rose above great over-burdening glaciers that were grinding out the broad, bathtub-shaped valleys of western Montana's Glacier National Park. The total weight of ice may have amounted to more than that of the mountains themselves."

Glacier's million acres extend from the Canadian border sixty miles southward down the Continental Divide. The huge mountain masses of the Glacier Rockies stretch across the international boundary to form Canada's Waterton Lakes

Park. Together the two preserves form Waterton-Glacier International Peace Park. Although rugged mountain peaks, beautiful streams and lakes, and remnant glaciers form the park's principal attraction, wildlife and wild flowers add greatly to its appeal. Bordering the park on the east is the enormous Blackfeet Indian Reservation. Two National Forests adjoin Glacier, the Flathead on the west and south, and the Lewis and Clark on the southeast.

Only one highway traverses Glacier, the fifty twisty miles of switchbacks called Going-to-the-Sun Road over 6,646-foot Logan Pass. It begins on the park's eastern edge at St. Mary, skirts St. Mary Lake, climbs over the high pass, then descends to McDonald Valley. Northward, beyond Gunsight Pass, Triple Divide Pass sheds its waters into three oceans, the Atlantic, Pacific and Arctic.

Glacier is a classical "railroad park:" it was conceived by railroad people, it was lobbied into law by railroad people and it was developed by railroad people. Which is not to belittle the role of the independent settlers who homesteaded the McDonald Valley in the years prior to 1890—but there were few sightseers and virtually no shelter for them until the Great Northern Railway Company built its tracks into Montana's Flathead Valley in 1891.

Great Northern president Louis W. Hill was instrumental in the lobbying effort that led Congress to establish Glacier National Park in 1910. Hill's motives were primarily economic: His father, GN's legendary founder James J. Hill, had always told him, "The value of a railway is its capacity to earn money." The elder Hill stands alone in America's railroading aristocracy as the man who relied entirely on private capital and earned revenues rather than government land grants, subsidies, or loan guarantees to build his empire. Glacier National Park provided a logical, convenient, and attractive stopping point for passengers on a transcontinental rail tour. Glacier National Park to Louis Hill was a way to increase the number of fares riding the Great Northern, and a competitive edge against the Canadian Pacific line to the north and the

Northern Pacific line to the south (which saw Yellowstone as a passenger attraction).

I have a feeling there was more to Glacier than money for Hill, because the year after it had been declared a national park he announced his semi-retirement as president of the railroad to devote full attention to turning Glacier into "The Playground of the Northwest." He told a Montana newspaper, "The work is so important that I am loath to entrust the development to anybody but myself." That was the same year Hill told the National Park Conference he didn't want to go into the hotel business. He spent the next six years building some of the finest and most elaborate concession buildings in all the national parks. Strange behavior for someone who didn't want to go into the hotel business.

The Great Northern built Glacier Park Hotel at Midvale (now East Glacier), and began a series of permanent Swiss chalets at Two Medicine Lake, Cut Bank Creek, St. Mary Lake (at the lake's east end and at the Upper Narrows), Gunsight Lake and McDermott Lake (now Swiftcurrent), all in 1912. Their major building projects lasted into 1927 when the Canadian Prince of Wales Hotel was completed. The Interior Department did little to hinder the Great Northern, regarding the railroad as a concessioner with the multiple virtues of capital, ambition and enthusiasm for national park values. When President Taft vetoed the Sundry Civil bill in 1913, which included all national park appropriations, the impoverished Interior Department virtually deregulated the wealthy Great Northern and encouraged their every project. As Interior Secretary Clement Uker said to the regional newspaper *Daily Inter Lake* on March 14 that year, "The way I see it is that the Great Northern had gone in here and erected these chalets and it is up to us to accommodate travel to them. All I want to do is move as expeditiously, harmoniously and as rapidly as possible."

Relations didn't remain so chummy. When Steve Mather joined the national parks in 1915, Louis Hill's Glacier Park Hotel Company was building Many Glacier Hotel at Swiftcurrent Lake and the Interior Department had allowed them to build a sawmill nearby in the park to supply necessary timber. Ten years later the supposedly temporary sawmill still stood, an eyesore to Steve Mather, a pet project to Louis Hill. On August 10, 1925, Mather was in Glacier for his daughter's nineteenth birthday outing. He had ordered the mill removed by that very day, but when Mather stepped out of the hotel, there it stood untouched. Mather ordered Glacier's trail construction crew to take a load of dynamite and plant it in the mill. He gathered a group of visitors on the veranda of Many Glacier and announced a fireworks display. He personally lighted the fuse and set off thirteen charges of TNT. That was the end of the sawmill. When a visitor asked what occasion he was celebrating, Mather replied, "My daughter's birthday!"

But now, after fifty years of concessioning at Glacier, Great Northern wanted out. And I was the heir apparent to its four major hotels with a combined room count of 571, three motel units, the Glacier Park Transport Company (a charter and in-park bus service), and a launch service on Waterton Lake. I looked over all the facilities except the Prince of Wales Hotel in one day. At East Glacier, outside park boundaries and surrounded by the Blackfeet Reservation, lay Glacier Park Lodge, the beautiful 178-room hotel built in 1912 and opened in 1913. This 630-acre site served as the center of Glacier operations, including the warehouse, garage, maintenance center, laundry and powerhouse, general offices and the reservation system.

On the shores of Swiftcurrent Lake stood the renowned Many Glacier Hotel, a four story structure in Swiss architectural style, comprising 220 rooms with auxiliary buildings for employee dormitories. Across the lake a mile and a half lay Swiftcurrent Motor Lodge, consisting of a general store, coffee shop and a combination of modern units and older ones in generally run-down condition, for a total of nearly 100 rooms.

On Going-To-The-Sun Highway we visited Rising Sun Lodge, which included a store, coffee shop, two motel units and a number of cottages along with employee dormitories. These were in better condition than Swiftcurrent, but lacked showers in the cabins.

Two Medicine, one of the 1912 chalets, had deteriorated during World War II to such an extent that the overnight facilities were abandoned and demolished, leaving only the lodge dining room, which had been converted into a camp store to serve the adjacent government-owned campground. The huge old fireplace once used by President Franklin D. Roosevelt as a setting for a fireside chat still remained.

On the west side of the park we stopped at Lake McDonald Lodge, a beautiful rustic facility owned by the government but operated by the concessioner, with a dining room, 33 sleeping rooms plus 14 cottages, most with four rooms but only one bathroom. Wood stoves provided room heat, and a central coal-fired system provided hot water. The night watchman tended the coal fire as a miscellaneous duty on his rounds, often resulting in either steam or icy cold at the hot water spigot. Lake McDonald also provided a soda fountain and counter service in a Louis Hill-vintage theater-like building mostly used for lectures, interpretive programs and employee gatherings. Three small dormitories and an old writer's home called Cobb Cottage rounded out the facility.

At the lower end of Lake McDonald lay the Village Inn Motel, a new unit which had been built by a private landowner and subsequently sold to the National Park Service.

At each location Kenady gathered the staff to introduce me as the prospective purchaser. I assured everyone that we needed an experienced crew and wanted them to stay on. I couldn't take the time to visit the Prince of Wales Hotel in Waterton Lake, Alberta, Canada—operated as part of the Glacier concession through international agreement—but looked over its plans. It was an elegant place in a stunning location, with 84 usable rooms, three dormitories and a year-around home for the caretaker, plus a powerhouse and water system. I was impressed with all of Glacier and decided to buy the concession.

A few days later Kenady came to Tucson where Gail and I negotiated the purchase. Great Northern had put a cash price of $1,300,000 on Glacier but wanted considerably more for installment purchase. We haggled a while and ended with an offer of $1,300,000; $250,000 down and the balance over 10 years. Kenady soon replied from Great Northern's St. Paul headquarters that our terms had been accepted. Now to the little detail of raising a quarter-million dollars.

My old law-school friend Don Ford agreed to help Gail and me find the money. He first tried the Mercedes Benz dealership in Hollywood, California. They were willing but wanted control of the operation. No deal, I told Don. A group that had just sold a motel in Nogales, Arizona, had $150,000 in cash and told Gail they'd come into the company, but demanded management control. No deal, I told Gail.

One day as I sat at my Mayor's desk a call came in informing me that Dudley Tower, president of Union Oil Company, happened to be in town for a Pima Mines Board of Directors meeting and wanted to talk with me. Union Oil, I knew, operated a refinery outside Cut Bank, Montana. Tower probably knew about my offer to Great Northern, I thought, and wanted to sell Union Oil products in the park. I was busy and Tower was tied up in a board meeting, so we arranged to meet at a motel lounge on Miracle Mile late that afternoon.

Several Union Oil representatives showed up. They had neglected sales in Montana, they said, and were interested in selling Union Oil products in Glacier National Park, just as I had expected. I told them I'd be pleased to arrange it. Everyone seemed happy. Shortly before the meeting broke up, Tower said to me, "Is there anything I can do for you?"

I said, "Yes, I need $250,000."

"Oh? Tell me more."

I explained the situation. Tower seemed receptive. I offered Union Oil preferred stock representing their $250,000 and a 25 percent equity interest in the company.

Without hesitation, Dudley Tower said, "We'll do it."

We shook hands to seal the deal. That's how I got the down

payment for the Glacier operation. I immediately contacted Jim Kenady and told him we were ready to sign the contract. T. J. "Terry" Slattery, Great Northern's assistant chief counsel, drew up the contract with me to be assigned to a firm I incorporated called Glacier Park, Inc. I gave Gail and Don Ford each a seven percent interest in the corporation for their efforts.

With my responsibilities as Mayor of Tucson and President of the National League of Cities, there was no way I could serve as general manager of the Glacier operation for the 1961 season. I had to find someone. Through the concessioner grapevine I learned that an experienced manager named George Golsworthy was available. He had occupied executive positions at Yosemite Park & Curry Company for almost 30 years and was presently handling hotel operations for the Winter Olympics in Squaw Valley. I contacted Yosemite Park & Curry Company's Hil Oehlmann and asked about George. He gave my candidate generally high marks, but failed to mention that George had a drinking problem.

We took possession of the Glacier premises at the end of December, 1960, which meant we'd be saddled with winter expenses and no income. One bright spot in this gloom appeared during our final negotiations with Great Northern. We learned that Glacier Park Transport Company, operated as a separate corporation, had $100,000 cash in its account. I asked Great Northern to leave this cash as part of the assets and add $100,000 to our purchase price, making it $1,400,000. Instead of taking the $100,000 out and paying dividends on it, GN could transfer it as a capital gain and I'd have an operating margin. We'd both be better off. They accepted my proposal.

Concessioning at Glacier

Now here I was at another significant milestone in my career, with interests in three national park concessions. Yet I had scant reason to celebrate. The first year operating Glacier became one of those "times that try men's souls." I couldn't stay in the park during the summer of 1961 but flew up every other weekend. I first installed the family along with Genee's mother Ruth Mitchell in a cabin at Lake McDonald for the season. The weather was perfect and the family enjoyed a wonderful time swimming and sunning themselves on the lake front.

But the operation was impossible. Lack of organization, failure to control costs, and overstaffing plagued the business. Had I been free to stay, I would have discharged many employees, but without a constant presence I knew I'd lose the good employees with the bad. I bit my tongue and said nothing—yet.

I tried to exercise tight financial control, routing all expenditures to me for approval. One cost-cutting opportunity stemmed from an exorbitant gift shop inventory—built up, as I discovered, by Don Knutson in expectation of taking over the operation. Payments to Great Northern on this inventory, which wasn't included in the purchase price, ran $52,000 per month for the four summer months. I immediately put the whole inventory on sale and used the proceeds to pay off the obligation. Our guests got rare bargains and I paid off an onerous debt.

Employee theft at Glacier had run rampant before I took over. Construction workers proved the worst culprits. Hired by Don Knutsen Company to refurbish the concession in preparation for its sale, they had loaded their cars with building materials at the end of each week and took them home. Glacier chief engineer Cy Stevenson protested to Great Northern officials in St. Paul, but to no avail.

The tight control that I instituted soon paid off. At the close of the 1961 season we had accumulated $200,000 in cash—not profit—on a total season income of $1,400,000. But I had an unexpected problem: Union Oil was not happy with our deal. Dudley Tower had evidently been replaced, and the new president saw the Glacier deal differently. Union Oil didn't mind selling their products in the park, but didn't like all that capital frozen in the concession. I called Don Ford and had him contact Union Oil's legal department, offering to return their $250,000 if they would release their preferred stock and their interest in the company. They said yes.

I needed more money to buy back Union Oil's interest and still have some funds to meet our expenses over the no-income winter. I went to the First National Bank in Great Falls and asked to borrow $100,000. They needed some security for the money, so I asked Great Northern if they would allow me to mortgage some facilities outside the park, primarily those around Glacier Park Lodge. GN said they would not co-sign the note, but agreed to let me take out the mortgage. As a result First National Bank of Great Falls extended me $100,000 in credit, but insisted that I purchase a life insurance policy to pay off my debt if I died.

Now I had an additional 25 percent interest in Glacier Park, Inc., of which I apportioned 10 percent to Don Ford and 10 percent to my brother Gail, and added five percent to my personal interests.

1962 was the first year I could spend full time at Glacier to direct its operations. My term as Mayor of Tucson ended on December 4, 1961, and with it a number of related obligations. I had been appointed by President Eisenhower as one of four mayors in the United States to serve on the Advisory Commission on Intergovernmental Relations, a 26-member commission of federal, state and local officials, and citizens at large, formed by Act of Congress in 1959. Although my mayoral membership expired with my term in office, President John F. Kennedy reappointed me to the Commission on February 22, 1962, as Public Member and Vice Chairman.

1962 was also the year of the Century Twenty-One World's Fair in Seattle, Washington, which materially increased travel to and through Glacier. Things looked rosy. That is, until June when I had to fly to Washington, D.C., to attend an Advisory Commission meeting. After a full day's work, a 140-mile drive to Great Falls for my flight to Washington, I checked into my hotel room at midnight, hit the hay and drifted off immediately into a sound sleep. At 1:30 a.m. the telephone rang. I had difficulty locating it. When I finally answered, a voice on the other end of the line said, "Hummel?"

I muttered, "Yes."

The voice said, "You're out of business. They just blew up the power plant."

It was my chief engineer Cy Stevenson, informing me in his best diplomatic manner that there had been an explosion at East Glacier's power plant. Cy was right: Without that boiler we were out of business. It provided all hot water for the bathrooms and kitchens and all the space heat for the entire hotel, as well as water for the central laundry. I decided I didn't really want to attend that Washington meeting anyway.

I immediately checked out and started back to Glacier, racking my brain for some solution. We had a full house at East Glacier. We *had* to get hot water somehow. Perhaps we could ask the Great Northern Railway Company to put a steam engine on a siding and hook into our boiler system.

When I arrived at East Glacier, Cy Stevenson and his assistant Howard Olson had already come up with a makeshift. They labored at re-routing the dormitory steam system to the Lodge's kitchen. I went to see the boiler room. It was a total disaster. The roof poked up some three feet higher than it should and all the sides bulged out except the one in front of the boiler. The boiler engineer must have led a charmed life, because that was exactly where he had been standing when the boiler blew.

The operator on duty was a professor with every type of boiler certificate you could get but not much common sense. An electrical storm had cut off the boiler ignition flame and its warning klaxon had summoned the operator. Our professor, instead of shutting off the fuel and starting the exhaust fans as he should have, decided to restart the system quickly. He put a torch down into the fuel-laden fire chamber. This promptly blew up the entire system.

"What can we do?" I asked Cy.

"Well," he said, "the railroad still has a crew that repairs boilers. They kept them over from the old steam engine days."

I immediately got on the telephone to Great Northern president John Budd, who assured me that a crew would be on the train for East Glacier within a couple of hours. When they arrived we put them on 24-hour work status with instructions to spare no expense to get our power plant back in operation.

Meanwhile, Cy had finished connecting the dormitory boilers to provide a minimum of hot water to the Lodge kitchens so we could prepare food. Our guests would not go hungry. But then came the real problem: linens. All linen service for the whole Glacier system was handled at the East Glacier laundry. I started telephoning every laundry company in the region to see if I could get temporary linen service.

A laundry service in Kalispell looked upon my misfortune as a golden opportunity. The proprietor immediately called his fellow laundry entrepreneurs adjacent to Glacier and told them to stick together and hold out for an exorbitant price. They approached me with a completely unreasonable proposal and I told them no dice. I would not be held up.

I finally made a deal with Quality Cleaners forty-five miles away in Cut Bank. Quality agreed to rent their entire plant to us from nightfall to morning if I handled the operations and provided my own crew. We had a van take our crew down to Cut Bank each evening with dirty laundry and bring them back in the morning with clean laundry. And that took care of our linen supply problem.

Cy Stevenson found that some of the local oil fields had small steam-operated power plants. We rented one from a drilling company and installed it outside the boiler room, which allowed us to reestablish limited services to the Lodge. We were in business again.

Seven days into the repair job, Great Northern's crew had the boiler room in full service. Everything was back to normal. I don't know what we would have done without the cooperation and support of Great Northern. They had no legal obligation, yet went completely overboard helping me. I think all their years working as the concessioner in Glacier National Park gave them complete sympathy with my problems.

12

The Dawn of Environmentalism

THE DECADE OF the sixties was to bring a new cultural reality to America: environmentalism. That fact could scarcely have been predicted in the early years. No prognosticator looking at a 1960 newspaper could have detected the faintest hint of the mass movement that would grab everyday headlines in 1970. Few premonitions of the drastic policy changes ahead revealed themselves to our sociological oracles in the last days of the Eisenhower administration.

One clue could be found in the Multiple Use - Sustained Yield Act of 1960, which for the first time explicitly disconnected the dollar value of natural resources from management calculations and how they should be allocated. Disregard for economics was to become a hallmark of the environmental movement by the end of the decade.

Wilderness Mystique

Another clue could be found in the passage of a Wilderness bill in the Senate in 1961, which failed to pass the House. Concern for wilderness protection could also have been found in the previous year's anti-economic Multiple Use - Sustained Yield Act, which said that "the establishment and maintenance of areas of wilderness are consistent with the purposes and provisions" of the act. The significance of the controversy over wilderness is difficult for many Americans to comprehend. The ordinary commonsense word "wilderness" conveys pleasant meanings related to any remote or scenic spot. Officially designated Wilderness, like most things official, does not resemble its commonsense counterpart. Official Wilderness Area designation—which I will hereafter indicate with a Capital "W"—virtually eliminates public use to all but hikers. No structures, no resource extraction, no roads, and no motorized traffic of any kind is allowed in official Wilderness. You cannot take a scenic drive with your children into a Wilderness Area, but most Americans are totally unaware of this fact. There is a distinctly anti-people overtone to the official designation of Wilderness, contrary to commonsense notions of wilderness. The campaign to create a National Wilderness System was an early signal that the age of environmentalism was dawning.

When the "Soaring Sixties" arrived, the Senate had already held half a dozen hearings on wilderness legislation. On June 7, 1956, the Wilderness Society's redoubtable executive director Howard Zahniser—regarded as the father of the Wilderness Act—saw his draft legislation introduced as S. 4013. And that was by no means the beginning of it. Zahniser appeared before Congress after a long evangelical crusade inspired by the man who thought up the wilderness idea in the first place, Aldo Leopold.

Leopold was a young forest supervisor on the Carson National Forest in New Mexico when he first articulated the idea of setting aside official wilderness areas in 1913. As Dennis Roth noted in the *Journal of Forest History* of July 1984, even though Leopold loved to hunt and ride and dress the part of a rugged ranger, he was in fact an eastern-trained intellectual who thought deeply about nature preservation. Leopold could see development coming and, as Roth wrote, "At the end of World War I, Leopold had become apprehensive about the expansion of Forest Service road systems into the backcountry. Wilderness, he felt, was the forge upon which the American national character had been created, and loss of wilderness regions deprived the country of a source of renewing this heritage." There was only one hitch to this lofty sentiment in the hands of an intellectual: he forgot that the American national character was forged by masses of economic developers, farmers and ranchers who *conquered* wilderness, not intellectual bureaucrats who *protected* nature museums for the loftily sentimental. And a nature museum for the loftily sentimental is essentially what Leopold conceived official Wilderness to be.

A key factor in the progress of the wilderness movement was the science of ecology, which inspired Leopold. Ecology had been coined as a term by the German biologist Ernst Haeckel in 1864 as "the study of the relationships between organisms and their environments." Members of the Ecological Society of America looked upon wilderness as an ideal laboratory for the study of natural processes and had in 1920 recommended the setting aside of untouched areas. In 1921, Aldo Leopold wrote an article in the *Journal of Forestry* recommending withdrawal of a wilderness of at least half a million acres in each of the eleven states west of the Great Plains—an ambitious idea in 1921, but a small fraction of the 80 million acres of official Wilderness locked away in America today.

Leopold found the opportunity to make his wilderness idea a reality after he became assistant district forester in Albuquerque in 1922: District Forester Frank Pooler on June 3, 1924, approved Leopold's plan to place the 500,000-acre Gila headwaters area under a ten-year wilderness recreation policy. Grazing and water power development were not to be impeded, but roads were to be limited and private inholdings were to be acquired through land exchanges. The Gila became the world's first official Wilderness Area.

In 1933 another key player in the wilderness campaign gained recognition: Robert Marshall (not Steve Mather's Robert Marshall), son of a wealthy New York attorney and Ph.D. plant physiologist. As a boy Marshall dreamed of exploring every wilderness like his heroes Lewis and Clark, and later espoused the cause of official Wilderness designations. Marshall wrote the recreation section of *A National Plan for American Forestry* (the 1933 Copeland Report), which gained broad public exposure for his Wilderness ideas. Marshall founded the Wilderness Society in 1935, but his premature death in 1939 cut short the mass activist campaign he had planned for the forties. Aldo Leopold, however, continued the efforts.

In 1945 Howard Zahniser joined the Wilderness Society as executive secretary (later executive director) and editor of its publication *Living Wilderness*. When Aldo Leopold died in 1949, Zahniser took on the mantle of the nation's foremost wilderness advocate. Zahniser, born in 1906, had worked for the U.S. Biological Service in 1930 and subsequently held several other federal government jobs.

Zahniser openly used the museum metaphor to describe wilderness areas, but he regarded them more as art museums containing national treasures—even people not destined to see them firsthand could appreciate them. A Berkeley forestry professor, Frederick S. Baker, in 1947 wrote to Zahniser that wilderness enthusiasts were only interested in self-gratification and escape. Zahniser's reply repeated Olmsted's 1864 "morally uplifting" thesis:

> Love of solitude, eagerness for adventure, and indulgence in romantic experiences are, as you point out, the most common motives for "fleeing to the wilderness" for recreation. Once there, however, many I believe, experience a better understanding of themselves in relation to the whole community of life on earth and rather earnestly compare their civilized living with natural realities—to the improvement of their civilization.

This moralistic view of wilderness may have been accentuated by the implications of interconnectedness of living in a nuclear age, as Stephen Fox suggested in *John Muir and his Legacy: The American Conservation Movement*. This idea of *interconnectedness* from the science of ecology was to find great public appeal in the Wilderness campaign in the 1960s.

Zahniser in 1949 persuaded Congressman Raymond H. Burke, chairman of the House Subcommittee on Merchant Marine and Fisheries, to commission the Library of Congress to complete a study of America's wilderness needs. The study consisted of questionnaires to federal and state agencies. The Forest Service recommended further study and the National Park Service recommended that more wilderness land be transferred to its jurisdiction. But the results gave Zahniser a good feel for the lobbying strategy he would need for a full-fledged Wilderness campaign.

By the early 1950s Zahniser had developed his plan for massive federal wilderness designation through a Wilderness Act and presented it to various conservation groups. Reaction was mixed. But by coincidence, the general public became aroused about wilderness issues through the efforts of the Bureau of Reclamation and Army Corps of Engineers to put dams in several western national park units, Echo Park Dam on the Green River affecting Dinosaur National Monument being the most notable. David R. Brower, executive director of the Sierra Club, helped Zahniser pull off a masterful publicity campaign to marshall the country's growing wilderness constituency. Hard-hitting pamphlets for mass distribution asked: "*Will you DAM the Scenic Wild Canyons of Our National Park System?*" and "*What is Your Stake in Dinosaur?*" A professional color motion picture was produced and widely shown throughout the nation. Novelist and historian Wallace Stegner edited a book of essays and photographs extolling the virtues of wilderness in Dinosaur. Of course, all this required immense amounts of money, which Zahniser obtained from the wealthy St. Louis chemical manufacturer Edward C. Mallinkrodt, Jr. By this time, the pattern of turning to such "leisure class" devotees for environmental funding had become routine. The money and notoriety stopped Echo Park Dam dead in its tracks.

In May 1955 Zahniser saw his chance: Following the classic pattern for developing support for a bill, he gave a speech to the American Planning and Civic Association in Washington, D.C., repeating his philosophical arguments and his specific legislative proposals. Senator Hubert H. Humphrey of Minnesota, who had vigorously opposed dams in the national parks, was much impressed and inserted the speech in the *Congressional Record*. Then—the long awaited turning-point—Humphrey asked Zahniser to develop a bill.

The draft bill was ready by the end of February, 1956 and copies were informally given to the Park Service and the Forest Service. Conrad Wirth, Director of the Park Service, replied that such a bill was not necessary and might even endanger national park wilderness areas by lumping them together with those of other agencies. The Forest Service feared that other special interests would seek similar guarantees for their uses of the national forests—National Stock Grazing Areas, National Timber Harvest Areas, National Mining Areas, National Petroleum Drilling Areas, National Hunting Areas, National Rockhound Areas, and on and on.

But on June 6, Senator Humphrey introduced Zahniser's draft as a study bill and then in February 1957, reintroduced it as S. 1176 for full process. Now the legislative battle began in earnest.

National Park wilderness had always been withdrawn from commercial development, which made any proposed Wilderness Act appear redundant to the Park Service. The Zahniser faction found itself having to chip away at Interior Department opposition for three years until 1960, when Director Wirth finally accepted the idea of statutory protection for Park Service wilderness areas.

Orville L. Freeman, who became President Kennedy's Secretary of Agriculture in 1961, had taken note of the growing support for wilderness among the traditional conservation constituencies, and began large scale redesignation of Forest Service "primitive areas" as official Wilderness Areas, which raised profound concerns among all natural resource producers. A Wilderness Act would give statutory power to such administrative elimination of grazing, logging, mining, settlement, farming, watershed improvement, recreation roads—a serious threat to the millions of people whose futures were tied to those ways of life. Zahniser's wilderness lobbying campaign with its distaste for and disregard of material development marks a significant turning point in the transformation of the traditional conservation movement into the modern ideological environmental movement.

Career Developments

Most concessioners and National Park Service personnel were unaware of these wilderness developments in the early 1960s and the shift of traditional conservation into environmentalism. We simply hadn't done our homework and lived to regret it. My own life was so busy that I probably couldn't have paid much attention to environmentalism even if I had seen it coming.

Among other things, my work as Mayor of Tucson involved me deeply in urban problems nationwide. While serving as president of the American Municipal Association in early 1960, a young Senator named Jack Kennedy began dropping in on our sessions. He was running for President of the United States, he said, and wanted to meet as many city politicians from throughout the nation as possible. I often invited him to sit at the head table and address the group. We pressured him for federal assistance to cities—the states weren't doing much and the huge population rush to urban centers was simply overwhelming us. He pledged, if elected president, to establish a Department of Urban Affairs, to be headed by a Secretary empowered to respond to city problems.

The young Senator won his election, and did not forget his promise. In December, President-elect Kennedy called me to meet with him at a hotel in New York City to discuss that Urban Affairs Department we wanted. Richardson Dilworth, president of the Conference of Mayors, was also invited. Dilworth suggested that I make the presentation, as I represented the strongest municipal association. I outlined the new Department to Kennedy and we ended with the understanding that after inauguration, he would submit legislation to the Congress urging a new Department of Urban Affairs headed by a cabinet-level officer.

Winter and spring came and went and nothing happened. 1961 was half gone. I called the President and asked for an appointment. Dick Lee, mayor of New Haven, Connecticut, had succeeded Dilworth as president of the Conference of Mayors, and together we met with President Kennedy in the Oval Office in June. We pressed him for action. He promised to move on the issue and soon submitted a proposal to Congress to establish a Department of Housing and Urban Development. Then an article appeared in the *Washington Post* reporting that President Kennedy planned to appoint a Negro to head the new agency. This immediately lost him the support of many Southern Democrats in Congress who had been the proposal's strongest supporters. It was an uphill struggle of hearings and compromises before we finally got our agency some years later in the Johnson administration.

Conference Chairman

As I've already noted, I left office as Mayor on Tucson in December 1961, but earlier that year, on top of my work with three park concessions and Democratic politics in Arizona, I was elected Chairman of the Western Conference of National Park Concessioners.

That event reflected changes not only in my own life, but also in the fabric of the Conference itself. No longer would the leadership be drawn only from among the "Big Three" concessions at Yellowstone, Yosemite and Grand Canyon. Election procedures now permitted a chairman and a secretary to be chosen by the membership. I don't know why they elected me as the first chairman under their new system; I would like to think they knew me as an activist deeply interested in the parks and their visitors.

Despite the newly democratized election process, some things hadn't changed since the Conference's founding in 1929 by Interior Secretary Wilbur: The chairman still held authority to make all Conference decisions during the interim between annual meetings. I was also confronted with the fact that the chairman's company remained responsible for any and all bills incurred by the Conference during the year, to be reimbursed by the membership at the following annual meeting. I found this practice very burdensome for a small company.

Nevertheless, I took my new position seriously and tried to lodge the democratic process more deeply in the Conference. I appointed an executive committee to provide advice to me between annual meetings. I felt it was poor business to have one man making decisions for the entire Conference without consulting fellow concessioners.

In January 1962 the long-awaited report of the Outdoor Recreation Resource Review Commission was released. Its lead volume, *Outdoor Recreation for America*, provided a broad-brush outline of the commission's work in fourteen chapters. While providing a revealing look at America's general recreation needs, the report devoted substantial attention to concessions generally:

> Private enterprise plays an important role in partnership with government in providing facilities and services on government-owned land. This arrangement—the concession system—is widely used by the Federal Government, by some States, and by local units of government. It provides services for the public without government expenditure and creates opportunities for private investment.

The commission gave the public a real eye-opener to federal concessions:

> Concessions are important on the recreation lands of the Federal Government. . . . The Forest Service has over 1,400 concession contacts in effect, the National Park Service 177, and the Corps of Engineers 278. These numbers are somewhat misleading in terms of total effect, since the individual concessions of the Forest Service and Corps of Engineers tend to be smaller than those of the National Park Service.

Most crucially, the commission explained to the American public both the legitimacy and problematic nature of concessions.

> Concession operations constitute a significant contribution to America's recreation resources, and the present system should be continued. . . .
>
> However, it must be recognized that there are limitations to the concession system. It is, quite properly, geared to the profit motive. It can, under certain circumstances, profitably provide lodging, food, and services which are normal business functions. But the role of profit-seeking capital is limited by a number of factors. The recreation industry generally is a highly speculative one subject to extreme fluctuation. The season of many operations, particularly in national parks, is quite short. Construction costs are often high because of the remoteness of location. Operation is complicated by the necessity of conforming to government regulations

I was particularly pleased to find that the commission had carefully delineated what few Americans knew about:

> The legal status of buildings and facilities is complex. Since concessioners cannot own the land upon which they build, they do not have fee title to their buildings. The contracts under which the concessioners operate allow a great deal of discretion to the administering agencies and little security to the concessioner.
>
> These factors combine to make it extremely difficult for concessioners to borrow large sums for capital expansion. Banks and institutional lenders have not been willing to advance long-term capital in the face of these adverse factors. The majority of concessions have been financed from personal savings and from money generated by the business. This works well enough in small operations, but it often is inadequate for the needs of large operations in the national parks.

The commission made several recommendations to strengthen the American concession system:

> A congressional review of the concession situation would be most helpful. There are actions which could be taken to ease the difficulty of concessioners in obtaining capital. These include a strong statement of policy at a high level to create confidence in the system; a government loan-guarantee program; contracts of long duration and on favorable terms; and tax incentives. Some aspects of these actions amount to a subsidization of the concession system.
>
> The problems of short seasons, high costs of construction and shifting desires of consumers were exacerbated by contradictory government attitudes and supervision, occasional introduction of political consideration, changes in public policies, vaguely worded contracts and legal concepts novel to the world of orthodox finance.

The commission had done a tremendous amount of work on outdoor recreation. A special study report examined concessions in minute detail. Even though commission members had interviewed me extensively about my acquisition of the Glacier National Park concession, I was astonished to find more than three pages devoted to Glacier.

> In January of 1961, a new concessionaire assumed operation of the Glacier complex. The Great Northern Railroad sold its interest to Glacier Park Incorporated, a company headed by Don Hummel. The Park Service granted Hummel a contract to operate the assets which he bought from the railroad.
>
> This may mark a major turn in the concession history of Glacier. Hummel has been the concessionaire in Lassen Park for some years and his Lassen Park Company in turn operates the Government-owned hotel in Mount McKinley Park in Alaska. . . . it must be said that the acquisition of the assets of the old concession was not without non-business considerations. Hummel points out that the railroad probably could

have gotten more for its assets in the park. The railroad was apparently motivated by its long-term interest in the public service and passenger promotion aspects. The sale to a corporation headed and largely owned by Hummel, a concessionaire who has profitably operated in the public interest, offered the railroad assurance that these long-term interests would be protected.

Everyone appreciates a few good words now and then. As I read the commission's report during February of 1962 I realized that it was speaking to me personally. I found in it a clarion call to stabilize federal concession policy by legislative enactment. One paragraph struck me in particular by its major recommendation to the President and Congress that:

A clear statement of federal policy toward the concession system be issued setting forth the role of concessions in a national recreation program; and a revamping of contracts and leases with concessioners that seem unduly weighted on the government side and unnecessarily stringent in light of actual operating conditions.

That was exactly what we needed and only Congress could do it. I felt that President Kennedy and his Interior Secretary Stewart L. Udall would be sympathetic to our cause and perhaps help with administration support. As Chairman of the Conference of National Park Concessioners, I informally took up the idea of seeking Congressional action on concessions policy with the membership in the weeks that followed. The reception was rather cool from some of our larger members. What if something went wrong in the legislative process and we lost favorable provisions instead of gaining them?

Then too, the large concessions didn't feel the pinch of current development demands as badly as the smaller ones. They were able to finance expansion for the public on their long and substantial records with their banks. Some concessions such as mine at Lassen had good banker relations, but could not swing loans for new visitor facilities because higher construction costs required investments far in excess of previous loans. The standard commercial loan had to be repaid in five years, which was insufficient time for a small concessioner to pay off the huge sums involved.

The Kirwan Investigation

As it turned out, politics was on my side. During the spring of 1962 disturbing noises began to emanate from the House Appropriations Committee and the House Government Affairs Committee, slapping at both concessioners and the Park Service. Most discomfiting, Representative Michael K. Kirwan of Ohio, chairman of the House Appropriations Committee's Subcommittee on Department of Interior Appropriations had initiated an investigation into national park concession policies. Kirwan particularly targeted the concepts of possessory interest, the preferential right of contract renewal and the preferential right to provide new facilities. While I was trying to convince reluctant members to back a legislative campaign, Kirwan's subcommittee staff contacted several concessioners and grilled them on their contract provisions, asking particularly how their investment could be completely amortized so that some other concessioner could come into the park. These inquiries focused their attention.

Hilmer Oehlmann of Yosemite reported back to me that he told the investigators most concession operations were for sale but no buyers could be found, blunting the criticism that our contracts were exceptionally favorable. Hil also informed his interrogators that constant reinvestment in the parks was essential, so that no investment could be completely amortized at any given time. Whatever previous reservations he may have had, Hil fully supported a legislative solution.

Kirwan's Congressional inquiries and criticisms made long-term lenders dubious of the security of concession investments, and that alarmed the concessioners. Obviously the Secretary's Statement of May 6, 1950, which essentially upheld our negotiated "standard language" contracts, was being undermined by politics. As Mr. Frisbee, our Lassen banker at Redding had told me back in 1952, "It's a good policy, Don, but a policy can be changed at any time and does not provide security for me to lend you bank funds." How right he was.

Kirwan also questioned our franchise fee payments. He felt the government should wring the maximum possible out of concessions. He was perfectly aware that long-standing Park Service policy sought good service to the public at reasonable rates rather than revenue to the government. Kirwan and his subcommittee wanted more money for the government. They and others thought franchise fees were too low for the privileges granted.

Kirwan harried the Park Service into putting pressure on concessioners. Their first pressurizing proposal was that franchise fees be collected on the basis of business *type* rather than gross receipts or profits—all hotels would pay one fee rate, all sales services another, and so forth. Such arbitrary disconnection between regulation and economics makes for bad business. Kirwan didn't care that every dollar taken for franchise fees went into the Treasury Department's general fund, not into the Park Service. Every dollar spent on franchise fees was a dollar not available to reinvest in needed facilities.

The Park Service was keenly aware of these facts, but the Congressional pressure was too much: They issued a whole series of proposals to increase fees and make them uniform. The Conference made its opposition clear: income, costs, and profits were the only rational basis for a fee structure. Any attempt to apply one fee to all concessioners was like making every human being wear the same size coat. This conflict between concessioners and the Park Service continued through the summer of 1962 without resolution.

After these stormclouds appeared on the political horizon, it was not too difficult getting the Conference's agreement: we would seek legislation from Congress to stabilize concessioner policy once and for all. When the Conference

members finally agreed, there was no halfhearted support—
that is, except from Utah Parks Company, which had signed a
20-year "Solicitor's opinion" contract and thereby became
subject to forfeiture of its buildings. The firm still experienced severe losses as a park concession operator and felt it
had little to fight for. The rest of us were more than ready to
go.

We launched our campaign at the annual Conference meeting on March 7, 1963, at the Ambassador Hotel in Washington. When I convened the meeting that spring Thursday
morning, my first agenda item was a review of the ten-point
Interior policy statement of May 6, 1950, the one that reiter-
ated our negotiated "standard language" contract provisions. I
pointed out to the Conference that in earlier years the Department of the Interior had been our worst problem, but
now congressional committees had usurped that dubious distinction. I told the Conference that if the private sector was to
continue in the parks, Congress had to make a strong policy
statement in the law. Our lack of security, the generally poor
economic climate, plus the rising tide of political harassment
made inaction untenable.

The sense of the Conference was that we should meet
directly, this very morning, with Interior officials, and tell
them what we had in mind. We knew that Secretary Udall
and Solicitor Frank Barry had both reaffirmed their support of
the May 6, 1950 Chapman statement. We knew that Assistant
Secretary for Public Land Management John A. Carver, Jr.
was particularly supportive of the private sector as the proper
source for funds to provide visitor facilities in the national
parks. We had made advance arrangements to meet with
various Interior officials during our annual meeting and now
the entire attending membership, nearly forty people, went
to the big gray Interior Department building.

The Meeting

We met at 10:00 a.m. in an office on the third floor with
National Park Service Director Conrad L. Wirth; Chief,

Division of Concessions Management Thomas F. Flynn, Jr.; and Park Service General Counsel Jackson E. Price. It was as cordial a meeting as could be expected under the circumstances. As chairman of the Conference I began by expressing our general concerns over recent events.

Director Wirth was informal and frank with us. He said, "I understand your concerns. But do you think that private enterprise is still able to do the job in the national parks? I'm not certain of that any more."

I said, "I can understand why you ask, Connie. We're both being criticized on the Hill. I know that better service is being demanded in the parks than is being provided. The Conference shares your concern about the criticisms being directed at both of us. But I think they're unjust and unfair."

"On what do you base that position?" asked Wirth.

"We in the private sector are being asked to provide services, but the very criticism we're getting from these congressional committees ties our hands so we can't provide better service. Our bankers don't like all this upset and uncertainty. We need stable policies that will permit access to adequate financing."

"I can understand that," said Wirth. "But I repeat my basic question: can private enterprise still do the job in the parks?"

"Connie, we feel the concession system offers the best chance of solving the problem in the parks. The Outdoor Recreation Resource Review Commission report confirms it. We know we have to serve the public better. But any shift to government ownership would only change the source of the problem. We feel that your policy is adequate, but we need legislation to remove the uncertainties, to make sure your policies remain constant. What I'm saying, Connie, is that we need to remove the possibility that the present policies will be retracted."

"Legislation?" asked Wirth, alarmed. "Do you think Congress will enact it?"

"I think it's consistent with the recommendations of the ORRRC Report. They called for legislative enactment of the concessions policy. We need your blessing before we can explore the idea with the Department."

Director Wirth was hesitant about the legislative approach. "That troubles me. Have you considered the possibility that you might lose some of your policy advantages?"

I felt that what he was really asking was whether the Park Service might lose some of its control over concessioners.

Wirth told us, "You have semi-legislative approval now with the Service submitting your contracts to the Interior and Insular Affairs Committee. That gives you the opportunity to complain about policy problems."

"But it doesn't stop the Appropriations Committee from scaring off our financing."

"That's true. But I don't know. Trying to pass legislation is fraught with pitfalls. Let me talk to Carver. Can you come back later?" I said yes.

The membership was generally pleased with the drift of our discussions. After a brief strategy session with our membership, I met alone that afternoon at 3:00 with Assistant Secretary Carver and Director Wirth. The Assistant Secretary for Public Land Management, as Carver's position was called in those days, was the immediate boss of the Director of the National Park Service. Carver had previously worked for Senator Frank Church of Idaho and was destined to become the architect of public land law review legislation. He was politically savvy and a good judge of policy. (In the conversation that follows I address Assistant Secretary Carver as *Mr. Secretary*, the proper honorific for both Cabinet and sub-Cabinet officers.)

Carver opened the discussion by stating that he had gone over the agenda of the Western Conference and that it completely paralleled his thinking.

"Don, I'm in favor of private enterprise in the national parks," he said. "And I recognize the need for security of investment made on public lands. But let me ask you the same question Director Wirth asked you. Can private enterprise do the job?"

"It certainly can, Mr. Secretary," I said, "if concessioners are given access to the money markets through proper security of their investments at proper rates."

Carver said, "I agree, Don. But let's talk about private enterprise for a minute. I'm bothered by the concessioner's preferential right to provide new services in a given national park. You talk about free enterprise in the parks. I don't understand why you don't want free competition in the parks."

"Mr. Secretary, I've been talking about *private* enterprise in the parks, not *free* enterprise in the parks. There's a difference. The conditions for free enterprise in the parks don't exist and the conditions for private enterprise do. The Park Service controls everything in the parks: Services to be performed, facilities to be built, opening and closing dates, prices—everything. That's not *free* enterprise, it's regulated enterprise, but it's also *private* enterprise. If you want free competition, you have to have a free market. You'd have to remove all government controls from the parks."

"We can't do that, Don," said Carver. "You know Congress has mandated that we protect natural values in the parks as well as provide for public use and enjoyment."

"That answers your question, then. Where you have such tight regulation in the public interest you have to offer some inducement to attract private capital, and one of those inducements is preferential rights. Mr. Secretary, you know that freewheeling competition did exist in the parks once, back before Steve Mather. If you were to have competition again, you'd have to at least double the visitor facilities in each park and I don't believe you want that."

Carver laughed. He told Wirth, "I'm going to recommended that the Conference proceed at once to secure concession policy legislation."

Wirth nodded his acquiescence.

Carver added, "I don't even think you should wait for the results of the Kirwan investigation. I'll support the Conference's efforts before Congress in any way I can."

Lobbying

In a joint session of the seven-man Conference executive committee and the Park Service leadership late on November 6, 1962, we agreed that the Conference would proceed with its lobbying effort. For the Conference were Trevor Povah of Yellowstone, Ray Lillie of Grand Teton, Leslie Scott of Yellowstone, Stuart Cross of Yosemite, Daggett Harvey of Grand Canyon, George Beal of Yellowstone, and myself. Carver, Wirth and Chief of Concessions Flynn spoke for the Department. We would strive to have the Mather-Albright policies enacted into law.

And we would seek a loan-guarantee bill for concessioners along the lines of Small Business Administration programs, primarily to assure access to capital for smaller concessioners. The Conference and the Park Service agreed to submit a loan-guarantee bill along with the policy bill. In fact, Connie Wirth favored a loan-guarantee bill over the policy bill—which you would expect, since the policy bill would place significant statutory constraints on Park Service decision-making power.

With my instructions to proceed approved, I asked Conference attorney Herman Hoss to get out his concessions policy bill from 1948 and go to work on our proposed legislation.

Hoss and Hil Oehlmann of Yosemite wrote most of the original draft, with contributions from several on the Conference executive committee and in the general membership. When the draft legislation was ready in late February 1963 I asked freshman Congressman Morris K. Udall of Tucson, Arizona, to sponsor the bill. He had been elected to the 87th Congress on May 2, 1961, and appointed to the House Interior and Insular Affairs Committee, an ideal position to help us with the bill. Mo represented my Congressional district and was readily accessible. He told me he'd have to first get the blessing of Committee Chairman Wayne Aspinall of Colorado, a tough and astute politician. And that might take some doing.

13

Policy Conundrums

N ATIONAL PARK CONCESSION policy was not the only long-
standing conservation issue clamoring for resolution in
1963: The wilderness question came to the fore. Ultimately,
the Wilderness Act of 1964 predated the Concession Policy
Act of 1965 by almost thirteen months, yet final congressional
hearings on both were held less than forty days apart in 1964.
Most astonishing, these incongruent measures both gained
support from many of the same legislators and administrators.

The matrix in which these two concerns solidified was the
Eighty-eighth Congress, convened on January 9, 1963 and
adjourned on October 3, 1964. One cannot grasp how the
Mather-Albright concession policies became law without an
understanding of the Eighty-eighth Congress. During its
term the administration of President John F. Kennedy ma-
tured and then dissolved in a hail of assassin's bullets. With
the hand of successor Lyndon B. Johnson at the government's
helm, Kennedy's objectives rode on a wave of public sympathy into law: civil rights, improved transportation, urban
housing, and many others.

It was the age of the New Frontier and the Great Society.
Under their banners, the Eighty-eighth Congress passed
crucial conservation legislation including the Wilderness Act,
the Land and Water Conservation Fund Act, the Outdoor
Recreation Act, and the Public Land Law Review Commis-
sion Act. It also heard the public testimony that shaped the
Concession Policy Act in the following Eighty-ninth
Congress.

Politics

The story of the Concession Policy Act and its formation is the tale of two committees. In 1963, the Interior and Insular Affairs Committees—one in the Senate, the other in the House—held responsibility for national park and wilderness legislation. The men who headed these two committees wielded power with equal skill but with utterly different temperaments. Senator Clinton P. Anderson, Democrat of New Mexico, and Representative Wayne N. Aspinall, Democrat of Colorado, clearly understood each others' talents and institutional constraints. Aspinall was a consummate legislative craftsman and a friend of concessions: He reaffirmed Congressman Peterson's 1950 policy statement by formal resolution dated August 30, 1960. Anderson, on the other hand, was the Senate's foremost proponent of the wilderness bill. When these two men disagreed, national park and wilderness legislation failed to move.

The story of the Concession Policy Act and its formation is also the tale of two bills. Although many congressmen supported both the Wilderness bill and the Concession bill, political maneuvering over the Wilderness bill grew so convoluted that it held up consideration of the Concession bill for a whole year. Here is an account of how it happened.

1963 Legislative Status:

February 18
Congressman Morris Udall accepts our draft Concession policy bill. The Wilderness bill has been bottled up in Representative Aspinall's House Interior Committee since the Senate passed it in 1961.

Aspinall bottled up the Wilderness bill because he had profound concerns over many of its specific provisions. He thought Congress, not the President, should have the exclusive power to proclaim an area Wilderness. He thought the whole Wilderness concept too narrow and restrictive for America's resource lands. He didn't like the provision requiring the Park Service to survey all national park areas over 5,000 acres for potential Wilderness designation. What would happen to visitor access? Aspinall felt that expanding Bureau of Outdoor Recreation lands would decrease pressures for more Wilderness by offering alternatives, and wanted a Land and Water Conservation Fund established to pay for acquisition of non-Wilderness recreational lands.

The Kennedy administration wanted to pry the Wilderness bill out of Aspinall's committee. As a pressure tactic, Kennedy's Agriculture Secretary Orville Freeman reclassified huge amounts of Forest Service land from "Primitive Area" status into the rigid "Wilderness" category. By 1963 total Wilderness stood at nearly 8 million acres.

February 26
Senator Henry M. Jackson (D-Washington) replaces Anderson as chairman of Senate Interior and Insular Affairs Committee.

Anderson's pro-Wilderness influence will remain, however: Historian Richard A. Baker called the relationship between Anderson and Jackson "in the sense of father to son."

February 28 and March 1
Jackson holds hearings on Wilderness bill to increase pressure on Aspinall.

March 7 and 8
Jackson holds hearings on Aspinall's pet Land and Water Conservation Fund bill.

March 11
Aspinall likes our Concession bill and tells Morris Udall to take it to the Parks Subcommittee. Udall spends substantial time framing our bill, truly becoming its author.

March 28
The House Appropriations Committee under chairman Clarence Cannon, Democrat of Missouri, issues a report critical of park concessions.

April 9
Wilderness bill passes Senate for second time. Under floor manager Frank Church (D-Idaho), ardent Wilderness supporter, the Senate passes the bill 73 to 12.

April 25
Concession bill introduced. Both Morris Udall and Interior Subcommittee on National Parks chairman Thomas G. Morris, Democrat of New Mexico, enroll identical bills. Both also introduce identical loan guarantee bills (which were never enacted).

May 2 and 3
Aspinall asks General Accounting Office for its views on the Concession Policy bill and the Loan Guarantee bill.

May 20
The Government Operations Committee under chairman William L. Dawson, Democrat of Illinois, issues hostile anticoncession report. The Appropriations Committee and Government Operations Committee reports appear to contradict long-standing concession policy stated by Interior Committee.

Government Operations Committee member Jack Brooks, Democrat of Texas, took our Concession bill as a personal insult, and began a long and sustained campaign to discredit not only our bill, but also national park concessions in general.

Also on May 20, President Kennedy insults Aspinall by saluting Anderson for "a lifetime of dedication to natural conservation" in a Rose Garden ceremony and vows to visit a number of Wilderness areas in support of the Wilderness bill.

May 29
GAO issues critical report to Congress berating certain park service policies and practices, especially possessory interest and preferential rights concepts.

Early June
No public hearings scheduled on our Policy bill. I contact Mo

Udall for information about Aspinall's intentions. Mo relays Aspinall's reaction: "The congressman wouldn't be pressuring the chairman now, would he?"

Early July
Aspinall settles on a new strategy to tie the passage of the Wilderness bill to a massive review of the nation's laws governing its public lands. Aspinall meets with our friend, Interior Department Assistant Secretary John A Carver, a former staff member for Senator Frank Church, to draft a bill that would create a Public Land Law Review Study Commission.

July 19
The Comptroller General of the United States writes Aspinall reinforcing the conclusions of GAO's May 29 report. Things appear to be going from bad to worse.

August 4
Aspinall introduces his Public Land Law Review Commission bill into the House. Aspinall addresses Chicago meeting of the American Bar Association, clearly promising support of a limited Wilderness bill.

September 24
Assistant Secretary Carver submits a report to Aspinall explaining the history of national parks concessions in some detail and vigorously defends the Mather-Albright policies.

At last we had some much-needed official support.

But in politics matters never remain simple for long. Now a changing of the guard was about to complicate things in the Park Service.

A Bad Scare

The stage was to be set at a Park Superintendents Conference held in Yosemite on October 18. Rumors flew that Connie Wirth wished to retire and that the announcement would be made at this meeting. Assistant Secretary Carver, for reasons that have never been made clear, rendered the occasion a near-disaster—a circumstance that could have imperiled both his job and our concession bill.

It was an important meeting, with a scheduled address by Interior Secretary Stewart Udall. I attended as chairman of the Western Conference of National Park Concessioners, and saw nothing amiss until Assistant Secretary Carver delivered his scheduled late morning address on the condition of the parks. I was shocked to hear him speak severely of the management performance in several parks, indirectly laying the blame at Connie Wirth's feet.

This did not sit well with the superintendents. Connie was a highly popular director within the agency and had rendered distinguished service to his country for many years. With Wirth's imminent replacement by George B. Hartzog, Jr. an open secret, Carver's critical remarks appeared harsh at best.

Secretary Udall's speech was the next scheduled event on the program and everyone expected it to officially announce Wirth's successor. But the Secretary had been held up in traffic and at this awkward moment approached the meeting hall unaware of Carver's gaffe. A conference organizer sent Hartzog and me out to meet the Secretary and escort him into the building. In the brief walk from Udall's car to the hall, I told Stew what had happened and what an angry audience to expect.

Forewarned, Secretary Udall delivered a glowing accolade to Connie Wirth's unflagging dedication to the parks in language befitting the situation, which mollified the crowd. As expected, he also announced Wirth's retirement and the appointment of George Hartzog as Director of the National Park Service effective January 8, 1964.

That evening Director-to-be Hartzog invited me to take a walk with him privately along the meadow trails of Yosemite valley. In that majestic setting he confided that Howard Hays of Sequoia and Don Hummel of Glacier were his real friends, and he expected us to tell him in the days to come if he was getting "off the track." Although I respect George as one of the last Directors to defend the "partnership" concept of concession policy, I have to admit that I must have taken this admonition more seriously than he did, because I often reminded him of the conversation over the years as he bent to environmentalist pressure. He listened but seldom responded to my advice.

Soon after the Yosemite conference, Aspinall's staff notified interested parties that three days of "Park Concession Policy" hearings had been scheduled for February 27, 28 and March 19 of 1964. At last, the concessioners were going to get their "day in court."

Concession Hearings at Last

As the witness list was assembled it became evident that the subcommittee hearings would take concessioners seriously. The full dress parade had been arranged: Carver for the Interior Department, Director George B. Hartzog for the National Park Service, Jackson E. Price, who had been elevated to Assistant Director of the Park Service, and no fewer than three officials from the hostile General Accounting Office. Senator Lee Metcalf of Montana, an avowed conservationist, not only agreed to introduce the Udall bill in the Senate as S. 1376, but also to testify on its behalf. And seven concessioners had been enrolled as witnesses.

On Thursday, February 27, 1964, Chairman Thomas G. Morris convened the seventeen-member Subcommittee on National Parks for hearings on Park Concession Policy in room 1324 of the Longworth Building on Capitol Hill. Subcommittee ranking minority member John P. Saylor (R-Pennsylvania) had indicated solid support of our bill, and this bipartisan unity bolstered our confidence. The first morning was taken up with the formalities of reading the bills and seven departmental reports into the record. The day's testimony led off with Senator Lee Metcalf of Montana who spoke with deep conviction in support of the policy bills. Assistant Secretary Carver came next, then a panel of three including Director Hartzog, Assistant Director Price and Concessions Chief Flynn. These information-packed sessions outlined virtually the entire history of national park concessions. Although I was pleased to see the subcommittee getting these valuable lessons, it put me in something of a quandary. I wondered what would be left to say when my turn came.

The next day I was the lead-off witness. At 10:00 a.m. Chairman Morris called the hearing to order.

> Mr. Morris. The subcommittee will hear from Mr. Don Hummel of Tucson, Arizona, chairman of the Western Conference. I suppose that is the Western Conference of Concessioners.
> Mr. Hummel. Yes, sir.

I asked the chairman if I could bring two other scheduled witnesses to form a panel with me, and he agreed. He asked if I had a written statement to offer.

> Mr. Hummel. Yes, sir; I have a written statement. Mr. Chairman, I find myself in the unenviable position that most of the material I have in the written statement was covered yesterday. With your indulgence, I would like to submit that written statement, but point out some highlights.

I submitted my written statement for the record and began my oral testimony.

> Mr. Hummel. Mr. Chairman, my name is Don Hummel. I am president of Glacier Park, Inc., and chairman of the Western Conference of National Park Concessioners. This is a voluntary association with membership of most of the major concessioners in the national parks. We have divided up our presentation here on behalf of the concessioners involved and our statements will try to give you a balanced presentation.
> I was to provide a statement on the need for legislation. Mr. Hoss will discuss the terms of the policy bill; Mr. Galusha, the guarantee bill. Mr. Stan Aby, of Kalman Co., a financial expert, is going to testify on behalf of the people who provide the money for these facilities, and then we have supporting statements by other concessioners and independent agencies who will present statements in support of the legislation.

Here I summarized my arguments on the need for legislation: the crucial importance of giving congressional approval to possessory interest and preferential rights, problems with access to financing, and most importantly, the recommendations of the ORRRC report to clarify and stabilize government policy.

The remainder of the hearings went overwhelmingly in our favor. Our financial and concessioner witnesses came well armed with factual information and tightly reasoned arguments. The hostile witnesses from the General Accounting Office who appeared the last day (March 19) obviously had neither historical perspective on concession policy nor practical grasp of the problems of the parks. Their testimony appeared to be mere carping, but contained several points that would lead to bitter debate on the House floor.

One fascinating sidelight of these 1964 hearings was the testimony of former NPS director Horace M. Albright. After all those years away from government, he still looked after the parks' well-being. He could not appear in person, but submitted written testimony to Chairman Morris restating the original Mather-Albright concession policy with about as much authority as a human being can possess:

> You are doubtlessly aware of the fact that much of the policy involving the concessioner system in the national parks was developed during Stephen T. Mather's and my tenure as Directors of the National Park Service (1917-34) and with the approval of our superior officers, Interior Secretaries Franklin K. Lane to Harold L. Ickes. I feel that these polices are sound, and have endured the test of time, and have produced results under the unique and difficult conditions that prevail in the national parks. The need to provide full-scale and balanced services and meet the need for preservation of natural features of the parks requires specialized handling . . .
>
> If we are to entrust private enterprise to provide these services, we must recognize the requirements of private capital. The first requirement is security of investment. A policy that recognizes these needs and provides this security will

permit the concessioner to compete with other demands for capital.

I would like to add my unqualified support to this legislative program, as I believe it necessary if the public is to be served.

With warmest regards and hoping our trails will cross again soon, I am,

> Very sincerely yours,
> Horace M. Albright

Our Bill Languishes

When the hearings concluded, we felt satisfied that we had done our best, that we had the subcommittee support we needed, and that Aspinall would obtain a speedy victory on the House floor. On May 26 of 1964 the House Interior and Insular Affairs report on H.R. 5886 was delivered to the Clerk of the House for printing and referred to the Committee of the Whole House on the State of the Union.

This "Committee of the Whole House on the State of the Union," incidentally, is a particularly bizarre cog in the machinery of American government. It means that the entire chamber sits as a committee to consider a bill referred to it. The historical foundation of this "committee of the whole" procedure was the desire of early parliaments to act on legislation in semi-secrecy, without recorded votes, and thus to be independent of the king's sanctions. The procedure has survived partly to give legislators the ability to act on bills free of the political consequences of recorded votes. With the modern move to openness in government, recorded votes are sometimes taken in "committee of the whole" sessions.

Aspinall also had our bill placed on the House Consent Calendar, hoping for easy passage. The "consent calendar" procedure is followed for bills identified by committee reports as noncontroversial. Consent calendar bills are voted on without debate.

On June 1, 1964, our concession bill met its first test and failed: it came up before the House on the consent calendar, but Rep. John J. McFall (D - California), chairman of the

House "committee of the whole," asked the Speaker of the House that the bill be passed over without prejudice—meaning it would not be considered that day, but would remain on the consent calendar for subsequent consideration. Chairman Aspinall had not gathered the support necessary for quick victory. The reason was the log-jammed Wilderness bill.

Aspinall's public land law review commission strategy had worked. Senator Clinton Anderson had correctly read Aspinall's August 1963 signal and began negotiations to trade Senate approval of the Land Law Review Commission bill for release of the Wilderness bill. After lengthy haggling, the agreements were made. If Aspinall would hold House Interior Committee hearings on the Wilderness bill, the Conservation Fund Act would be released from the Senate Rules Committee as a sign of good faith that the Land Law Commission Act would meet no Senate resistance. The intricate legislative logjam was broken. Both the Wilderness Bill and the Concession Bill could now proceed.

Aspinall gave the go-ahead for Wilderness hearings in the House Interior Subcommittee on Public Lands, chaired by Walter S. Baring (D-Nevada). The hearings went smoothly. All sixty million acres of *de facto* wilderness in America would not suddenly become official Wilderness Areas: only the nine million acres already classified as "Primitive Areas" would be declared "instant Wilderness." Other areas would have to be considered by Congress one at a time. The most land the Wilderness bill would ever encompass would amount to about fifty million acres, or about two percent of the nation (as an ironic footnote, current Wilderness designations now blot more than 80 million acres of America and are growing every year, which shows how much you can trust Congress to resist environmentalist demands).

The process by which Wilderness would be created would be orderly: all federal agencies managing roadless areas including the National Park Service would prepare Wilderness Study Area plans to be completed and submitted to Congress ten years after the bill's passage. On April 28, Howard

Zahniser testified in support of the wilderness bill for the nineteenth time in seven years. He told chairman Baring that he hoped it would be his final appearance. It was. A week later Zahniser died.

Now instead of a feisty lobbyist Aspinall had to deal with a revered memory. He announced Zahniser's death to the House in a tone of great respect, pointing out, as Zahniser had, that the long battle was nearly over, and that, "like the patriarch of old," the nation's greatest wilderness advocate "was denied the opportunity to experience his moment of victory."

Now the machinery of Congress continued its deliberate course. In early May the House passed Aspinall's Public Land Law Review Commission bill and sent it to the Senate for action. Near the end of the month, Senate Rules Committee chairman "Judge" Howard W. Smith (D-Virginia) agreed to release the Conservation Fund bill for Senate floor consideration. All this was why Aspinall devoted little work that year to the Concession bill.

Back To Business

After the Park Concession Policy hearings I had returned home and then went to Glacier to take care of pre-season business. Everything seemed to be going as usual. I looked forward to a busy summer and passage of the Concession bill.

On June 8, at about 4:00 a.m., everything turned upside down. Cy Stevenson pounded on my door, stating in his usual blunt manner that we had a terrific torrent of water rushing down Midvale Creek. Cy's daughter Kathy and her children lived in a house close by the stream and he had to try rescuing them. Midvale is a substantial creek that provides all the water for the hotel, the laundry and many local residents of East Glacier, who, with or without permission, had attached to our water system.

We almost lost Cy that night. He tried to cross a side stream on the way to his daughter's place but the swift waters caught him. Fortunately he grabbed a hanging willow branch and pulled himself out. He should have saved his strength: A little after dawn a Civil Defense chopper airlifted Kathy and her children to safety.

As the gloomy Monday morning dragged on we learned that the flood was more than a local problem. One terrible fact piled on another: We had lost the entire East Glacier water system. Our storage reservoir's dam and several hundred feet of flume had vanished completely. All communication lines were down. What reports people brought to us indicated a serious disaster. We set up a temporary car radio system and agreed with the Park Service on times to go to our automobiles to transmit from our respective positions in the park. Our reports were grim.

The flood had come without warning. True, we knew the late snows might pose some problem, but June has always been a variable-weather month around Glacier, so they caused no concern. But we didn't anticipate the warm Chinook rains that followed. The new-fallen snow melted in record time, turning every mountainside into a literal cascade. The streams and valleys filled with this rushing torrent and the dams gave way, inundating everything, even high mesas bordering the watercourses. Our oldest "old-timers" could not recall such a flood.

Interior Secretary Stewart Udall had scheduled a speech at the Blackfeet Indian Reservation in Browning for that very Monday. Reports of the flood left him undaunted. He arrived in an Army helicopter and invited me to Many Glacier Hotel on a damage reconnaissance.

As we flew together over the route to Many Glacier the enormity of the flood unfolded. The road to Many Glacier was out in five or six different places. Great landslides gouged the mountain flanks mile after mile. Every stream seemed to be out of its banks and choked with fallen trees. Udall shook his head at the destruction.

When we landed in the parking lot at Many Glacier manager Ian Tippet told me that Swiftcurrent Lake had risen to a foot and a half above the Hotel's lower floor. Tippet had ordered our banquet tables set up and most of the furniture stacked on top, averting great loss. Many Glacier's water and sewer systems were out, requiring the hotel staff to dig temporary latrine trenches until the sewer system could be restored.

The Swiftcurrent Motor Lodge area was completely flooded and without power. The big electrical transformers in the basement were submerged and non-operational.

Udall had other obligations, so I thanked him and flew on to West Glacier in a Glacier County Civil Defense helicopter for a full inspection. We soon discovered that the east-west transportation corridor of Glacier Park was in ruin. Fourteen miles of railroad roadbed were gone. In some places floodwaters had completely undermined the tracks, leaving the rails suspended many feet in the air. On U.S. Highway 2 the big bridge at Walton was swept away. Fifteen miles of U.S. 2 had been washed away by gullies cut in parallel rows down the mountainsides like zebra stripes. The only west-side access into the park, a bridge over the Middle Fork of the Flathead River, was so badly undermined by the tree-clogged river that engineers had to condemn it.

We flew into the Village Inn and inspected the damage. Ten-mile-long Lake McDonald had risen six feet in eight hours. I waded through the Inn with water up to my thighs, pushing aside all the furniture floating around. My manager said they could have moved the furniture to the second floor, but were assured by a ranger that it would be foolish—they would never have water that high. Some 13 large plate glass windows had been smashed and the place was filled with silt and debris. Incredible.

We then flew to Lake McDonald Lodge. The damage was appalling. Snyder Creek had rampaged down the mountain, undermining huge cedar trees which formed a dam that diverted the flood directly into the hotel. The dining room had been undermined, an empty shell hanging over eroded streambanks. Its floor lay at the bottom of the creek. The big stone fireplace that had stood at its far end was completely gone. Ragged logs and the tattered remains of its roof hung over empty space. The mounted elk and goat heads still hung intact on what remained of the walls, dangling above the creek.

Every one of our sites had suffered serious damage except for the Prince of Wales Hotel at Waterton Lakes in Canada. We lost only our pumping station and power plant there. The destruction surrounding the hotel, though, was enormous. We offered the Prince of Wales Hotel, standing high and dry on a glacial moraine, as the rescue site for the nearby village and our hotel filled with refugees—at no charge, of course.

I worried particularly about our 250-passenger sightseeing launch *International*, a 73-foot twin diesel-powered vessel that could itself have become a dangerous juggernaut in the unruly waters of the lake. Our skipper, though, had the presence of mind to moor her to the trees in the picnic area—that's how high the water rose.

All roads in and out of this natural wonderland, rail or highway, lay in ruins. The public could not get to or through Glacier National Park. It was completely shut down. And the season was on us.

Our employees took first priority. Manager Ralph Erickson had established an outdoor campfire kitchen at Lake McDonald Lodge where cooks fed the employees who had already reported for the season's work. We had to move some of these people to East Glacier. The flood had struck with most employees in transit to the park. We had no way of knowing the whereabouts of many or even if they were alive. My secretary Emily Moke spent practically all her time on the telephone with a list of employees who had reported safely. Distraught relatives called day and night. Emily could only tell them, "They are here, they are safe," or "We don't know."

I faced a classic manager's quandary. None of our hotels except Glacier Park Lodge were accessible by rail or highway. We already had 600 employees on the job—most gathered now in our central headquarters at Glacier Park Lodge—and not a single guest. I realized that even if we got into operation, there was a good chance we would lose most of our reservations. We had seen what happened after the Good Friday earthquake in Alaska in March: our lodgings at Mt. McKinley National Park had suffered no damage, but sensational media reports drastically reduced our season patronage. For every thirty reservations Mt. McKinley received, we got ninety cancellations in the same mail. I could just imagine the same thing happening to us in Glacier with all the publicity on our damaged facilities and disrupted transportation.

Each evening I assembled all our employees and gave them the latest news. On the third evening I had bad news. I would be unable to pay anyone until we could get the facilities open and establish a cash flow. I promised everyone room and board without charge. I offered all an opportunity to leave without any reflection on their employment records. Not a single employee left.

Reconstruction began immediately. The job was overwhelming: Some 114 bridges out in Glacier County, miles of severely damaged highways, more miles of destroyed railroad. The agency response was phenomenal. Normally competitive bodies—the Bureau of Public Roads, National Park Service, Glacier County Road Crew, the Corps of Engineers and Montana State Highway Department—all came together as a single organism with one purpose: rebuilding.

The Air Force sent in three helicopters for emergency evacuation and personnel transport to inaccessible sites. Cy Stevenson routinely flew with them to supervise repair work. One day he flew to Many Glacier Hotel and didn't return by dinnertime. This was worrisome because the Air Force was not supposed to fly these aircraft after 6:00 p.m. I wondered what could have happened. A call finally came.

"Hello, Hummel. It's Stevenson."

"Cy, where are you?"

"Many Glacier."

"Cy, what in the world are you doing there? The Air Force isn't supposed to fly this late."

"We crashed."

"What?"

"Something happened to the helicopter and we crashed into a tree about 30 feet up. I got the lieutenant out and we walked back to Many Glacier."

That was about as flustered as Cy ever got.

A soon as the Great Northern Railway found out about the disaster they immediately began shuttle service out of Minneapolis to the east side of the park and out of Seattle to the west side. They also sent their passenger agent Kent Van Wyck to East Glacier and each morning he and I reported on conditions and accommodations to travel agencies nationwide. We were thus able to salvage a great number of our reservations, particularly the tour groups which formed the bulk of our business. The Great Northern was fantastic.

We soon had many guests to take care of. The Montana Junior Chamber of Commerce had scheduled a convention at Many Glacier Hotel, which was now inaccessible. We couldn't afford to lose the business so we transferred the JayCees to Glacier Park Lodge at East Glacier. We managed to construct a temporary water system, but couldn't extend it to the fourth floor and certainly had no capacity to deal with a fire emergency. With the prospect of some pretty wild drinking parties and careless cigarettes I placed four fire spotters twenty-four-hours-a-day on each floor.

Sadly, in the midst of this turmoil we found the manager of Glacier Park Lodge wandering up and down the lobby saying, "Gee, what a beautiful hotel." He had suffered a small stroke and did not know he was the manager. I called on Ken Gelston, our long-time assistant manager at Rising Sun, to set up the front desk and serve as acting manager until things settled down.

As the days wore on, I followed the reconstruction work keenly, making frequent helicopter trips around the park, opening each facility as it became accessible. Our big problem still lay in the western gateway over the Middle Fork of the Flathead. The main bridge had been condemned, but an

old bridge downstream still stood with its concrete arch intact, yet without a deck. Rebuilding this deck was the quick-
est alternative available, narrow though it was, and a reconstruction contract was soon let. For some reason the crew on
this deck took many coffee breaks and few work breaks, in
contrast with the others who struggled to speedily reopen
Glacier National Park.

Exasperating! Then I remembered Rex Whitten, Chairman
of the Bureau of Public Roads, whom I had met while serving
as President of the National League of Cities. I called him at
about 1:00 a.m. Washington time, got him out of bed and told
him how disgusted I was with his contractor for slowing down
the park reopening. The next afternoon a Bureau of Public
Roads supervisor arrived and the dilatory bridge crew thereafter hastened its efforts. On June 29, three weeks after the
flood, Glacier National Park opened for visitors.

Congress Again

Needless to say, I took no notice whatsoever when the
House on June 15 once again passed over the concession bill
without a vote. Politics was the farthest thing from my mind.
Nor did I pay attention to Chairman Aspinall's July 21 decision to have our bill passed over again because Rep. Harold
Royce Gross, Republican of Iowa, objected to the fact that no
provision for General Accounting Office audits of concessioner accounts had been included. But I certainly noticed
when on August 3, chairman Aspinall said, "Mr. Speaker, I
ask unanimous consent that H.R. 5886 be stricken from the
Consent Calendar." The concession bill was dead for the
Eighty-eighth Congress. We had lost!

We had reckoned without the growing force of environmentalism. Aspinall's tangle of conservation bills had monop-
olized his attention and left none for national park concessions. Now, one by one, all his cherished dreams came true
while the Conference wondered why we had failed. At 10:30
on the morning of September 3 in the White House Rose
Garden, with Aspinall watching, President Johnson signed

the Wilderness Act and the Land and Water Conservation Fund Act. On September 19 the Public Land Law Review Commission Act became law. Aspinall got the chairmanship of the commission and didn't even have to resign from Congress to do it.

In the Eighty-ninth Congress, it was our turn. On January 7, 1965, Mo Udall, having himself been duly reelected, reintroduced our policy bill as H.R. 2091. Five days later Lee Metcalf introduced an identical bill in the Senate as S. 397 and obtained "Scoop" Jackson's blessings for its passage. Clinton Anderson's interests lay elsewhere, and Jackson was completely his own man on this Senate bill. Aspinall had the free attention to maneuver the House bill himself now and decided it was time for it to become law.

The Interior Department reported favorably on our bill to Chairman Aspinall May 14, saying,

> We believe that legislative consideration of national park concession policy is very timely, in light of the positions taken by the various congressional committees. We recognize fully the legitimate concern of each committee involved, and we believe it is appropriate to have a policy reduced to a legislative directive at this time.

To the Mat

The 1965 battle for the concession bill was shaping up as a spite-fight joined by the House Government Operations Committee against the Interior and Insular Affairs Committee. Rep. Jack Brooks of Texas, as expected, remained our most vociferous opponent. He had found a loose thread in the fabric of our legislation and yanked it as hard as he could: our bill was a piecemeal solution to a government-wide problem, he asserted. Instead of granting national park concessions any stable policy, all concessions in the entire government must be studied and a uniform strait-jacket law applied to them all, he asserted.

Brooks convinced Government Operations Committee

Chairman Dawson to write President Johnson on June 24 asking that the Bureau of the Budget comment on H.R. 2091 and a possible study of overall government concession legislation.

Unperturbed, Aspinall and his committee completed its study of our concession policy bill and on July 7 committee-member Ralph J. Rivers (D-Alaska) delivered to the Clerk of the House the committee's Report No. 591, recommending H.R. 2091 for passage.

Bureau of the Budget Deputy Director Elmer B. Staats on July 22 reported back to Dawson what he wanted to hear:

> . . . should an overall policy be developed for the management of concessions generally throughout the Government, the provisions of H.R. 2091 would have to be reconsidered in the light of that policy.
> We would expect that such a study might lead to the submission of recommendations for appropriate legislation, either in an omnibus bill on a Government-wide basis, or in a series of bills for the agencies concerned.

Several July negotiation sessions between the leaders of the Government Operations Committee and the Interior and Insular Affairs Committee failed to produce a compromise bill, thanks to Jack Brooks. Brooks had become sufficiently hotheaded to want the bill killed outright. Aspinall shrewdly decided to let him try.

On July 29 Aspinall wrote a "dear colleague" letter to the chairman and members of the Rules Committee asking support for an "open rule" with two hours of general debate and limited amendments on our bill. He had been counting noses and knew he could beat Brooks easily. Otherwise he would have pressed for a suspension of the rules to prevent "tampering" with the bill on the House floor. On August 17 the Rules Committee granted Aspinall's 2-hour open rule request. The bill waited its customary 21 days for floor consideration—and then some.

At noon on September 14, 1965, after a Call of the House

established that a quorum of 377 members was present, Rep. Claude Pepper of Florida called up House Resolution 520. Its ornate and arcane language read:

> *Resolved,* That upon the adoption of this resolution it shall be in order to move that the House resolve itself into the Committee of the Whole House on the State of the Union for the consideration of the bill (H.R. 2091) relating to the establishment of concession policies in the areas administered by National Park Service, and for other purposes. After general debate, which shall be confined to two hours, to be equally divided and controlled by the chairman and ranking minority member of the Committee on Interior and Insular Affairs, the bill shall be read for amendment under the five-minute rule. . . .

Rep. Gross, who now emerged as opposition manager for the measure, objected to allowing the bill onto the floor, but lost a voice vote. Rep. Aspinall knew the bill's time had come. He arose and said: "Mr. Speaker, I move that the House resolve itself into the Committee of the Whole House on the State of the Union for the consideration of the bill. . . ." There was no objection.

And now Aspinall's legislative drama played itself out. Speaker of the House John McCormick surrendered the gavil to Rep. John J. McFall of California, who took the Chair of the Committee of the Whole. As Chairman of the bill's originating committee, Aspinall led off the debate, detailing our measure and its rationale. He then assured all members that "this bill is not a hasty product and . . . it is not the product of doctrinaire thinking. . . . It is the result of an honest attempt to get to the heart of a problem and to solve it as best we know how."

Aspinall told how he and his committee's ranking minority member, Congressman Saylor of Pennsylvania (who had been instrumental in passing the Wilderness Act of 1964) had dealt with concession issues as long as they had been in the House, back into the 1950s. Aspinall knew that Rep. Gross would demand an amendment allowing the General Accounting Office to audit concessioner books, and knew he could not resist it without endangering the bill. He said, "Such an amendment is acceptable to me and I shall support it."

But he knew he could resist Brooks entirely. One by one, Aspinall set up the objections he knew Brooks would soon cite and knocked each down with carefully measured arguments. Numerous members then questioned Aspinall about how the bill would affect their districts. By the time Brooks got to speak he was fuming. He opened with the only trump card he held: the "piecemeal vs. government-wide" objection. After Aspinall remarked that the idea had been "kicking around for at least 10 years and nothing has happened yet," he deferred to Mo Udall, who gracefully sliced Brooks to ribbons without once mentioning his name. Among Mo's remarks:

> Mr. Chairman, as the author of this bill I urge my colleagues to approve it because it is a good bill. . . .
>
> We have a great system of national parks. On the one hand we want to preserve all the scenic and natural wonders for posterity and for ourselves; on the other hand we want to make them reasonably accessible to visitors, and have the visitors provided services when they get there. Sometimes these two goals conflict. So what do we do?
>
> You can do one of three things: You can have the Government run them, and there have been suggestions in the past that the Government run it, with Government ownership. Certainly, while they do not say it, and they do not mean it, this would be the result if we do not get sound policies where a private enterprise man can survive.

The unstated reference to objectors such as Brooks hit home. Aspinall then taunted Brooks for several minutes in oh-so-gentlemanly terms, reminding him of Udall's many strong arguments and Udall's genuine concern for concessioner well-being. Brooks came back full of gall:

> I should like to reply to my distinguished and able friend

(Mr. Udall), who mentioned me and was worrying about the concessionaires.

When we worry about how long these people can survive, how difficult their lives are, I want to read a couple of little examples of initial contract dates of concessionaires now serving in the national parks.

I do not want to be unkind but I want to be factual . . . The National Parks Concessions, Inc., at Mammoth Cave National Park, have an initial contract date of January 1, 1942.

The initial contract date at Cedar Breaks National Monument is January 1, 1930.

These people have been worried all this time, and some of them were worried before I was born.

Here is one who started worrying—the Crater Lake National Park—and sweating it out in 1912. . . . There is another group at the Grand Canyon National Park. I do not know these people, but I want to give you an example of the rough life these boys and girls and their in-laws and grandchildren have in these concessions.

Now Brooks made a serious tactical error: he began to name concessioners as individuals in the most disparaging manner. He continued in this petty vein for five minutes, walking straight into Aspinall's trap:

I just want to point out that it does not look to me like it is such a risky business. If it is not, why should we not let the . . . Howard Johnsons or other professional caterers go in there and give the American people decent food at prices they can pay . . .

Brooks then called preferential rights "reprehensible" and possessory interest "disgraceful." Wayne Aspinall sat and smiled, counting votes Brooks was sending his way.

The debate adjourned at 2:44 so the House could welcome the Gemini 5 astronauts and resumed shortly after 3:30. At the end, Gross tried to block the bill by moving to recommit it to the Interior committee. When he lost the voice vote, he demanded a roll call. It is recorded as 298 against sending our bill back to committee, 73 for, 61 not voting.

Then the final voice vote on our bill itself was taken. The *Congressional Record* noted in elegant simplicity: The bill was passed. There is no way of knowing the actual count of a voice vote in Congress, because it is a matter of saying "Aye" as a group and "Nay" as a group, and nobody counts. But the "recommit" roll-call vote that Rep. Gross demanded is indicative: those who voted *against* sending our bill back to committee probably voted *for* the final bill.

The Senate passed our bill on the September 23 Consent Calendar. On September 28 the Speaker of the House and President of the Senate signed our legislation and sent it to the President. Jack Brooks couldn't take the stinging defeat: he visited his friend and fellow Texan, President Lyndon B. Johnson, who was laid up in the Bethesda Naval Hospital recovering from a gall bladder operation, and asked him to veto the bill. Johnson refused, as it had received overwhelming support in both houses. But in deference to his friend, Johnson signed the bill on October 9, 1965, with an executive constraint to the National Park Service not to implement its provisions until the Bureau of the Budget explored its terms and determined whether they should apply generally to other federal agencies with recreational lands.

The long fight was over. We had Public Law 89-249, the Concession Policy Act of 1965.

14

Environmental Politics

O VER THE NEXT two decades, the environmental movement grew into one of the most powerful and wealthy lobbies on Capitol Hill. By the mid-1960s its political clout could be felt in every federal land management agency. The direction the movement was going grew more apparent. Twenty years of ideological wildernism had stiffened the Sierra Club's 1947 repudiation of its original purpose: Now the exclusionist philosophy "to render inaccessible the mountains" was explicit. Historian Susan Schrepfer stated in a *Journal of Forest History* article "Conflict in Preservation," "By 1960 the Club viewed roads as the most destructive of human threats to parks . . ." Roads bring people and environmentalists did not want that. With the passage of the Wilderness Act of 1964 they had the legal tool to keep those roads and people out.

Environmental group leaders visited NPS Director Hartzog regularly during 1965, pressuring him to "render inaccessible the mountains" through vast Wilderness allocations. By early 1966, the Park Service estimated that 22.5 million acres of national park system land were subject to becoming Wilderness Study Areas under the Wilderness Act. NPS eventually identified for review 63 units covering over 28 million acres. Leaders of major environmental organizations began to drool—each Wilderness Study Area represented a potential fund-raising and membership-recruiting campaign to augment their burgeoning clout. The concessioners—and the public—became aware of this mercenary self-serving aspect of environmentalism nearly too late.

As an effect of the environmentalists' highly organized
pressure for wilderness, Park Service attitudes turned against
concessioners even as Congress approved the Concession
Policy Act of 1965. Before the ink of President Johnson's
signature dried, the Park Service began methodically strip-
ping away the guarantees concessioners had achieved in Congress, which is the story of this chapter.

How naive we were to believe that an Act of Congress
could bring concessioners stability. As time went on, the
National Park Service scuttled huge sections of concession
policy a step at a time in response to the rising political clout
of environmental organizations. We in the Conference had
only ourselves to blame. We did not follow the application of
the Wilderness Act to the national parks. We did not notice
changing environmentalist tactics that turned obscure technical procedures such as Master Planning into potent policy
weapons. We did not fully understand the new objectives of
the conservation movement as it evolved into the environmental movement. We did not grasp that organizations such
as the Sierra Club and Wilderness Society now intended to
first reduce and then eliminate visitor facilities in the national
parks.

The Park Service, we believed, had successfully administered our park areas to leave them "unimpaired for future
generations." We failed to recognize that environmental organizations did not share our trust and wanted to protect the
parks from the Park Service. We didn't hear people like
Sierra Club board member Martin Litton—himself a motor-
less-boat concessioner in Grand Canyon—saying of the parks
that they wanted "to make it harder to get in and harder to
stay once you get there." We learned the hard way.

Into The Bureaucracy

Because we had no idea what lay ahead, things seemed to
be going reasonably well in the world of concessions. At the
February 1966 meeting of the Conference, even lingering
regionalism among concessioners fell away. The Western

Conference of National Park Concessioners officially changed
its name to simply the Conference of National Park Concessioners. But soon more personal business took me away from
the focus of the parks. As the spring of 1966 approached I
went to Grand Canyon with NPS Director George Hartzog to
speak on concession problems at the Horace M. Albright
Training Center. Director Hartzog and I sat together listening to a presentation when a message came that "the Secretary was trying to reach Don Hummel." George was visibly
upset: Why would the Secretary want me instead of him? It
wasn't the Secretary of the Interior, said the messenger, but
the Secretary of Housing and Urban Development. George
relaxed.

But I didn't. I returned the call and found that the Johnson
administration wanted to appoint me Assistant Secretary for
housing and urban renewal programs. I gave a noncommittal
reply—I had enough to do with my concession operations in
Glacier, Lassen and McKinley National Parks.

I left the Grand Canyon unsettled and thoughtful. At home
in Tucson, Genee talked to me at length about the proposition. I should take this position, she said. A hired manager
ran McKinley for us, so that was no problem. My nephew Al
Donau readily agreed to take over Glacier while his wife
Frankie agreed to manage Lassen. I reported to Washington
in May 1966.

I said goodbye to concessioning for a while, resigned my
chairmanship of the Western Conference, and became a federal bureaucrat. After Senate confirmation, I found myself
with responsibility for 61 percent of the entire Housing and
Urban Development departmental program—housing for
college students, the low-income and elderly, and a variety of
urban renewal projects—with an annual budget of $1.9
billion.

Policy Progress

While I delved in the federal fields, concession policy continued to evolve. In October 1966, the Bureau of the Budget

released the concession study report requested by President Johnson. As Brooks had demanded, the survey reported on the question of extending possessory interest, preferential rights and other provisions of the Concession Policy Act of 1965 to all federal land management agencies providing recreational services.

The report rebuffed Congressman Brooks' importunings. In a sweeping examination of practices in the Corps of Engineers, Bureau of Land Management, Bureau of Reclamation, Bureau of Sport Fisheries and Wildlife, Tennessee Valley Authority, Defense Department and Forest Service, the Bureau of the Budget vindicated the provisions of the Concession Policy Act of 1965.

The report concluded:

> As a result of the lack of specific guidelines on use of concessioners, the agencies have gone diverse ways. In part, this flexibility has been useful and desirable and has permitted agencies to adopt policies and procedures suited to their particular objectives and to meet specific situations.

Its comments on the privileges and benefits offered concessioners:

> Most of the criticism concerning the various agency concessioners policies relates to the granting of privileges and benefits not normally given either in a free competitive environment or in normal governmental contractual relationships. The granting of these privileges and benefits has been justified on the basis of the conditions under which the concessioners are required to function. The business is usually seasonal, with exceptionally short seasons in many of the northern national parks and forests. Contracts are generally of short duration. Prices, services and facilities are all determined by federal agencies. Concessioners do not have title to the land upon which they construct their facilities. Federal agencies are free to change their policies towards concessioner operations to the detriment of such operations. Concessioners are required to remain open at the beginning and end of extended seasons

when the volume of business would not normally allow operations to continue. Concessioners have difficulty recruiting and retaining sufficient qualified help because of the seasonal nature of the concessions business.

As a result of these conditions, particularly the lack of title and sufficiently long contracts, concessioners have difficulty in borrowing money from commercial sources, especially for long-term periods, to build facilities on recreational lands. They have cited this as their biggest single problem.

In an effort to offset these conditions and encourage additional private investment, some agencies have offered a number of special considerations to concessioners, including; (1) granting of possessory interest; (2) relatively long-term contracts with renewal preferences; (3) monopolies in business locations; (4) the opportunity to construct and operate any additional facilities required in an area; and (5) relatively low fee payments.

The report also noted:

The legislative history of Public Law 89-249 clearly demonstrates that Congress gave careful consideration to the NPS practice with respect to possessory interest. Public Law 89-249 provides that a concessioner who constructs or has constructed any structure, fixture, or improvement, pursuant to a contract on land administered by the National Park Service shall have a possessory interest in that facility. This law further provides that the possessory interest shall not be taken for public use without just compensation.

We have found that the incorporation of the possessory interest concept into Public Law 89-249 has already added significant credibility to previous administration interpretations of the value of a possessory interest.

We believe that while there are problems associated with granting a possessory interest to the concessioners on National Park Service lands, there is no useful way to change the policy without seriously disrupting future investment in our national parks.

. . . It is generally agreed that the use of concessioners offers the best means of providing the bulk of needed recreation facilities and services on federal lands.

. . . It would be contrary to general federal policy to have the federal government directly engage in such operations which private enterprise is willing to provide on reasonable terms.

Concessioners should be selected on their ability to provide the necessary facilities and services to the public rather than on the amount they are willing to pay the government.

On April 21, 1967, President Lyndon Johnson wrote:

The recommendations made in the report are consistent with the intent of Congress in passing Public Law 89-249 which established concessions policies for the National Park Service. Implementation of these recommendations does not require changes in that law. Therefore, I hereby rescind the constraint which I placed on the terms of concession contracts granted by the National Park Service in my signing statement of October 9, 1965.

The Ninetieth Congress, convened in 1968 and adjourned in 1969, reflected the environmental movement's rapidly growing power. Its sobriquet, "the Conservation Congress," was well-earned: It passed the National Wild and Scenic Rivers Act, the National Trails System Act, it created North Cascades National Park, seized private timberlands to create Redwood National Park, and defeated a bill to permit a dam on the Colorado River within the boundaries of Grand Canyon National Park.

But, as the Sierra Club's Political Handbook says, legislation is not enough: the key to capturing policy lies in the art of "hassling administrative agencies." By the time the Concession Policy Act became law, the Park Service had found out all about being hassled by environmentalist leaders pushing for Wilderness plans. And the Park Service found itself in a bind. Knotty problems prevented NPS from rapidly developing their Wilderness Study Area plans: The Wilderness Act had failed to spell out an explicit allocation procedure and it was nearly impossible to determine specific boundaries in the national parks for Wilderness study.

The Master Plan Scam

And here is where another "lock-it-up-and-keep-'em-out" device came to the fore: Master Plans. On September 1, 1967, the Park Service released a compilation of administrative policies for natural areas. On page 31, the compilation described Master Plans:

> It has long been the practice of the National Park Service to prepare and maintain a Master Plan to guide the use, development, interpretation and preservation of each particular park. Graphics and narratives specify the objectives of management. These Master Plans in the true sense of the word are *zoning* plans. They not only define the areas for development, but also define the areas in which no developments are to be permitted.

In an effort to create wilderness allocation guidelines, Hartzog decided to take a lesson from the Master Planning process: After all, hadn't Yellowstone's Master Plan zoned much of the park's *de facto* wilderness "Roadless?" The Park Service already had numerous experienced Master Plan Teams to help determine land use. They had even modified the six land classes developed by the Outdoor Recreation Resources Review Commission for applicability to the National Park System. They included Class I: High-density recreation areas, Class II: General recreation areas, Class III: Natural environment areas, Class IV: Outstanding natural areas, Class V: Primitive areas, and Class VI: Historic and cultural areas. Roadless areas within a national park commonly fell within Class V, but sometimes Class III, IV and VI lands were included for special reasons. The Master Plan concept already contained classifications similar to Wilderness and offered ready-made guidelines by which Wilderness Study Areas could be rationally defined.

However, when environmentalists became familiar with the Master Plan idea, they realized it contained a framework for even more sweeping people-exclusions than the Wilderness Act. Master Plans could do what the Wilderness Act could not: They could eliminate concessions and crowds entirely. One excuse or another could easily be manufactured for downgrading one at a time Class I sites (where most concessions are) to Class II (where fewer concessions are). Then these Class II lands could be lobbied into Class III and IV (where only key concessions are) and finally Class V (where no concessions are). In the hands of politically savvy and ruthless lobbyists for the Sierra Club and Wilderness Society, the Master Plan was to become the Frankenstein monster of the 1970s.

A bitter irony lies in the origin of the Master Plan concept, which not one environmentalist in a million can tell you, and not one Park Service planner in a hundred can tell you. Master Plans originated in the Economic Stabilization Act of 1931, "An Act to provide for the advance planning and regulated construction of public works, for the stabilization of industry, and for aiding in the prevention of unemployment during periods of business depression."

Section 8(a) of that law, "Advance Planning," declares that it is the policy of Congress to "assist in the stabilization of industry and employment" and "to further this object there shall be advance planning" in the form of "a six-year advance plan with estimates showing projects allotted to each year." National Park Service Director Horace Albright assigned head landscape architect Tom Vint to implement this policy for the parks and the Master Plan was the result.

The Interior Secretary's Annual Report for 1933 tells us:

> The Office of National Parks, Buildings, and Reservations has planned ahead on its developments and has established a 6-year development program in accordance with the Employment Stabilization Act. Though not yet in their ultimate form, master plans for each park, developed in cooperation between the park superintendent, the landscape architects, and the engineering staff proved of invaluable assistance in enabling this office to submit immediately, in connection with the

public-works program, an outline of national-park development accompanied by plans, estimates, and justifications. They have also served many other purposes and their use is on the increase."

What irony! It is a sad commentary on the human condition that such a humanitarian process as master planning should be deformed into a weapon of misanthropy at the hands of wilderness purists. And the wildernists remain ignorant of the irony. They cannot see that their hallmark has become the distortion of original intent to suit shifting political expediency. Just as the Sierra Club struck "to render accessible the mountains" from their founders' creed to reinforce their political program, so the entire environmental leadership mutilated the Master Plan into a people-exclusion-fence around the national parks. They stray because they have no respect for history. But this proves what folk-singer Utah Phillips once said: The most revolutionary thing in the world is a long memory.

In the late 1960s Master Plans (today called General Management Plans) offered the Park Service its best solution to the allocation problems caused by the vaguely written Wilderness Act. Even though George Hartzog's experienced teams struggled daily to meet the mandate of Congress, the Director sensed that Sierra Club and Wilderness Society leaders would soon be accusing him of acting in bad faith, even of defying the law of the land. With such a powerful and organized constituency pressuring him, he appeased them by picking away at concessioners. It didn't bring about Wilderness designations any faster, but it made him appear sympathetic to environmentalists who detested roads, people, and developed services.

Hartzog's Harpoon

Early in 1968, while I struggled with intractable problems in the Department of Housing and Urban Development, I got the first indications that concession policy was in serious trouble again.

On the morning of Monday, March 18, Al Donau called me from Tucson with a problem. As a federal officer I had recused myself from all direct management of concessions upon confirmation by the Senate, but still retained the right to render advice. The National Park Service, Al said, had just sent him a letter demanding that Glacier Park, Inc. repair or replace some old balconies on Lake McDonald Lodge by the opening of the summer season. Such a demand, while unusual, was within the Park Service's province. But in this instance, Al told me, Park Superintendent Keith Neilsen insisted that we waive our possessory interest in the capital improvements we were to make to this government-owned building. I wondered who was behind this. Neilsen worked too far down the hierarchy to have originated this policy interpretation. It must be from Washington.

"There's no way we're going to do that," I told Al. "That flies in the teeth of everything the Concession Act stands for."

Al delivered our refusal to Neilsen and a few days later the mail brought back a hardnosed threat: Make the repairs under our terms or we'll shut you down. Superintendent Neilsen did more than threaten, too. He asserted that Public Law 89-249 does not permit concessioners to acquire possessory interest in government-owned buildings and requested Harvey B. Reynolds, Chief, Office of Programs Coordination, NPS Regional Office, Omaha, Nebraska, to amend Glacier Park, Inc.'s contract—unilaterally waiving our possessory interest. The request had already gone for approval to Washington and Director Hartzog.

This was outrageous, not to mention illegal. Al immediately contacted Stuart G. Cross, who now served as Chairman of the Conference of National Park Concessioners. He agreed to put the Glacier situation on the agenda of the upcoming annual Conference meeting only a few days away in late March. The Verkamp's Store concession in Grand Canyon National Park was having some trouble with its contract renewal terms, another issue scheduled for discussion as well. NPS Director Hartzog attended the Conference annual meeting sessions and listened to our problem. He then arose and made a strong statement denying possessory interest to concessioners for any improvements on government-owned buildings. Hartzog's stand on our contract language harpooned concession policy through his administrative misinterpretation. It would not be the last time we saw contract manipulation used as a weapon against concessions.

The entire Conference was outraged. Cross put attorney Herman Hoss to work on a reply and in mid-April sent a powerful and lengthy rebuttal to Hartzog. Herman, is his usual methodical way—he was still known as "that technical bastard"—explained virtually every facet of possessory interest to the Director, but explicitly stated about Glacier's situation:

> The recognition of possessory interest in concessioner's improvements to government improvements has been established policy ever since the adoption of the concept of possessory interest, and is now confirmed in Public Law 89-249.

Soon after the Conference annual meeting we seemed to be getting a softer line from Washington: NPS Assistant Director Jackson Price replied to Chief of Programs Coordination Reynolds' request to unilaterally amend our contract:

> We shall, of course, be pleased to amend the contract as proposed by Mr. Neilsen, if the concessioner requests it, or advises that he is willing to accept such an amendment. However, we cannot unilaterally amend the contract as requested.
>
> In this connection, we would like to correct the references made by Mr. Neilsen, that Public Law 89-249 does not permit concessioners to acquire possessory interest in government-owned buildings. On the contrary, the Act provides for such possessory interest, making it necessary for the concessioner to waive it if it is not to acquire the interest.

Congressional Concern

At least someone in the Park Service grasped the Concession Policy Act! But one was not enough. Conference chairman Cross contacted Congressman Morris K. Udall after our annual meeting to let him know what the Park Service was doing at Glacier National Park with the law he authored. Mo, already trying to deal with the Verkamp's situation at Grand Canyon, was deeply upset. On March 27, 1968, he wrote a letter to his brother, Secretary of the Interior Stewart L. Udall.

Dear Stew:

Reference is made to the complaint made by the Glacier Park Company concerning the replacement of balconies on the Lake McDonald Lodge in Glacier National Park.

The Glacier people advise me that the National Park Service has demanded that they repair or replace the balconies by the opening of the summer season, or close the facilities to public use in toto, or at least 22 of the 31 rooms. The Glacier people respond that according to the terms of their contract with the government, this work which constitutes a major capital investment is to be done by the Park Service or if performed by the Park Company, they are entitled to a possessory interest in the building to the extent of this new capital investment. The concessioner already has a substantial possessory interest in this building.

The Park Service refuses to do the work, or to acknowledge the company's investment requiring that the company waive its rights under the law and the terms of the contract under threat of closing the facilities.

Public Law 89-249 which I authored specifically provides that the concessioner shall be given a possessory interest representing its interest in the Park, which is not to be terminated without just compensation. The law is clear and Glacier's contract is clear that the company is acting within its rights; and a demand to the company to waive this right under threat of closing is a flagrant violation of the law and its contract with the government.

This is not the first time that concessioners have complained to me that the Director of the National Park Service is violating both the spirit and the terms of the law. This is not consistent with the reasons for the adoption of this law which was intended to encourage private investment in concession facilities in the parks to serve the public by giving the concessioners security for their investments.

The continued disregard of the terms and intent of law is largely negating the purpose of encouraging private investment to serve park visitors.

Sincerely, Morris K. Udall

Secretary Udall discussed the matter with Director Hartzog, and got a surprisingly tough answer in light of Price's earlier defense of the Concession Policy Act: No possessory interest for a concessioner in a government-owned building. In early April Udall telephoned me saying that Director Hartzog felt very strongly about the issue.

I said, "Stew, I feel strongly, too, and if the Park Service insists on its waiver or closing of the facility, I would have no alternative but to sue the National Park Service and you as Secretary of the Interior."

Secretary Udall said, "I'll call you back."

He did, and asked me if I had any objection to the Park Service doing the work.

I said: "Only as a taxpayer, as I believe it is our responsibility, but the Glacier Company could not object to the government making the improvement on their own building."

Although that settled our problems for the moment at Glacier, the Verkamp's conflict continued. On the morning of June 21, 1968, Mo Udall met with Stuart Cross and others from the Conference to discuss the situation. Congressman Udall wrote of their discussions to his brother Stewart that same day:

At the heart of this exchange, of course, is the question of whether the Park Service is following both the letter and

intent of Public Law 89-249. In my judgment, as author of the
act, it is not. It seems to me that the Park Service position on
length of contracts as well as on handling of possessory interest
in government improvements is at variance with the letter and
intent of that act. The situation at Lake McDonald Lodge in
Glacier National Park, about which I wrote you on March
27th, 1968 is a case in point.

Time did not heal these wounds. Eight years later, on July
17, 1974, Mo Udall again wrote to his brother Stew a poignant
outcry against the National Park Service:

> Implementation of Public Law 89-249 has been one of my
> more frustrating experiences since coming to Washington. To
> pass a bill with overwhelming support, send it to the President
> and then get an approval that sounds like a veto, and finally to
> have the administering agency extract from it precisely the
> opposite meaning than that intended by its author has left me a
> little shaken.

This is a good place to ask ourselves a few questions. First,
is this the kind of National Park Service our nation needs?
Second, should the pressure of environmental group lobbyists on an executive agency supercede the law of the land?
Should an elected lawmaker of Mo Udall's stature be forced to
voice such frustration? Should an agency of the federal government be allowed to scurry off in its own direction as an
independent fiefdom? We'll talk this over more thoroughly in
Chapter Nineteen.

Silent Scourge

While this clearly defined situation riveted our attention in
early 1968, an obscure technical report by the U. S. Geological Survey quietly prepared the doom of our Lassen concession. On April 1, 1968, the Survey released *Chaos Crags
Eruptions and Rockfall-Avalanches* by four government geologists. It wasn't published in an accessible journal until 1974.
Had I but known of the report! But I was deep in the throes of

urban problems. Under the heading "Potential Volcanic Hazards," the four authors wrote:

> A potentially more hazardous event than an eruption would be the formation of another rockfall-avalanche at Chaos Crags, or from a newly erupted dome. Such avalanche could becaused by volcanic explosion during the eruption of the dome or by an earthquake unrelated to volcanism. A rockfall avalanche might not be preceded by any warning and an extremely high velocity would surely preclude evacuation in time to prevent loss of life. Because of this, we regard as hazardous, the area within a distance of about five kilometers down-slope from Chaos Crags to the east and to the west. There seems to be no way to warn or protect persons in the path of such an avalanche and we think that future use of the area which might be affected should be restricted.

Manzanita Lake Lodge, the building I had helped build with my own hands, lay directly in the path of this hypothetical and highly improbable catastrophe. The report was to lay dormant for a full year before the growing environmentalist faction in the National Park Service realized what a handy justification it would provide for eliminating our Lassen concession.

A Farewell to HUD

In November of 1968, Richard Milhous Nixon was elected thirty-seventh President of the United States. Throughout the Johnson government, all Democratic appointees from the Secretary of State to the last Assistant Secretary—including me—submitted their resignations. As is traditional, I agreed to stay on during the transition to the new administration. Under law, every outgoing administrator continues to wield authority until the Senate confirms a successor, creating a very awkward situation for everyone. Unconfirmed nominees may show up, hired by the new government as "consultants" in the time-honored manner, but they may not sign papers or take part in any official business until confirmed.

One day in January, 1969, I received a frantic call from a finance employee telling me that $300 million worth of treasury notes for HUD projects were scheduled for sale the following Monday, but new HUD Secretary George Romney had rescinded my obligating authority. Outgoing Secretary Weaver had delegated this vital Secretarial authority to me years earlier and I had routinely handled it. Obviously the incoming Republicans didn't trust the outgoing Democrats! However, in their fear of an embarrassment, the Republicans were about to "shoot themselves in the foot."

Normally the government sells treasury notes on 90-day term and then redeems them by selling new notes—like rolling over a bank loan. I walked to Secretary Romney's office and explained that someone had better authorize these notes or the government would be in $300 million worth of default—an embarrassment I was sure the Nixon administration could do without. Romney authorized me to keep signing for treasury notes but did not restore my decision-making authority to select and approve projects for funding. Then, about two weeks after the Nixon inauguration, the powers that be told me my services were no longer required.

I cleaned out my desk in early February, 1969. On my way out I dropped by Secretary Romney's office to say goodbye. He peered over foot-high stacks of urban renewal and housing files, studying project reports and signing authorizations for the sale of treasury notes. He did not seem too happy with the work load. He said wryly, "Hummel, if I hadn't taken away your authority, you'd have done all this work for me." Somehow I felt less than sympathetic with his plight. And that was the end of my career with the Department of Housing and Urban Development.

It was back to Glacier and concessioning. I was glad to return to the park and its scenic beauty. Al Donau had done a good job at Glacier as his wife Frankie had at Lassen. But none of us knew that the 1968 geologists' report on Chaos Crags—which had heretofore been ignored—had been discovered by the Park Service. Questions of shutting down

Manzanita Lake had been bouncing around the Park Service for several months when one man clearly grasped the implications of this report: Lassen Superintendent Richard Boyer was flabbergasted when he sensed in 1969 that the Manzanita Lake concession might be closed. On April 29, 1969, Boyer appealed to NPS Regional Director Howard Chapman in San Francisco for "a hard and fast administrative decision" on the issue. Boyer put it concisely: "There are only two alternatives: do we go, or do we stay?" Boyer favored staying. The Master Plan, of course, would reflect other views.

United States Natural Resources

As this question simmered quite unknown to us, great changes were brewing in the status of all my concessions. In late August an old friend from the Redding Chamber of Commerce named George Fleharty called me and made an interesting proposal. He wanted me to merge my three concession operations with U. S. Natural Resources (USNR). USNR was a multi-resource firm rejuvenated by a highly-touted "brain trust" in 1969 from a floundering oil and gas exploration and development company first founded in 1926.

Stock analysts favored U.S. Natural Resources. The new management had brought their company's stock price up 21 points to 31⅛ in only six months. The executive roster looked like something out of *Who's Who in American Business* with former vice-presidents of Boise-Cascade, a president of American Standard, consultants for General Electric—talent galore. But what was George Fleharty doing with this outfit?

I had known George Fleharty as staff director of Redding's Chamber of Commerce. He and another local named Russell Olson had joined forces in the early 1960s to form the Shasta Company, a television broadcast outlet in Redding, and parlayed their $100,000 investment into $1,300,000. With the proceeds from their TV station they bought the Ice Follies, which they turned around and sold for $5 million.

But George and Russell then set their sights on Yosemite Park & Curry Company, which suffered declining profitability. At first they tried a merger, but the old-line Curry family and their hand-picked "Stanford Connection" successors would have none of it. So the Shasta Company tendered for Yosemite stock. George and Russell had acquired 395,000 of the 1,045,000 outstanding shares when they ran out of money. Many Curry loyalists declined to sell, even though Shasta's tender offer of $11.00 a share far exceeded the price posted by Dean Witter, which made the market in this stock.

Needless to say, the Yosemite Park & Curry Company directors were not pleased by these "adventurers" and their takeover bid. George tried to make it plain he had no intention of liquidating the firm even if he gained a controlling interest. Nevertheless, in a special meeting on August 5, 1969 at Yosemite George managed to alienate just about every director on the board with his criticisms of management. General discord descended on Yosemite.

There had to be another way to acquire control of Yosemite. George approached newly revitalized U.S. Natural Resources with a proposition to exchange his Yosemite stock for U.S. Natural Resources stock and a position as head of USNR's Recreation Division. They accepted. George nursed great expansion plans for USNR's Recreation Division. And that's why he contacted me one August day in 1969 with a proposal to merge Lassen National Park Company, Mt. McKinley National Park Company and Glacier Park, Inc. into USNR.

This was a serious move. George's deal would mean losing ownership control of my concessions, even though I was promised an employment contract with USNR to continue managing them. But it would provide me with USNR stock—a hot item at that time—and that would provide my family with something my concessions never could: security in the event of my death. Estate taxes from a national park concession leave virtually nothing for anyone to inherit except the business—and not every descendant of a concessioner will be constitutionally or temperamentally fit to respond not only to the operation but also to the politics that accompany the contract. Most importantly, a concessions contract is not very liquid when cash for taxes is needed. I decided to do it.

We made our deal on the Lassen and McKinley Companies, but stalled on the Glacier operation. USNR was beginning to run into difficulties caused by their rapid expansion and weakness in operational talent. USNR said no to the Glacier deal. But they wanted me to sign a five-year employment agreement to manage the Lassen/McKinley Companies and to provide executive services for Yosemite and other USNR subsidiaries. As part of the package I was to reorganize Yosemite Park & Curry Company as soon as USNR gained control. I accepted this task with some trepidation: many personal friends, including Conference chairman Stuart Cross, would be subject to my business decisions, always an uncomfortable position.

U.S. Natural Resources president Robert L. Katz wrote the Yosemite Park & Curry Co. board on December 16, 1969, advising them of the Shasta Company acquisition. Yosemite director Eric Stanford realized that USNR's entry into the picture lent substantial muscle to George's ambitions. He appointed a committee to propose ways and means of cooperation with the new thirty-eight percent minority stockholder. The committee realistically recommended a merger as the best way of protecting Yosemite's minority stockholders, pointing out that U.S. Natural Resources very likely had the leverage to acquire fifty-one percent of Yosemite's stock.

In January 1970 six of Yosemite Park and Curry Company's fifteen directors were elected through U.S. Natural Resources stock. I was one of them.

15

The Times, They Are A'Changin'

THE EARLY 1970s were years of ferment in the national parks. Overriding social changes shook park policy to its roots—we could feel the impact of war in Vietnam with its noisy dissent and divisiveness, the growing counterculture, the advent of the affluent society with its mass automobile traffic, and the growing cult of wildernism.

The Nixon Interior Department brought wealthy environmentalist Nathaniel Reed to power as Assistant Secretary for Fish and Wildlife and Parks—Director Hartzog's boss. We thought it was the worst of times. But that was yet to come.

Among the problematic legacies of the late sixties, the National Environmental Policy Act of 1969 (NEPA) stood out. NEPA is the Sherman Act of environmental law, a seminal enactment that strengthened the hand of Congress in overseeing agency actions with adverse environmental effects. As legal scholar William H. Rodgers, Jr. complained in his textbook *Environmental Law*, NEPA "sets forth a ringing and vague statement of purposes." It also imposed the exceedingly clear requirement that any federal action potentially affecting the environment first undergo the scrutiny of an Environmental Impact Statement (EIS). In the hands of zealous environmental lawyers the EIS was to become the perfect tool for obstructing economic development generally and a marvelous weapon for delaying national park projects specifically.

Most ominously, without fanfare or public notice, a new paragraph was inserted in the Park Service Administrative Policy Manual in 1970:

Sound park management in these instances requires that the national parks and monuments be preserved in their natural condition. In the long range, this management objective is best achieved when exploitative and private uses are eliminated by acquisition of the property by the federal government.

It was, as yet, not quite a statement that all concessions and public access be eliminated from the parks, but the shape of the future stood there for all to see.

At least one ray of light shone through the gathering murk. In June of 1970, Wayne Aspinall's Public Land Law Review Commission released its final report, *One Third of the Nation's Land*. The three pages it devoted to federal concession policies for the most part reinforced the Mather-Albright principles. "We approve the principle of the 1965 Act," wrote the commission, "and believe that Congress should extend it so that it is applicable to other Federal areas. . . ."

Specifically, the report recommended that:

1. A range of services should be available to the public.

2. The Federal Government should finance and build public accommodations in areas that do not attract private capital and lease them to private concessioners.

3. Increased emphasis and special attention should be directed to the credit requirements of Federal concessioners.

4. The security of investment offered under the Concessioners' Act of 1965 should be extended. The full text of this recommendation touched our Glacier problem directly:

> The 1965 Act recognizes a possessory interest in facilities constructed by concessioners and provides for compensation for their values upon termination of the concession agreement. We believe that this policy is sound and should be uniformly applicable. However, we understand that the National Park Service does not recognize such an interest where the concessioner improves or adds to government-built facilities. Since all such concessioner improvements become the legal property of the United States, we see no reason for any such distinction and believe that the concessioners in such cases should be recognized as having a compensable interest.

The commission's fifth and final recommendation: Concession privileges should be priced so that rates charged the public for concession services can be kept at a reasonable level, and quality service to the public can be sustained.

Yosemite Problems

The Yosemite Park & Curry Company board of directors meeting on June 26, 1970, was not so encouraging. U.S. Natural Resources shares had suffered a substantial drop in market price and Yosemite's anticipated earnings were down. Merger was no longer feasible. In this difficult situation U.S. Natural Resources demanded evidence of having working control of Yosemite operations. The Stanford Connection had no choice: like it or not, Yosemite Park and Curry Company's fate was now tied to USNR. YPCC president Stuart Cross acquiesced in the election of USNR president Robert Katz as chairman of their board and explicitly recognized USNR's control position.

Katz demanded that I be given operation management power, and the board elected me chairman of a newly created executive committee with members John Curry, Stuart Cross and Eric Stanford.

After this power shift, which was not without acrimony, the board took up an important visitor policy problem: automobile traffic into the magnificent scenic valley had swollen to such proportions that existing roads, parking lots and campgrounds congested. The quality of visitor experience had definitely declined. Some type of voluntary group transport system within the valley was the best available solution—it would spread out visitor density, but not deny visitor access. The board approved Chairman Katz's proposal that $125,000 be allocated to establish a shuttle bus system on an experimental basis for 10 weeks, beginning July 15, 1970. We understood that the Park Service might not be able to reimburse the company. We hoped it would significantly reduce automobile traffic in the valley by 1972—by visitor choice, not government fiat. H.L. "Spud" Bill, deputy director of the National Park Service, was delighted when we informed him of the project. He told the board that the Service had been unable to pry a supplemental budget out of Congress for such a system. Mr. Bill and Director Hartzog agreed to inaugurate the system on July 9 and 10.

But now I faced the task of reorganizing the Yosemite operation. Immediately after the board meeting I made three visits to the major concession sites, talking with Yosemite Park & Curry Company top management. I uncovered more problems than I expected.

Finance: A thorough review of the company's financial position revealed its inability to raise further capital and the need for tight cash control. The company's June statement revealed no working capital. Cash projections through September 30, the end of the summer season, would fall $300,000 short of 1969 results, insufficient to meet winter expenses.

Visitors: Arrivals, house counts and meals served had dropped substantially during the past two years, a result in part of increasing counterculture settlement in the park: The average park visitor did not enjoy being confronted by the youth movement asserting its liberty at the price of everyone else's.

Staffing: I was not surprised to find most of the units overstaffed. Compared with Glacier National Park, Yosemite had a considerably higher employee-per-room ratio. Then too, Yosemite employees worked a five-day week, Glacier six. Yosemite provided free meals in lieu of 50 cents per hour employee meal charge—with employees working five days and getting food for seven, costs were out of line. Yosemite employees did not consider food part of their remuneration, and often took more than they required, which went into garbage cans. I suggested that we increase wages and give them discounts at our cafeterias.

Personnel: I found that the personnel department had no recruitment program, did not use the college campus applicant system, but hired only by personal interview at Yosemite. At some other period in American history this casual approach might have yielded adequate service to the public, but during the rise of the counterculture few but drifters and dropouts came to Yosemite asking for jobs. Employee quality was far below the standards required for good service to the public.

Supervision: Yosemite employees also had a complete lack of supervision. Managers stayed in their offices and seldom visited their operations. A weekly breakfast provided the only contact between top management and unit managers. I attended one and felt it more a social gathering than management seminar.

Warehousing: Practically everything came to a central warehouse for redelivery to the operating units. Many supplies could have been delivered directly to the user. No one had standardized purchasing procedures; each unit ordered whatever it preferred—this brand of cleanser and that, a dozen different kinds of disinfectant—with no thought to discounts on bulk orders or other economies of scale.

I also had an unpleasant legacy to deal with. On July 4, 1970—the year I came to Yosemite—the growing counterculture presence in the park had erupted into violence. It was not altogether unexpected, for young people had been gathering in Stoneman Meadow adjoining Camp 14 near Curry Village to rap, sing, smoke marijuana, go naked, engage in sex openly, and generally do as they pleased. The participants were not traditional college students out on a spree: known dissident and radical leaders were clearly identified in the more "laid-back" counterculture milieu. This island of authority-flaunting youth offended park users and also resulted in considerable destruction to the meadow area.

Over 1970's Memorial Day weekend, the National Park Service had one evening attempted to clear the meadow with a small force of rangers. They were violently driven out by a jeering mob egged on by hard-core anti-establishment agitators.

In preparation for the Independence Day weekend, the Park Service announced its policy of closing the meadow to public use every evening at 7:00 p.m., posting signs to that effect. On the Thursday and Friday evenings just before the holiday, rangers succeeded in clearing the meadow with little trouble. But on Saturday night a far larger number gathered, perhaps as many as four or five hundred, obviously bent on confrontation. Shortly after 7:00 p.m. the Park Service moved in with 12 or 15 rangers mounted on horseback. The mob met them with stones, chunks of wood, empty bottles and other objects.

After a brief skirmish the rangers retreated. The young rioters threw up barricades blocking all access to the upper end of Yosemite Valley. On advice of FBI agents assigned to augment the ranger force, the Park Service sent an emergency call to the police departments of communities as far away as Fresno. More than a hundred law enforcement officers responded. Sometime after midnight they joined forces and moved back into the meadow, taking into custody over a hundred persons charged with various offenses.

By morning the Park Service again had control of Yosemite Valley. A force of United States marshalls and Border Patrol officers remained in the park. The only personal injury reported involved the Sheriff of Mariposa County who made a wrong turn and ended up in the middle of the troublemakers. He was beaten and his car burned.

The riot lingered in aftermath. The bad press was incredible. The bureaucracy reacted with unaccustomed swiftness: Immediately training, equipment, and protective philosophy was restructured. Law enforcement rangers shed hard-nosed attitudes, grew mustaches and long hair, led "rap sessions" to build rapport, but simultaneously learned to use clubs, pistols and Mace. Congressional action was likewise swift: new appropriations infused Yosemite with professionals experienced in dealing with social change. A mall replaced a stretch of parking lot in front of the Yosemite Village complex to provide more interpretive programs and encourage visitor use. New emphasis was placed on walking, bicycling and busing in the valley. It came none too soon. Hundreds of unruly individuals invaded Yosemite, ignoring all park regulations and the rights of other visitors. Some blocked the entrance to Yosemite Village store to play their guitars. Others stretched out to sleep on the boardwalk. Others ate their lunches there, harassing park visitors trying to get by. The more defiant pilfered the store. They called stealing "ripping off" and bragged about it. We had five-hundred theft arrests in a single week.

This disorderly conduct carried over into the restaurants and cafeterias. The more timid came in to scavenge food scraps. The bold waited for visitors to get up for a second cup of coffee and then stole the food right off their plates! This was beyond toleration. I ordered professional security forces into all trouble spots. The Park Service objected that uniformed security guards with badges gave the public the wrong impression in a national park.

"If you assign rangers to enforce the rules, we'll withdraw our guards," I replied, "but we have to protect both our own property and the rights of our clients."

The Park Service did not want to send in their personnel. They consented to our security officers.

The campgrounds also suffered from this influx of counter-culture transients. Theft became rampant. Law-abiding visitors could not leave anything in their cars. Yosemite resembled an urban jungle while they held sway. The Park Service partially solved the problem by assigning a particular campground to counterculture "do your own thing" use at fifty cents a night. The fee was seldom collected, for the Park Service feared the assaults that became common when they attempted to collect fees. The "hippie campground" became a no-man's-land. Dope smoking and psychedelics were the order of the day. Panhandling grew rife throughout the park—a fact visitors found highly objectionable.

It was a summer of confusion and noise, with Hells Angels cruising back and forth on their motorcycles, riding down the footpaths and bridle trails, waving to hippies in their old bread trucks. One segment of this group enjoyed drinking wine on Centennial Bridge, another invaded the meadows, yet another panhandled in front of the stores. In 1972 arsonists burned down the government stables and then burned

Camp Curry's dining room on Easter Sunday, 1973. The disorder continued a long time. But the national parks were set aside for everyone, and no move was made to exclude even the anti-social and criminal.

The Master Plan

While this cauldron bubbled, I stepped into the Yosemite Master Plan Study Team—but only as an observer to the process. The team had been meeting, as I gathered, for something over a year. They faced intractable problems. Automobile traffic and social unrest refused to let up. The task seemed impossible. How could use and preservation coexist in this atmosphere? The Master Plan team had to answer that question successfully.

NPS Director George Hartzog knew full well the travails with which this crew struggled. He sent them a message of greeting to help continue their efforts. Hartzog urged them to consider all possible alternatives in solving Yosemite's visitor problems, especially where significant patterns of public use were involved and important resource values were at stake. He stressed the needs of society for outdoor recreation of the type available in national parks. He also emphasized America's burgeoning population, its growing leisure time, and the rise of the youth society. He concluded that the Yosemite of tomorrow must be responsive to these needs and pressures. His message was long on ideals and notably short on practical advice.

The Master Plan team should have been qualified to render sound advice: Team captain Ronald Mortimore from the Park Service Western Service Center in San Francisco brought long planning experience to the group. Dr. Morgan Harris, professor of zoology, University of California at Berkeley, understood ecosystems as well as any professional in the field. Laurence C. Hadley, superintendent at Yosemite offered veteran management talent. Yosemite Park & Curry Company president Stuart Cross, vice-president Robert Maynard, and honorary chairman Hilmer Oehlmann ably represented the park's major concession. Ansel Adams of Best Studios—the world-renowned photographer and conservationist—spoke for the park's small concessioners. The National Park Service sent its Western Regional director, its deputy director and its wilderness coordinator John Henneberger.

This Master Plan team was to struggle with the problem for five years and see only one solution: remove all cars from Yosemite Valley. Their initial proposal would call for immense government expenditures in removing most administrative functions and employee housing from the valley. Realizing this was unlikely, they would then proposed an interim measure: Parking areas outside the valley would concentrate visitors for mass transport to the scenic attractions. Big Meadow was the favored concentration site with Illilouette Ridge a distant second. Neither plan had a prayer of acceptance. The Illilouette Ridge site required construction of a gondola to transfer visitors down to the valley floor. The Big Meadow solution required a mechanical transportation system such as a monorail or a vast fleet of buses. Both ideas were politically and financially impractical.

Later they were to propose to allow automobiles as far as Bridalveil Falls and stop them there. This, however, would have required a four-story parking building in the lower end of the valley. Impossible again.

Seeing that all these solutions were expensive and far in the future, Superintendent Hadley would propose a one-way road system combined with a greatly expanded shuttle bus system. It would cost little and eliminate most private car and truck traffic in the eastern half of the valley. The Park Service would adopt the Hadley plan in 1971. Unfortunately, the new traffic pattern was to eliminate a connecting road between Curry Village and The Awhahnee, resulting in great confusion and terrible access problems.

Hartzog's message emphasized the need for High Sierra camps or chalets in backcountry and Wilderness areas, a concept clearly expressed in a memorandum dated June 18, 1969, from Interior Secretary Wally Hickel. The team was also to consider such camps and chalets to lie within a short walking distance of automobile trail-head points.

In 1974 the team's final report would be completed and submitted to the public in three separate hearings. Ninety days of Comment Period was to provide more opportunity for public suggestions and changes. It was this Master Plan that would in late 1974 be approved by Park Service Director Ronald Walker and sent on to Assistant Secretary Nathaniel Reed, who was to throw it out on December 13 for permitting too much use. Reed would sneer that it sounded as though the concessioners had written it, which to an environmental extremist seems the vilest of insults.

But nobody knew any of this on July 9, 1970, so these dedicated planners set to work thinking their efforts meant something. Not long after the Master Plan team began its arduous task I began my reorganization of Yosemite Park and Curry Company at a board meeting on July 20, 1970.

I recommended that management's lines of authority be clarified and enforced. I recommended that each unit manager prepare a personal budget supported by schedules to justify staffing levels and stick to it. I recommended a personnel pool giving each hotel, store and food service operation a basic staff complement with a reserve pool to draw from during peak visitor days. I recommended an advertising plan directed to those likely to patronize Yosemite's concessions. I recommended inventory control, tighter management of the pension fund, and absolute accountability of all managers for their performance. I made few friends that day.

It had the desired result, however. By December 1971 net profits before taxes increased by $1,500,900 as contrasted with $492,900 in 1970. Then, the fortunes of U.S. Natural Resources began a serious decline. It was headed for one of the more spectacular failures in American business annals. George Fleharty must have seen it coming, for he became increasingly disgruntled with USNR and finally convinced them to sell him the Mount McKinley National Park Company. As soon as the papers were drawn up in

1972 George departed for Alaska to operate the concession himself.

This left only Yosemite Company and Lassen in the U.S. Natural Resources Recreation Division. When the decline in USNR's fortunes became unmistakable to all in early 1972, their board replaced president Bob Katz with John Del Favero. Part of USNR's public relations problem lay in the fact that it could not file consolidated financial reports with Yosemite Park and Curry Company because they did not own the requisite eighty percent of its stock. The board of U.S. Natural Resources instructed Del Favero to either acquire the necessary stock or sell the company. He duly tendered for additional Yosemite stock and succeeded in acquiring a controlling 52 percent interest. Now USNR secured its management control: At a special meeting held at Wawona on June 25, 1972, I was elected chairman of the board and chief executive officer of Yosemite Park and Curry Company.

The Conference Again

In March of 1972, the Conference of National Park Concessioners came to occupy a central position in my life once more. At their annual meeting in Williamsburg, Virginia, I was elected chairman again.

The work sessions of the meeting brought the long-stalled NPS Wilderness Study Plan program to the fore. Director George Hartzog told the Conference, "The Park Service is developing new vistas. Change is the order of the day. The visitor load in the parks is growing beyond all expectations. Overcrowding has become a regular feature in the parks. Great pressure will be put on us all in the weeks and months ahead. And that means that we must take our policy responsibilities seriously. In particular, I consider environmental policies to be one of the concessioner's major responsibilities. You should handle those responsibilities with pride."

Hartzog then rambled on about "implementation of the Secretary's directives," and "improvement in the quality of the park experience," and "preserving a proud heritage for posterity." In concrete terms, he admitted for the first time to the Conference that the Park Service intended to restrict visitor use and eliminate automobiles from the parks as a partial solution to their problems. Now the Interior Department and Park Service policy that we had all suspected for years was being openly stated: Preservation would supercede public use and enjoyment.

I responded as chairman of the Conference: "Director Hartzog, we concur with your remark that change is the order of the day. That doubles the importance of keeping open lines of communication. We're concerned about change, perhaps more than you are. Private investment, once made, loses some of the flexibility to change and change can alter services and cause losses."

Hartzog listened, knowing where I was leading.

I went on. "We've seen the statistics on overcrowding. But we often see crowding on specific days and in specific locations exaggerated to look like total over-crowding. I don't believe the parks are overcrowded. Excluding visitors is not the answer to peak-time problems that do exist. I think we should explore other approaches—extensions of the season, more entrances to the parks to avoid back-tracking, opening new areas in the parks, emphasis on less visited parks. George, I request that concessioners be given an opportunity to participate in decisions being made by the National Park Service which affect our responsibilities."

Director Hartzog responded: "Don, I recognize that the parks are not actually overcrowded. But public perception is quite the opposite. You know the rule of government: Government deals only with *perceived crises*. I've been subject to great pressure from the wilderness groups ever since the Wilderness Act of 1964 was passed. You talk about having an opportunity to participate in the decision-making process. At all the hearings we've held since 1964 the wilderness groups were present en masse and made presentations. But the hearings lacked other interested organizations such as the Hotel Association, the automobile clubs, and chambers of commerce. The groups who represent the majority of visitors to the national parks didn't show up."

Every concessioner in the room heard Hartzog's unspoken reproach: You weren't there, either.

We all had the ominous feeling that bad times lay ahead.

The Reed Memo

In June 1972, Assistant Secretary Nathaniel Reed issued a memo to NPS Director Hartzog defining criteria to be followed in determining an area's suitability for Wilderness designation. The memo specified conditions that were sufficient or insufficient to exclude an area from Wilderness consideration.

1. Areas should not be excluded from Wilderness designation solely because established or proposed management practices require the use of tools, equipment, or structures [forbidden by the Wilderness Act] if these practices are necessary for the health and safety of Wilderness travelers, or the protection of the Wilderness area.

2. Areas that otherwise qualify for Wilderness will not be excluded because they contain unimproved roads created by vehicles repeatedly travelling over the same course, structures, installations, or utility lines, which can be and would be removed upon designation as Wilderness.

3. Areas which presently qualify for Wilderness designation but which will be needed at some future date for specific purposes consistent with the purpose for which the National Park was originally created, and fully described in an approved conceptual plan, should not be proposed for Wilderness designation.

Even this memo, which clearly favored Wilderness designation, brought howls of protest from environmental leaders. The Wilderness Society published an article in its magazine *Living Wilderness* arguing that these criteria were too stringent and merely intended to disqualify areas from classification as Wilderness. The environmentalists were honing their central tactical principle: No victory is ever big enough.

The National Park Centennial Commission

The end of the year 1972 was a time of revelation. The political cunning of environmentalists was brought home to me most powerfully, and through a most unexpected avenue: the centennial celebration of the national parks. On July 10, 1970, President Nixon signed Public Law 91-332 creating the National Park Centennial Commission in commemoration of the establishment of Yellowstone in 1872.

The President and U.S. Senate appointed a thirty-five-member advisory committee to the commission to suggest policy directions by 1972 for the second century of national parks in America. The Conservation Foundation was selected to assign thirty others to five task forces which would make concrete recommendations for future park policy. The Conservation Foundation, a Washington, D.C. environmental group, came to this position of power through the good graces of NPS Director Hartzog. The selection of this environmental organization automatically set the tone of the interim report, *National Parks for the Future: An Appraisal of the National Parks as they Begin Their Second Century in Changing America*, which would be available to the five task forces prior to their symposium to be held November 13 through 15, 1972, in Yosemite. Preservation would be the dominant theme. Limitation of visitor facilities would be the means to reduce visitor use. And it's all there in black and white.

As head of the Conference of National Park Concessioners, I was appointed to the advisory committee. And here the revelation came. This appointment showed me the deceitful and unscrupulous nature of environmentalist leaders in no uncertain terms: The Conservation Foundation never notified me of my membership or gave me any opportunity to participate! They knew I was a concessioner and in their minds that blackballed me from the club. I had been a commission advisory committee member for nearly two years before I discovered that fact, and then I found out by reading my name on a draft of *National Parks for the Future*. When the revelation came, I asked that my name be deleted from the committee roster. I did not want my name associated with the Conservation Foundation's recommendations. Even this request was denied.

I also thought that the concession viewpoint ought to find some representation in this rigged commission. Thus I requested an opportunity to speak at the plenary session of the upcoming Yosemite Symposium. It seemed the appropriate forum for a belated message. The symposium would unveil the reports of the five task forces and hear panels of other invited participants. Among these "other invited participants" were concessioners—invited for the first time, of course, after all the decisions had been fashioned. What cunning manipulation of national park policy! What consummate skill in coopting power! You have to hand it to the environmentalists. Or they'll take it from you.

Conservation Foundation powers-that-be promised me thirty minutes at the plenary session. They later reduced it to twenty minutes. I prepared my remarks carefully, thinking the Conservation Foundation would keep its word. Then came November and the Symposium. It was another revelation.

Symposium In Yosemite

Occasional autumn showers descended upon Yosemite along with the environmentalists. It was not one of the valley's more serene moments as we experienced one downpour after another.

The Conservation Foundation report *National Parks for the Future* was available in quantity. A disclaimer at the front of the book admitted that the report's recommendations were not those of the Centennial Commission:

> The commentary and conclusions, while formed by the findings of all who contributed to the work, are *the Foundation's own.* They do not necessarily reflect the positions held by participants, or consultants—some of whose contributions are set forth separately in the remaining sections of the volume. (Emphasis added.)

The book's overriding theme was "concessioners too often bring people to the parks for the wrong reasons." From this Godlike stance, the authors handed down the gospel:

> If the parks are to be meaningful to all Americans, everyone must feel welcome. For many visitors this requires a somewhat civilized base of operations; a dry room, a bed with sheets, a recognizable kitchen or public eating place. At the same time, resort accommodations and shopping centers do not belong in national parks. Nor do camping and picnic areas which are designed and congested to bring urban scenes with urban problems.
>
> There was a time when concessions were clearly needed to provide basic services for accommodations, food and the like. Today, however, the concessioner has a disproportionate influence on planning and policy-making for the national parks. His objective is to generate as much demand for the services he provides as is possible.
>
> We recommend that a long-term program of concessioner replacement be started on a pilot basis and proceed according to an equitable timetable until the parks are free of major private entrepreneurs and the public has regained full control of facilities planning and operations.

Then came the Symposium proper. NPS Director George Hartzog called me over to sit beside him and the task force reports were delivered to the Symposium by panels of chairmen. We were to see all five task forces comment on the concession system adversely, and three of them recommend removal of concessions and/or government acquisition of concession facilities. It is interesting that environmentalists dominated *every* task force, and *no* concessioner was named to any task force.

The panel on "The Role of National Park Concessioners" reported that one task force categorically recommended moving all facilities outside the parks; another advocated removal when practical; and a third, no facilities be left in the parks other than those essential. The report contained this caveat:

In determining the practicality of removal of visitor facilities from the parks, consideration should be given to: (1) geographic and aesthetic implications of alternate locations; (2) practicality of transporting huge numbers during primary entrance and exodus periods; (3) impact on visitor experience; (4) effect of scheduled transportation approach on individual's park experience; (5) insure against proliferation of undesirable development on the periphery; (6) inequalities of exclusion which might result; and (7) review of economic imperatives of concessioners and permitting of democratization of services and facilities.

It was nice of them to remember economic imperatives while democratizing our concessions. What a marvelous word that is, "democratization." It almost sounds like it means something. As time went on, I began to realize what.

Jack Strain, Director of the Nebraska Bureau of State Parks, and the chairman of a panel on "Facilities in the National Parks" dissented from this majority view:

With great respect and admiration for the purist and the highly skilled, whatever his special interest, but with a greater concern for the average American, we concluded that visitor accommodations are a legitimate part of the national park scene and make an essential contribution to the quality of the visit of most Americans.

We oppose the banishment of visitor accommodations outside park boundaries on these grounds: (a) there is no effective means of quality control; and (b) without control, high quality environment outside the park equal to much of that within the area may suffer disproportionally.

He went on to say that the concessioner, to survive, must furnish desirable goods and services to make a profit. To resolve this and insure control, the panel endorsed public ownership with private operation with a subsidy, if necessary.

The task force panel on the "National Park System and Urban America" also dissented:

Shall the National Park Service permit itself to become a "wilderness land bank" increasing concern with preservation and conservation and oriented only to the accommodation of people to the extent that they don't threaten the land? Or shall the Park Service look first to the needs of Americans and then place parks and recreation services to meet those needs, viewing the land as a resource?

The wilderness in current National Park Service terms is neither available nor accessible to most of the urban population. Transportation is inadequate, education inappropriate and interpretation falls far short of providing the basis for identification among minorities of color and women.

In addition, we are aware of a certain insular tendency on the part of the National Park Service to deal more closely and comfortably with those elements of society who are most sympathetic to the natural preservationist preference and supportive of its basic management approach. These individuals, as Roger Revelle has observed, are "more concerned with the enhancement of the resources than with the needs of the people."

We think the full range of consumer preference needs representation on the National Advisory Board.

After all the discussions concerning the problems of concession operations and the recommendations for removal from the parks, the Chairman called on me to make my presentation. He had conveniently left no time for my remarks—the meeting was now scheduled to recess for a sightseeing tour of Yosemite (the weather had cleared enough after a night of intermittent downpour to see up to the valley rim).

The crowd was restless, so I stood up at my seat and did not go the speaker's podium. I asked everybody to remain seated, as I would take only two minutes of their time. I announced that I had filed a prepared statement for those who might be interested in the concessioner's point of view which had not been expressed to this symposium. I said, "I have listened with interest to the recommendations to remove all visitor accommodations from the park so as to restore the pristine nature of the natural features without discussion of this effect on the park visitor."

I reminded them that concessioners had not been included on any task force, although they were probably in the best position to report how the park visitor felt about having accommodations for his convenience and use removed from the parks. Reminding them of the weather, I said: "I am curious and would like a show of hands of the participants who slept out in the open last night, rather than in the concessioner's facilities?"

A gasp went up, then loud laughter and tumultuous applause. Startled, Director Hartzog nearly leaped out of the chair next to me. He turned around and said to the man sitting behind him, "If you're going to clap that loud, warn me—I thought I had been shot!"

Not one of those armchair environmentalists had raised a hand!

So concessioners' views on removing visitor facilities from the parks were not only excluded from all task force reports, but they were also conveniently squeezed out of the symposium by time constraints. The statement I filed for the record never appeared in the commission's final report. The Conservation Foundation knows all about democratization.

Parks are for People

For the record, here is what the Conservation Foundation didn't want the public to know—excerpts from my written statement.:

> It is my understanding that the charge to this symposium is to develop a statement of philosophy, long-range objectives and goals, and means of implementation for the national park system to enable it to better serve the needs of all American people.
>
> I stress the word *all* because the parks are for people—all of the people. They are not just for the ardent preservationists who would remove them from most of the people by expanded

wilderness designations and by restricted access; not for just those who would use them as laboratories for scientific investigations; not just for those who have the physical stamina to backpack, ride a horse, to hike; but also for those who, by reason of age, physical handicap, or temperament, can enjoy the grandeur from the seat of a sightseeing bus or from a chair on a lodge veranda.

Nor have these areas been set aside for the affluent only but also for the poor and the minorities among us, for otherwise the system would not be truly national. Each segment of our population has a right to have its needs recognized, for we are dealing here in large measure with the natural, historical and cultural heritage of our entire nation.

We are under directive to preserve these resources for the use and enjoyment of all generations, and that means present as well as future. The dichotomy of preservation and use has been debated and fought over since the passage of the basic act. This debate will continue long after our departure, for it is in the day-to-day struggle for balance between these potentially antagonistic concepts that solutions lie.

We are not acting responsibly if we project fearful speculations about the year 2000 which prevent today's generation from enjoying the parks in a manner that does not harm the resource.

Many of the solutions you have proposed suggest that the parks serve fewer, not more, people.

I submit that those who propose quotas, limitation of access and wholesale removal of visitor facilities might prevail in an autocratic system but they must not prevail in a democracy unless there is no other way to conserve the resource. The nation's heritage should be available to as diverse and wide a population as possible consistent with preservation.

The only reason for a concession system is to serve the needs of people. People need food and drink and shelter for the night. Removing these services from the park creates more problems than it solves and materially reduces the quality of the experience for a very large proportion of present park visitors. Last year concessioners provided services to 117 million visitors.

Areas like Yellowstone, Yosemite, McKinley, Grand Canyon and others cover vast land masses, with park features located at great distances from each other and from park boundaries. Much of the land inside our parks is no different in character than large areas outside. The location of the park boundary line in many instances was established by historical accident or log-rolling legislative compromise. The boundaries include many acres of land which, of themselves, do not call for the same degree of preservation as the features for which the park was created. The development of concession facilities on these lands to help visitors enjoy their parks does not and should not impinge on the scenic values sought to be preserved.

The approach of some task forces appears to be concerned with the value of the land and the physical resources, and not with the needs and enjoyment of people. Even in the founding days of the park system, when men were more rugged and used to a minimum of physical comforts, Steve Mather made his famous comment, "Scenery is a hollow enjoyment to a tourist who sets out in the morning after an indigestible breakfast and a fitful sleep on an impossible bed."

Today, as we search for ways to allow more and more of our citizens who are more and more used to creature comforts to enjoy their parks, it is proposed to deny them the right to spend a night in their national parks unless they camp. This is rank discrimination against that vast majority of park visitors who have no disposition to camp.

Why is it meritorious to sleep under a tent but not under a lodge or cabin roof? You attempt to justify this injustice on the basis of damage to the resource. I believe a good case can be made that the controlled atmosphere of a stable concession-operated facility causes far less damage than the helter-skelter, repetitious erection and dismantling of thousands of tents where ever the camper sees fit.

Do not be misled, nature is not as fragile as some would have you believe. Yosemite has been singled out in horror as the epitome of an over-crowded, smog-ridden, desecrated area. While you are here, look at it. It has absorbed the living and the trampling of millions of men's feet for a century. It is still blessed with green meadows, beautiful forests, clear and sparkling streams, waterfalls and incomparable granite cliffs.

One old-timer, the late Ansel Adams, has said it is more beautiful today than it was a half century ago.

Serving people where they want to be decreases the need for expanded transportation systems which in themselves impinge on park values. Can you imagine the congestion and pandemonium of 30 to 40 thousand people all starting out at Mariposa in buses to get into Yosemite Valley between seven and nine in the morning, and all leaving the park at the close of the day? Have you ever witnessed a Disneyland exodus? Is that the atmosphere you want to create for the national park visitor?

Anyone familiar with the history of concessions is aware just how unsatisfactory the freewheeling competitive system was in early parks: harassment of tourists, price gouging, poor quality service, and the complete absence of certain desirable but uneconomic services. The Park Service carefully and deliberately replaced these chaotic multiple concessions by a single controlled concessioner who was required to provide balanced service at reasonable rates. Are we willing to go back to the old unsatisfactory system by placing it at the park entrance rather than in the park?

My real concern with the recommendations is the preeminence given the protection of physical values as opposed to people enjoyment. In this park the Master Plan proposes to set aside as wilderness 80 percent of the land for less than one percent of the visitors. This is bad enough, but now you propose to exclude the other 99 percent except on a day-use basis.

The role of the concessioner, whoever he may be or whoever owns the facilities, is to make the parks available to the ordinary American on terms that permit him maximum enjoyment and that leave the park intact for future generations. To dismantle concessions is to deny the vast majority of Americans the right to use and enjoy their national parks.

Unfortunately, these remarks remain as timely today as they were then. The Yosemite Symposium was not the end-all, however. The final report by the National Park Centennial Commission had some merits. Titled *Preserving A Heritage*, it reaffirmed the parks' use/preservation duality in the following words:

In keeping with the 1916 Organic Act and the tradition of the Service, the Commission strongly recommends that the dual purpose of preservation and use be maintained as the dynamic principles undergirding the National Park System.

It is clear that Congress intended the national parks to be used by people to the fullest extent possible without impairing those features for which the parks were established to protect.

The Commission recommended that when a needed service is being well performed by a private concession, it be continued and upgraded; that when the facilities and services had outlived their usefulness, they be eliminated. They also recommended greater citizen participation and the creation of a Citizens Advisory Commission.

The report called attention to the fact that the establishment of Wilderness designation in the parks provides for a higher level of preservation than the 1916 Act establishing the National Park Service:

> Members of the Commission realize that many of their fellow conservationists feel that no development would be best. This is not realistic. The public will demand access to these areas and access requires certain improvements or development, if for no other reason than public safety. In addition, certain types of creature comfort are demanded and must be built. Excluding the public because they might cause damage is unacceptable.

Democracy and Democratization

The Park Service soon proved its intent to democratize the national parks for wilderness purists. They proved their intent to ignore the law as Congressman Udall had complained before: they selectively adopted only those recommendations of the Centennial Commission that suited their increasingly politicized wilderness constituency. The Wilderness Act of 1964 would be enforced to the hilt. The Concession Policy Act of 1965 would be ignored. The national park visitor was to be excluded; the majority ignored. The Park Service was going to democratize America right out of its parks. After all, a group of experts clearly stated in the government publication *Wilderness Users in the Pacific Northwest* the classic rule of environmentalist democratization: "Wilderness Management—Not a Majority Vote Problem." Democracy is only for environmentalists. They'll democratize everybody else.

And now the Park Service set out on a program to destroy concessions without public hearings and without approval of the Interior and Insular Affairs Committee. They joined the environmentalists who intended to steal the national parks. They increasingly ignored the rights of the people. And that is the sorrowful story of the next chapter.

16

Our Park Service As Enemy

A S THE DECADE of the 1970s developed, the environmentalists grew bolder and their influence on the Park Service grew more evident. In time, employees and volunteer leaders of environmental organizations were to find positions within the Interior Department, spreading their ideological gospel of environmental purism into an already rigid system.. The years from 1973 to 1975 saw the overt change of the Park Service from guardian of the Mather-Albright principles to betrayers of the public in the name of political and social change.

The changes did not pass over Yosemite: At the annual board meeting on January 15, 1973, I was elected to three simultaneous positions: president of Yosemite Park and Curry Company, chairman of the board, and chief executive officer. Shortly thereafter I received a visit from a Mr. Sidney Sheinberg, president of Music Corporation of America, a Los Angeles-based entertainment conglomerate known today simply as MCA. Among its other holdings, MCA owned Universal Studios. Mr. Sheinberg brought with him Jay Stein, head of their recreation division. They had business in mind: U.S. Natural Resources, was suffering severe financial troubles and MCA decided to purchase the Yosemite concession. Sheinberg told me negotiations were under way and that he had also spoken with National Park Service officials who advised that the company was well-run and at the peak of its profits. The tight management policy I designed had increased after-tax profits from $232,000, to $1,500,000.

Sheinberg and Stein wanted to know what I thought of the company. I told them it was the largest single concession in the national parks, even larger than Yellowstone Park Company. Our valley operation had a substantial physical plant that brought visitors a complete range of lodgings in 1,498 units from luxury rooms in The Ahwahnee to rock-bottom-price tents. It included 3 restaurants, 2 cafeterias, a hotel dining room, a seven-lift garage, 2 service stations with a total of 15 pumps, 7 gift shops, 2 grocery stores, a delicatessen, a bank, a skating rink, 3 swimming pools, a pitch-and-putt golf course, 2 tennis courts, 33 kennels, stalls for 114 horses and mules, a barber shop, and a beauty shop. But as far as economic potential, I candidly told them it was at the bottom of its profit potential. I told them our Wawona operation outside the valley opened only two and a half months each year and capital had not been directed to its development. Visitors constantly suggested that we lengthen Wawona's season. The place could be improved into a separate recreation area if handled properly, I said.

I also told them that sixty percent of Yosemite's in-valley facilities were substandard and needed upgrading—particularly some of the four-hundred-and-six dilapidated tents and cabins lacking modern facilities built at Camp Curry in 1922. With the advent of car-camping, these low-cost units had lost most of their market and now rented only as options-of-last-resort. Besides, guests had nagged us for years to do something about these poor accommodations. Upgrading those facilities with modern cottages could quadruple the unit's profits. In fact, I already had construction plans prepared to replace a hundred-fifty of these tents and Park Service approval from Regional Director Howard Chapman (who later rescinded his approval when the political pot boiled over).

I urged the two men, if they succeeded in acquiring the Yosemite concession, to promote year-round occupancy. I had replaced the T-bar tow at our winter operation at Badger Pass with a chairlift, materially improving our winter patronage. I assured Sheinberg and Stein that a properly capitalized and operated Yosemite could not only yield better profits, but also give visitors what they had wanted for years: a quality accommodation within one of the greatest national parks at prices the working or retired American could afford.

In August 1973, MCA consummated their purchase of Yosemite Park and Curry Company from U.S. Natural Resources and tendered for the balance of the stock. They were successful. I contracted to run the company for a year until they could hire an executive and build their organization. Jay Stein said he would send me executive candidates and act on my recommendations. Jay sent me several applicants but I turned them all down until Edward C. Hardy walked through the door. Hardy had managed the Riviera Country Club in Pacific Palisades, California, and understood the hospitality industry. MCA hired him as chief operating officer in September 1973. Ed came on-site in the valley in January, 1974, the Curry Company's tenth head, coincident with the arrival of Leslie Arnberger, Yosemite's eleventh superintendent. After five months, I was sure Ed could run the company and asked MCA to release me from my contract.

I wanted to get back to my Glacier operation—thank the Lord I hadn't been able to package it for U.S. Natural Resources with McKinley and Lassen, which were now lost to me forever. USNR's stock had plunged into the nether basement of market oblivion. I had a great deal of it. As the old joke goes, it made attractive wallpaper. And USNR's operations were coming to the end of their rope. I was fortunate to lose only my entire investment in my first two concessions. At least I had something to go back to. Al Donau had run the Glacier concession from the time I left for HUD in May 1966. How long ago that seemed as I left the splendor of Yosemite. It was May 1974 when I returned to Glacier.

Era of Discord

I returned to those "new vistas" Director Hartzog had promised in the national parks. But George had left the scene. Ronald Walker had assumed the title of Director of the

National Park Service in January 1973. He did not fit well in the organization. Some called him a Nixon political hack. Park Service personnel never gave him their support. His downfall came less than two years later under the shadow of multiple scandals—one, a deal with a friend to set up a nationwide visitor reservation system called "Ticketron" for the parks, another, the infamous *Sierra* painted rocks episode, which we will get to shortly. Of greatest permanent significance, however, Walker was to preside over the first overt destruction of concessions in the history of the national parks.

When I returned to those familiar places, Many Glacier, Lake McDonald, Swiftcurrent, Rising Sun, the Prince of Wales in Canada, a pall was descending over the national parks. Director Walker had approved, without prior notice or public hearing, an order dated April 26, 1974, permanently shutting down Manzanita Lake in Lassen Volcanic National Park. I took it like a physical shock. Manzanita Lake shut down! I couldn't help remembering the days when Dal Dort and Charley Keathley and I set out with great expectations to build the Lodge there, to greet the visitors, to open the area to public use and enjoyment. How primitive but happy our first tent-store had been! How delighted we were when President Hoover's party came to fish and bought out our entire stock! How we struggled and sacrificed to make it work for all those years. And now—shut down.

It made me sad. It made me mad. Obviously the environmental purists had grasped the highest levers of policy power. Their influence could be clearly seen in this abrupt decision. They had to be stopped before they shut down other parks. But how had they done it? As I was to learn, pressure from the outside, relentless orchestrated environmentalist pressure was part of the answer. And cooperation by purist Park Service employees from the inside, using a six-year-old geologic report to justify the exclusion of the public.

NPS Regional Director Howard Chapman, who actually issued the April 26, 1974, Manzanita Lake execution order, claimed to be acting on the basis of the 1968 U.S. Geological

Survey report of Dwight Crandall, et al. The gist of the justification was that a rockslide from Chaos Crags might destroy the concession facilities and endanger the people occupying them. With more stagecraft than veracity Chapman dramatically stated: "The evidence at hand is so compelling that no other decision than closing out the operations at this location is consistent with our responsibility."

What evidence was that? I wondered. Evidence that the Chaos Crags could soon experience a rock avalanche and crush Manzanita Lake Lodge? Not likely. In a feat of imagination bordering on science-fiction, Park Service planners worried that the Manzanita Lake concession buildings *might* be destroyed by a *possible* rock slide from Chaos Crags, the volcanic ridge that rises above the valley floor.

That 1968 Geological Survey study stated that some three hundred or more years ago, a rock slide had swept two and a half miles down the cliffs creating the Chaos Jumbles. The cause of this ancient disaster was unknown, but the geologists speculated that the volcanic extrusion which built Chaos Crags had reached too high and had tumbled, or a buildup of steam had caused an explosion which in turn caused the rock slide. *If* this were to happen on a busy weekend in July, 1974, everybody in its path *could* be killed! Of course, none of these Park Service planners gave the slightest indication that such a landslide *would* happen, or was even *likely* to happen, just that it *could* happen.

The USGS report had gathered dust on Park Service shelves for almost six years with no action. But now, on April 26, 1974, Manzanita Lake Lodge—along with the Park Service visitor center and museum—were ordered shut down. Remarkably, the government campground adjacent to the lodge was briefly closed and then reopened—some genius had decided that the campground would magically not be affected by any impending landslide! Then too, in another stunning display of planning logic, the main Lassen park road which passes directly beneath the Chaos Crags was never closed. Something distinctly inconsistent was going on.

The outrage was universal. It was obvious to everyone that the Park Service was only using the USGS report as a handy excuse for implementing an anti-concession policy they tried to pretend didn't exist. How could Chaos Crags be a threat to Manzanita Lake Lodge but not to the adjacent campground? Ben Avery, a member of Lassen park's citizen advisory council, was the first to say it openly. At a meeting in Redding August 1974, he said "It is a hazard because USGS says so." His caustic opinion was shared by the vast majority of Northern Californians.

One of the four geologists who wrote the 1968 report, Dwight Crandall, Chief of the U.S. Hazards Projects, was a also bit puzzled by the Park Service's belated overreaction to the Chaos report. He said, "I don't think the Lassen situation is unique. We have right now the towns of Weed and Mt. Shasta and McCleod around the base of Mt. Shasta." Dan Miller, another USGS geologist from Denver said, "The idea is that once a community or town becomes established in a hazard area, it becomes a little hard to pack 'em up and move 'em out." A newspaper reporter commented, "Indeed, the citizens of Weed, McCleod and Mt. Shasta might frown upon such an enterprise."

The public clamor to reopen Lassen extended to Congress. Northern California Congressman Harold T. "Bizz" Johnson, co-sponsored a House resolution asking the Park Service to reaffirm its duty to assure adequate lodging in the parks. Members of the California congressional delegation intervened requesting the Park Service hold off the shutdown and reconsider any future shutdown plans. Their instructions fell on deaf ears. The arrogant Park Service, as I have pointed out, is an independent fiefdom within the Department of the Interior that listens politely to everyone and then proceeds in its own direction. As a local newspaper put it, the Park Service "reacted to expressions of puzzlement and outrage by the public with all the patient paternalism of a colonial government which had been summoned for a native uprising in some back-water province." Regional Director Howard Chapman said: "We did it for your own good."

Now that was too fishy for the media to swallow whole. Everyone in the area suspected that a deeper reason lay behind the Lassen closure, and most reporters had a good idea what it was. It would take until 1975 for the media to react, but the editor of *The Redding Record Searchlight* put reporter Glenn Hassenpflug to work on the puzzle. Hassenpflug confirmed what was obvious to any knowledgeable person: The Park Service was merely using the hazard report to justify its new nature-purist campaign to destroy visitor facilities.

First Hassenpflug asked himself "Why did the Park Service *really* shut down Lassen?". He knew certain things already: For one, that all the overt steps to deal with the alleged avalanche threat occurred between January and April 1974, although the Park Service had been alerted in 1968 by the four geologists' report. Why did it take so long for the Park Service to start worrying about the danger?

At Park Headquarters in Mineral the reporter searched public documents and found a revised draft of the Lassen Volcanic National Park Master Plan dated November 12, 1973, containing curious references to visitor elimination not related to geologic hazards. On page 29 he read:

> Lassen Volcanic National Park, a park already hosting near capacity crowds at times of peak travel, cannot face the future passively or in isolation. The National Park Service must consider new systems of receiving the public so that visitors may enjoy a quality experience in a manner not leading to degradation of an outstanding national resource.
>
> At the north entrance on the trans-park road, the Manzanita area will continue to serve as the major developed center of the park. However, in view of the rockfall-avalanche hazard, and increasing human pressures on a primary and limited scenic site, all functions other than those necessary for reduced day-use activities will be relocated to sites outside the present park boundary (the only exception is the campground which will be retained in its present location south of Manzanita Lake)

So . . . The Park Service explicitly intended to limit public use and enjoyment—"reduced day-use activities" indeed! Even the closure of nature-interpretation facilities at the visitor center! It sounds like something the Sierra Club wrote. And the Park Service already knew they were going to keep the government campground open back in November 1973. Its short closure was merely for show.

Hassenpflug then discovered in an appendix to the Master Plan an astounding document. It led him to interview Lassen superintendent Robert J. Murphy, the author of the document. Murphy quite candidly admitted writing it, and explained that shortly after he arrived in Lassen in early 1973, a new set of management objectives was outlined for the park with approval at the Regional Office level. Murphy showed Hassenpflug the astonishing 6-page "Management Objectives" document he had written—and which had been approved May 17, 1973 by Howard H. Chapman, director of the Park Service's western region. These were the Park Service's management objectives for Lassen:

1) Restore park lakes to their natural condition, where recent use, visitor use or fish-stocking has adversely affected the normal ecosystem.

2) Actively promote the development of campgrounds, trailer courts, overnight visitor accommodations and associated recreational facilities outside the park.

3) Limit formal campground developments and the total number of campsites to those presently existing.

4) Eliminate concession overnight visitor accommodations from the park. Limit existing Manzanita Lake and Drakesbad facilities to their current overnight visitor capacity, as long as they continue to operate.

5) Phase out the concession operation at Drakesbad.

It should be noted that the concession facility at Drakesbad is located some 10 air miles away from the alleged danger of Chaos Crags. Glenn Hassenpflug was appalled. The public had never been notified of these management objectives. Nor had I or USNR. Here were government documents plainly stating a hidden policy intent to limit public access to the national parks by destroying concession facilities, a blatant violation of the Concession Policy Act of 1965.

Hassenpflug carefully evaluated Murphy's management objective document. The emphasis throughout, he later wrote, "was on erasing man-made changes and restoring Lassen to its natural state. The avalanche hazard was mentioned only once briefly in the six-page report." The tone of the report was established in the introductory paragraph which stated:

> Current and projected visitor use statistics indicate that if continued (they) may jeopardize the integrity of park values and quality of the visitor experience.

Visitation to Lassen had increased from 399,000 to 500,000 during 1962 to 1972. Now Hassenpflug saw the environmental hustle: visitors jeopardize the integrity of park values. Therefore, visitors must be removed. The covert motives of the Park Service were clear. Hassenpflug's editor spurred on his detective work.

Hassenpflug asked Murphy why he wanted to shut down Drakesbad, since it was clearly not in any danger: Superintendent Murphy answered:

"That particular action comes from the development of a policy where certain concessioners were marginal. I think we were taking the total visitation as opposed to Drakesbad, where they were accommodating guests in the primary purpose of a dude ranch. There was some feeling that private interests [outside the park] had a desire, in some areas, to develop their facilities quality-wise above those existing in the park. In such instances, it was viewed in the best interest to encourage private development outside and reduce private development inside, where it proved marginal or of limited interest."

Reporter Hassenpflug pointed out that the question of overcrowding seemed to be a mere smokescreen like the avalanche threat. He produced a letter dated August 13, 1972, from Lassen concessioner U.S. Natural Resources to the Park Service, saying:

"Lassen does not appear to be in any overuse danger at the present during the summer season."

It went on to say that projections over the next five years showed "an essentially continuing non-pressure visitation." By contrast, noted Hassenpflug, the Park Service was already thinking of closing the Manzanita Lake development for a reason that had nothing to do with either actual visitor overcrowding or a possible avalanche, but related more to a philosophical change toward turning our national parks into "vignettes of primitive America." Murphy did not deny it.

However, Murphy asserted that he had taken the Manzanita Lake avalanche hazard seriously, as his predecessor Boyer had. Boyer, as you may recall from Chapter 14, asked Regional Director Chapman for an immediate decision whether to go or stay at Manzanita Lake, and that as early as April 29, 1969. Chapman said to stay despite the risk. Boyer continued to ask about it. Chapman, on May 12, 1971, repeated his decision to take "a calculated risk" and keep the development open. In a 1972 memorandum to Regional Director Chapman, Murphy advised that he thought the matter "from a legal standpoint should be aired with the public." On January 23, 1974, he wrote Chapman a memo saying, "The lack of an action plan appears to be long overdue and any attempt to further defer positive solutions, in view of longstanding recommendations, could prove embarrassing to the service." Despite Murphy's recommendation, the public knew nothing until the closure announcement on April 26, 1974.

Thereafter, every public effort to expose the true Park Service policy of eliminating all concessions met with some variation of the standard line: "We have no policy as such; when such possibilities exist they must be considered on a case-to-case basis."

But, Hassenpflug wondered, what finally triggered the

Park Service's sudden action to shut down the concession? And why didn't the concessioner fight back?

Unfortunately, the concessioner could not fight back. U.S. Natural Resources had sunk into profound economic distress. It had been forced to sell its concession at Yosemite just as the profits there were taking on some semblance of normalcy because it desperately needed the cash. With only Lassen left, which had never been a profit generator, USNR was in worse condition than ever. And the news of the hazard came as a sudden surprise.

January 18 and 19, 1974, the Park Service's Western Regional Advisory Committee met in San Francisco. John Del Favero attended for USNR. There the news of a possible avalanche hazard in the Chaos Crags seeped out from the Lassen Master Plan. Denver Service Center planning representative Frank Collins, who had been working on the Plan, told the committee: "The planners have strongly indicated that they *must* reduce the hazard to the visitor by removing the visitor from the hazardous area." Del Favero was shocked. His liability insurance writers would not be pleased. USNR couldn't possibly allocate its vanishing cash to buy insurance for a possibly imaginary danger in a money-losing concession. And if there was danger in the park, the Park Service had to take positive steps to avoid it. Del Favero warned the committee that "this is not a problem necessarily that relates to a long-range plan. It is a problem that relates to opening the concession area up again this next summer."

Regional Director Chapman then agreed to "find out what the legal ramifications were of . . . the concession's closure."

At Chapman's request, on March 4, 1974, Ralph G. Mihan, San Francisco field solicitor for the Department of the Interior, rendered a legal opinion calling attention to the government's liability under the Tort Claims Act. If there was injury to person or property at Lassen on Park Service property the government was ultimately liable. Mr. Mihan stated later that he did not know why the service, if it cared deeply either about human life or liability, took six years to act.

After absorbing the implications of this Solicitor's opinion, John Del Favero, president of USNR and owner of Lassen National Park Company, gave the Park Service an ultimatum on April 5, 1974: Announce its steps to protect employees and visitors by April 15, or he would shut the resort himself. He said: "We will, of course, hold you responsible and liable for all damages." The Solicitor had clearly placed the liability onus on the government, whether the geological threat was real or imagined. Had the concessioner been financially healthier, he would have fought Chapman's next move.

Regional Director Chapman had found his reasonable excuse for shutting down *all* concessions in Lassen. There was danger at Manzanita Lake and the concessioner was too weak to keep the ski area and Drakesbad guest ranch as their sole operations. And even here Chapman made no pretense of actual rationality: He didn't seem concerned about safety because he left the main highway directly under Chaos Crags and the government campground open. The string of events leading from the USGS report to the Advisory Committee meeting to the Solicitor's opinion to Del Favero's ultimatum was a most practical and credible justification for beginning the Park Service concession-slashing campaign. So it was goodbye, Lassen. And how bitterly reasonable the justifications sounded.

But the plans to shut down Drakesbad and the ski area at the park's southwest corner ran into trouble. Both areas lay far away from Chaos Crags. Not even planning voodoo could stretch an avalanche that far. The raw face of purist ideology was about to be exposed. Rush M. Blodgett, M.D., of Redding, California, a long-time patron of Drakesbad and its nearby ski area, wrote dozens of letters to the Park Service protesting the Lassen closure and accusing them explicitly of having a concession-destruction policy. In a letter dated June 10, 1974, Imogene B. LaCovey, Acting Assistant Director of Concessions Management in Washington, D.C., replied:

In regard to the Drakesbad and ski areas, the National Park

Service has not proposed or encouraged the closure of these facilities. U.S. Natural Resources, the present operator, has taken action to close these facilities.

Well, that's *almost* the truth. U.S. Natural Resources took action to make the United States accept liability for any injury at Manzanita Lake resulting from a potential Chaos Crags disaster or it would close its facilities. When Interior's field solicitor accepted that liability on behalf of the United States, Park Service officer Chapman, not the concessioner, closed *all* concessions in Lassen. It's simply marvelous the skill with which the Park Service molds the truth.

With congressional intervention, Regional Director Chapman had to do some fancy verbal dancing. These are his words:

> In the event the concessioner expresses a wish to continue the Drakesbad and ski operations, as there was strong public political pressure to continue, they could be continued in operation on their concession contract or through a successor concessioner.

Chapman knew full well that USNR had made a strong push to expand the ski area at the Southwest corner of the park with some major improvements and that the public would not stand for a closure of the ski area. He also knew full well that USNR's financial condition would not allow it to devote any capital to Drakesbad, even though the little operation had always yielded a small profit—miniscule compared to the needs of USNR.

As reporter Hassenpflug later wrote, "The much harassed Chapman assured Doctor Blodgett that Drakesbad's continued existence depended upon its ability to pay its own way. Blodgett had his accountant prepare a financial statement to prove that Drakesbad was not a loser. The Park Service denied that there was a desire to move concession facilities out of the park. . . ."

Reporter Hassenpflug finished his investigation and wrote

a five-day series for the *Redding Record Searchlight* from Monday, December 1, 1975, to Friday, December 5. It stood as a scathing indictment of Park Service arrogance. As a preface to an epilogue dated December 18, the editor wrote:

> A reporter's job is to report facts as he finds them and the opinions of others as they are expressed to him. When it comes to his own opinions, the disciplines of his profession require that he put them on the shelf—neither expressing them directly in what he writes nor allowing them to color what he writes.
>
> *Record Searchlight* reporter Glenn Hassenpflug spent several months recently probing both the steps and the motivations involved in the U.S. Park Service's closure of visitor facilities at Manzanita Lake in early 1974. His five-part report appeared in the newspaper early this month. We asked Hassenpflug to share with our readers the personal impressions and opinions that he formed as a result of his investigation.
>
> Here is his report:
>
> As a reporter, I have spent hours trying to get a specific question answered, been shunted from desk to desk, disconnected, lectured to about who's doing what and who isn't, and finally been given the answer, off the record. Had I not been a reporter, but a "mere" citizen, I would not have gotten the answer at all.
>
> It is the news media's dubious distinction to have become an institutionalized information-collector for the citizen and, conversely, information-dispenser for the government.
>
> The closure of the Manzanita Lake development in Lassen National Park is an excellent example of how the system functions.
>
> When the National Park Service, without notice, shut down its visitor center and a private resort, it told the public, "We did it for your own good, to save you from a possible hundred mile per hour rock slide off Chaos Crags."
>
> Partly because the closure was made so suddenly, while the Crags had stood unmoved for centuries, many citizens and Shasta County officials suspected that they were being avalanched by the Park Service. They were.

But service spokesmen stuck to their justification. It was a good one, sealed and delivered by another government entity, the U.S. Geological Survey, but not understood or seriously challenged.

On request from county officials, the service even released its file of memoranda, telephone calls and lectures on the closure—or at least enough of the files to start a damning circumstantial case for the prosecution.

But Shasta County lacked the time to flesh out the file with endless telephone interviews and inquiries to Utah and Denver and San Francisco. And, had it assembled the case, it lacked a forum for pressing it effectively.

By contrast, a newspaper is a forum and it has the time, if it chooses. An investigation of several weeks revealed the true reason why the Park Service closed Manzanita Lake:

It wanted to.

Everything else was sheer pettifoggery.

It wanted to, because human population pressures had begun to imperil the natural ecology, and because commercial pressures at other parks, such as Yosemite, had embarrassed it politically.

Quietly, and for the public's own good, it had decided to limit public access to the parks and to begin buying out private interests.

Yet how painfully hard it was to make the Park Service explain its intention!

Service spokesmen took refuge in bureaucratic loyalties, in elaborate quibbling over terms, in manufactured statements and appeals to altruism and in buck-passing both petty and grand.

The combined effect was obscurity—a tangle of words and circumstances that could hardly have been more difficult to separate had they been designed deliberately to obscure.

I don't think park service officials sat in their offices and decided: "Let's deceive the public." I think instead, the service—like the bureaucracy in general—had learned it functions with the greatest freedom in a climate of obscurity.

For example, regional director Howard Chapman, who acted as the service's field marshal for the closure, is uniformly described by his fellow bureaucrats as honest and conscientious, a hard worker.

But county officials and private citizens who dealt with him described a different man—aloof, hard to reach, noncommital.

The point about the whole Lassen controversy is not just whether people's access to the park should be limited or whether the service made the right decision in closing the lake complex.

The point is that the people cannot afford to let administrators whom they can't locate or understand make their decisions for them.

The government doesn't need more good men—it needs more responsive men.

It doesn't need better reasons—it needs more clarity.

Epitaph

Drakesbad remains open. But at Manzanita Lake the grocery store, gift shop, all the housekeeping cabins and hotel bungalows, the service station, the two-story dormitory, the manager's home and the beautiful 53-year-old lodge all have been dismantled and removed—every accommodation I had built over forty years to provide for the peoples'use and enjoyment. It is bitter irony that the only three buildings left standing, a stone museum, the superintendent's home, and a stone residence built by B.F. Loomis, the early photographer, belong to the government. There is no nature interpretation in the park. There is no visitor center. I feel like I lost an old friend—a part of my life. In an unexpected economic fallout, the visitor flow to Lassen fell off so drastically—from 496,600 in 1973 to 380,000 in 1979, a loss of 116,000 annual visitors—that nearby businesses outside the park have failed. The Park Service's predictions were monstrously wrong.

In another tragedy for the public, Mammoth Cave National Park Superintendent Albert A. Hawkins grew angry at the concessioner's opposition to a restrictive Master Plan. National Park Concessions, Inc., the non-profit corporation that

had operated the charming old Lodge at Historic Entrance
since 1941, had publicly objected to the planned removal of all
visitor facilities to the outer periphery of the park and busing
visitors to the cave. After the Park Service told a congressional
committee that no concessions would be removed anytime
soon, Superintendent Hawkins ordered a safety inspection of
the Lodge and then served notice to make certain improvements or vacate the premises. NPCI made the improvements.
Hawkins then ordered the second floor vacated. NPCI complied. Hawkins ordered the building vacated. NPCI complied.
Hawkins ordered the Lodge at Historic Entrance razed to the
ground. The government wrecking crew complied. Easy as
pie. The purist design had prevailed.

During the last days of Lassen I made a systematic study of
twelve national park Master Plans. Every one of them called
for a limitation or removal of concession and visitor facilities
out of the park. Every one. At Yellowstone the overnight
accommodations at Old Faithful were to be shut down and
West Thumb left an unpeopled wilderness. At Yosemite all
"non-essential" visitor accommodations were to be removed
out of the park. At Mammoth Cave all overnight accommodations were slated for destruction and the ground restored to a
"natural condition"—humans "aren't natural." At Rocky
Mountain no overnight lodgings were to remain in the park.
At Zion, Bryce and Cedar Breaks all overnight lodging was to
be torn down and removed. At Glacier only 82,600 acres of its
total 1,013,500 were to be left for human use including roads,
campgrounds, Park Service and concession facilities. At Great
Smoky Mountain a fine old lodge was to be closed and destroyed. North Rim Grand Canyon was scheduled for a 1980
"review" to decide whether all overnight accommodations
should be removed.

I wish it was better today. It's not. As far as visitors are
concerned, the parks are dying. The environmentalists are
stealing them. The National Park Service is their willing
instrument.

Coda

In a terrible irony, in 1985 some park personnel and others interested in Lassen sponsored a solicitation program to build a visitor center at Manzanita Lake. It was like reading something written by someone with no comprehension of cause and effect. The solicitation said:

> The whole picture has been aggravated by the closure of Lassen's major visitor center complex at Manzanita Lake in 1974. This area was the hub of summertime activities at Lassen; now little remains of what was once a memorable national park experience there. The park is still without an appropriate visitor facility, and federal funds for a planned replacement are not likely to be available in the near future.
>
> This is an exciting time for Lassen. There is a spirited rebirth of the private initiative that created our national parks and aid in protecting their precious natural resources. Continuing a portion of the protection in the face of limited governmental funding is again in the hands of the American people. Each of us, through your active support, can join in the same effort that Peter Lassen, John Raker, Arthur Conrad and Stephen Mather worked so tirelessly to achieve.
>
> Sincerely yours,
> W. Stephenson
> Former Superintendent

Well, you could write them a stinging reminder of why they lost their park in the first place, but they would just ignore you and ask for money. I suggested reopening that wonderful lodge as a visitor center—it was still standing, and had been cited as a valuable historical structure. "A spirited rebirth of private initiative," Stephenson wrote. How bitterly that falsehood rings! Perhaps somewhere there *is* a young person in whom the spirit of Steve Mather and Horace Albright will be reborn. I don't know. I can only hope.

A few months after I received my invitation to help pay for reopening what the Park Service had shut down, a crew on government orders came in with a wrecking ball and destroyed the lodge and all concessioners buildings. All those years of perseverance, sacrifice and pride. . . .

Yosemite Under Attack

MCA's purchase of Yosemite Park & Curry Company in August 1973 created a real furor among environmental organizations. The idea of a *big business* owning a national park concession was intolerable to the anti-capitalist ideology of environmentalism. A *corporate conglomerate* was even more horrendous. An *entertainment conglomerate* was absolutely outrageous—it catered to *people*, nasty *people* who insisted on using their national parks. Environmentalists looked to Congress to see who would minister to their power most amicably. They found Representative John Dingell (D-Michigan).

By July 17, 1974, Mr. Dingell was firing off letters to Interior Secretary Rogers Morton complaining about MCA, "I am greatly outraged that the Music Corporation of America, a concessionaire at Yosemite National Park, is aggressively promoting the Park as a convention center." As we shall see in a few chapters, Mr. Dingell knew all about aggressiveness.

Of course, Park Service officials had always encouraged Yosemite concessions to find uses for their facilities over slack seasons as a way to spread costs and keep summer rates down in a highly seasonal operation. What had prompted Mr. Dingell's complaint was a photograph. Environmentalists zeroed in on a photograph of a large number of auditorium chairs set up for an event *years* before MCA arrived. They sent the picture to Mr. Dingell representing it as an MCA outrage against nature, a typical environmentalist distortion of the facts to create an emotional response.

But the real conflict erupted over a television series. In 1974 MCA subsidiary Universal Studios invaded the valley to film an ill-fated television series called *Sierra*. The original idea sounded good on paper: to dramatize the problems and effectiveness of National Park Rangers.

The National Park Service, yearning for a competitive series to rival the Forest Service soap-opera *Lassie*, not only encouraged MCA, but also assigned rangers to them as technical assistants. Orders to help any way possible came all the way from NPS Director Walker. The crass and technically complex production process, however, caused unexpected problems. Traffic on the valley floor was slowed or stopped during months of filming. And the result was less than stunning. The quickly-canceled series was as memorable as old what's-his-name.

But what gave the environmental purists their *cause celebre* was the July 1974 staging of a mountain rescue scene. A scene had been partially filmed in a truly dangerous location and a Park Service consultant stopped the shooting in mid-take because of safety problems. A new location, hurriedly selected, proved safe and dramatically adequate to continue the shoot. But it was photographically problematic: the darker rock in the new location did not match the extensive footage already shot. If editors intercut this dark background with the previous footage, all visual continuity in the scene would be destroyed. So, the technical crew came out with some washable clay paint of the proper reflectance and nine square yards of color-corrected rock appeared behind the actors. The color matched and the scene was completed.

Now, this was during the heyday of the margarine commercial with the punch line "It's not nice to fool mother nature." The environmental purists looked at that nine square yard patch of paint—which was immediately removed without a trace—and concocted the myth that MCA was painting *all* the walls of Yosemite Valley! "Obscene desecration" was one of their milder accusations. It was certain proof that MCA was turning Yosemite into Disneyland North. *Sierra* became the worst skeleton in concessioning's historical closet, even outstripping the lease-fraud shenanigans of Hobart and Douglas in early Yellowstone. It remained for years the symbol of concessioner irreverence. The press was unbelievably brutal and self-justifying.

The outcry against the painted rocks of *Sierra* combined with the Ticketron scandal ultimately drove Park Service Director Ronald Walker from office. And, completely aside from Nathaniel Reed's own elitist view of the parks, the furor convinced him on December 13, 1974, to throw out the entire Yosemite Master Plan. Anything tainted by *Sierra* was the kiss of death —even a Master Plan that arch-conservationist Ansel Adams helped to write.

Environmentalists immediately seized upon the trashed Master Plan as proof that MCA had bullied the Park Service to further commercialize Yosemite—with their usual carefully careless disregard for facts. The Master Plan, of course, had been developed long before MCA came to the park.

The Sierra Club quickly realized that the public glare now scorching park concessioners could be used to turn policy further in their direction. In mid-March of 1975, the House Interior and Insular Affairs Committee heard testimony on national park matters including concessions. Brock Evans, the Club's Washington lobbyist revealed that Club executives had carefully analyzed the concession system's weak points and decided to push them to see what would happen. On March 14, Evans told the committee, "We share the view of the Conservation Foundation that visitor facilities within the parks are ideally to be operated by a nonprofit, quasi-public corporation, whose primary allegiance is to appropriate public use of the parks. Where private enterprise is required, it should operate facilities outside the parks." The Sierra Club correctly perceived that non-profit concession organizations would be easier to remove from the parks and that a practical first step in eliminating all visitor facilities from the parks might very well be the conversion of private for-profit concessions to quasi-public non-profit operations.

The Sierra Club had already grasped the opportunity to shape the national park Master Plan process in its image, to become the master of the Master Plan. When a series of National Park workshops were announced throughout the country, the Club had jumped on the bandwagon with both feet. A March 3, 1975, Club release invited those with expertise in the fields of planning, wildlife, biology, plant ecology, geology, sanitation and engineering to join their Yosemite Task Force and get trained for dominating the workshops. They would draw up their own Master Plan this time.

As the year unfolded, the Sierra Club loaded every Yosemite Master Plan workshop. The instructions to members were clear: a Sierra Club Letter dated May 3, 1975, distributed to all Bay Area Master Plan Meetings said, "We urge the following actions be taken regarding Yosemite Valley: concession facilities be removed to a location outside of the park—possibly El Portal . . . Study of the feasibility of removing visitor accommodations from the Valley." At the public meetings Club members objected to everything human. They protested the High Sierra camps in the Wilderness Area, and wanted them removed. They objected to Yosemite Wilderness boundaries being set back from roads or developed areas by buffer zones—they wanted Wilderness right up to the roads, or the roads removed.

They protested Badger Pass Ski Area as a "non-Park use" which should not be expanded; that Glacier Point should be dedeveloped and the road to Glacier Point closed; that ranger housing and support facilities be removed outside the park; that all private automobiles be eliminated within the valley. They demanded that all visitor accommodations be ultimately removed from the valley; in the interim, all for-profit business must be forbidden and existing concessioners replaced by nonprofit concessioners.

The *Los Angeles Times*, May 4, 1975, ran a long article under the banner "The Battle Over Yosemite." The conservation organizations' position was enunciated by Connie Parrish, the California representative of Friends of the Earth.

The overriding issue in the battle over Yosemite is the rights of an increasingly conservation-minded public vs. the projected profits of a privately owned conglomerate.

Act one of the Drama ended Dec. 13 when the Interior

Department, pushed by major conservation groups, rejected the National Park Service's tentative master plan for Yosemite. The plan has gone back to the drawing board and the public's voice at last is being heard . . .

Thanks largely to the protests of Friends of the Earth, the Sierra Club and other conservation groups, the Interior Department rejected the draft master plan on the grounds that there had been no public participation. . . .

As a matter of fact, there had been three widely advertised public hearings on the master plan, but the final results did not please the environmental organizations.

The article continues:

A Congressional investigation also grew out of our protests. Hearings were held in December by U.S. Rep. John Dingell (D-Mich.), chairman of the House subcommittee on energy and the environment in conjunction with the subcommittee on conservation, energy and natural resources. Dingell heard testimony that the park service let MCA push it into recommendations which were overly commercial . . .

What MCA wanted to do, in our opinion, was to turn Yosemite into a year-round luxury resort. The company proposed to tear down 150 of the primitive tent cabin units in Curry Village at park headquarters and replace them with modern lodge facilities with indoor plumbing—at higher rent.

In fact I made these proposals as president of Yosemite Park & Curry Company and had Park Service approval in 1972 before MCA purchased the company, but it was never honored. And Parrish neglected to mention that at those Dingell hearings Park Service Deputy Director Russell Dickenson (who later served as Director) defended concessions and the park service's ability to keep them in line. He told Representative Dingell, "Our position as administrators of public parkland is to reflect the appropriate requests and views and needs of public services." Neither Dingell nor other purists, of course, wanted to hear that.

Rudy Aversa, *Los Angeles Herald Examiner* staff writer sympathetic to environmentalist goals, reported:

The major conservationist problem seems to be putting up a united front against the Yosemite Park & Curry Company, a subsidiary of MCA, the prime concessioner and unnamed candidate to implement future development of Yosemite.

There is a faction of conservationists and environmentalists such as the Sierra Club, Friends of the Earth, Wilderness Society and other "Save the Yosemite" groups who not only want no more development in the park, but want all development removed.

In the midst of this media hubub, the National Parks and Conservation Association (NPCA) joined the free-for-all attack on concessions. They filed suit against the National Park Service under the Freedom of Information Act of 1974 to gain access to concession financial records. Hoping to find something to embarrass concessioners—unconscionable profits, Machiavellian manipulations by the new corporate conglomerate owners of several large concessions such as MCA, or some such—NPCA asked for every financial detail of eight national park concessions to be made public. Of course, these figures had been regarded as confidential since before Steve Mather—even the hostile General Accounting Office recognized their confidentiality when it demanded (and got) the right to audit private concessioners in 1965. Despite the regulated-monopoly status of national park concessioners, the court found that genuine competition does indeed exist in the field, particularly from unregulated operations near the parks. To release detailed operating cost information would severely compromise the competitive position of existing concessions.

Within a year, a Washington, D.C. lower court held that detailed concession cost information was exempt from the requirements of the Freedom of Information Act and denied the National Parks and Conservation Association access to the material.

But NPCA was playing to the gallery as much as to the court: It wanted to be able to point an accusing finger and say,

"Public efforts to obtain the data, however, have been un-availing; the service releases some aggregate data for conces-sioners as a whole, but does not provide the data on individ-ual concessioners that would allow public scrutiny of dealings between the concessioners and the park service. Operating on public land, often under contracts that confer a long-term right to operate with little or no competition, concessioners are subject to a regulatory commission—yet that process is not fully open to public accountability." That is a quote, incidentally, from NPCA's fellow purists in the Conservation Foundation—it appeared in the 1985 anti-concession chapter of *National Parks for a New Generation.*

I might also note that the financial records of environ-mental groups which influence billions of dollars worth of resources and jobs on the public lands are likewise unavail-able for public scrutiny. Most of the top ten environmental groups won't even reveal the salaries paid to their hired executives or head lobbyists, and none will reveal the names of their major cash donors. When it comes to their own multi-million-dollar operations, which are vastly larger than all concessioners combined, environmentalists are not so con-cerned about public accountability. And they're not audited by any oversight group, whereas all concessioners are.

But as for Yosemite and its Master Plan, the *Christian Science Monitor* on August 13, 1975 summed up the contro-versy by asking:

> What is the public's will? The basic question lingers; just what is the public's will? What does the park visitor want— better and more modern facilities, easier access to hiking, camping and scenic wonders? Or is he or she more concerned with preserving the natural state of things, with restoring forests, protecting wildlife and maintaining a rugged outdoor ethic?
>
> The conflict between these divergent outlooks is what the Yosemite controversy is all about. It surfaces in terms of pro-posals to limit visitor use, ban concessioner facilities from the interior of the park and replace auto traffic with bus transit.

The Park Service . . . says the issue gets down to preservation vs. use. They admittedly lean toward the former goal.

The National Park Service under new Director Gary Everhardt was now staffed with numerous willing accomplices helping the environmentalists steal the national parks. Steve Mather would never have put up with them.

17

The People Strike Back

THE DESTRUCTION that began in 1974 at Lassen has spread throughout the National Park System like a cancer. Millions have been denied the right to overnight lodgings in our national parks. In a 1986 *Seattle Times* article, former ranger-naturalist Kim Heacox wrote: "The Park Service in Alaska has taken a small yet important first step: Visitors were turned away at Denali (Mt. McKinley) last summer." The Park Service itself has become the head thief in the campaign to steal the national parks. How can the people fight back?

Conscience of a Concessioner

The first part of the answer is, "Know the principles you're fighting for." Concessioners expressed their philosophy resoundingly March 14, 1975 in the words of Jay S. Stein, president of Yosemite Park & Curry Company and vice president of MCA. He told the Subcommittee on National Parks and Recreation of the House Interior and Insular Affairs Committee:

> We recognize that it is our duty not only to meet our contractual obligation to provide a public service but also to do so in a manner that preserves the priceless natural beauty that is Yosemite. . . .
> The NPS has long championed the necessity for master planning within the national parks. . . . The NPS has historically followed the policy of involving the public and the concessioner in the planning process. . . .

The public, the NPS and the concessioner all have a vital role to perform as members of the planning team. By practical necessity the concessioner has traditionally played his role at an earlier stage in cooperation with the NPS. Subsequently the public reviews a draft master plan. . . .

Our company was criticized for its involvement in the planning process in Yosemite National Park. These criticisms have centered on the contention that the concessioner should not be involved to any greater extent than the general public. . . . We submit this is an unjustified indictment of a process which the NPS and Congress have designed to provide for the best possible plan in the most expeditious manner. . . .

It seems reasonable to involve the concessioner in the early processes of planning since he has a contractual relationship with the NPS, has developed expertise as the result of his experience in operating park concessions, and will be called upon to make some of the major capital investments. . . .

We believe that the historical process described above is an intelligent process. . . . We submit concessioner involvement in the planning process with the NPS is neither an abrogation of the NPS's responsibility to the Congress and the public, nor an anathema to the public interest. . . .

The second part of the answer is, "Keep in mind the atrocities of the Park Service in its campaign to rid the parks of the people." In this chapter we will follow the story of concerned citizens who fought back against the Park Service and won at least a partial victory. And here we have to backtrack to 1972 and come forward again.

A Deal Goes Bad

It happened to Utah Parks Company, a subsidiary of the Union Pacific Railroad. As you will recall, they built the concession facilities in Cedar Breaks National Monument, Zion, Bryce Canyon and the North Rim of Grand Canyon national parks because Steve Mather told them "they'll never make a profit, but the good will you'll generate with them will set bolshevism back twenty years." Mather proved to be a poor prophet about the march of bolshevism, but he was right on the mark about never making a profit. With the coming of better highways and mass automobile travel and the decline of rail traffic in the 1960s, the losses grew impossible. By 1970 the Union Pacific wanted out of the concession business.

My brother Gail heard of the railroad's desire through other concessioners and contacted Union Pacific with a proposal. The popular non-profit Up-With-People organization, a private youth-development group headquartered in Tucson, was interested in taking over three of their concession contracts—North Rim Grand Canyon, Zion, and Bryce—and hiring Gail to run the operations. The large facilities would provide perfect housing and rehearsal halls for their young entertainers during the off-season. By donating their concessions to Up-With-People, Union Pacific could exit the concession business and come out with a tax advantage at the same time—and the concessions would stay in private hands.

Union Pacific chairman James H. Evans accepted the proposal and told Gail to take possession. Gail got to work on the deal with zest. He inspected the buildings, prepared menus and proposed rates for submission to the Park Service. He worked with Union Pacific's Transportation Department on plans to renovate the lodges and cabins in preparation for the next season. He made an appointment with NPS Director George Hartzog to formalize the change of ownership, but the Director failed to show up.

As his transition work progressed, Gail protested that he had nothing in writing to guarantee the changeover, but Union Pacific assured him that he had no reason to worry: the operations were his. Gail's attorney suggested that he pay a personal visit to Union Pacific's Chairman Evans. Gail agreed and travelled to New York on behalf of Up-With-People to formalize the transfer.

In the meantime, unknown to Gail, Union Pacific Chairman Evans telephoned NPS Director Hartzog for final permission to transfer their contract to Up-With-People. Hartzog replied, "Look, if you're going to give away those concessions, why not donate the three operations to the National Park

Service Foundation?" This Foundation is a non-profit quasi-public corporation chartered by Congress in 1967 to encourage private gifts to the parks and to provide grants for projects of direct benefit to the National Park Service. The Secretary of the Interior serves as chairman of the foundation's board of directors, which includes the Director of the Park Service and generally wealthy individuals appointed by the Interior Secretary for six-year terms.

Hartzog told Evans to leave Gail and Up-With-People out of the deal and the foundation would give him the same tax break. So the government got the concession. Gail went home from New York empty-handed. Hartzog ignored the language about encouraging private enterprise in the national parks from the Concession Act of 1965.

A Prospectus for Trouble

The National Park Service quickly took formal possession of the Cedar Breaks, Zion, Bryce and North Rim Grand Canyon operations. In May they issued an operating prospectus looking for a new concessioner. The prospectus seemed deliberately designed to subvert every provision of the Mather-Albright concession principles—stability, service to the public, security of investment, possessory interest—but since it was merely a prospectus seeking a new concessioner, this flagrant violation of the Concession Policy Act went unheralded and escaped the notice of Congress.

The prospectus stated among other things: lodging facilities would be phased out at Zion National Park at the end of three years (1975); lodging facilities would be removed from Bryce Canyon National Park in five years (1977); and that continued service at the North Rim of the Grand Canyon would be reevaluated at the end of the 10-year contract (1982)—more hidden influence of environmental purists.

The prospectus stipulated that the successful applicant would be assigned government-owned buildings, structures and improvements for use in providing facilities to the public. It described the extensive facilities in detail. The prospectus also provided for the concessioner to rehabilitate and modernize the physical plant at an estimated cost of $130,000, adding this provision:

> In order to avoid the concessioner acquiring a possessory interest in a government acquired or constructed facility to be assigned to the concessioner, the concession contract contemplated hereunder will require the concessioner to relinquish and waive any right to possessory interest in all government-owned facilities which may be assigned.

In a ridiculously classic government Catch-22, the prospectus generously promised that the chosen concessioner would acquire a possessory interest in any new facilities constructed by him with approval by the National Park Service, but that no new facilities would be permitted.

A number of companies responded, but declined to make proposals when they discovered the limits on the operations. I made a proposal on behalf of the Yosemite Park & Curry Company, of which I was president, but reserved the right to raise the question of removing the facilities. My proposal was summarily dismissed.

The National Park Service finally found a concessioner willing to put up with its nonsense: TWA Services (now TW Services, Inc., a subsidiary of Canteen Corporation, which is a subsidiary of Trans World Corporation), headed by M. J. Kennedy, president, and headquartered in Chicago, Illinois. This contract, in contravention of the Concession Policy Act, provided for the phasing out of operations as provided in the prospectus, but the Park Service went them one better: Before turning the sites over to TWA, government crews removed the cabins and camper service building in Zion and destroyed the camper services in Bryce Canyon.

Bad Times

As I look back on it, 1974 was not at all a good year for concessioner public relations. The General Accounting Office

(GAO) published a study complaining that in seven western parks 143 conventions or group meetings were held, 53 of them during the peak visitation season. The implication is that groups and conventions have no right to use national park facilities. GAO stated: "In 1974, during Yosemite's peak season of May through September, 19 percent of the total room nights were scheduled for conventions and other group meetings." GAO insisted that some of these visitor "facilities and services in Yosemite were inconsistent with the natural surroundings."

And then the National Parks and Conservation Association, with all the finesse of a meat-ax, blurted in its magazine:

> All new concessions belong outside the boundaries of the parks where tourist traffic may boost small town revenue. [We saw how well that worked at Lassen.] Further, to the extent possible, the Park Service should phase out current concession operations to locations outside the parks. . . . How can parks be preserved in an unimpaired state for present citizens or future generations when bulldozers are busy carving out new sites for gift shops at the behest of powerful concessioner firms?

Preservationists were pushing their philosophy that "only those demands consistent with park purposes—use and enjoyment of park resources, not urbanlike services—should be satisfied inside the parks. In the provisions of goods and services, no less than in other management decisions, the park service is expected to lead rather than follow consumer demands," as the Conservation Foundation was to write in its 1985 *National Parks for a New Generation*. As in 1985, the 1974 preservationists weren't specific about what constituted an "urbanlike service"—hotels? gas stations? souvenir shops? grocery stores? indoor plumbing? And they certainly didn't specify *who* is doing the expecting when they say "the park service is expected to lead rather than follow consumer demands." Consider that a moment: the *government* should lead consumer demand for public access to public areas. The converse of that proposition is that the public's demands should remain subservient to government orders. Such logic raises the interesting question of who elects who in the American system. No doubt it's another aspect of the environmentalist principle of *Democratization* expressed in the Yosemite Symposium. Democracy is for environmental purists. Everybody else gets Democratized.

And then we had the performance of NPS Director Ronald Walker giving his testimony in response to congressional questioning on concession management that

> We have not been tough with them. They, in turn, have been able to cut deals, and to confuse or to hoodwink a superintendent because he is not knowledgeable in hotel management, in food management, in the sale of curios and souvenirs . . . [We] expect the poor superintendent, who came out of park recreation management, a zoologist or botanist to be a businessman and handle these programs involving large sums of money and assets.

This was the unkindest cut of all. Walker cast unwarranted aspersions upon concessioners and superintendents alike. He represented his own people as lacking the intelligence to deal with concessioners. Concessioners may have called park superintendents a lot of names over the years, but "stupid" isn't one of them. And the concessioners, since their Conference was founded at the call of Interior Secretary Wilbur in 1929, have given seminars, training sessions, and other help to park superintendents in understanding the problems of concessioning.

Being Heard

It was time to do something about all this. The first opportunity arose on September 26, 1974 in Salt Lake City where the National Park Service had scheduled Master Plan hearings for Zion National Park. (Keep in mind, too, that this was only two years after the Conservation Foundation's anti-concession Yosemite Symposium). I attended on behalf of the Conference of National Park Concessioners and said my piece.

In the State Office Building auditorium at Utah's State Capitol before a crowd of about a hundred-fifty, I reminded my fellow citizens that the Concession Policy Act of 1965 gave the Park Service no power to remove visitor facilities. Yet, I pointed out, the Act had been quoted by the Park Service as authority for its proposed destruction of visitor facilities at Zion.

I read the section in question:

> . . . the Congress hereby finds that the preservation of park values requires that such public accommodations, facilities, and services as have to be provided within those areas should be provided only under carefully controlled safeguards against unregulated and indiscriminate use, so that the heavy visitation will not unduly impair these values and so that development of such facilities can best be limited to locations where the least damage to park values will be caused. It is the policy of the Congress that such development shall be limited to those that are necessary and appropriate for public use and enjoyment of the national park area in which they are located and that are consistent to the highest practicable degree with the preservation and conservation of the areas.

This language, I pointed out, is solely a caution against over-development. It neither mentions nor implies the discontinuation or removal of existing concessions. Nor does it allow the prevention of new construction. The Park Service had completely invented its power to remove concessions. Congress never gave it such power. I told the hearing panel that I was tired of the charade, that Master Plans and Environmental Impact Statements (EISs) were convenient justifications for bypassing the Concession Policy Act and eliminating visitors from the national parks.

"Here is a prime example of how these instruments can be used to implement a policy of exclusion," I said, holding up

Zion's Master Plan and EIS. "You simply endorse development that fits your concept of park use and you damn development that is contrary to your objective."

I opened the Master Plan. "This is a classic of contradictions," I said. "The Plan calls for removal of 83 cabins that can provide overnight lodging for 372 people each night. The cabins occupy only 12 acres of the park's 187,000 acres. This, according to the Plan, is an intrusive development and therefore should be removed."

I turned to another page of the Plan. "On the other hand, development of 10 picnic sites and limited camping is approved with the statement that this development will disturb less than 25 acres of land."

I held the two pages open for the audience to see. "In other words," I said, "we approve development of 25 acres of land to serve 10 picnic sites and limited camping, but forbid lodging for an overnight experience of some 372 people a night on 12 acres. Who do you think you're fooling? This plan simply and solely intends to exclude people and nothing else."

I went on. "And look how your planners had to strain to show that replacement facilities were available outside of Zion in the community of Springdale so they could justify keeping people out. They faced some real problems. Water is the major problem. In fact, there was a congressional act of May 28, 1928, which permitted the diversion of water from inside park boundaries to enable the community of Springdale to exist at all. If a visitor facility is going to be built in the community of Springdale, it has to have park water. In other words, develop outside and use park water, but don't use park water inside for visitor facilities! Don't you think there's something patently absurd about that?"

I picked up the EIS and showed it to the audience. "This document says that sewage is a problem in the Zion concession. So you get rid of the sewage by getting rid of the concession. The problem was transferred to Springdale. Now this EIS says that Springdale has no sewage system except for septic tanks. But that could be solved by developing a sewage system in the town. The EIS doesn't disclose by whom or how this sewage development will be financed. The Park Service thought process is clear: If the problem was transferred out of the park it would not be a problem. There is grave doubt that the small community of Springdale can cope with the vastly expanded development that will be caused by the transfer of park sewage treatment from Zion to Springdale."

I turned back to the Master Plan. I said, "Here is an excellent statement that everyone should try and figure out. It says here, 'The elimination in the park of concessioner overnight facilities will allow Zion to implement a more meaningful concept of personalized visitor services.' What these services are and how they are to be accomplished is not divulged. There will be no persons left in the park to give any kind of service. The meaning of this sentence is a big secret. Nor does this Master Plan report disclose why overnight facilities in the park interfere with meaningful experience."

I put the documents back on the table and spoke directly for a moment. "I submit that the opportunity to spend the night in the park and the opportunity to experience a sunrise or sunset on the multi-colored Zion walls, or to observe the stars on a clear Utah night from the valley, is to enhance—not limit—the park experience. I believe that it is clear that Congress intended to make these parks available for the use and the enjoyment of the people, and that people are entitled to those facilities they need to make the park available for their use and enjoyment."

Zion, I said, "is the guinea pig for those who advocate the reduction of park use by reducing facilities available. It's not because Zion is different from other parks, but because the government now owns the facilities and feels that by removing them it can dictate the terms of park use. The decisions made here today will in large measure determine whether our national parks may be used and enjoyed by all the people, or are to be reserved for an elitist few. It will also in great measure determine whether Congress sets park policy or whether some ideologically pure bureaucrat will usurp that power to saddle our national parks with an inhumane exclusionary policy."

I sat down and hoped for the best. I felt I wouldn't get it.

Uproar

The situation rapidly deteriorated. We saw what kind of treatment concessioners were getting at the hands of the environmental lobby at the Yosemite Symposium. We saw what kind of treatment concessioners were getting at the hands of the Park Service at Lassen. By early 1975 the Park Service showed every intent to illegally dismantle all concessions in Zion, Bryce and North Rim Grand Canyon. It was time for congressional intervention. The Conference of National Park Concessioners together with TWA Services and other Conference members, contacted their congressional representatives, protesting the removal of concessions from Zion National Park. The chambers of commerce and businesses from surrounding communities for miles around Zion National Park joined the call for public hearings.

When the hearings came in 1975 to Cedar City and Salt Lake City in Utah and Kaibab, Arizona they were not soon forgotten.

Governor Calvin L. Rampton of Utah and the entire state congressional delegation—Senator Jacob Edward "Jake" Garn, First District Congressman Gunn McKay, and Second District Congressman Allan T. Howe—led by Senior Senator Frank E. Moss, resoundingly objected to the proposed destruction of the concession in Zion National Park. They requested the Federal Research Committee of the State of Utah to examine the proposed closure of Zion's concession and report back. At each hearing the audience expressed almost universal objection to removing the lodge from Zion. The Park Service people listened politely and, as usual, "took the matter under advisement" for later decision.

On April 29, 1975, Senator Moss issued a press release asking for a postponement of the Zion closure until the Utah

Federal Research Committee completed its study. Moss had the backing of the entire Utah delegation.

The furor soon broke into the media in a big way. The *Salt Lake Tribune*, on June 14, 1975, blared "Park Service May Close Zion Lodge:"

> According to a university researcher, no negotiation has transpired for a contract for overnight accommodations in Zion National Park for next year. Tom Wilson, a spokesman for the National Park Service in Washington, D.C., said Friday no final decision had been made. "However, a study of moving concessions out of the park and a tentative decision to eventually phase them out has been reached," he said.
>
> TWA Services' contract was predicated on this possibility, according to Mr. Wilson, who said it had been a long-standing policy to build up business on the outside of the park and try to cut down some park traffic. Unofficial reports this week say the National Park Service is moving ahead with plans to phase out concessions in most of the parks, including Yosemite and Yellowstone, with Utah's going first, because it would not cost anything to locate the services outside the parks.

Trevor S. Povah, president of Hamilton Stores, Inc., a concessioner in Yellowstone National Park, found out about the article and wrote several worried letters to Washington. One went to NPS Director Gary Everhardt. Povah wrote "since the *Salt Lake Tribune* article quotes unofficial reports saying the National Park Service is moving ahead with its plans to phase out concessions in most of the parks, including Yosemite and Yellowstone, we are again concerned as to what is transpiring."

Director Everhardt wrote back on July 16, 1975:

> Tom (Wilson) is the National Park Service Chief of Media Information in our Office of Public Affairs, and has dealt many times daily with the press for a number of years without controversy. I am satisfied that this flap resulted from a misunderstanding and I explained this the other day to Representative Allan Howe.

Howe, of Utah's 2nd District, also answered Povah:

> I thank you for writing me your feelings concerning this
> most important issue. I have been trying for some time to
> extract from the National Park Service what their long-term
> policy is concerning the phase-out of facilities in the national
> parks, and as of this date I have as yet to receive a direct
> answer concerning this policy. However, in a conversation
> with the National Park Service Director, he did indicate that
> each park would be considered on its own individual merits as
> to whether a phase-out of facilities would become a reality.

But just to make sure Director Everhardt understood congressional intent, Utah's delegation admonished him on July
24, 1975:

> You have previously stated that pursuant to Public Law
> 89-249, it is your policy to close down existing lodging facilities
> inside the parks when such facilities can be provided outside
> park boundaries. However, there is no provision in Public Law
> 89-249 which directs that lodging facilities within national park
> boundaries should be precluded when lodging facilities exist
> outside the park boundaries.
> The language which you cite in Section 1 of the Law—that
> concession development should be limited to that which is
> necessary and appropriate for public use and enjoyment of an
> area, is merely a word of caution against over-development
> and use, since Congress recognized that this law grants to the
> Secretary of the Interior increased discretion in promoting
> concessioner development. However, reading Public Law
> 89-249 in its entirety, reveals that the law is designed to pro-
> vide for concession facilities—not to restrict them.

To add official sanction to this position, Senator Moss then
introduced a Resolution calling on the Secretary of the Interior and the Director of the National Park Service to repudi-
ate the policy of removing concessions from the national
parks:

. . . Whereas the Congress of the United States enacted, and the President approved, Public Law 89-249, to provide for lodging, facilities and services to make these parks available for the use, enjoyment and benefit of all people; Whereas the policies of Public Law 89-249 cry for reaffirmation,

Now therefore be it resolved: that the National Park Service, as the federal agency entrusted with the responsibility for administering these areas, be advised that it is the sense of the Senate of the United States that the National Park Service should take all appropriate action to carry out the terms of Public Law 89-249 to assure the availability of lodging and other services and facilities where appropriate in the national park system, thus enabling all of our citizens to use and enjoy their national parks, said use and enjoyment to be consistent with the obligation of said National Park Service to protect the parks from irreparable harm,

Be it further resolved: that this resolution be spread on the records of the United States Senate and a copy thereof be furnished to the Secretary of the Interior and the Director of the National Park Service.

Utah Senator E. Jake Garn then sent an undated "dear colleague" letter to the other senators from the West calling for support of the Moss resolution:

I am writing this letter to request your help in preventing the National Park Service from proceeding with their plans to close lodging accommodations inside Zion and Bryce Canyon National Parks. The lodging facilities at Zion are slated to be closed at the end of this year, while those facilities at Bryce Canyon will be closed two years hence. This action is a direct result of the Park Service's interpretation of Public Law 89-249 to mean that when adequate commercial services exist adjacent to the national park, then such services will be unnecessary and inappropriate inside the national park. Furthermore, the Park Service has expanded their policies in their current Management Policies Manual, April 1975 edition, to include not only those areas where adequate commercial facilities exist, but also to where they can possibly be developed.

The ramifications of this alternative accommodations policy have a bearing on more than just Zion and Bryce Canyon. It applies to all national parks—Yellowstone, Grand Teton, Mesa Verde and Glacier National Park—are just a few examples of the parks with support communities in close proximity to present concession sites.

In order to calm the opposition to this policy, the Park Service utilizes an escape valve by saying that the policy is implemented only on a case-by-case basis, but if Congress tolerates and is pacified by this pretext, each time a new case arises, then the Park Service will remove concessions case-by-case from the entire national park system.

The War of Letters

The Park Service "kept a low profile." Alarmed by the murky situation, Povah wrote on August 2, 1975, to Senator Clifford P. Hansen of Wyoming, quoting from the Yellowstone Master Plan and Environmental Impact Statement, which included a statement that the 9300 concessioner-provided pillow spaces in the park would be reduced to 8300.

Povah was particularly concerned about Old Faithful. The report recommended that "High priority should be given to gradually converting the Old Faithful development into a scenic day-use area, an objective that necessarily will take many years to achieve."

One section of the report got downright fierce about it:

Old Faithful should be restored to day-use area with the obliteration of all non-historic facilities. In the meantime, no overnight accommodations will be constructed. At Fishing Bridge, overnight facilities should be phased out of the Fishing Bridge area. The existing campground there, the Village Store and service station will, however, be retained for an interim period. At West Thumb, the gas station and other service facilities should be phased out.

Povah concluded to Congressman Hansen:

While the threat of removal in Yellowstone concerns the future, it is nevertheless a very real threat and when combined

with past and immediate situations such as those at Lassen and
Zion and Bryce, serves to illustrate that congressional intent
most recently enunciated in Public Law 89-249, is not being
followed by the National Park Service.

Now came the last straw. NPS Director Gary Everhardt on
September 18, 1975, wrote Utah Congressman Howe:

> The National Park Service has no overall policy concerning
> the closure of all over-night facilities at all national parks which
> are in close proximity to the community that can accommodate
> the park visitor's needs. Each park is treated as an individual
> case study.

Where had we heard that before? But Everhardt then got on
his high horse.

> With regard to the position that the National Park Service
> lacks the statutory authority for closing park facilities, we
> [NPS] offer the following comments:
> The Act of August 25, 1916, as amended and supplemented,
> directs the Secretary of the Interior to administer areas in the
> national park system in accordance with the fundamental pur-
> pose of conserving their scenery, wildlife, natural historic ob-
> jects and providing for the enjoyment in a manner that will
> leave them unimpaired for the enjoyment of future genera-
> tions. The Act of October 9, 1965, 79th Statute 969, 16 USC
> Section 20 et seq.
> In our judgment, this congressional mandate, as well as
> other authorities of the Secretary contained in 16 USC Section
> 1 et seq., as amended and supplemented, provides authoriza-
> tion pursuant to which the Secretary may exercise discretion as
> to the extent, if any, of permissible development within any
> park area. We consider that the exercise of this discretion is
> on-going and that . . . the Secretary shall have the authority to
> eliminate such developments, so long as proper compensation
> is paid affected concessioners.

This was just too much. Senator Henry M. Jackson of
Washington, Chairman of the Senate Interior and Insular

Affairs Committee, placed in the Senate Congressional Record on September 23, 1975, an impassioned plea on behalf of concession policy:

> Mr. Jackson: Mr. President, I bring to the attention of my colleagues a matter which is of critical importance to the State of Utah at this time, but which could appear at any time to any other state in the country. I am referring to the policy of the National Park Service toward overnight accommodation in national parks. The National Park Service has recently announced in its Administrative Policy Manual, Chapter 8, page 2:
>
> If adequate facilities exist or can be developed by private enterprise to serve the park visitors' needs for commercial services outside park boundaries, such facilities shall not be provided within the park area.
>
> The Park Service has initially singled out only lodging accommodations in implementing its policy of excluding commercial services inside the park, when they exist or can be developed outside the park; however, the language of the Park Service is much broader and more comprehensive. Commercial services such as campgrounds, restaurants and curio shops are not logically exempt from this recently announced policy and, therefore, could become victims also of such far-reaching decisions.
>
> The ultimate effect of this policy may be that people will be allowed access to the parks only on a limited daytime basis. An aesthete standard is being imposed by this policy which specifically affects those people who believe that a park visit is enriched by being able to spend a night inside the park.
>
> There is no adequate substitute for the overnight experience inside the park. There are only less desirable alternatives to this experience. Take the case of the park visitors who derive their greatest enjoyment of visiting the park by just being able to relax beside or near their cabin, taking in the park's natural beauty, and not having to rely on constant commuting to and from an external motel in the area. Such an alternative accommodation would not be surrounded by the beauty of the park in its natural setting, but would be surrounded by an environment similar to that of the city which he left.

While the policy that is currently being implemented may reduce the administrative problems of the National Park Service, it is in direct opposition to their charge to provide for the enjoyment of the national parks.

The lodging facilities being phased out in Zion and Bryce Canyon National parks are not for the purpose of protecting scenery, natural or historic objects or wildlife; in fact, the removal of log cabins at Bryce Canyon could be interpreted as a direct violation of the mandate to protect historical objects.

The Park Service, in its effort to conserve the park environment, has neglected the equally important duty to provide for the enjoyment of the environment. It must consider that there are different types of park visitors and that it should respond where reasonably possible.

It was Jackson, recall, who pushed the Concession Policy Act of 1965 through the Senate. If anybody knew its congressional intent, he did.

When the smoke cleared, the uprising had worked. The Senate's strong voice prevailed. The Park Service recanted and extended TWA Services's Zion and Bryce Canyon contracts for an additional seven years. At the end of the seven years, the Park Service issued a new 20-year contract. It shows that the Park Service can be convinced to listen to consumer demand, regardless what environmental purists "expect" it to do.

Perhaps the greatest lesson to be learned from this brouhaha, though, was summarized in the *Iron County Record*, of Cedar City, Utah, on August 28, 1975, in an article titled "Who's to Decide?"

> The implication of the issue is that the Park Service is considering each park on an individual basis. The handwriting is on the wall, that the "phase-out" is a definite goal of the department in all national parks. Like Senator Jake Garn told a Cedar City Chamber of Commerce meeting, "The departments are very courteous to congressmen. They answer their questions and respond to their letters; then they do just as they please."

But the peoples' victory was not complete. One day in the fall of 1975 the Park Service wrecking ball shattered Zion's rustic bath house while bulldozers ripped out its swimming pool. That same autumn day they smashed the historic lodge and cabins at Cedar Breaks National Monument into dusty debris. What a loss. Even with all the public outcry and political objections destruction of facilities can still take place.

Only direct intercession by Congress stopped Park Service barbarians from devastating the fine old lodges at Zion and Bryce Canyon.

The third rule in fighting back is obviously: "You can no longer trust the National Park Service to abide by the law."

18

Crisis With Everhardt

IN EARLY 1975 the signs became unmistakable: Michigan Representative John D. Dingell (D-Trenton) decided he was an environmental hero and wanted to run the Park Service. The trouble was, he sat on the wrong committee. The House Interior and Insular Affairs Committee possessed statutory oversight powers over all agencies of the Interior Department, including Dingell's coveted Park Service. Congressman John sat on the Interstate and Foreign Commerce Committee. He sat on the Merchant Marine and Fisheries Committee. He sat on the Small Business Committee. He even chaired the Small Business Committee's Subcommittee on Energy and Environment. But he did not sit on the Interior and Insular Affairs Committee. Being a Congressman of nimble wit, he decided that since the environment included national parks, and he was chairman of a Subcommittee including the Environment, that he would run the national parks anyway through his subcommittee. This was often referred to as "The Dingell Committee," despite the fact that it was only a subcommittee.

John Dingell quite obviously has no love for concessioners. It is also quite obvious that he regards the Concession Policy Act of 1965 as sincere but misguided demagoguery requiring his corrective hand. On July 25, 1975, the good Congressman lent powerful credence to those observations as he convened hearings on National Park Service Management of Concessions Operations. He and Pennsylvania Representative William S. Moorhead (D-Pittsburg), Chairman of the House

Government Operations Committee's Subcommittee on Conservation, Energy and Natural Resources, had decided to hold joint hearings, a slap at the Interior and Insular Affairs Committee. Mr. Dingell's opening statement conveys the atmosphere:

> Mr. Dingell: I think the nature of the matter before us demonstrates gross indifference of the National Park Service of its responsibilities under the law, and one of the functions of this gathering today is hopefully to procure—I must confess I say this with some doubt—statements from the Park Service indicating a change in the handling of their responsibilities to protect the public interest from predaceous actions of the concessioners.

Upon seeing fellow concession-hater Jack Brooks of Texas in his hearing room, Congressman Dingell spoke:

> Mr. Dingell: The Chair is delighted to acknowledge at this time the Chairman of the distinguished Government Operations Committee, who is a very good friend of us all here. We are certainly glad you are here, Mr. Chairman, and if you would like, we would be glad to have you join us.
>
> Mr. Brooks: I am going to have to go to another meeting, but I would just like to commend you, Mr. Dingell, and Mr. Moorhead, for this look at the concessions operations of the National Park Service, which for 20 years has been a disgrace. I tell you, I know from personal experience and personal investigation, that the Park Service gives, not by trade or by sale, but by inheritance, concession rights to the major park facilities in the United States. Families just inherit them from generation to generation, and there is no refuting the evidence. It has been clearly laid out before us. I am very delighted that both committees are now looking at it. It may be that now, on a bipartisan basis, we can reestablish some kind of equitable competition in the granting of these concessions and help protect the rights of people who drive with their kids to see the beauties of this nation.
>
> Mr. Dingell Mr. Chairman, we are in entire agreement with

you. We would be delighted if you would sit with us. I believe
your thoughts and views are certainly identical with my own
on these thoughts and viewpoints.

Mr. Brooks: Well, I have confidence in you—get after
them, John. My theory is, "if they won't follow the law, maybe
you can cut their appropriations." We can get the Appropriations Committee in here with us as well. Surely the Park
Service will pay some attention to Congress, now that we have
Republican and Democratic awareness of the problem of third
generation and fourth generation concession operators.

Mr. Dingell: Mr. Chairman, you echo our thoughts. As a
matter of fact, you say them first. We are proud of you, Mr.
Chairman. Thank you very much for being with us.

That was a lot of sweet talk even for people of this ilk. But
we can sort out several thematic elements in this lush and
impressionistic overture. Dingell, of course, was playing the
politician, saying what he thought the most influential pressure group wanted to hear. Unfortunately the whole history
of challenges to the legitimacy of national park concessions
was coming into focus here—but among people who had no
historical memory. They didn't know the evolution of the
Mather-Albright principles. They didn't realize that concessioners virtually created the great western national parks with
time, money, lobbying, and visitor accommodations. They
didn't understand that the Conference of National Park Concessioners had been called into existence originally by a respected Secretary of the Interior. They didn't know that the
words of their challenges had been spoken by others years
before.

In departing after his exchange with Dingell, the Texan
spoke nobly.

Mr. Brooks: I want it to be a fair and objective hearing.

As I sat awaiting my turn to give testimony on behalf of the
Conference of National Park Concessioners I didn't at all feel
this hearing would be either of those things. And I got a

distinctly uneasy feeling as the Honorable William S. Moorhead spoke up.

Mr. Moorhead: Mr. Chairman, I would first like to commend you and my predecessor, Mr. Reuss, for the hearings [on concessions] you held last year. I think they have already had some results. I would also like to join you in commending the GAO and I want to welcome them before this joint hearing.

I remembered the GAO only too well. Theirs was the first witness, Henry Eschwege, Director, Resource and Economic Development Division. Mr. Eschwege testified that, based on his review of the concession operation at Yosemite National Park, he concluded that the Park Service does not have sufficient information to determine whether existing concessioners are performing satisfactorily and, therefore, are entitled to consideration when the contract is expanded or renewed. He criticized having one large business control all the concessions in the parks, stating that from a practical point of view, the Service cannot close down the concessioner to force compliance, because the concessioner's sizable investment makes it difficult for the Service to obtain funds to buy them out. He said:

We believe that the Act allows the Park Service to institute a policy of asking the concessioner to waive his possessory interest. This would obviate some of the problems of acquiring concessioner facilities.

He further testified that the Concessions Policy Act encourages continuity in concession operations; that if Congress wished to provide for more competition in the award and renewal of such contracts, it could do so by encouraging construction of facilities by the government whenever possible. [But, remember,this would require the government to advance the construction funds up front.] Eschwege further testified that Congress could encourage competition by amending the Concession Policy Act to limit preferential renewal rights.

While I was trying to figure out how government ownership encourages competition, my turn came to testify. I was an old hand at it now. I was no longer green in the ways of Congress, though perhaps a little gray. After all these years I noticed myself getting tired of sitting in congressional hearing rooms.

I told the august body that I had testified before a number of congressional committees and that the concessions movement had probably been investigated more than any contractor for government services in the history of the country. Its policies had been challenged on at least three separate occasions, two of them before congressional committees and, despite any weaknesses the system may have, on each occasion the Mather-Albright principles had been reaffirmed.

By now you undoubtedly have a good idea what the rest of my testimony was like, so I'll spare you the details. You can guess the outcome of these fair and objective hearings by the title of the resulting Government Operations Committee report, which is self-explanatory: *National Park Service Policies Discourage Competition, Give Concessioners Too Great a Voice in Concession Management.*

Cultural amnesia institutionalized! The report concluded that the role of the concessioners in planning had been disproportionately greater than the public's. The report claimed that concession contracts had protected the government's interest inadequately and that some typical provisions—for example, the granting of monopolies, preferential rights, and possessory interests—were "creating windfalls no longer necessary for the large businesses operating concessions."

This kind of anti-capitalist thinking is quite typical of the environmentalists' approach to concessions. They do not like the idea of profit. It is a dirty word to them. They look at the world of concessions and sees subsidiaries of large conglomerate corporations such as MCA, ARA Services, Greyhound,

AMFAC, and Del Webb operating concessions in 16 parks. They don't think of the other 321 park units (mostly smaller ones) or the nearly 500 other concessioners. They don't see the service rendered, the people pleased, or the jobs generated by these conglomerate corporations in those 16 parks, either. TW Services, with concessions in six units (Bryce Canyon, North Rim Grand Canyon, Yellowstone, Zion, Death Valley and Everglades) employs nearly 3,000 people and had gross receipts in 1983 of more than $27 million. Their main product is happy people who've enjoyed America's national parks. By comparison, the National Wildlife Federation had gross receipts in 1985 of $43 million, and their main product is unemployment for loggers, miners, and petroleum drillers.

In his rush to rip up the Concession Policy Act of 1965, Mr. Dingell forgot to mention the ratio of little concessioners to big concessioners. Most concessions have always been small. I remember Lassen well. Out of more than 500 concession contracts in 1983—a statistically typical year—only 113 had gross sales of as much as $250,000, and most had much less. At Grand Canyon, for example, some 20 river-rafting concessioners employ between 10 and 30 people each and earn gross receipts averaging around $300,000 a year, the smallest earning about $100,000 (most typical), the largest about $1.6 million.

But Congressman Dingell doesn't care about any of this. He wants concessions eliminated to please ideological purists. That's exactly what his proposals would do if enacted—eliminate all national park concessions. He knows it. I know it. And now you know it. And Congressman Dingell knew what his hearing report was going to say before his hearings got started.

Internecine Strife

While all this flak was coming at us from the usurping committees of Congressmen Brooks and Dingell, the Conference of National Park Concessioners was generating some of its own flak from the inside. In early 1975, the Conference voted to incorporate as a non-profit organization. As Lincoln might have put it, the solutions of the quiet past were no longer adequate to the stormy present. The informal structure that had worked for so many years was simply not up to handling our problems with various congressional committees and the fact that a new law required any organization attempting in any manner to influence legislation to register as a lobbying group.

The Conference had for many years retained a Washington representative in a capacity that amounted to a lobbyist in some respects. Former Interior Assistant Secretary Dale E. Doty had been our first "Washington Rep" after he retired from government in the late 1950s. He handled day-to-day contacts with the Washington crowd under the executive authority of the Conference's board chairman and enjoyed a distinguished reputation on Capitol Hill. Another retired Interior official, Imogene LaCovey, had followed Doty. In late 1974 we hired former Lockheed Corporation lobbyist Edward M. Lightfoot—our first Washington representative without prior concession-related government experience.

In January of 1975 the Conference board instructed Lightfoot to prepare Articles of Incorporation for approval by the membership. He submitted them to me on February 3, along with a proposed set of By-Laws. I looked them over and saw that Ed had modeled them after the usual trade-group setup: a hired executive director with day-to-day administrative powers and an elected chairman to make general policy. Environmental groups are organized the same way; most lobbying groups are set up that way regardless of their purpose.

I objected to these proposed By-Laws because I thought control should be vested in someone who had been elected, not hired. I had seen too many cases of executive directors who betrayed the best interests of their groups because they constantly had to "play ball" with the bureaucracy, compromising on marginal questions and hoping to call in the chit when a really important issue came up.

And I now knew the nature of the environmentalists we were up against. They would insist upon compromise, because they knew that compromise was the legislative ideal. But when an environmentalist wants you to compromise, it's over how much he gets to take away from you. He wants everything you've got and the compromise you reach is that he only gets half. To an environmentalist, what's his is his. What's yours is negotiable.

I changed the By-laws to read:

> The Chairman is charged with the executive and administrative responsibilities in the management and continuing conduct of the affairs of the Conference. He shall be the chief policy spokesman for the Conference.

And I kept my eyes open. I knew this little incident with Ed meant there would be a power struggle one day. Worse, I knew this meant that someone outside would find out about it and take advantage of the split.

On January 13, 1975, a new National Park Service Director had come into office. This time he was not a political appointee but a Service professional, a man named Gary Everhardt—we've seen a bit of him in the last two chapters. Now it's time to tell his whole story.

As soon as I got word of his appointment I contacted him as Chairman of the Conference and asked for an opportunity to discuss our mutual problems. Nothing. I tried on six different occasions to arrange a meeting with Everhardt, but somehow he was always too busy. I sensed his uneasiness in the new job. I didn't know him, but the Washington scuttlebutt was that Everhardt had come to his lofty position at the behest of the Rockefellers. Gary had served a stint as superintendent of Grand Teton National Park—the area around Jackson Hole had been bought up and donated to the Park Service by Rockefeller cohorts—and was said to enjoy the Rockefeller favor. He was also said to be out of his depth in the new job.

Well, I figured, everybody is a little intimidated by their

first days in that job. So I conveyed to Everhardt the Conference's full support. I let him know that in the past we had always conducted Conference affairs through the Chairman and that the Conference position was the collective voice of the concessioners.

But I soon saw that Everhardt was deliberately avoiding me. Too much was happening with too little communication from the bureaucracy. Park Service relations with concessioners were sinking to an all-time low. The first indicator appeared in February when Everhardt designated Phillip O. Stewart, former head of park land acquisition, as Concessions Management Representative, the Conference contact point in the Park Service. We found him to be not only arbitrary and inflexible, but also totally unfamiliar with concessions. Most of our members absolutely refused to negotiate with him.

We became concerned as well over the growing bureaucracy sent in to supervise concessions. Concession "specialists"—who in fact knew next to nothing about concessions—were placed in positions of power and authority. Their net effect was not to improve service to the public but to lower efficiency and raise costs.

Then Everhardt, through Stewart, began to issue unilateral changes in contract language, a provision here, a term there, stretching the Concession Policy Act beyond reason and recognition. It was a foreshadowing of much worse to come. I sent sharp reminders to Director Everhardt that the law had a definite meaning and he had no right to break it. Our relationship ebbed to the vanishing point.

William Briggle then entered the picture and appeared to offer some hope of reconciliation. An experienced administrator, he was appointed Deputy Director of the Park Service on June 13, 1975. Shortly thereafter, Conference executive director Lightfoot met with Briggle and Director Everhardt. In an effort to remove the main stumbling block to rapport, Lightfoot told them bluntly that more than half the concessioners would not deal with Phil Stewart. Park Service-

Conference relations would be bad as long as Stewart remained as contact point.

"Let me tell you something," Director Everhardt responded, "You people may not be able to talk to Phil Stewart, but I can't talk to Don Hummel."

Lightfoot had been fully informed of the fundamental disagreement between Everhardt and me over contract manipulation. He said, "Are you thinking of a *quid pro quo*?"

"What would you suggest?" asked Everhardt.

"You take Stewart out of contract negotiations and the Conference will take Hummel out of the chairmanship."

They both knew who would be left as the voice of the Conference of National Park Concessioners. There was only one problem with Lightfoot's deal: the Conference knew nothing about it.

While Lightfoot sought some way to bring his plan to fruition, concessioners whose contracts were coming due for renewal began to adopt stalling tactics rather than deal with Stewart. This did not improve Gary Everhardt's mood. In September 1975 the Park Service released its Management Policies Manual, containing the overt statement:

> If adequate facilities exist or can be developed to meet people's commercial needs outside park boundaries, such facilities will not be provided in the park.

Senator Jackson, as you will recall from Chapter 17, was to decry this statement a few days later in the Congressional Record. Official admission of this long-denied policy came as another serious blow to all Conference members. No longer was there any question about what the concessioner and the visiting public faced from the Park Service. It seemed like one thing after another: Master Plan biases, Environmental Impact Statement obstructions, contract manipulations, unilateral policy changes. But the worst thing I had to deal with as Conference chairman during 1975 was not Everhardt, but a genuine concession scandal brewing in Yellowstone.

Yellowstone Park Company had entered into a 1966 contract that stipulated they were to invest $10 million in facil-
ities by mid-1975. The company's profit had declined for
several years in the early 1970s and their facilities and service with it. By the time the $10 million was supposed to
have been invested, a new owner had taken over and soon
thereafter became part of General Host. In August, 1975,
the Park Service extended the investment deadline two
years.

In 1976 the Park Service would assemble a Yellowstone
Concessions Study Team composed of representatives from
Yellowstone Park Company and Hamilton Stores, Inc. (the
two principal concessioners in the park), representatives of the
Service's Denver Service Center, the Regional Office, and
the Yellowstone Superintendent's staff. The team was to
study the growing crisis for eight months. Their final report,
*Yellowstone National Park Concessions Management Review
of the Yellowstone Park Company*, would reveal grave faults
with General Host's management of the concession. Everhardt's inflexible contract policy hovered over all the problems, but the concessioner was failing in its obligations.

The situation was so serious that word had gotten out to
every concessioner in the system. This could become the
test case nobody wanted to see: What would happen when
the new environmentalist-ridden Park Service terminated a
contract because of unsatisfactory performance? Would the
government pay fair market value as the Concession Policy
Act required or would it demand the much lower book
value? In such a dilemma over concessioner performance
there was nothing I or the Conference could do under the
best of circumstances—we had repeatedly rejected becoming each others' policemen. And with the Everhardt
impasse, we couldn't even talk to the Park Service about it.

Despite this rash of troubles, there were a few bright spots
in the winter of 1975-76. At least one congressman stood up
and strongly challenged the environmentalists. Joe Skubitz, a
congressman from Kansas, and seven-term member of the

House of Representatives, made a statement on the floor of the House on January 21, 1976. He said:

> During my **seven** terms in this house, I have been a member of the Interior Committee and I have spent considerable time on the problems of the national park system. Over the years, I have watched a growing national debate, arising like hot lava in the plumbing of a volcano. It is a debate between conservationists, who would restrict and limit the use of the national parks, and those like myself who believe that the parks are for people; that their use and enjoyment should be encouraged.
>
> Some extremists would only be happy when all man-made structures are completely eliminated from the national parks, right down to the roads and overlooks everyone uses to view the scenery. This course, if implemented, would eliminate all visitation except for a few young healthy backpackers.

Another bright spot paradoxically came as a result of increasingly restrictive Park Service Master Plans calling for limitation or removal of concession services from the parks. The Conference had commissioned Stanford Research Institute of Menlo Park, California, to perform a substantial study of the question. The results, released in January 1976, were quite revealing. These were the questions and answers:

	Oppose	Favor
1. Do you favor or oppose removal of *all* overnight hotel and lodge type facilities?	92.2	5.6
2. Do you favor or oppose removal of *some* hotel and lodge type facilities?	74.7	20.6
3. Do you favor or oppose removal of *all* established campgrounds?	83.5	7.0
4. Do you favor or oppose removal of *some* established campgrounds?	61.8	26.1

Park visitor preferences had been polled with statistical error factors of less than plus-or-minus 4.3 percent at 95 percent confidence level for yes-no type response results.

The Stanford Research Institute report's executive summary went into considerable detail on the costs of removing visitor facilities from Yosemite:

> A 1973 Park Service evaluation of moving of what were termed "non-essential" facilities out of Yosemite was projected at a cost of between $110 and $113 million in 1973 dollars— close to twice the $65.9 million in 1976 planning/construction/ reconstruction dollars requested for the entire System.

Another interesting fact:

> Assuming concession elimination, an examination of operational logistics reveals other problems to be overcome. At Yellowstone, for example, a visitor must travel a 140-mile loop to view the park's principal natural features. Without overnight facilities inside the park, each visitor would have to complete the loop between sunup and sundown, substantially diminishing the park experience and congesting the park entrances at sunup and sundown hours.

But the new year did not bring improved relations with Everhardt. On March 10, 1976, Lightfoot and I went to see Assistant Secretary Nathaniel Reed about it. We told him our problems in some detail, including Everhardt's unilateral imposition of new contract provisions. Assistant Secretary Reed deplored the situation. He promised that we would all get together at the Denver Service Center, which was a more central meeting place, and work out some solutions. Lightfoot and I went away feeling that perhaps things would improve now. But somehow the promised meeting never took place.

And now came a move that caused the most profound concern. Everhardt broke all precedent and unilaterally changed our entire standard-language contract (the "boiler-plate" form) without consulting the concessioners about it in advance. On July 12, 1976, Everhardt placed in the *Federal Register* a total standard-language contract revamp as *fait accompli*. The Conference was stunned. We had always been asked for Conference comment on all standard-language contract matters before Park Service adoption. We had fought small unilateral changes here and there for years—including Everhardt's—but this was totally unheard-of. Concessioners had been given no opportunity to discuss the new standard-language contract's effect on operations or its compliance with the Concession Policy Act. All we had was a thirty-day comment period *after* the contract's publication.

The significance of Everhardt's tactic cannot be overstressed: The contract is the legal basis of all Park Service/Concessioner relations. It is the foundation of concessioners' rights and responsibilities. The terms of these relations and rights are clearly spelled out in the Concession Policy Act of 1965. They protect the concessioner, the government and the public. For the Park Service to unilaterally manipulate contract terms as an instrument of policy change is to undermine all concessioner security. Most disastrous for the concessioner and the public, there is virtually no recourse against contract manipulation. And most ominous, the long-standing oversight that Congress had once exercised over contract changes—insisting that all changes must win the agreement of the Conference of National Park Concessioners and the National Park Service—had been weakened by the incursions of the House Government Operations and Small Business Committees, and now stood virtually abandoned.

At first the thought that Everhardt was beginning a deliberate assault on contract provisions seemed too incredible to consider. But the fact soon became obvious. As Conference chairman I protested firmly that his behavior constituted a breach of trust and perhaps a breach of law. I was absolutely adamant. No compromise. I would not let the Concession Policy Act of 1965 be repealed by default.

A turning point came that fall. On September 2, 1976, at Hamilton Stores in West Yellowstone, Montana, I called a special meeting of the Conference Board of Directors. I reported that I had received a message from executive director Lightfoot, a message that had come to him from NPS Director Everhardt and Deputy Director Briggle. The Park Service had requested that representatives of the Conference meet with Deputy Director Briggle to discuss ways and means of improving communications between the Conference and the Park Service. The request specifically stipulated that neither Director Everhardt nor Chairman Hummel be present.

I had pondered this situation seriously before calling the board meeting. Perhaps I had become a stumbling block instead of a help. I privately decided to decline another term as Conference Chairman. But I said nothing to the board meeting, only transmitted the Park Service message in a businesslike manner. The Board of Directors ordered that Director Edward Hardy of Yosemite, Director Vern Johnson of Grand Teton, and Executive Director Lightfoot should arrange the proposed meeting, subject to these two instructions:

1) No matter of substance be discussed.

2) Director Everhardt, Acting Assistant Director Stewart and Chairman Hummel not attend.

The meeting with Deputy Director Briggle was held on September 27, 1976, at Dulles Airport in Washington, D.C.

Vern Johnson, Trevor Povah of Yellowstone—sitting in for Hardy of Yosemite, who could not attend—and Ed Lightfoot represented the concessioners. The minutes of this meeting were reported back to me as follows:

Concessioners: Why had Briggle asked for the meeting and what did he think it would accomplish? Also, what, in his opinion, had caused the Conference/Park Service impasse?

Briggle: Obvious answer—there are personality clashes. We recognize Hummel has been an outstanding member and Chairman of the Conference almost since its inception. He has more than satisfactorily operated several of our finest concession operations. He literally has more background and knowledge regarding the concessions operations and problems than anyone else today. His devotion to the concession cause is legendary and we wish we could work with him. His views should be considered. But Hummel has an uncompromising attitude that we can no longer accept. We wonder about the Conference really representing all concessioners as long as Hummel is in the chair. Hummel is brilliant, but dogmatic. The Conference needs to give Ed Lightfoot more authority so he can act for them.

Concessioners: Why Lightfoot?

Briggle: He is here in Washington. He gets along very well with Gary. We know that the Hummel problem is aggravated by Everhardt. Gary is a compromiser. He plays on human relations. A specific system of positive communication should be developed with your Washington office. If you need to change your rules, change them.

Concessioners: Why is Gary Everhardt so uptight?

Briggle: He can't be pushed; he must be led. Hummel has tried to push him. Hummel doesn't seem to recognize or want to recognize NPS problems. Then too, NPS personnel must be made aware that the concessioners are not bad people just because they are concessioners. The concessioners really need to police their own operations by establishing standards and insisting on adherence to those standards. When it comes to communicating, you just can't refuse to talk, even under the very worst of circumstances and still hope to establish satisfactory communications.

Concessioners: Under what conditions will Everhardt relax his repeated statement that he just won't talk any more with Hummel?

Briggle: The Conference must impress on Hummel that there is a problem; that he is a contributor to the problem and that to reopen a satisfactory discussion, there must be a capability and a desire to recognize the Park Service's side of the problem, and discuss it from both points of view.

Concessioners: Why can't Everhardt more easily and quickly say "yes" or "no," and then stand by it?

Briggle: It is the very nature of the guy—he ponders and ponders and ponders. He is a brilliant man, but he allows fear and concern of bad reactions somewhere to influence his actions.

Concessioners: Why, after so many years of mutually satisfactory operations, do we suddenly have so many more costly, effort-consuming controls placed on us?

Briggle: The pressure from outside groups, environmentalists and all, highlighted by Dingell/Brooks Committee actions, and focused on the MCA and Yellowstone situations have pressured Gary into the action being taken. The Conference has not endeavored to be of assistance, but has steadfastly, unpleasantly, objected to any proposed or adopted position. The Conference could help us a great deal in the Yellowstone Park Company situation.

Lightfoot: Why didn't you ask us to help you draft proposed standard contract language?

Briggle: We should have, but unfortunately, this was done at the lowest ebb in our communications cycle. I acknowledge it was a mistake.

Concessioners: Why has NPS so suddenly, in the last 18 months, apparently acceded to the great pressure from the environmentalists?

Briggle: We had to because it came to us from all sides, as well as from above. You know Reed's views.

Briggle's conclusions: He believed the meeting showed progress. Everhardt believed, and Briggle concurred, that Hummel must be replaced by a less uncompromising Chairman. No decision was made to remove Phil Stewart. The NPS would like this or a similar Conference group to meet with them two or three times a year. A self-policing program should be developed. Finally, a positive system of communications was needed. All communications both oral and written should flow through the Conference's executive director in Washington. This would expedite action.

The report was signed by Vern Johnson, Edward Lightfoot and Trevor S. Povah. Povah insisted that a letter be appended to the meeting report:

To: Edward Lightfoot: I would like to go on record that although the minutes do not reflect this, we did not just listen to Bill's answers. We did discuss the issues and spoke out in favor of our Chairman's position. Nobody can deny that our

Chairman knows more of the concession system policy, history and why the original policies were enacted than Don Hummel. He has also been the one person who has devoted more time and effort to the concessioners' problems than any one of us in the concessions business today. I am sure everyone agrees we all appreciate Don's hard work and the continued help he will give us all in the future.

Trevor Povah

So there it was. Everhardt wouldn't talk to me because I refused to compromise away our rights guaranteed under the Concession Policy Act of 1965. And Ed Lightfoot was only too eager to do so. I reconsidered my earlier resolve. My tenure in office was the Conference's decision, not the National Park Service's or our hired lobbyist's. I therefore ran for office again in 1977 and was reelected Chairman of the Conference each year until 1980 when I voluntarily stepped aside.

But now, as 1976 drew to a close, the contract manipulation problem absorbed our attention. Everhardt's new "standard-language" contract published in the *Federal Register* had aroused such furor that the "30-day comment period" had been extended from August 12 to October 12. This "standard-language" contract was so bad it allowed the Park Service to unilaterally abrogate nearly any provision of an existing concession contract at any time.

Specifically, the new contract proposed to 1) authorize competing concessioners to pre-empt existing preferential rights; 2) deprive concessioners of the use of land and buildings at the whim of the Secretary; 3) give the Secretary power to arbitrarily increase franchise fees; 4) empower the Secretary to terminate any contract "for the convenience of the government"; and 5) empower the Secretary to impair possessory interest. In short, the proposed contract effectually repealed the Concession Policy Act of 1965 without the inconvenience of having to obtain congressional approval.

My protest on behalf on the Conference finally reached Assistant Secretary Nathaniel Reed. I had strongly stated that the Concession Policy Act's whole point was to create a "bankable contract" to enable concessioners to borrow money to make the capital improvements needed by the public. In late November, Assistant Secretary Reed evidently heard me— he never told me so—for he submitted the proposed contract to the Bank of America and Chase Manhattan Bank asking, "Does our proposed modification of contract language in any way change the loanability as contrasted with the existing contract, disregarding the capital position of any particular concessioner?"

Bank of America's vice-president and assistant general counsel Winfield Jones began his reply by saying,

"As you may know, loans to such concessioners have never been as attractive to lenders as loans to most other businesses." Jones pointed out that lenders want assurances that the business will survive long enough to pay off the loan, and that some assets can be secured as collateral in the event of foreclosure. National Park concessions offer neither assurance. Jones ended each section of his detailed point-by-point response to Reed's inquiry with the comment, "This might give lenders some concern," or "This would give lenders some concern."

Chase Manhattan's vice-president and assistant to the chairman Joseph V. Reed, Jr. wrote a "Dear Nathaniel" letter back to Assistant Secretary Reed (his brother) on December 2, "I have had several people read the proposed contract and I have read it a couple of times myself. Overall, the concensus is that the contract leaves decisions in it, most all of the key financial areas, totally to the discretion of the Secretary of the Interior . . . Quite frankly, this . . . gives the Secretary extremely broad powers and leaves the concessioner in a rather tenuous position."

In his detailed analysis, Joseph Reed stated that the proposed contract provisions were "generally unacceptable to most commercial bankers," and they leave "very little that can be relied upon as an asset value against which a banker would prudently lend money."

The message was clear: No banker in his right mind would lend money to anyone foolish enough to sign a contract such as the Park Service had proposed. The Everhardt contract never received approval. Refusing to compromise has its points. The NPS however, still holds concessioners hostage by demanding that they sign contracts that forfeit their security rights.

On July 5, 1977, William Whalen took Everhardt's place as Director of the National Park Service. Whalen welcomed my initial contact and we had several friendly meetings. It appeared to be the beginning of a new era. It turned out to be something quite different.

19

Saving The National Parks

We've finally come to the last chapter. My story is about over. There's just a little more personal business to cover before we size up America's national park concessions today and see what we can do to preserve the human face of our parks. So bear with it a few pages more. Then I'll be through.

The Thrill Is Gone

In 1977 I entered into negotiations to sell our Glacier operations to TWA Services, the concessioner at Zion, Bryce and North Rim Grand Canyon. The vast expansion of government regulations, the appointment of concessions specialists and general bureaucratic intervention in the operations had taken out all the fun. Watching private enterprise in the parks being eroded by government zealots pained me. Concessioning in America's wonderlands was no longer a partnership to provide service to the public. It had become a grueling contest with the purist-suborned Park Service for sheer survival. New Park Service Director Whalen and his friendly posture seemed to make little difference in the day-to-day business of the parks.

TWA and I came to tentative agreement on a sale, but they did not want to buy the whole company—only the national park portion, excluding East Glacier's Glacier Park Lodge and the Prince of Wales Hotel in Canada. We couldn't come to terms because of the tax implications so the deal eventually fell through.

By law I had to inform the Park Service of my attempt to sell so the press became involved while TWA and I were still dealing. The *Hungry Horse News* of Columbia Falls, Montana, contacted me and I confirmed that negotiations were in progress. Dick Munro, Glacier Park Acting Superintendent, released the following story:

> Don Hummel and his associates rebuilt the business into a successful venture in spite of a 70 to 80 day visitor season, old facilities and an inflationary economy. Over the years Glacier Park visitors have been well served by the company. This is evident by the lack of visitor complaints. Written complaints averaged less than 10 per year. When we consider that in 1977 Glacier Park Inc. housed over 98,000 persons and served approximately 448,000 meals to visitors, the complaint factor is infinitesimal. Glacier Park Inc. has provided valuable services to Glacier National Park visitors and will be missed.

The Montana Tourist Promotion Bureau saw the story and asked me to attend their annual conference. They prevailed upon me to continue our operations in Glacier. Well, why not? I might as well give it another try.

The Yellowstone Matter

While I carried on business as usual the concession situation simmering in Yellowstone exploded like one of its famous geysers. Everhardt's contract abrogation tactic seemed to be continuing under Whalen.

The Yellowstone problem had admittedly started with the concessioner. When a new owner took over the failing Yellowstone Park Company, the existing 1966 contract requirement to invest $10 million by 1975 still stood. General Host soon took over the new owner and also did not meet this obligation despite two contract extensions. By 1978 it had met only about 59 percent of the $10 million investment requirement. It was clearly in the wrong. It had misjudged its financial returns. I'm an advocate for concessions, but I will not justify any concessioner's failure to comply with its contract.

Much to every concessioner's sorrow, the Park Service began proceedings to terminate General Host's contract for unsatisfactory service. However, the firm negotiated an agreement for the Park Service to buy out the contract. The idea of selling out to the government, of course, did not please the rest of the concessioners, but they had no say in the matter. The Park Service had already bought out General Host's Everglades contract for $1.2 million because the company also failed to meet its contract obligations in that park.

But now, in Yellowstone, the Park Service applied a new contract abrogation tactic: As a condition of coming to a settlement with General Host, it demanded that all possessory interest be sold to the government and never assigned to a successor, much as it had done in the Zion/Bryce/North Rim Grand Canyon contract with TWA Services. Although it was completely illegal under the Concession Policy Act of 1965, Director Whalen approved this kind of contract abrogation as a deliberate and open policy.

Anti-Concession Policy Intensifies

The Carter administration surrounding Whalen had come into office on a strongly environmentalist platform and soon huge numbers of environmental organization members found positions in the Interior Department. These zealots had none of the spirit of service to the public that had built America's historic conservation administration. They were religiously dedicated to an ideology, not to the public. The public consisted of people and people were anathema to them. They hid their distrust of everything human behind pat phrases such as "professionalism"—Potomac lingo for "We don't care about people. People are definitely at the bottom of the totem pole."

Now their anti-concession policy came to Yellowstone: As the Conservation Foundation put it, "The government was convinced that it could exercise sufficient control over subsequent concessioners only if it bought General Host's interest." The Park Service had originally insisted upon paying compensation equal only to the book value of the facilities—practically nothing, as many buildings had been built in the early days—but General Host insisted on "sound value"—reconstruction cost of the structures (not to exceed "fair market value") minus physical depreciation. A government appraiser established a low figure under $10 million, General Host asked for $43 million, and they compromised at $19.9 million. The Park Service in 1979 bought out the Yellowstone Park Company's possessory interest and terminated General Host's contract. Part of the funds had been appropriated by Congress, the rest scrounged from other Park Service budgets.

No one was happy with this buy-out except General Host. Virtually every concessioner felt the price was much too high. They only wanted *sound* value, not *inflated* value. And the environmentalists complained that some Park Service officials who knew nothing about the deal told them the value of General Host's possessory interest was closer to $4.5 million. The Park Service thus put itself at odds with the environmentalists and through their lobbyists, with Congress. The House Appropriations Committee's Subcommittee on Interior Appropriations subsequently tied a rider to the Park Service's 1980 appropriation calling for payment of book value in cases of breach of contract by any concessioner. This flies in the teeth of the Concession Policy Act of 1965. However, this rider was never called into action.

Disintegration

And now, on our final leg of the discovery trail, I must take you with me through my departure from my long devotion to concessioning. The beginning of the end came at the annual spring meeting of the Glacier concession with the park superintendent and his staff on April 23, 1979. It was the last of the good relations. All seemed well, even cheery. Superintendent Phillip Iverson did not express any criticism of our concession operations for the past year. In fact, he had praised our operation before a Rotary club meeting. But soon afterward, the Yellowstone fiasco's shock waves spread to Glacier like ripples in a pond.

The splash that started the ripples was a General Accounting Office survey of the government's newly acquired assets at Yellowstone. The GAO report severely criticized fire and safety conditions there and censured the National Park Service for lax enforcement. As a result, NPS Director Whalen issued a memorandum requiring the Park Service to make a thorough inspection of all park and concessions facilities, particularly older buildings—a special survey over and above the routine annual fire and life safety inspection programs.

The first of September, a team of sixteen government inspectors arrived at Glacier Park headquarters for the survey. We gathered in the Park Service conference room. As a goodwill gesture I brought Cy Stevenson, our retired Chief Engineer, to make available his vast knowledge of our facilities.

After a businesslike discussion, we agreed to meet in five days when the team would alert us what to expect from their written report. We parted amicably and Cy agreed to show them everything. That night he called and said, "Hummel, I don't know what I can contribute. This gang of sixteen arrived at Many Glacier and scattered like a covey of quail. Each one has a notebook and is making his own inspection."

Five days later we gathered in the Park Service conference room as agreed. I asked for the promised preliminary reports. They refused to say anything. Park Superintendent Iverson and I protested without avail. The reason came out later. No one had coordinated the inspections and no one knew what was in the sixteen notebooks. We would find out in due course.

Whalen's Outrage

In late October the Conference of National Park Concessioners held its annual mid-year meeting at Wahweap Lodge on Lake Powell in Arizona—a Del E. Webb concession. Our first order of business was a board of directors meeting called in specific response to a request by National Park Service Director William Whalen. He wanted a chance to talk over our problems prior to addressing the general session. As a courtesy, I introduced Whalen to the Conference's new Washington representative, former congressman from Utah Allan Howe. Our outgoing representative Imogene LaCovey was retiring after a year and a half's good service.

Director Whalen blew up at the idea of us hiring a former congressman, saying that if we were going to go around him, he could play the game. And if he couldn't lick us in Congress, he could lick us in the press. He said he could get editorial support from the *New York Times*, the *Washington Post*, and the *Los Angeles Times*. I explained that our policy had not changed and we expected to cooperate with the Service as we had in the past.

Despite this assurance, Whalen, accompanied by a number of his staff people including Lloyd "Buddy" Surles, Chief of Concessions, went before the Conference general membership and repeated his threats.

> I hope that I am not misreading some of the signals, but to walk in here and find that you hired an ex-member of Congress to be your Washington representative, I hope that is not a signal to me that you intend to go around the Administration and around me and to deal on the Hill. If it is, fine, because I can play the game also and I want to assure you that you will be hearing about it in the editorial pages of the *Los Angeles Times*, *New York Times*, and the *Washington Post*, because I can play rough too, if you want to play that way. I don't want to get into an editorial war, but want to lay my cards on the table, and if that is the direction you want to take, okay, we'll play it that way. If you want to work out a good working relationship between Allan and ourselves, we want to work that relationship out. He is a respected attorney in Washington and we are very happy to work with him, but if it is going to be a behind

the scenes relationship that begins, well then I guess we're just going to have to go to the mats also.

No citizen of the United States should be subjected to such abuse from a public servant. Our tape recorder took it all in. When Whalen finished his session, Concessions Chief Buddy Surles saw the tape recorder and asked, "Was that thing running when the Director was speaking?" I told him, "It was on the table in clear view the entire time." He gave me a look that required no translation. I had thirty tape copies of the Director's remarks made and distributed to the concessioners. The Director knew it. There is an old saying that biographer Robert Shankland mentions in *Steve Mather of the National Parks*: "It's fatal to get in the way of the Park Service." I was about to find out what he meant.

First I found out what was in those fire inspectors' notebooks. A 300-page report came from the Park Service Regional Office reporting on the state of Glacier Park, Inc.'s concession. It was a hatchet job pure and simple. Someone had assembled it with great cunning. In one section, the written text praised the general condition of Rising Sun Motel, but the accompanying photograph showed a row of plastic trash bags and cited them as evidence of our bad housekeeping. In fact, the bags were routinely left behind the laundry about noon for garbage pickup later in the day.

The section on Swiftcurrent was the same: written text approving our operation, photograph showing a work-table needing repainting. It was the same throughout—not just about fire and safety, but a great many other references calculated to discredit the general operation. The "rehabilitation" requirements listed in this document were absurdly extensive. The "Special Life/Safety" program, as they called this general repair program, had to be completed before the next season opening date of June 7, 1980 or they would not let me open. It didn't matter that the roads into the facilities were snowed-in until late spring. It didn't matter that it would be impossible for me to hire, house, and feed a crew until late spring. They told me that was my problem. The final cost estimate: $1,750,000. It's fatal to get in the way of the Park Service.

Pressure Point

Now I had a good idea of what lay in store for me. In January 1980 the bureaucracy descended on Glacier in grandeur. Washington Concessions Chief Buddy Surles brought with him Denver Regional officials James B. Johnson, Assistant Regional Director, John Spurgeon, Regional Chief of Concessions, and a long memory about tape recorders.

We had "frank and useful" discussions, as the diplomats say. I told these men that I had only five years remaining on my contract and the law provided that I could not be required to make an investment without a reasonable opportunity to make a return on the investment. I pointed out that this $1,750,000—much of it applying only to new construction, not our historic buildings—would not produce a dollar of revenue in any period of time.

They said a new contract couldn't be approved before the Special Life/Safety program had to be completed. They offered to extend my present contract. I agreed based on their assurances.

By mid-January the tapes of Director Whelan's imprudent remarks had made their way to Congress. Within days Congressman Morris K. Udall wrote as chairman of the House Interior and Insular Affairs Committee to Interior Secretary Cecil D. Andrus:

> I was outraged by the remarks of the Director of the National Park Service at a meeting with the Conference of National Park Concessioners on October 19.
>
> In spite of what some bureaucrats may think, the citizens of this country are entitled to fair and civil treatment by government officials. I believe that the remarks of the Director were

extremely arrogant, a discredit to the Service, and a disservice to you and to the Department.

I am personally offended at the Director's suggestion that any group—whether it be the concessioners organization, the Sierra Club, the American Mining Congress, or any other group—should not be free to express its views to any Member of Congress and to employ any spokesman it may choose. I'm not familiar with any requirement in the Concessions Policy Act that concessioners waive their right to free speech as a condition of doing business with the National Park Service.

From the remarks and comments of the Director, and from the action of the National Park Service in recent years, it is blatantly apparent that those responsible for interpreting and administering the law dealing with national park concessions have the utmost contempt for its provisions and have no intention to adhere to either the letter or spirit of the Act. . . .

Administrators like Mr. Whalen have already driven many small businesses out of the national parks. It is a discredit to the Administration's effort to improve its image to continue to harrass small business concessioners to the point that they prefer to quit their operations and turn them over to conglomerates that have the financial wherewithal and muscle to absorb or combat autocratic domination of such bureaucrats. . . .

I strongly urge that the Department review Mr. Whalen's performance. I think that you will find you can do far better in this key position which has been usually held by sensitive, outstanding conservationists.

> (Signed) Morris K. Udall
> Chairman

The headlines were not so gentlemanly. The *Federal Times* of February 18, 1980, read: *Udall Calls for Firing of U.S. Parks Director.* The grounds for firing Whalen were "persistent discourtesy to the public." It was a new cause for discharging federal employees written into the 1978 Civil Service Reform Act at Udall's insistence. Cecil Andrus took Mo Udall's letter very seriously.

While this situation roiled in the background, Regional Director Glenn Bean and John Spurgeon flew to Tucson from the Denver office and presented me with a five-year contract extension. Why only five years? I asked. They said the maximum term of a contract was 30 years and since my contract was for 25 years, they could not give me more than a five-year extension. It's fatal to get in the way of the Park Service.

In the interest of getting on with the job, as time was fleeting, I protested but agreed to proceed with the Special Life/Safety work until they showed me their "extension." It was not an extension at all. It contained numerous new contract provisions which the Park Service had been unsuccessfully urging concessioners to approve. I refused to accept it and demanded a long-term contract if I was to proceed.

They agreed. But when I saw the long-term contract provisions, the Park Service had added another three million dollars of required improvements. It's fatal to get in the way of the Park Service.

Then they insisted that I had to perform the Special Life/Safety program work, contract or no contract. Fatal or not, I contacted my congressman, Mo Udall.

Mo called Interior Secretary Cecil Andrus and set up an early March meeting to discuss the Special Life/Safety program requirements with Assistant Secretary for Fish and Wildlife and Parks Robert L. Herbst, two of his staff members Richard Myshak and David Hales, Director Bill Whalen, Assistant Director Jim Tobin and Concessions Chief Buddy Surles. Mo sent his Committee counsel, Lee McElvain, with me, a signal that the congressman expected fair treatment.

After a short but serious meeting, Surles, McElvain and I cloistered ourselves in a small office and worked out a compromise on what would have to be finished before Glacier's season opening and what could be delayed. The settlement was onerous but possible. Our agreement stipulated that the Park Service would proceed with notice for a new contract and I was to start on the Life/Safety program.

In due course the Park Service issued a prospectus calling for a new concession contract at Glacier National Park. The final document called not only for the $1,750,000 Life/Safety program, but also for that $3 million worth of improvements. The meeting had only bought me a little time.

One day shortly afterward, the flap over NPS Director Whalen's indiscretion came to a head. Secretary Andrus called Whalen in and summarily discharged him.

It was not the only change in the wind. I could feel time closing around my days as a concessioner. At the annual spring Conference meeting I announced that I would not seek another term as chairman. I had been quietly grooming Rex Maughan, who was elected to succeed me. The Conference bought me a silver tray and service as a memento of fourteen years serving as chairman.

Shortly another passage was announced: On May 14, Russell Dickinson became the eleventh Director of the National Park Service. In some quarters of the bureaucracy, I got the credit for Whalen's release.

When I returned to Glacier to open the season, as if I didn't have enough problems with the Park Service, I had to fire my new chief engineer because he was padding purchase orders for equipment and pocketing the extra. Then, as we started on our Life/Safety work, Many Glacier Location Engineer Ray Wyatt suddenly resigned. I soon found out why. At the end of last year's season he had failed to drain about half the hotel's water system. We had 176 broken pipes in the walls and ceilings. Wyatt hadn't drained the fire extinguishers either, and they burst. The auxiliary steam pump for the fire sprinkler system likewise cracked open. It was a trying time. And Many Glacier was only one of six locations we had to change so we could open on June 7th.

It soon became obvious that certain Park Service officers not only blamed me for Bill Whalen's ignominious departure but also had decided to get even. I saw it plainly when my old friend Park Ranger Dick Munro had to retire on medical disability and some strange things happened to his replacement. Superintendent Iverson requested the standard list of ten candidates and selected the third man on the list, an able young fellow named Robert Reyes. Reyes was an hispanic and entitled to preference, so he got the job. In our first few contacts Reyes and I got along well: He was intelligent, knew his duty, and performed competently.

Then suddenly Buddy Surles from Washington pressured Superintendent Iverson to dismiss Reyes and appoint one Joe Shellenberger as Munro's replacement *and* management assistant in charge of Glacier concessions. Reyes was beside himself. Iverson was not thrilled, either: such replacements were properly his decision. When Reyes told Iverson that he planned to file a discrimination complaint, Iverson told him that if he did, Washington would end his park service career. If he shut up, he would receive a promotion to some position in a small Park system unit. Reyes shut up and took his promotion.

Joe Shellenberger was an interesting one. He had a long park service record but had never been to Glacier. He was Buddy Surles's personal choice for Glacier concession supervisor—an obvious plant. His assignment: Get Hummel. He set about his duty with gusto.

First, Shellenberger replaced C. W. Brinck, our U.S. Public Health Service sanitarian of two seasons, with a stranger, James Lodge. The sanitarian is a food safety officer. His word has the force of law. We at Glacier Park, Inc. had gotten along well with all previous sanitarians. Now, in the midst of a fight against time to comply with Park Service demands, Shellenberger's man Lodge subjected us to a series of microscopically detailed inspections, some lasting for six hours. He was obsessed with food temperature. He considered any reading between 45 and 140 degrees Fahrenheit to be dangerous. He opened any refrigerator, stuck a thermometer into the nearest food, and regardless when it had been put there—five seconds or five hours earlier—wrote us up for improper storage. On one occasion this obstreperous official went into the dining room and thrust a thermometer into a guest's plate of food!

In years past our sanitarian had always scored us in the middle- to upper-90s. Lodge scored us at 50 to 60 and usually supplemented his scoring with a dissertation from the Sanitation Code. One of our best chefs, a man with over 40 years' experience in top restaurants, resigned rather than take Lodge's harassment. Another with 45 years' experience threatened to resign if he had to deal with this tyrant of a sanitarian. We had the storekeeper deal with Lodge and kept our chef.

Park Service officials in Denver sent "concession specialist" James Miller from Yellowstone sent to inspect our Life/Safety work progress. He was known in Yellowstone as a "nitpicker." We found the term inadequate to the reality. His frequent inspections often lasted as long as Lodge's. He was rude and obtrusive. He took pictures of guests and employees during mealtimes, disrupting service and antagonizing everyone. He often sneaked into kitchens when no one was present and without notice.

I protested to Miller's superiors without result. The park service reminded me the government has a legal right to make unannounced inspections. I told them that unannounced did not mean surreptitious entry.

Miller routinely issued orders to my employees and managers, although he had no authority to do so whatever. One young inexperienced manager obeyed a Miller order and painted the front of a coffee shop without my knowledge or permission. It was a color Miller knew the Park Service objected to and the storefront had to be repainted.

I complained bitterly of this Park Service obstructionism and sabotage. Superintendent Iverson, who had always been supportive to our concession, called me into his office. To my surprise, Joe Shellenberger sat there with Iverson. Shellenberger—supposedly the assistant—was obviously running things. He threatened to give me an unsatisfactory rating if I didn't shape up. I told the two that our concession was entitled to cooperation and assistance but had only had criticism and obstruction from Park Service personnel. I reminded Iverson that in times past the Park Service had cooperated with concessioners but now policy appeared to be deliberate opposition.

Superintendent Iverson wrote me this letter dated July 11, 1980. In a way it is a requiem for the park visitor.

You have often lamented the decline and deterioration of relationships between the National Park Service and concessioners throughout the system. There could be numerous explanations for this change, but the change is not necessarily bad. We have evolved from a sort of buddy system to a more professional relationship. The Service now employs more specialists and professionals, i.e., sanitarians, law enforcement specialists, concessions specialists, building fire experts. You are encountering these professional people more often and obviously resent it, regarding it as an intrusion into your domain.

In bygone days park concessions operated more independently. Let's face it, some of the big companies, Union Pacific, Great Northern and Santa Fe Railroads barely acknowledged the presence of the National Park Service. They played a dominant role in establishing some of the parks, provided a great service to the public but at the same time displayed a possessory interest in the real estate.

During George Hartzog's era, this term "partnership" between concessioners and the National Park Service became a pet phrase. I think it was not so much an acknowledgment of the concessioner's role as a new assertion of NPS responsibility. Today, the Service has reached, in my opinion, a proper position of responsibility.

So, human decency has a season, Mr. Iverson, a time to flourish and a time to perish. The environmentalists were winning. First they democratized us, now they professionalized us.

I knew it was hopeless. It's fatal to get in the way of the Park Service. I began negotiations to sell the stock of Glacier Park, Inc. to Del E. Webb Corporation, the concessioner at Glen Canyon National Recreation Area. Our stockholders signed a contract for the sale of their stock. Del Webb principals signed with two conditions: 1) They had to sell their half-interest in the Rosenzweig Center in Phoenix (to get out from under a debt); and failing that, 2) get permission from a consortium of banks to whom they were indebted for loans for two hotel casinos in Atlantic city.

I immediately notified Director Dickenson of our intention to sell and to whom as required by our contract. Now I would turn my attention to negotiating our new contract as favorably as possible so I could pass on the greatest value to the new owner. Any thought of staying in concessions faded into the world of lost dreams.

On September 1, 1980, I telephoned Lorraine Mintzmyer, NPS Regional Director in Denver, and asked if I could come to Denver to negotiate my new contract. I told her I had reservations to take my wife to China on September 10th. Mintzmyer said she needed thirty days to evaluate the responses to the prospectus. It seems that I was not the only respondent. A small group of former Glacier employees calling themselves the Glacier Park Foundation had responded to the prospectus with a proposal based upon total capitalization of under $10,000. I called to Mintzmyer's attention that ours was the *only* acceptable response: we had a preferential right to renewal under the law. Mrs. Mintzmyer said she would not be able to negotiate until the end of September and urged me to continue with my travel plans. I got the distinct impression that the Regional Office did not want Don Hummel to get a new contract. I asked Conference of National Park Concessioners Chairman Rex Maughan to keep in touch with the Park Service for me and I left with Genee for China.

On September 24, 1980, the Denver Regional Office wrote me as follows:

Dear Mr. Hummel:

We have reviewed the proposal submitted on August 26, 1980, by Glacier Park, Inc. for the negotiation of a contract for the operation of accommodations, facilities and services within Glacier National Park.

While Glacier Park Inc.'s proposal offers some additional commitment to maintain and improve facilities, it does not provide sufficient consideration to justify abandonment of the present contract and entering into a new long-term contact. Our position is, therefore, that the present contract with Glacier Park Inc. should remain in effect for the time being.

> Sincerely yours,
> James B. Thompson
> Acting Regional Director
> Rocky Mountain Region.

Enclosure: letter from R. E. Dickenson dated September 24, 1980.

Director Dickenson's letter was addressed to:

David L. Johnson,
Executive Vice President,
Del Webb Recreational Properties Inc.

Dear Mr. Johnson:

The National Park Service has determined through extensive analysis that a long-term contract is needed for a private operation to economically return the investment required to accomplish improvements in concessions facilities and services in Glacier National Park.

In accordance with the stated intention of Del E. Webb Corp. to purchase the stock of Glacier Park Inc. for a term of 25 years, providing that the agreed-to contract contains adequate consideration from the government's interest to justify the length of term, and further provided the stock transfer of Glacier Park Inc. to Del Webb is consummated.

Sincerely,
Russell E. Dickenson, Director.

No, you didn't miss anything. Both letters refer to exactly the same contract. The letter to me turns it down, the letter to Del Webb accepts it. The odd thing is, Del Webb Corp. never responded to the Park Service prospectus and had no standing to negotiate for this contract.

On October 1st, Lorraine Mintzmyer and John Spurgeon told the press that Glacier National Park and her staff had recommended that our proposal not be accepted. When I returned from China Lorraine Mintzmyer refused to negotiate with me saying she "would rather negotiate with Del Webb." I told her that Del Webb had not responded to the prospectus and until they bought Glacier Park, Inc.'s stock, they had no standing. She still refused to negotiate with me. I called Rex Maughan and told him to have Director Dickenson straighten out Mintzmyer or I would sue the Park Service. This was getting ridiculous. The Park Service was even making it hard for me to *get out* of the concession business!

Somebody got to Mintzmyer. She wrote me on October 10th, setting a contract negotiation meeting for October 17-18th:

> Since the proposed sales agreement for the transfer of stock to Del E. Webb states that the terms of the negotiated contract must be agreeable to Webb we assume a representative of Del Webb will be present.

On the same day, Mintzmyer wrote Del Webb, "We hope to begin negotiations for a new concessions contract for Glacier with Del E. Webb Corp. as soon as possible. We propose to meet with you and other Del E. Webb representatives in Denver." How eager she seemed to be to give Del Webb a contract!

We met in Denver and negotiated a contract for 25 years based on Glacier Park, Inc.'s proposal—the one their office claimed did not contain sufficient consideration to justify a new long-term contract. On October 22, 1980, I signed, on behalf of Glacier Park, Inc. The contract was then submitted to the congressional committees for 60 days for their comment.

The Glacier Park Foundation, whose proposal had been rejected, sued the National Park Service, asking an injunction to stop them from signing the contract with Glacier Park, Inc. Their complaint alleged that since the National Park Service had rejected Glacier Park, Inc.'s proposal, it had no right to sign a contract with us.

In a U.S. District Court hearing in Missoula to decide the issue, Glacier Park Foundation called John Spurgeon, chief of concessions of the Denver Regional Office, as an adverse witness. He said under oath that in his statement "rejecting" Glacier Park, Inc.'s proposal he had indeed used the word "reject," but denied that it was a "real" rejection.

How easily he spoke those words under oath. In a matter as important as a legal contract he felt perfectly justified in causing me baseless delay and distress. How *professional!* At any rate, the judge denied the Foundation's request for an injunction.

Soon afterward, Del E. Webb Corporation notified the National Park Service that it no longer intended to purchase the stock of Glacier Park, Inc. They had money problems of their own and backed out.

Then Buddy Surles told Rex Maughan that NPS had no intention of signing a contract with Glacier Park, Inc. unless a successor came into the picture. He needn't have worried about it. I had no intention of staying. I had seen the Park Service's future and there were no people in it—just *professionals.* I asked Rex to search for another buyer. He approached Greyhound Corporation on our behalf to negotiate the purchase Glacier Park, Inc.'s stock. This deal was successfully sealed and agreements signed to take over all the stock of Glacier Park, Inc.

But I wasn't out yet. Things got more complicated. Glacier Park Foundation took their case to the Ninth Circuit Court of Appeals in San Francisco, which supported their claim and remanded the case back to the District Court for trial. And if the Foundation won, ordered the Ninth Circuit, the Park Service would be required to solicit new proposals, as they had violated their own regulations.

The lower court, however, found for the Park Service, which permitted them to proceed with our contract. The rest was anticlimax. In March 1981, Glacier Park, Inc. stockholders sold all their stock to Greyhound Food Management Company, Inc., a subsidiary of Greyhound Corporation, Inc. And that was the end of it. My forty-seven-year concessioning career was over. I was out.

State of the Concessions

Now I've come back to haunt those who are trying to steal your national parks. And I've brought you with me as a witness this time. Together you and I may be able to do something about it. Something good. Something important. Something necessary. Together we may be able to save the national parks from their saviors.

We've just been through a lot together. I've tried to let you see the world of concessions as I've seen it. I've tried to give you a true picture of how I feel about it. It isn't a complete picture, but it's as honest as I can make it. I've checked the facts as best I could. I've shown you a lot about myself. Maybe I would have been better off keeping some of the less attractive things out of sight, but I believe in honesty. I've had my weaknesses and failures. I can get tough when I have to, and sometimes aggressive. And maybe I'm a little vain about my achievements. I could have smoothed all that out. But it wouldn't have been true to life.

There's only a little left now, and I'll stick to the point: Saving the national parks. The environmentalists showed us what they would do in power. Theirs was a record of shame. It was a record of blind destruction of visitor accommodation and visitor access. It was a record of abnegation of everything human. We must close that age, the age of harsh environmental imperialism. We must find an ethic of civilization that cherishes the natural world without hating the human world. We must take that last good step toward encompassing man and nature with equal vigor and respect, and for all social classes. After all, man is a part of nature.

If we're to do something effective about access to the national parks, we have to size up the parks's condition now. The past few years have seen a mixture of good and bad. The concessions in the early 1980s suffered from years of administrative deterioration by an increasingly rigid and stratified National Park Service. The Park Service concession bureaucracy grew from 20 full-time positions in 1971, 16 of them in Washington, with a budget of about $386,000, to a 1985 total of 87 full-time-equivalent positions with a budget of $3.5 million.

The Reagan administration took the first of many badly needed steps: It reaffirmed the place of private enterprise in the American park system.

On March 9, 1981, about the time I retired from concessioning, Interior Secretary James Watt spoke words that predecessor Cecil Andrus should have spoken, and Kleppe and Hathaway and Morton before him should have spoken. Jim Watt told the annual meeting of the Conference of National Park Concessioners:

> It is time for a new beginning and the private enterprise system must be looked to for rejuvenation and enthusiasm as we try to make the parks more accessible and usable for the people. . . . You folks are going to play a tremendously important role and a growing role in the administration of our national parks and we are going to reach out to involve you in some areas that you haven't been asked to be involved in before.

Unfortunately, no such actions were ever taken. There is no reason why an Andrus should not say the same words. Liberal Democrats and conservative Republicans alike treasure both the private enterprise system and the national parks. Today we are on the verge of a new awakening to that fact. The era of harsh environmental imperialism is waning. Environmental protection has become so deeply institutionalized in America that the angry extremism of the past has, I hope, lost its place in our society. Oh, the thieves are still out there looting the national parks of their public access. But there is a growing segment of sensible, balanced environmental opinion in our nation that will rise to put an end to it—*if* it's informed.

Just where do concessions stand in the mid 1980s? According to NPS Concessions Division, of the 337 park system units in 1985, 111 had concessions. (That is roughly equivalent to all the Natural Areas in the system—about 140 of them in 1985—many of the system's approximately 135 Historical Areas are so small they require no concessions.) But today, food service is provided by concessioners in only 70 units, lodging in only 36.

As a result of the environmentalist assault on concessions, few new visitor facilities have been built in the national parks since the 1970s. At the risk of being repetitive, let me remind you that Yosemite has been stymied, although substandard units there badly need replacing. Additions proposed in Glacier have been denied. Yellowstone's building program in Grant Village has been approved only as a tradeoff for removing visitor accommodations at West Thumb, Old Faithful, and Bridge Bay. At Lassen—well, you know what happened at Lassen. This tells you how well the environmentalist's anti-concession program is doing.

Financially, the concessioners are doing as always: some good, some bad. In 1983 the gross receipts of all 500-odd concessions was $340 million, up from $318 million in 1982. The combined income of all concessions before taxes in 1983 was $30.6 million, down from $30.9 million in 1982. In 1983 the concessions paid the national treasury $6.2 million in franchise fees, up from $5.8 million in 1982.

The government spends $3.5 million a year, an amount equal to a tenth of all concessioners' combined income, just doing *administration*. And remember too that the tax-free income of the National Wildlife Federation was $43 million in 1985, while the combined tax-free income of the top ten environmental groups that year exceeded $110 million. Environmental groups, of course, pay nothing to the national treasury. The top ten groups of the organized environmental movement alone command more than three times the income dollar power of all 500 national park concessions combined.

Concessioning is not a glamour industry and seldom gets good press. Its critics such as John Dingell and Jack Brooks and the Sierra Club and Friends of the Earth have received sympathetic press coverage. Concessions face nearly a million people every day and have to deal with every kind of individual imaginable under a great variety of conditions. The government bureaucracy which was imposed on concessioners at the demand of environmentalists has as its primary goal the removal of all benefits conveyed by the Concession Policy Act of 1965—possessory interest, preferential renewal rights, the full range of Mather-Albright principles.

Saving the National Parks

What can we do to stop the national parks from being stolen? First, keep in mind the truth about the big lies:

1) The Truth: The natural integrity of our National Parks is not threatened by visitors. Even the four or five most-used parks suffer crowding very few days of the year. The carrying capacity of the entire park system is immense and barely touched. As respected scientist J. E. Lovelock pointed out in his widely acclaimed book *Gaia: A New Look at Life on Earth*, nature is not as fragile as the environmentalists would have you believe. Assert your rights of access!

2) The Truth: Wilderness is not an evocative general term, it is an official government designation that keeps the vast majority of the world's citizens from visiting more than 80 million acres of America. Official Wilderness means absolutely no development. Make these areas available for people's use and enjoyment. Reduce Wilderness boundaries!

3) The Truth: Environmentalism has more on the agenda than protecting nature, it has distinctly anti-people overtones that are hidden and denied but that nevertheless powerfully

impact our national policy. Environmentalists may tell you anything. Be skeptical!

4) The Truth: The media refuse to tell the concessioner's side of the national park story and make a mere pretense of objectivity by devoting a few quotes to concessioners while carefully explaining environmentalist views. Be wary!

5) The Truth: The Park Service is a working partner in stealing the national parks despite its claims of innocence and its haughty dismissal of critics. They work in obscurity, bow politely to the Mather-Albright principles, and do what they please. Don't trust them!

But just keeping your eye on the truth isn't enough. A practical, down-to-earth activist program is the basis of all change in this country. If we want to preserve public use and enjoyment of our national parks, then we have to fight for it. The opposition is powerful and intelligent, but they can be beaten.

Here's a blueprint for success:

Future Needs:

Exposing Anti-Concession, Anti-Access Intent

All National Park policies should be analyzed for anti-concession, anti-access intent and consequence. This analysis should become a required part of every Master Plan, Environmental Assessment, and Environmental Impact Statement. The true anti-private enterprise intent of environmentalists too often is hidden in deceptive words and seductive phrases. A "hard-look" doctrine needs to be brought to every step of the National Park planning process to explicitly state whether any given policy will harm or help concessions and public access. The findings must be stated in clear, plain English. Public and private penalties should be imposed against any Park Service employee or pressure group representative who attempts to hide or disguise the harmful effect of a policy on concessions and public access. Members of the public should have the right to sue the Park Service and environmental groups for denying public access to the national parks.

Release of Information on Anti-Concession, Anti-Access Lobbying Groups

A Right-To-Know measure concerning environmental groups should be adopted. It should require any group that lobbies or otherwise pressures agencies or legislatures to adopt policies with the intent or consequence of limiting national park public access to disclose the names and addresses of its sources of income including private memberships, donations, and grants. The salaries of all officers should likewise be released. The public is entitled to know who wants to keep it out of its own national parks and how much they're paying their lobbyists to keep you out.

Sell-Backs: Uniting Ownership With Operation

Strengthening concession ability to manage is essential to ending the bureaucratic mess imposed on public services in the parks at the demand of environmentalists. One of the most sensible programs would be to sell back to private parties all government-owned public service facilities. Another would be to place new private facilities in park areas where public demand exists. Still another is to increase the concessioner's investment to increase his incentive to manage well in order to make a profit. All possessory interests that have been seized by contract abrogation should be *given* back to the concessioner or his successor along with a penalty payment for denial of private enterprise.

Increasing Protections

The present degraded state of concession policy is a direct result of environmentalist pressure on a few congressmen who were willing to wreck the Concession Policy Act of 1965 for the sake of political popularity. The power of all congressional committees other than the House Interior and Insular Affairs Committee and the Senate Energy and Environment Committee to create national park policy should be statutorily limited and ultimately eliminated. Peripheral committees are too powerful today for their influence on park policy to be immediately eliminated, but as in all national park matters, here one must take the long-term view. The present leaders of these committees will not be re-elected forever. As opportunities arise, small steps toward refocusing national park oversight into its proper committee should be taken.

Enlightening Park Service Oversight

Park Service control over virtually every aspect of a concessioner's operation and public access is complete. Unfortunately, Service personnel entertain strongly anti-private-enterprise attitudes and are vastly ignorant and incompetent to run business operations. Civil Service guidelines for all concession specialists should require degrees in business administration and previous experience in a successful for-profit, non-government private enterprise. Universities should offer degree programs for the national park concession specialist stressing the needs of profit-making private enterprise in a public land setting.

Park Service Reorganization

Wallace Stegner once said the national parks are one of the best ideas we ever had. I agree. Unfortunately, the National Park Service cannot be ranked in that high category. A new Interior Department *Division of Mandate Protection* is obviously needed to keep the balance between use vs. preservation closer to center. This division should be situated in the present Solicitor's Office with a corresponding legal overseer assigned within the National Park Service. All Park Service files should be open to the Division of Mandate Protection. This division should have the legal authority to nullify any Park Service policy that strays too far from a genuine balance between use and prservation. The solicitor is the only Interior Department officer with the legal power to stop even the Secretary dead in his tracks and is less susceptible to the pressuring of environmentalist groups. Without such a reorganization, public access to our precious parks is doomed to slow strangulation.

The Need for Continual Reassessment

Growing pressure on park access by self-serving environmental groups, coupled with increasing demands for visitor access, create a continual need to reassess the place of environmentalist dogma in national park management. Changes will not come rapidly. Park Service policy is already clear in dealing with environmentalist pressure: bow down and ignore public access. The Park Service must be made to understand its legal responsibility to provide "public use and enjoyment" of the parks for the common person and not just for the highly sensitive and elite nature lover. The non-affiliated park-going public must be included in the policy decision-making process to bring some balance to the present overwhelming domination by large powerful environmental organizations that are out to exclude the general unaffiliated public.

The Personal Touch

What can just one person do? A lot! Many public issues have been won by the concerned action of a single person. Here's a list of a dozen actions from the easy to the hard to accomplish.

1. If you're a member of an environmental group (and about five million of us are) and you didn't realize *your* organization was doing such things as I've revealed in this book, you can do several things:

A: Ask your group leaders what their policy is about national park concessions. Ask them what they think of access for everyone to the national parks. Ask them what they think about overnight accommodations in the parks.

B: Insist that a Parks Are For People policy be adopted by your environmental group's local chapter and the national organization. If they don't want to talk about it, *make it an issue*. It's *your* group.

C. Get your environmental organization to put together a periodic Concession Appreciation Day. Take people to the parks to enjoy the natural beauty and include a meeting with a concession representative. They'll be happy to tell you what their concession does and show you around.

2. If you're a member of a social or civic group, have a

meeting on the national park situation. Have a speaker, a discussion, a debate. Get the issues out in the open.

3. Start a local Concession History Society centered around your nearest national park concession. You'd be surprised how little historical knowledge has actually been collected and preserved by concessioners—they've been slightly busy housing and feeding a few hundred million people, minding the store, and coping with a few floods and snowstorms here and there. There's a wealth of material just waiting for an interested organizer and interpreter.

Concession history is an area where volunteer citizen help can make a truly meaningful difference. The more we know about a subject the more we appreciate its significance. There are many national park history societies, but not many national park *concession* history societies. Old papers by the thousands are just stuffed away in back rooms here and there waiting for interested people to bring the past alive. Tape record interviews with retired concessioners. Make your trips to the national parks a personal experience by finding about about the people who accommodated the people.

4. Take on national park concessions as your personal cause. If you're looking for something to do, there's a lot to be done. People must be informed. The threat of losing our precious access to the national parks must be explained. The role of concessions in keeping the parks open must be made clear to everyone. As you can see by this book, concessioning is an involved subject. It needs good interpreters among those who have never been concessioners. It needs good people to explain it to others. It needs citizen champions to stand up for it in the public limelight.

5. Buy a share of concessioner stock. It won't cost much and it won't earn much, but it will be a symbol of your support for open parks and sound park concessions.

6. Get the media interested. You've learned a lot about concessions reading this book. You can see their importance. A letter to the editor of your newspaper, a short article in your club news, even a visit to your local television station to

tell them about the problem—you never can tell what will help.

7. Join a private enterprise support group. A number of national groups touch on concession issues. You can't join the Conference of National Park Concessioners—and they should think seriously about creating a Citizen Supporter Associate Membership—but you can join The Center for the Defense of Free Enterprise, a non-profit, tax-deductible educational foundation that defends private enterprise through many worthwhile programs (address: 12500 N.E. Tenth Place, Bellevue, Washington 98005). Their Free Enterprise Press published this book. And you can join the National Inholders Association, a group directly related to national parks and the protection of private interests in federal lands (address: 30 West Thomson, Sonoma, California 95476). It's an action-oriented lobbying and public interest group that doesn't even mind butting heads with Congressman Brooks and Dingell and others when necessary!

8. Get political. Support candidates of any party who pledge to support public use and enjoyment of the national parks and respect for the Mather-Albright principles of sound national park concessions. Let your own congressman and those who serve on the House Interior and Insular Affairs Committee and the Senate Energy and Environment Committee know how you feel about access to your national parks. Maybe one day we'll see the Park User's Protection Act or equivalent.

9. Be informed about Park Service actions. Receive their notices of intent to close down accommodations, campgrounds, and trails—you can get your name added to the Park Service mailing list by writing to Director, National Park Service, Washington, D.C., 20240. Attend NPS public meetings to let your voice be heard. If you can't attend, write your comments and urge your friends to do the same.

10. Let the National Park Service know directly what you think about public access to public lands. Remind them that you're the landlord and they're just the hired help. Put the

same kind of pressure on them to keep the parks open for people—all kinds of people—that the environmental groups put on them to keep people out. If we complain loud enough long enough they'll bend to *our* pressure instead.

11. When you finish this book, lend it to a friend. Send copies for gifts. Help Americans find out what's happening to their national parks.

12. This book contains many notable examples of what one person can do. I want to be one of those people who makes a difference. I urge you to be one too.

Fare Thee Well

Well, that's it. You're done with me now. It's been a rousing ride and I hope you've enjoyed it as much as I have. Now don't let all this experience we've shared go to waste. You know what to do. I'm counting on you. The parks are counting on you. America is counting on you.

Sources

W riting source citations is one of those chores that your friends don't need and your enemies won't appreciate. But so much misinformation has been spread about national park concessions by overzealous environmentalists that a reasonably complete set of source notes is essential to a book like this.

I am indebted to chief editor Ron Arnold for applying his vast knowledge of environmentalist literature in digging out many of these citations. The following sources will help the industrious reader verify every major point I make.

Sources completely identified in the text will not be repeated here. After first citation, only author and abbreviated title are used.

1: Thieves

Environmentalist attitudes: Ron Arnold, *At the Eye of the Storm: James Watt and the Environmentalists* (Chicago: Regnery-Gateway, 1982); Lester W. Milbrath, *Environmentalists: Vanguard for a New Society* (Albany: State University of New York Press, 1984); William Tucker, *Progress and Privilege: America in the Age of Environmentalism* (New York: Doubleday, 1982). Bernard J. Frieden, *The Environmental Protection Hustle* (Cambridge: Massachusetts Institute of Technology Press, 1979). Rael Jean Isaac and Erich Isaac, *The Coercive Utopians: Social Deception by America's Power Players* (Chicago: Regnery Gateway, 1983). **Martin Litton**: Robert Wallace and the Editors of Time-Life Books, *The Grand Canyon* (New York: Time-Life Books, 1972), p. 136.

Wilderness Society: "Wanted: Your Ideas on Yosemite National Park's Future" *Wilderness Report*, Vol. 12, No. 2., April, 1975, p. 4.

National Parks and Conservation Association: "Help Plan Yosemite's Future," *National Parks and Conservation Magazine*, June 1975, p. 22. **Edward Abbey**: quoted in "Working to control the opportunists in land of opportunity," Kim Heacox, *Seattle Times*, June 19, 1986, p. A19. **Environmental group income**: Ron Arnold, *Ecology Wars: Environmentalism as if People Mattered* (Bellevue, Washington: The Free Enterprise Press, scheduled 1987), p. 153. **Environmentalist clout**: R.C. Mitchell "Public Opinion and Environmental Politics in the 1970s and 1980s" in Vig. and M.E. Kraft (Eds.) *Environmental Policy in the 1980s: Reagan's New Agenda*, Wash. D.C., Congressional Quarterly Press, 1984, 51-74. **Wildernist demographics**: John C. Hendee, William R. Catton, Jr., Larry D. Marlow, and C. Frank Brockman *Wilderness Users in the Pacific Northwest - Their Characteristics, Values and Management Preferences*, U.S.D.A. Forest Service Research Paper PNW-61 1968 Pacific Northwest Forest & Range Exp. Sta., Portland, Oreg.

Environmental elitism: For two studies a decade apart see W. B. Devall, "Conservation: An Upper-Middle Class Social Movement, A Replication." *Journal of Leisure Research*, 1970, 2 (Spring), 123-126; and S.F. Cotgrove and A. Duff, "Environmentalism, Middle Class Radicalism and Politics." *Sociological Review*, 1980- 28 (2), 92-110. **Roszak**: Theodore Roszak *Where the Wasteland Ends: Politics and Transcendence in Postindustrial Society* (Garden City: Doubleday, 1972), p. 24, 25. **Esteem for Parks**: A Roper Organization poll of 2,000 Americans interviewed between August 11 and August 18, 1984, found the National Park Service the most highly esteemed government agency. *Roper Reports, Issue 84-8* The Roper Organization New York 1984. For general-issue environmental opinion that touches upon national park issues, see R.C. Mitchell, *Public Opinion on Environmental Issues: Results of a National Survey*. Report for the Council on Environmental Quality. GPO, 1980. **Structure of Interior Department**: *The United States Government Manual 1985/86* Office of the Federal Register National Archives and Records Service, General Service Administration GPO, 1985.

The First National Park: For a discussion of which was the "first park," Hot Springs in Arkansas, Yosemite or Yellowstone, see John

Ise, *Our National Park Policy: A Critical History* (Baltimore: Published for Resources for the Future by the Johns Hopkins Press, 1961), p. 13. **Yellowstone**: A classic of interest is Hiram M. Chittenden, *The Yellowstone National Park, Historical and Descriptive, 1915* (Cincinnati: Stewart and Kidd Co., 1917). Merril J. Mattes, "Behind the Legend of Colter's Hell: The Early Exploration of Yellowstone National Park," *Mississippi Valley Historical Review, 36* (1949). Essential histories: Richard A. Bartlett, *Nature's Yellowstone* (University of New Mexico Press, 1974); Richard A. Bartlett, *Yellowstone: A Wilderness Besieged* (Tucson: University of Arizona Press, 1985); Aubrey Haines, *The Yellowstone Story* (Colorado Associated University Press, 1977). A good popular account may be found in Ruth Kirk, *Yellowstone, The First National Park* (New York: Atheneum, 1974). **The Folsom-Cook Expedition**: David E. Folsom, *The Folsom-Cook Exploration of the Yellowstone in the Year 1869* with a preface by Nathaniel P. Langford (St. Paul Minnesota: H.L. Collins Company, printers, 1894). **The Washburn Expedition**: Nathaniel Pitt Langford, *The Discovery of Yellowstone Park: Journal of the Washburn Expedition to the Yellowstone and Firehole Rivers in the Year 1870* (Lincoln: University of Nebraska Press, 1972). **Catlin Creator of National Park Idea**: George Catlin, *North American Indians: Being letters and Notes on their Manners, Customs, and Conditions, written during Eight Years' Travel amongst the Wildest Tribes of Indians in North America* (2 vols. Philadelphia, 1913) I-294-95.

Expeditioners' lobbying: Nathaniel P. Langford, "The Wonders of the Yellowstone," *Scribner's Monthly,* 2 1871. Gustavus C. Doane, *The Report of Lieutenant Gustavus C. Doane upon the so-called Yellowstone Expedition of 1870,* 41 Cong., 3 Sess., Senate Ex. Doc. 51 March 3, 1871. Walter Trumbull, "The Washburn Yellowstone Expedition," *Overland Monthly,* 6 1871. **The worthlessness of Yellowstone**: For a lively debate on this point, see "The National Parks: A Forum on the 'Worthless Lands' Thesis," *Journal of Forest History,* Vol. 27, No. 3, July 1983, p. 130 ff. A number of secondary sources cover the founding of Yellowstone National Park adequately. See Robert Shankland, *Steve Mather of the National Parks* (New York: Alfred A. Knopf, 1951), p. 43; Ise, *National Park Policy,* p. 14. The definitive work on all national park legislative history to 1951 is Edmund B. Rogers, *History of Legislation Relat-*

ing to the National Park System through the 82nd Congress 108 volumes Departmental Library U.S. Department of the Interior **Hayden Expedition**: Ferdinand Vandeveer Hayden, *The Great West: Its Attractions and Resources. Containing a Popular Description of the Marvelous Scenery, Physical Geography, Fossils, and Glaciers of this Wonderful Region: And the Recent Explorations in the Yellowstone Park, "The Wonderland of America." Being an Article for a Work Entitled, "The Great West."* (Philadelphia, Pennsylvania: Franklin Publishing Company; Bloomington, Illinois: C. R. Brodix, 1880).

Northern Pacific's Role: Richard A. Bartlett, *The Genesis of National Park Concessions Policy* Colloquium paper 1980 National Park Service Archives Harpers Ferry, West Virginia (restricted). Richard A. Bartlett, *Great Surveys of the American West* (Norman: University of Oklahoma Press, 1962). Ellis P. Oberholzer, *Jay Cooke: Financier of the Civil War* 2 vols. (Philadelphia: 1907). Henrietta M. Larson, *Jay Cooke: Private Banker* (Cambridge, Mass.: 1936). **Yellowstone Park Act**: United States *Statutes At Large*, *17*, p. 32. **Subsequent Park Acts**: A handy compilation of national park act texts to 1933 is Hillory A. Tolson, *Laws Relating to the National Park Service, the National Parks and Monuments* (GPO, 1933). **National Park Service Act**: Public Law No 64-235. Although this law has no official short title, it is commonly called the "National Park Service Organic Act." **Environmentalist Tampering**: U.S. Department of the Interior, National Park Service, *Yellowstone National Park Master Plan*, 1976.

Yellowstone Acreages: *National Park Index 1985* (GPO, 1985). **Park Visitor Statistics**: *National Park Statistical Abstract 1985* Statistical Office Denver Service Center National Park Service (GPO, 1986). **Park Nomenclature**: *Index of the National Park System and Affiliated Areas as of June 30, 1977* (GPO, 1977). **Demolishing Visitor Accommodations**: see Chapters 16 through 19. **Congress and the Parks**: A standard source on Congressional Committees and government departments including Interior is the annual *Congressional Directory*. See *1986 Congressional Directory 99th Congress 2nd Session* (GPO, 1986). **Phillip Burton**: Ron Arnold, "Eureka Arises in Wrath to Oppose Burton's Folly" *Western Conservation Journal* June-July 1977 p. 23-25. **John Seiberling**: His pro-environmentalist tactics are examined in *For the Good of All*, broadcast

June 6, 1983, television news series "Frontline," Jessica Savitch reporting, Public Broadcasting System, written transcript published in *Congressional Record*, July 12, 1983.

Concessioners as Nature Interpreters: C. Frank Brockman, "Park Naturalists and the Evolution of National Park Service Interpretation Through World War II" *Journal of Forest History* Vol. 22, No. 1 January 1978 24. **Aspinall on Concessioners**: *Congressional Record* - House September 14, 1965 23637. **The First Concession Lease**: Richard A. Bartlett, *The Genesis of Concessions Policy*. Shankland, *Steve Mather*, p. 114 ff.

2: The Discovery Trail

Grand Canyon: Introductions to the area may be found in Merrill D. Beal, *Grand Canyon: The Story Behind the Scenery* (Las Vegas: KC Publications, 1975). Wallace, *The Grand Canyon*. **Indian lore**: Earl R. Forrest, *The Snake Dance of the Hopi Indians*, (Tower Publications, 1961). Clyde Kluckhohn, *Navajo Witchcraft* (Boston: Beacon Press, 1962). **Canyon Science**: *Geology and Natural History of the Grand Canyon Region* Fifth Field Conference, Four Corners Geological Society 1969. **Sandburg**: "Good Morning, America" in *The Complete Poems of Carl Sandburg*, Revised and Expanded Edition (New York: Harcourt Brace Jovanovich, 1969), p. 464. **Concession Buildings**: An unexpected and welcome addition to the literature is Bill McMillon, *The Old Lodges & Hotels of Our National Parks* (South Bend, Indiana: Icarus Press, 1983). **Hance Legends**: Michael Collier, "The View from Bright Angel Point," in T.J. Priehs, Elizabeth Johns Simpson (Eds.), *The Mountain Lying Down*, (Grand Canyon: Grand Canyon Natural History Association, 1979).

Cameron: Horace M. Albright, *The Birth of the National Park Service: The Founding Years, 1913-33* as told to Robert Cahn, Howe Brothers Salt Lake City 1985 p. 169 ff. **Mather's Dictum**: Shankland, *Steve Mather*, p. 134. **Powell**: John Wesley Powell, *The Exploration of the Colorado River and Its Canyons*, (New York: Dover Publications, 1961). **Mapping**: A definitive map of the most-visited national park area of Grand Canyon is National Geographic Society Cartographic Division, *The Heart of the Grand Canyon* Washington, D.C. July 1978.

3: Concessions and Conflict

National Park History: Many notable histories cover park concessions *inter alia*. Among the best are Ise, *National Park Policy*; Alfred Runte, *National Parks: The American Experience* (Lincoln: University of Nebraska Press, 1979); Joseph L. Sax, *Mountains Without Handrails: Reflections on the National Parks* (Ann Arbor: The University of Michigan Press, 1980); Conrad L. Wirth, *Parks, Politics, and the People* (Norman: University of Oklahoma Press, 1980); An anti-concession bias is revealed in William C. Everhart, *The National Park Service* (Boulder, Colorado:Westview Press, 1972, 1983) Also indispensable is Ronald Foresta (Ed.), *America's National Parks and Their Keepers*, (Wash. D.C.: Resources for the Future, 1984). The only reliable secondary source on National Park Service organizational change is Russell Olsen, *Administrative History: Organizational Structures of the National Park Service 1917-1985* (Wash. D.C.: NPS, 1986).

Vest and Ingalls: *Congressional Record*, 47th Congress, 2d Sess., 14 (March 1, 1883), p. 3488. **Park Establishments**: See Tolson, *Laws Relating to the National Park Service, the National Parks and Monuments*. 1864 **Yosemite Grant**: Hans Huth, "Yosemite: The Story of an Idea," *Sierra Club Bulletin*, 33 (1948), 47,78. **Nabob Lobbying**: Holway R. Jones, *John Muir and the Sierra Club: The Battle for Yosemite* (San Francisco: 1965), 25 ff. **Noble's Designations**: *John Ise, The United States Forest Policy* (New Haven, Conn., 1920), 109 ff. **Stewart**: Shankland, *Steve Mather*, p. 45. **Muir on the Southern Pacific**: Alfred Runte, *Trains of Discovery: Western Railroads and the National Parks* (Flagstaff, Arizona: Northland Press, 1984). **Olmsted and Yosemite**: Frederick Law Olmsted, "The Yosemite Valley and the Mariposa Big Tree Grove," *Landscape Architecture*, 43 (1952), 12-25. The original advisory report is in Frederick Law Olmsted Papers, Library of Congress, Washington, D.C., Box 32.

Yosemite Pioneers: James Mason Hutchings: *In the Heart of the Sierras* (Oakland: Pacific Press, 1886). Shankland, *Steve Mather*, p. 128 ff. Shirley Sargent, *Yosemite & Its Innkeepers: the story of a great park and its chief concessionaires* (Yosemite: Flying Spur Press, 1975). **Unsystematic Park Designations**: C. Frank Brockman, *Story of Mount Rainier National Park* (Longmire, Washington: Mount Rainier National Park History Association, 1940). Ise, *National Park Policy*, 13-182. Shankland, *Steve Mather*, p. 42 ff. **Muir and Pinchot**: Linnie Marsh Wolfe, *Son of the Wilderness: The Life of John Muir* (New York, Alfred A. Knopf, 1945) and William F. Bade, *The Life and Letters of John Muir* (2 vols. Boston: Houghton Mifflin, 1923). M. Nelson McGeary, *Gifford Pinchot: Forester-Politician* (Princeton, N.J.: Princeton University Press, 1960) and Martin L. Fausold, *Gifford Pinchot: Bull Moose Progressive* (Syracuse, 1961). **Conservation**: Samuel P. Hays, *Conservation and the Gospel of Efficiency: The Progressive Conservation Movement 1890-1920* (Cambridge, Mass.: Harvard University Press, 1959).

Antiquities Act Proclamations: a handy compilation of all park-related presidential proclamations to 1945 is *Proclamations and Orders Relating to The National Park Service up to January 1, 1945*. Compiled by Thomas Alan Sullivan, Attorney, Office of the Chief Counsel National Park Service. (GPO, 1947). **Hetch-Hetchy**: Elmo R. Richardson, "The Struggle for the Valley: California's Hetch Hetchy Controversy, 1905-1913," *California Historical Society Quarterly*, 38 (1959), 249-58. **McFarland-Pinchot Feud**: Hays, *Conservation* tells this episode in detail, p.196 ff. **McFarland's Lobbying**: Shankland, *Steve Mather*, p. 51 ff. Ise, *National Park Policy*, p. 188 ff. **Miller**: Albright: *Birth of the National Park Service*, pp. 1-12.

4: Steve Mather

Biographies: This chapter relies heavily on Shankland, *Steve Mather*; Donald C. Swain, *Wilderness Defender: Horace M. Albright and Conservation* (Chicago: University of Chicago Press, 1970); and Horace Albright: *The Birth of the National Park Service*. **Mather's Thoughts on Concessions**: Of course, there is no way of knowing Mather's thought processes literally, but this section is culled from numerous later summaries of his final concession principles that I believe fairly represent his developing ideas, particularly: Annual Report of the Secretary of the Interior 1946 p.312-17; **Mather's Yellowstone Concession Overhaul**: I have included these details at the behest of Horace Albright, who in a letter to me dated January 27, 1986, said, "any history of concessions must include the actions taken by Stephen T. Mather in 1915, when we completely reorganized the Yellowstone concessions . . . I think I'm the only living person who can give you an account . . ." He is, and I'm grateful. The documentation is also intact in Shankland, *Steve Mather*, 114 ff. **Tresidder and the Stanford Connection**: Sargent, *Yosemite & its Innkeepers*. Mather's "No Competitive Bids" Legislation: *Congressional Record* 70 Cong. 1 sess. Ch.137 (1928) p. 235.

5: Lassen

Lassen Region: Richard L. Williams, *The Cascades* (New York: Time-Life Books, 1974). Stewart L. Udall, *The National Parks of America* (New York, G.P. Putnam's Son, 1966). A National Park Service Booklet of historical interest is J.S. Diller, *The Volcanic History of Lassen Peak* (GPO, 1918). **Tehama**: Freeman Tilden, *The National Parks*. (New York: Alfred A. Knopf, 1970). **New Lodge Design**: *Park Structures and Facilities*, prepared by the United States Department of the Interior, 1935.

6: Getting Organized

The Ahwahnee: The Lady Astor story, probably apocryphal, is told by McMillon in *The Old Lodges*, pp. 114-15. McMillon also describes the doorman excluding registered guest Herbert Hoover in his fishing clothes because no one so poorly dressed could possibly belong in The Ahwahnee. **Conference Origins**: Concessioner and Park Service tradition has clouded the Conference's origins in needless mystery. Even Horace Albright, according to his daughter Marian Schenck, insists that Secretary Wilbur's 1929 Conference meeting as described in this chapter was not the beginning of today's Conference, stating "The Conference actually began years after I left office as Director. That Conference in 1929 was insignificant." Albright's own documents from 1929-33 show that he had a different opinion at the time. The relevant documents, although scattered in half a dozen archives across America, form an unbroken chain and leave no room for doubt that today's Conference began on December 6, 1929.

Conference Names: First name, Conference of National Park Operators: *Memorandum* from NPS Chief Auditor Charles L. Gable to Horace Albright dated October 28, 1931; Second Name, Western Conference of National Park Operators: Account of name change in a letter from Howard H. Hays to Roe Emery dated December 7, 1933, Both letters in University of California Library, Horace

Marden Albright Papers, Collection 2056, Box 131, Envelope, "Concession Affairs, National Park Service, 1930" (Contains 1931 and 1933 items despite "1930" envelope notation). **Conservation Department**: U.S. Department of the Interior Departmental Library *History of Natural Resources Agencies and Proposals for their Reorganization* Unpublished internal document July 1977. **Wilbur Background**: Eugene P. Trani, *The Secretaries of the Department of the Interior, 1849 to 1969* (Wash. D.C.: National Anthropological Archives, 1975).

Edwards as originator of the Conference organization idea: No explicit documentation ever existed, but only three men in 1929 had the power to call the Conference into being: Secretary Wilbur, Assistant Secretary Edwards, and NPS Director Albright. All relevant documents and Conference traditions point decisively to Edwards. In addition, Horace Albright says that Dr. Wilbur by December 1929 was still too unfamiliar with concession problems to originate the Conference idea. Albright says he himself did not originate it. Albright further states "It was probably Edwards." Albright did not attend the Conference meeting's second day, December 7, and so did not see Edwards launch the Conference. Personal communication to Horace Albright September 1986 relayed by Albright's daughter Marian Schenck. **Importance of the Conference**: Albright to Wilbur, December 3, 1929 Ray Lyman Wilbur Papers - National Parks Herbert Hoover Presidential Library, West Branch, Iowa.

Albright's Questions: The list of "questions I would like you to raise" attached to Albright to Wilbur, Dec. 3, 1929, has been lost. However, the questions survive in restatement as asked by Secretary Wilbur at the Conference meeting in the 136-page *A Report of the National Park Operators to the Secretary of the Interior* December 4, 1930 UCLA Albright Papers Collection 2056 Box 131. The points Albright wanted broached: "What type of service and facilities should be furnished in the National Parks? Ways and means of providing for accommodations to meet the transient motorists' demands. More medium priced accommodations for people wishing to stay over in the Parks. More uniform hospitality to visitors throughout the Parks. How can reasonable standardization of such services and facilities in and among the various parks be attained? Housekeeping camps. How can rates be made approximately the same in all Parks for the same or similar service to the public? How can the Operators prepare and submit to us their building and other plans as the Government advances with its development programs? Publicity. De Luxe Busses."

Time and Arrangements of Conference Meeting: Horace Albright's daybook, 1929 Albright personal collection. **Wilbur Speech**: Memorandum for the Press Department of the Interior December 7, 1929 Wilbur Papers - Press Releases Hoover Library. **Tresidder First Conference Chairman**: Numerous documents identify Donald B. Tresidder as the Conference's first chairman, see Charles L. Gable to Albright, October 28, 1931 UCLA Albright Papers Collection 2056 Box 131. **Conference Statement of Purpose**: *A Report of the National Park Operators to the Secretary of the Interior.* p. 1. December 4, 1930 UCLA Albright Papers Collection 2056 Box 131.

Albright's Post-Meeting Views: Albright to J. E. Haynes, president, Haynes Picture Shops, Inc. (a Yellowstone concessioner), February 3, 1930. Haynes Collection, Montana State University Libraries, Bozeman 1930 Folder 2 - U.S. Department of the Interior. Albright wrote, "The formation of the permanent association of operators should lead to better understanding between the operators, and be of real assistance to the Service in the advancement of park ideals and in the improvement of our administration." **Second Conference Annual Meeting**: Report of Director of National Park Service (GPO, June 30, 1931), pp. 35-36. **Third Conference Annual Meeting**: Report of Director of National Park Service (GPO, June 30, 1932) p. 29-31. **Confidential Report**: Wilt to Albright March 9, 1932 Wilbur Papers - National Parks Hoover Library. **Fourth Conference Annual Meeting**: Report of the Secretary of the Interior, 1933 p. 187. **No Conference Meeeting in 1933**: Report of the Secretary of the Interior, 1934 p. 202. Howard H. Hays to Roe Emery, December 7, 1933 UCLA Albright Papers Collection 2056 Box 131.

Albright's Retirement from NPS: Albright, *Birth of the National Park Service*, p. 298 ff. **Ickes**: The authoritative source on National Park Service change in the 1930s is Harlan D. Unrau and G. Frank Williss, *Administrative History: Expansion of the National Park Service in the 1930s* (Denver: Denver Service Center, National Park Service, September 1983). See also Barry Mackintosh, "Harold Ickes and the National Park Service" *Journal of Forest History* Vol.

29. 2 April 1985 p. 78. Harold L. Ickes, *The Autobiography of a Curmudgeon* (New York: Reynal and Hitchcock, 1943). **Albright's Roosevelt Meeting**: Albright, *The Birth of the National Park Service*, p. 285 ff. **Reorganization**: Horace M. Albright, *Origins of National Park Service Administration of Historic Sites* (Philadelphia: Eastern National Park and Monument Association, 1971), p. 23. **Conference Name Change**: Hays to Emery, December 7, 1933, UCLA Albright Papers, Box 131. **CCC**: John A. Salmond, *The Civilian Conservation Corps, 1933-1942: A New Deal Case Study* (Durham: Duke University Press, 1967). For a more personal account see Clair E. Nelsen, "Remembering the CCC: Buck Meadows, California, 1933-1934 *Journal of Forest History*, October 1982 p.184.

Ickes "purist" views: Donald C. Swain, "The National Park Service and the New Deal, 1933-1940," *Pacific Historical Review*, 41 (August 1972): 323. **Pinchot vs. Ickes**: Richard Polenberg, "The Great Conservation Contest," *Forest History* 10 (January 1967), 22.

7: Hard Times

Ickes and WRAPBG: Report of the Secretary of the Interior 1936 (GPO, 1936), p. 133. **Mammoth Cave**: I am indebted to Garner Hanson, president of National Park Concessions, Inc. for his detailed history of NCPI's experience at Mammoth Cave. Hanson to Hummel, July 14, 1986. Author's collection. Additional documentation is found in Ise, *National Park Policy*, p. 264 ff. and 459. **Government Buildings at National Colonial and Shiloh**: Report of the Secretary of the Interior (GPO 1936) p. 133. **National Conference on Outdoor Recreation**: Organized at the request of President Calvin Coolidge, met in Washington, D.C. with some 309 delegates from 128 national organizations. See U.S. Congress, Senate, National Conference on Outdoor Recreation: *Proceedings of the National Conference on Outdoor Recreation, May 22, 23, and 24, 1924*, 68 Cong., 1 sess., 1924, S. Doc. 151. **Graves Remarks**: Henry S. Graves, "A Crisis in National Recreation," *American Forestry*, XXVI (July 1920), 39.

Ickes's Lobbying of Recreation-Area Act: Ickes to DeRouen and Robert F. Wagner, May 28, 1934, U.S. Congress, House, Committee on Public Lands, *Aid in Providing the People of the United States with Adequate Facilities for Park, Parkway, and Recrea-*

tional-Area Purposes, Etc., 73 Cong., 2 sess., 1934, H. Report 1895, p. 2. **The Park, Parkway, and Recreational-Area Act of 1936**: Public Law No. 770-½, U.S. *Statutes at Large 49*, p. 1894. **Mather and Mount Rainier's Concession**: Shankland, *Steve Mather*, p. 76-78. **Timberline Lodge**: Jean Burwell Weir, *Timberline Lodge: A W.P.A. Experiment in Architecture and Crafts*. Unpublished Ph.D. dissertation, (Ann Arbor: University of Michigan, 1977)

8: The Parks and War

Alaska Railroad: A good summary of the Alaska Railroad's history—that hardly mentions Mount McKinley National Park, showing the railroad's original purpose as a tool of resource development rather than tourism—with excellent source citations is William H. Wilson, "Developing Central Alaska's Forest Resources: The Alaska Railroad 1923-1941," *Journal of Forest History*, January 1981 p. 26-35. **Mount McKinley Lodge and Painted Desert Inn**: Report of the Secretary of the Interior (GPO, 1937), p. 58-59. **Ickes's Concession Nationalization Bill**: Report of the Secretary of the Interior (GPO, 1939), p. 299. **Wartime in the Parks**: A stark account of World War II on the parks homefront, all the more poignant for its blunt bureaucratic tone, is Report of the Secretary of the Interior (GPO, 1940 to 1945). A contextual summary of the parks during wartime is in Ise, *National Park Policy*, p. 447 ff.

9: New Challenges

Davidson Concession Memo: Author's collection. **Chicago Conference Meeting**: Annual Report of the Secretary of the Interior (GPO, 1946), p. 311. **Krug and Chapman**: Trani, *Secretaries of the Interior*, p. 270 ff. **Solicitor's Opinion**: The Memorandum dated December 3, 1946 is in Record Group 79, National Archives, Washington, D.C.

The Chapman Memo: Memorandum for the Director, National Park Service, June 6, 1946, (Chapman to Drury), is in Record Group 79, National Archives, Washington, D.C. It was mailed "by Axtell" from Washington. **The Drury Memo**: Memorandum for the Secretary, July 8, 1946 (Drury to Chapman), is in Record Group 79, National Archives, Washington, D.C. Its letterhead gives the Park Service address as Chicago. **Ickes "I wanted to take your concessions"**: Tresidder told me of this incident. **Hoss saw the Solicitor's**

Opinion coming: Quotes from Hoss's analysis of the problem appear in a letter to Drury from Howard H. Hays of Sequoia dated September 20, 1946. It was included as an appendix to the Solicitor's Opinion and remains attached thereto in Record Group 79, National Archives. Hoss never mentioned it to me. I found out about it while researching this book. This gives the reader a clear idea how informal our Conference organization really was.

Appropriations Committee Rumblings: The 1946 Annual Report of the Secretary of the Interior spent five and a half pages explaining concession policy history in an effort to fend off an Appropriations Committee investigation. p. 312-17. **The Concessions Advisory Group**: The Annual Report of the Secretary of the Interior for 1947 gives an account of this group's appointment, formation, and makeup. p. 330. In an ironic foreshadowing of future troubles with "professionalism-as-uncaring-arrogance," the Secretary's 1947 report also explains new regulations "to preserve the wholesome atmosphere of service engendered by the use of nonprofessional help." The National Park Service's turn to cold "professionalism" in the late 1970s was distinctly unwholesome and in part prompted my retirement from concessioning. **Old Contracts Extended**: U.S. Congress, House of Representatives, *Concessions in National Parks*, Hearings before the Subcommittee on Public Lands of the Committee on Public Lands on H.R. 2312, a bill authorizing the Secretary of the Interior to acquire on behalf of the United States government all property and facilities of the Rainier National Park Co., May 21, 27, June 1, 11, 12, 15, 16, 1948, Committee Hearing No. 41, (GPO, 1948), p. 207.

Union Pacific Signing Confiscatory Contract: Annual Report of the Secretary of the Interior (GPO, 1949), p. 301. The subject is discussed in greater detail in the House Public Lands Subcommittee *Concessions in National Parks* document cited above, p. 88 ff. **Albright Statement**: Quoted in Don Hummel, *The Concession System in National Parks*. (Washington, D.C.: Conference of National Park Concessioners, undated pamphlet). **Sierra Club Purpose**: The original statement is contained in *Articles of Association, Articles of Incorporation, By-Laws, and a List of Charter Members of the Sierra Club*, Publications of the Sierra Club, 1 (San Francisco, 1892), p.4. The repudiation is found in all Sierra Club statements of purpose since 1947. An account of the policy change is in Richard

M. Leonard, *Mountaineer, Lawyer, Environmentalist*, interview conducted by Susan R. Schrepfer (Berkeley: University of California, Regional Oral History Office, 1975) pp. 18-21.

Concessions Advisory Group Report: The Advisory Group's Report was never formally published that I know of, but the Annual Report of the Secretary of the Interior (GPO, 1948), p. 345, states, "In multilith form, this report has been given wide distribution," and summarizes its contents on pages 346-7. The 1948 House Subcommittee on Public Lands *Concessions in National Parks* record cited above provides the text of an advance report dated October 4, 1947 along with a recommended sample contract, pp. 145-158. **Ise Summary**: *National Park Policy*, p. 461. **Albright Reply to Chapman**: *Congressional Record*, 80 Cong., 2 Sess., Appendix, 4149, 4150. **Dawson Resolution**: House Res. 639, S. Res. 254, 80 Cong. 2 sess. **Hummel Testimony**: House Public Lands Subcommittee *Concessions in National Parks*, p. 202 ff.

10: Drakesbad and McKinley

Negotiations with Interior: No written evidence of these negotiations survives except the outcome, which was expressed in Secretary Krug's early November 1948 statement of concession policies. See Annual Report of the Secretary of the Interior (GPO, 1949) p. 298. **Chapman's Last Try to Take Over Concessions**: Annual Report of the Secretary of the Interior (GPO, 1949), p. 301. **Definitive Policy Statement**: Memorandum to the Director, National Park Service, from Oscar L. Chapman, Secretary of the Interior, dated May 6, 1950. The complete text may be found in U.S. Congress, House, Hearings before the Subcommittee on National Parks of the Committee on Interior and Insular Affairs, *Park Concession Policy* (GPO, February 27, 28 and March 10, 1964), p. 23-24. **Peterson Resolution**: House Interior hearings of 1964 cited above, p. 25. **Doty Policy Statement**: House Interior hearings of 1964 cited above, p. 26.

Later Bill Passed Requiring Concession Contract Deposit with Congress: U.S. *Statutes at Large 70*, 84 Cong., 2 sess., Public Law 712, July 14, 1956, p. 543. **Lassen Background**: Ise, *National Park Policy*, p. 222-225.

11: Glacier National Park

Glacier Concessions Generally: Michael J. Ober, *Enmity and Alliance: Park Service-Concessioner Relations in Glacier National Park, 1892-1961*, Unpublished Master's Thesis, University of Montana, Missoula, 1973. **Tourist Invasion**: Ise, *National Park Policy*, p. 537. **Mission 66**: National Park Service: *Mission 66: To Provide Adequate Protection and Development of the National Park System for Human Use*, U.S. Department of the Interior, January 1956. See also Conrad L. Wirth, "The Mission Called 66" in *National Geographic*, Vol. 130, No. 1, July 1966, p. 7. **Early Glacier History**: Madison Grant, *Early History of Glacier National Park*, Montana, National Park Service, 1919. **Mather Blowing Up Hill's Sawmill**: Everyone tells this story. See Shankland, *Steve Mather*, p. 209; Albright, *Birth of the National Park Service*, p. 171.

12: The Dawn of Environmentalism

Multiple Use - Sustained Yield Act of 1960: U.S. *Statutes at Large 74*, 215; 16 U.S.C. 528-531. **Wilderness Act**: U.S *Statutes at Large 78*, 890; 16 U.S.C. 1131-1136. For a detailed study see Jack M. Hession, "The Legislative History of the Wilderness Act," M.A. thesis, San Diego State University, 1967. **Wilderness Act Background**: Dennis Roth, "The National Forests and the Campaign for Wilderness Legislation," *Journal of Forest History*, Vol. 28, No. 3, July 1984, p. 112. Richard A. Baker, "The Conservation Congress of Anderson and Aspinall, 1963-64," *Journal of Forest History*, Vol. 29, No. 3, July 1985, p. 104. **ORRRC Report**: *Outdoor Recreation for America*, A Report to the President and to the Congress by the Outdoor Recreation Resources Review Commission (GPO, January 1962). The ORRRC also released numerous Study Reports on specific problems; concessions are covered in *Paying for Recreation Facilities: A Report to the Outdoor Recreation Resources Review Commission by the National Planning Association*, ORRRC Study Report 12. (GPO, 1962). **Meeting with Wirth**: No documentation survives beyond a few notes in the author's collection.

13: Policy Conundrums

Anderson and Aspinall: Richard A. Baker, *Conservation Politics: The Senate Career of C.P. Anderson.* (University of New Mexico Press, 1985). **Wilderness Bill Legislative History**: Dennis Roth,

"The National Forests and the Campaign for Wilderness Legislation," *Journal of Forest History*, Vol. 28, No. 3, July 1984, p. 112. **Critical Appropriations Report**: U.S. Congress, *House Appropriations Committee Report No. 177*, 88 Cong., 1 sess., 1963. **First Concession Bill**: Introduced as H.R. 5872 by Rep. Udall, *Congressional Record*, April 25, 1963, p. 7159. **Critical Government Operations Report**: U.S. Congress, *House Government Operations Committee Report No. 306*, 88 Cong., 1 sess., 1963 **Kennedy Insult to Aspinall**: Richard A. Baker, "The Conservation Congress of Anderson and Aspinall, 1963-64," *Journal of Forest History*, Vol 29, No. 3 July 1985, p. 111. **Critical GAO Report**: Comptroller General of the United States: *Report on H.R. 5873 and H.R. 5887*, (GPO, 1963). **Comptroller's Letter**: Comptroller General of the United States to House Committee on Interior and Insular Affairs concerning concessions contracts, dated July 1963. **Carver's Favorable Report**: Interior Department on H.R. 5872 and H.R. 5886, dated September 24, 1963. **Concession Hearings**: U.S. Congress, House Interior and Insular Affairs Committee, Subcommittee on National Parks, *Park Concession Policy*, February 27, 28, and March 19, 1964, 88 Cong., 2 sess., Serial No. 19 (GPO, 1964). **Consent Calendar Failures:** June 1, 1964, *Congressional Record* - House, p. 12249; see also June 15, July 21, and August 3 entries. **Concession Bill Floor Debate**: *Congressional Record* - House, September 14, 1965, p. 23634 - 23654. **Johnson Signs Concession Bill**: *Congressional Record*, October 13, 1965, "Message from the President," p. 26875.

14: Environmental Politics

Bureau of the Budget Report: *Study of Concessions on Federal Lands Available for Public Recreation*, Bureau of the Budget, Executive Office of the President, October, 1966. **Ninetieth Congress Conservation Acts:** The generic laws cited are Wild and Scenic Rivers Act of October 2, 1968 (82 Stat. 906; 16 U.S.C. 1271-1287); National Trails System Act of October 2, 1968 (82 Stat. 919; 16 U.S.C. 1241-1249); **Sierra Club Political Manual:** Gene Coan (Ed.), *Sierra Club Political Handbook: Tools for Activists* (San Francisco: Sierra Club, 1979), p. 35. **NPS Wilderness Problems:** John C. Hendee, George H. Stankey, and Robert C. Lucas, *Wilderness Management* U.S. Department of Agriculture Forest Service Miscellaneous Publication No. 1365. October 1978, p. 106-107. **Master Plans**: National Park Service, *Compilation of the Administrative Policies for the*

National Parks and National Monuments of Scientific Significance (Natural Area Category) U.S. Department of the Interior (GPO, September 1, 1967), p. 31. **ORRRC Land Classes**: ORRRC, *Outdoor Recreation for America*, p. 96-117.

Master Plan Origin: Public Law 71-616, Employment Stabilization Act of 1931, 71 Cong., 3 sess. February 10, 1931. **Balcony Repair Letter**: Keith Neilsen, Glacier National Park Superintendent to Al Donau, General Manager, Glacier Park, Inc. March 15, 1968 Author's collection. **Udall letters**: In author's collection. For public record, *see* U.S. Congress, Joint Hearing before certain House Subcommittees of the Committee on Government Operations and the Permanent Select Committee on Small Business, *National Park Service Planning and Concession Operations*, 93 Cong., 2 sess., December 20, 1974. Udall's March 27, 1968 letter is on pages 470-471. The July 17, 1974 letter is on p.458. **U.S.G.S. Report**: Dwight R. Crandell, D. R. Mullineaux, R. S. Sigafoos, and M. Rubin, "Chaos Crags Eruptions and Rockfall-Avalanches, Lassen Volcanic National Park, California;" *Journal of Research*, U.S. Geological Survey, Vol. 2, No. 1, January-February, 1974. p.49-59, (publication of original 1968 report).

15: The Times, They Are A'Changin'

Chapter Title: From the song. Words and music by Bob Dylan, published by M. Witmark & Sons, 1963. **NEPA**: William H. Rodgers, Jr., *Environmental Law*, (St. Paul: West Publishing Company, 1977), p. 679. **Hippie Riot**: *New York Times*, "Rioters Overturn, Burn Car in Yosemite," July 6, 1970. **Reed Memo**: Cited in Hendee, et al., *Wilderness Management*, p. 107. **Centennial Parks Book**: The Conservation Foundation, *National Parks for the Future*, (Washington, D.C.: The Conservation Foundation, 1972)

16: Our Park Service as Enemy

Manzanita Lake Shutdown Order: Howard Chapman, Regional Director, NPS Western Region, *Closure Order*, April 26, 1974. **U.S.G.S. Report**: Crandell, et al., "Chaos Crags Eruptions and Rockfall-Avalanches." **What Evidence?**: In 1979, Woodward-Clyde Consultants of San Francisco reviewed the rockfall-avalanche hazard in the Manzanita Lake area and concluded, "It appears that the rockfall-avalanche at the Chaos Crags was unique both in size and triggering mechanism, and that, in event of any future instability or rockfalls in that area, they will probably be of a smaller magnitude and not of sufficient size to reach the existing facilities in the Manzanita Lake Area." Charles L. Taylor, Senior Project Engineering Geologist, *Review of Rockfall-Avalanche Hazard, Manzanita Lake Area, Lassen Volcanic National Park, California*, Project No. 14508A, Report of July 9, 1979, Author's collection.

Redding Record Searchlight Articles: Glenn Hassenpflug, five sequential articles beginning Monday, December 1, "Volcanic Hazard Study Leads to Shasta," p. 9, and ending Friday, December 5, 1975, "Park Service Vows to Change its Ways," p. 21. **Dingell's Yosemite Complaints**: U.S. Congress, Joint Hearing before certain House Subcommittees of the Committee on Government Operations and the Permanent Select Committee on Small Business, *National Park Service Planning and Concession Operations*, 93 Cong., 2 sess., December 20, 1974. **Brock Evans Testimony**: U.S. Congress, House Interior and Insular Affairs Committee, Subcommittee on National Parks and Recreation, *National Outdoor Recreation Programs and Policies*, 94 Cong., 1 sess., March 6, 7, 14, 20..p. 258. **Connie Parrish**: "Nature Wins First Round," in *Los Angeles Times*, Sun., May 4, 1975, Part VIII, p. 5. **Aversa Article**: Rudy Aversa, "Wilderness or Development: Which for Yosemite's Future?", *Los Angeles Herald Examiner*, April 27, 1975, p. A3. **NPCA Lawsuit**: NPCA v. Kleppe, 7 ELR 20052 (D.C. Ct. 1976).

17: The People Strike Back

Kim Heacox: reprinted in *Seattle Times*, "Working to control the opportunists in land of opportunity," June 19, 1986, p. A19. **Stein's Philosophy**: U.S. Congress, House Committee on Interior and Insular Affairs Subcommittee on National Parks and Recreation, Hearings on *National Outdoor Recreation Programs and Policies*, 94 Cong., 1 sess., March 6, 7, 14, 20, 1975, p. 263, 264. **Prospectus for Trouble**: U.S. Department of the Interior, National Park Service, *Prospectus for Concessions, Zion National Park, Bryce Canyon National Park, and Grand Canyon National Park (North Rim)*, May 25, 1972. **TWA Contract**: U.S. Department of the Interior, National Park Service, Concession Contract with TWA Services, March 30, 1973. **GAO Report**: U.S. Comptroller General, *Concession Operations in the National Parks—Improvements Needed in*

Administration (GPO, 1975). **National Parks and Conservation Association Article:** "Concessions: A Continuing Threat to Park Quality," *National Parks and Conservation Magazine*, March 1974, p. 26. **Walker Testimony:** U.S. Congress, House Appropriations Committee, *Appropriations Hearings, Testimony of Ronald Walker, Director, National Park Service*, 94 Cong. 1 sess., 1975, pp. 151-52. **Senate Resolution:** U.S. Senate, Resolution 232, 94 Cong. 1 sess., July 31, 1975. **War of Letters:** All letters cited were copied to me as Conference chairman and are from the author's collection.

18: Crisis With Everhardt

Dingell Committee: U.S. Congress, House of Representatives, Joint Hearings before certain Subcommittees of the Committee on Government Operations and the Committee on Small Business, *National Park Service Management of Concession Operations*, 94 Cong., 1 sess., July 25 and 28, 1975, p. 2. **Dingell Report:** U.S. Congress, House of Representatives, *National Park Service Policies Discourage Competition, Give Concessioners Too Great a Voice in Concession Management*, 94 Cong. 2 sess., 1976. **Rockefellers and Grand Teton:** Nancy Newhall, *A Contribution to the Heritage of Every American: The Conservation Activities of John D. Rockefeller, Jr.*, (New York: Alfred A. Knopf, 1957). See also Albright, *Birth of the National Park Service*, p. 158 ff. **Yellowstone Scandal:** For the environmentalist telling of the tale, see Conservation Foundation, *National Parks for a New Generation*, p. 179, 180. **Visitor Preference Data:** Stanford Research Institute, *The Concession System in United States National Parks: Background, Services Performed, Public Attitude Toward, and Future Considerations*, Executive Summary, SRI Project ECC-4268, (Menlo Park: January, 1976). **Everhardt's Standard Concession Contract Language:** *Federal Register*, Vol. 41, No. 135—Tuesday, July 13, 1976, p. 28809. The Conference of National Park Concessioners responded with a 24-page detailed analysis submitted to the Park Service October 6, 1976, author's collection.

19: Saving the National Parks

Anti-Concession Zealots: For a typical insult-laden environmentalist tirade against concessions see Dyan Zaslowsky, "Black Cavalry of Commerce: Hotels, Hot Dogs, and the Concessioner Syndrome." *Wilderness* 46 (Spring 1983) 25-32. Perhaps most interesting is the case of Michael Frome, a leading environmentalist critic of concessions. He wrote "Park Concessions and Concessioners" for *National Parks*, June 1983, p. 16, stating, "It would be one thing if park concessioners over the years had demonstrated concern and responsibility for park resources. But the concern of the most vocal and powerful of them has been for the protection of their vested interests—of the public subsidy they receive for private profit. . . . They have allowed park visitors to stay overnight in buildings that constitute fire hazards and have marketed the worst kinds of trashy trinket souvenirs at exorbitant profit."

In a letter to Concessioners Conference Washington Representative Dale E. Doty dated February 12, 1959, Mr. Frome solicited us to accept his proposed public relations program to "tell the story of the contributions of the concessioners to the National Park System where this story is needed and will do the most good." He offered his services "at the rate of $100 a day and expenses," and suggested "a 25- to 30-day program to start with." He promised not only "my physical presence" for $3,000 a month, but also "that I will be working for you in many ways at other times. For example, I would be serving the concessioners through my membership and activities in such groups as the Outdoor Writers Association of America, Society of American Travel Writers, National Press Club and others. I would be happy and honored to be associated with the Western Conference of National Park Concessioners." We turned him down. I've never wondered why Mr. Frome was thereafter so critical of concessions.

Dick Munro's Comments: *Hungry Horse News*, Columbia Falls, Montana, January 12, 1978, p. 1. **Yellowstone 1966 Contract:** Concession Division, National Park Service. **Conference Mid-Year Meeting:** Minutes of the Meeting, October 18, 19, 20, author's collection. **Congressman Udall's Letter to Secretary Andrus:** Udall to Andrus, January 29, 1980, author's collection. Udall copied the letter to Congressmen Phillip Burton, and Don H. Clauson, Senators Henry Jackson, Dale Bumpers, Mark Hatfield, and Sidney Yates, Director Whalen and the author. **Newspaper Article:** "Udall Calls for Firing of U.S. Parks Director" *Federal Times*, Washington, D.C., February 18, 1980, p. 3. **Political and Educational Solutions to the Theft of Our National Parks:** I am indebted to Charles S. Cushman, executive director of the National Inholders Association for suggesting some of the political actions listed, and to Ron Arnold, executive director of the Center for the Defense of Free Enterprise for suggesting several of the educational actions listed.

Index